Thank you!
Thank you!
Mary Jane Wilson

European history as you've never read it before!

⁘

Journey with the Busy Body and discover . . .

In Brittany, Claude Monet was trying to paint at Belle Isle. He wrote to his wife "There was so much hail, I was afraid it would make holes in my canvases."

Overheard outside Notre Dame Cathedral in Paris: "Ah, de Gaulle! The only man I was ever faithful to."

General Lafayette was "the perfect director for a Cecil B. de Mille mob scene. He calmed thousands of crazed people."

During the French Revolution, future Citizen King Louis Philippe toured America on horseback with his three brothers. As a reward for curing an Indian chief, he was invited to spend the night sleeping on a straw mattress between the chief's grandmother and great-aunt.

The Knights Templars' lay brothers or sergeants were forbidden to play chess or cards. Hopscotch was okay.

The French novelist George Sand was "always on the lookout for a new lover to analyze."

At George Sand's ancestral home, Nohant, Benjamin Franklin's picture was supposed to be hanging over Sand's bed, but it wasn't. She loved his

(continued)

Poor Richard's Almanac, and never knew that the author of "early to bed and early to rise" stayed up half the night.

Chopin, being dragged through foggy England on a concert tour, lamented "I am out of my element, like a violin string on a bass viol."

The poet Petrarch wrote to his brother reminiscing about their youthful days, including "our curling irons and our artful locks which cost us labor and pain and robbed us of our sleep! . . . In the morning we saw red wounds on our foreheads. . . . To show off our beautiful hair, we had to hide our faces."

There were medieval guidebooks for every purpose, including table manners: "When you are through gnawing a bone, do not put it back in the dish."

The wife of King Louis XIV's brother, "Monsieur," wrote that she had to sleep on the edge of the bed and kept falling on the floor "like a sack of corn."

Outside their hotel on Mont Saint Michel, the author and friend discovered a statue of Saint Anthony, "the saint who finds things" (below), wondering where <u>he</u> is!

Back to Europe with the
Busy Body

Back to Europe with the
Busy Body

MARY JANE WILSON

Waldo Bruce Publishers, Inc. • Dallas, Texas

Copyright © 2006 by Mary Jane Wilson
Published by Waldo Bruce Publishers, Inc., Dallas, Texas
All rights reserved. No part of this book may be reproduced in any form by any electronic or mechanical means (including photocopying, recording, or information storage and retrieval) without permission in writing from the author.

First edition.

© The paper used in this book meets the minimum requirements of the American National Standard for Permanence of Paper for Printed Library Materials, ANSI Z39.48-1992. Binding materials have been chosen for durability.

This book was set in Utopia and Foundry Form Sans with Spumoni display by Graphic Composition, Inc., Athens, Georgia, and was printed and bound in the United States of America.

Library of Congress Cataloging-in-Publication Data

Wilson, Mary Jane
Back to Europe with the busy body : Mary Jane Wilson
   p.   cm.
Includes bibliographical references and index.
ISBN: 0-9773637-0-8 (pbk.)

Library of Congress Control Number: 2005934200

10 9 8 7 6 5 4 3 2 1

Contents

Heartfelt Thanks	xiii
Acknowledgments	xv
Preface	xvii
Back to Europe with the Busy Body	xix

ENGLAND

1	London's "The Savoy"	1
	London to Paris: With American Teenagers	5

FRANCE
Paris

2	Notre Dame	7
3	The Louvre	13
	Empress Eugénie and Géricault	13
	Eugène Delacroix	15
	The Life of Marie de' Medici	19
4	Café Procope and Mirabeau	25
5	Saint Sulpice Church	33
	Father Francis Libermann	36
6	Garnier's Opera House	41
7	Opéra Comique and Bizet's *Carmen*	45
8	Napoléon III	51
9	Chopin	58
10	The Palais Royal	63
	The Regent, Philippe	64

Contents

	Citizen Égalité	65
	Louis Philippe, the Citizen King	65
11	In Memory of Molière	69
12	Place de la Bastille and Beaumarchais	73

Paris Suburbs

13	Passy: Maison de Balzac and Honoré Balzac	79
14	Rueil Malmaison: Château Malmaison	85

Les Provinces

15	Normandy	92
	Mont Saint Michel	92
16	Aquitaine	100
	Chivalry and the Courts of Love	100
	Saint Émilion (The Famous Wine Town)	103
	Château Monbousquet	106
	Hospice de la Madeleine	109
	The Abbey of Fontevraud	111
17	Brittany	113
	Nantes	114
	Nicolas Fouquet	114
	Dauntless Duchesse de Berry	115
	Jules Verne	117
	A Seventy-Nine-Year-Old Pilot	119
	Saint Anne d'Auray and Her Messenger	121
	Gaugin, Monet, and Flaubert	122
18	Auvergne	125
	Le Puy en Velay	125
	Chavaniac	127
	Lafayette and Chavaniac	129
19	Berry	139
	The Jacques Coeur Tour	140
	Gutsy Gien	140
	Gien's La Musée de la Chasse	141
	Château le Verrerie and the Scotch Guard	142
	Sancerre	144
	Castle Maupas and the Dauntless Duchess	145
	Bourges and Saint Étienne's Cathédrale	145
	Jacques Coeur	148

Contents

Jacques Coeur's Palace	150
Meillant	152
La Commanderie and the Crusades	153
Castle Ainay le Vieil	161
Jean Baptiste Colbert	162
George Sand's Nohant	165
20 Touraine	**171**
Tours	171
Saint Martin of Tours	172
Château Ussé	173
Charles Perrault	175
Château Saché	177
21 Lorraine	**180**
General George S. Patton, Jr.	180
Art Nouveau: Émile Gallé	181
The Battle of Nancy and Two Cousins	183
Joan of Arc (Jeanne d'Arc)	188
Orléans	195
Cathedral of Saint Croix (Holy Cross)	196
The Bishop's Palace	196
Hôtel de Ville	197
Parcs	197
22 Burgundy	**199**
Dijon	199
Alexandre Gustav Eiffel	202
Dukes of Burgundy	204
Beaune	205
Hôtel Dieu (House of God)	207
Burgundy Wine	209
23 Provence	**213**
Grignan Castle	213
The Poet of Provence	218
The Holy Marys of the Sea	220
The Gypsies' Patron Saint	220
The French Naturalist	223

LUXEMBOURG

24 The Grand Duchy of Luxembourg	**229**
Cathedral of Our Lady of Luxembourg	230
Vianden	231
The Battle of the Bulge	234

Luxembourg City	238
The Luxembourg Story	239

BELGIUM

25	**Belgium**	**254**
	Brussels	254
	Antwerp	256
	Ghent	257

THE HAGUE

26	**The Hague**	**260**
	Kurhaus	260
	Madurodam, The Miniature City	261
	Rembrandt and Vermeer	262

HOLLAND

27	**Delft**	**265**
	The Father of International Law	266
	William the Silent's Prinsenhof	267

POLAND

28	**Kraków**	**269**
	Thaddeus Kosciuszka	271
	Count Casimir Pulaski	273
	Adam Mickiewicz	275
	Ignace Paderewski	276
	Sister Faustina	278
	The Wieliczka Salt Mines	279
	Czestochowa	280

GREECE

29	**Greece**	**283**
	Athens	283
	Cape Sounion	284
	The Acropolis and Dionysus' Theater	285
	The Acropolis and the Museum	293
	The Agora (Marketplace) through the Centuries	295

Contents

The Persian Wars	297
The Peloponnesian Wars	299
Notes	305
Places of Interest	337
Bibliography	363
Index	383

The author with Père Abel de Bourhis, in front of the hotel where
Benjamin Franklin stayed after landing at Auray

In Memoriam

PÈRE ABEL LE BOURHIS, parish priest,
Basilica Sainte Anne d'Auray, Brittany, France
M. HENRI LABY, Dijon, France
EMILY ARDELL CROFFORD, St. Paul, MN
and
JACQUELINE BENNING, Gap, France

**Dedicated to John
from Mary Jane**

Heartfelt Thanks

TO THE HOLY GHOST, Saint Francis de Sales, and my Guardian Angel and all the saints who retrieved everything I lost and got me to trains on time. And miracle of miracles, for sending me Michel in Tours. Also my Cheering Section: Family, friends and notes from complete strangers for their can-do attitude and loving enthusiasm. A very special debt to the friendly, helpful staff of The Dallas Public Library, editors Susan May Patterson and Keith Nichols, my computer experts Gretchen Payne, Nancy Sutton, and Gloria Servin; also Danielle Habitzreiter and Frances Carpentier, translators, and John Anton, my *bon chauffeur*. And special thanks to my daughter, Marty Ledenham, and son, Clancy Wilson, for their invaluable help in seeing this project through to completion.

Alain Querre, founder of the pottery museum Hospice de la Madeleine in Saint Émilion, with brother François, wife Sheila, and the author

Acknowledgments

LONDON

"Stompin' At The Savoy," words and music by Benny Goodman, Edgar Sampson, Chick Webb and Andy Razaf. Copyright © 1936 by EMI Robbins Catalog Inc., Copyright renewed by Rytvoc, Inc., Ragbag Music Publishing Corporation (ASCAP), EMI Robbins Music Corporation and Razaf Music Co. All rights for Ragbag Music Publishing Corporation controlled and administered by Jewel Music Publishing Co., Inc. All rights for Razaf Music Co. administered by The Songwriters Guild of America. International copyright secured. All rights reserved.

SAINT ÉMILION

Hospices de la Madeleine: Permission granted by Alain Querre, owner.

DEIKIRCH

The Battle of the Bulge: General Patton's letter while stationed in Nancy. Permission granted by Luxembourg National Tourist Office.

NANCY

General George Patton section: permission granted by *L'Est Republican*. Note 6: "Give My Regards To Broadway," permission granted by George M. Cohan Music Publishing Co.

Sampling Sancerre wine with Marie-France de Peyronnet, director of the Jacques Coeur Tour, in the French province of Berry

Preface

IT WAS ALL Dr. Bowie's fault (with his little black mustache, bow tie and sexy French accent) that I fell in love with France. Dr. Bowie was my French teacher at Skidmore College in Saratoga Springs, New York. Since then, I've been sneaking in and out of France from different countries, always with some very good excuse. Even a trip to Greece called for a detour. Tours included a three week tour-de-force with a seventeen-year-old boy at the wheel, a tour of shrines, a needlepoint tour, a serendipity trip to Luxembourg and a funny tour with teen-agers. There was even a tour in a wheelchair when I hurt my leg riding a bike. In Paris there was much smiling and making way for pitiful Pearl. When we came to an intersection, the invalid would jump out, run across the street and hop in again.

Each trip, with various companions, ended in France and wherever I roamed, most people spoke English. Even when they didn't, they appreciated any attempt to communicate in their language. Bus drivers and ticket agents wrote directions, and a beautiful girl at the metro actually led me to the train—the right one.

The chapters are arranged for a tour starting in London, across the channel to France. From Notre Dame Cathedral in Paris the tour continues down to Place de la Bastille, then to the suburbs of Passy and Rueil Malmaison and into the provinces and other countries—or maybe you would rather stay home.

"We ate dinner and were merry"
The author with a plastic bag—too many souvenirs

Back to Europe with the Busy Body

THE BUSY BODY IS BACK with memories of Benny Goodman's band "Stompin' at the Savoy" at London's Savoy Hotel. Also checking out the Gilbert and Sullivan rooms in the hotel, then on to Paris to tour Garnier's Opera House. (The only door open was in the basement.) Statues and paintings come to life with the Busy Body. A statue of a handsome man around the corner from Place de la Bastille is Beaumarchais, author of *The Barber of Seville* and *The Marriage of Figaro*. Like Figaro, Beaumarchais was "welcomed in one town, imprisoned in another."

Famous people are real. Two streets from the Palais Royal is Molière's home, where he was carried to the second floor still in makeup and costume after collapsing on stage at his nearby theater during a hilarious performance in *The Imaginary Invalide*. Molière, the very serious clown, masked his personal sorrows under the role of comic actor.

In Square d'Orléans where Chopin lived in an apartment complex with his mistress the author George Sand and her children, you can visualize the little garden in winter with "snow balls, sugar swans, cream cheese, and Solange's hand and Maurice's teeth."

In Balzac's split-level home, run down the back stairs he used to escape from creditors. Visit Château Malmaison where Josephine spied on Napoléon's mistresses. Admire the theater off boulevard des Italiens where Bizet's *Carmen* failed so dismally and learn why the chapter is subtitled, "A Girl's Picture and a Recipe for Gazpacho Soup."

And so it goes — throughout France, Luxembourg, Belgium, Holland, Poland and Greece. Whether you stay home or travel, it is another Busy Body book with the author's off-the-wall sense of humor and the essential ingredient, universality.

The author riding high in Vianden, Luxembourg, with
Romain Schwartz from the National Tourist Office

1

London's "The Savoy"

"Stompin' at the Savoy"

STATUES DRIVE ME CRAZY. Who are those people? In Paris a plaque on a statue of Henri IV on horseback says, *Vert Gallant. Vert* in French means green, but what is a green gallant? I should have guessed the other meaning—"fertile." Now we have a fertile gallant. I still didn't get it. "Oh! Merci, monsieur. Je compris; a ladies' man!" In London at the Savoy Hotel, it was the same guessing game; who was that gold-leafed man outside the entrance?

Count Peter of Savoy has been greeting guests on the site of The Savoy Hotel in London since the Middle Ages. Now, as a glistening gold leaf statue, he receives twentieth-century guests.

Peter was an uncle of Henry III's wife.[1] Three of her eight uncles, especially Uncle Peter, were given high positions in England. Uncle Peter was made Earl of Richmond and built a medieval palace on the site of today's Savoy. A thirteenth-century plaque in the hotel says, "Peter lodged there the many beautiful ladies whom he brought in 1247 from courts of Europe before marrying them to his wards, a large number of rich young nobles."

Chaucer lived at the palace during the fourteenth century under the patronage of John of Gaunt (Ghent),[2] and was married in the palace chapel. The palace was destroyed by starving peasants in 1381; it remained in ruins

Back to Europe with the BUSY BODY

for more than one hundred years until replaced by a hospital and almshouse.

During the Victorian era the little impresario, Richard D'Oyly Carte, arrived on the scene as manager for the musical team of Gilbert and Sullivan.[3] D'Oyly Carte noted the long lines waiting to hear Offenbach's rollicking operettas and decided, "We can do that!" And they did—for eighteen years. *H.M.S. Pinafore, Pirates of Penzance, The Sorcerer,* and *The Mikado* were such hits, D'Oyly Carte built a theater[4] for Gilbert and Sullivan productions. The plot of land he chose, where Count Peter's palace once stood, is in today's West End theater district. D'Oyly Carte's Savoy Theater, named for the original landowner, seated 1,100 and was the first London theater lighted by electricity. Opening night performance (October 10, 1881) was *Patience*, named for the village milkmaid who marries her childhood friend instead of her suitor with the funny name, Bunthorne.

Eight years later D'Oyly Carte opened The Savoy Hotel below his new theater, on a lot that stretched down to the Thames. The seven-story hotel equaled or surpassed the most luxurious American hotel. In addition to electric lights and elevators (lifts), the hotel boasted sixty-seven bathrooms with showers, 200 rooms, and three speaking tubes. Guests could command anything from a cup of tea to a cocktail.[5] When the French artist Monet stayed there while visiting his son[6] he could see three bridges, and behind them, Westminster, from his fifth-story balcony.

Lily Langtry, the Isle of Jersey "Lily," suggested Swiss hotelier César Ritz[7] as manager. At first he declined, but after spending a week as D'Oyly Carte's guest, he not only agreed, he also brought the famous French chef, Escoffier,[8] as *Maître Chef des Cuisines*. Escoffier made Savoy cuisine world famous. For Queen Victoria's Diamond Jubilee, he created *Cherries Jubilee*. When the racy Prince of Wales, later Edward VII, dined at The Savoy, his favorite Escoffier creation was frog legs served cold in a jelly of cream and wine, flavored with paprika. Italian singer Luisa Tetrazzini was honored with *Soufflé Tetrazzini,* and when world renowned Australian opera star Nellie Melba sang the role of Tosca in Covent Garden, Escoffier invented a special chicken recipe for her, *Poularde Tosca*. When she requested a peach, he served *Pêche Melba,* a fresh peach poached in vanilla syrup, served on a layer of vanilla ice cream and coated with raspberry purée. When Melba had to diet after too many chicken Toscas and peach Melbas, Escoffier consoled her with bread left in the oven too long—Voilà! Melba toast! For Melba's French lover, the duc d'Orléans, Ritz had a *fleur-de-lys* engraved on the duke's crystal, china, and linen. For the Americans—pumpkin pie!

The Savoy legend began with César Ritz and Escoffier. Ritz replaced the magnificent chandeliers, unflattering to the ladies, with table lamps and soft, rose-colored shades. Johann Strauss III, in town for a concert, played waltzes, and select, elegantly dressed guests were escorted as "very important people" to "reserved" tables. They were seated with lavish ceremony as the maître d' whisked away the reserved card with a flourish. Everything was done with panache—whether it was deboning a fish or unfolding a napkin.

Ritz and Escoffier knew psychology and their clientele. They understood why audiences applaud a stage set when the curtain rises. Their "Let Us Entertain You" showmanship included music, champagne, beauty, and action; from flaming sauces and cherries jubilee to the show-stopping performance of a tossed salad.

When both Ritz and Escoffier left The Savoy after eight years, George Reeves-Smith, manager of the elegant Berkeley Hotel in Picadilly, took over. To lure him, however, D'Oyly Carte had to buy the Berkeley.

When D'Oyly Carte died in 1901, his son, Rupert, expanded the hotel to make a total of 400 bedrooms and one hundred suites with separate baths. A favorite tall tale recalls the lady from Texas who said she started to get into the enormous bathtub but lost her nerve because she couldn't swim.

The original entrance to The Savoy was on Savoy Hill, through a large courtyard. At one time, the courtyard was flooded to make a lake. Guests dined in lighted gondolas while the Italian tenor Caruso serenaded them. In 1904, the courtyard was transformed into the Lancaster ballroom where Pavlova, the Russian ballerina on tour with Diaghilev, performed.

In the Thames Foyer, with its surprise gazebo, George Gershwin played his "Rhapsody in Blue" for the first time in London. Other entertainers in the Foyer were Noel Coward and Maurice Chevalier. Art deco mirrors and a Gilbert and Sullivan painting reminded guests to laugh, sing, and have a jolly good time. A fantasy painting depicts Koko, the Lord High Executioner in *The Mikado,* Jack Point, the nimble court jester in *Yeoman of the Guard,* and *Iolanthe,* the fairy who broke the rule and married a mortal.

From the River Entrance and the Lancaster Room, down a flight of stairs, the copper and marble Abraham Lincoln Room contrasts with Tiffany stained glass in the Manhattan Room. Gilbert and Sullivan meeting rooms

Back to Europe with the BUSY BODY

The New Thames Foyer at The Savoy

are named for different operettas: *The Gondoliers, The Sorcerer, Princess Ida,* and others. How could anyone not have a happy hour, or two or three, in the Patience Room, where jolly notes on musical staffs dance to the score of *Patience* on a decorative room divider?

Kaspar, a black cat, presides over the Pinafore Room. Three feet high, curved and slinky, carved from a plane tree, Kaspar, perched on his shelf, surveys the scene. To avert bad luck for a party of thirteen, Kaspar graciously accommodates the host by occupying the fourteenth chair. When Prime Minister Winston Churchill dined here, Kaspar, his friend, sat next to him, both with napkins tucked under their chins.

Churchill founded a club of cronies who met there every Thursday. Recalling Samuel Johnson's seventeenth-century literary club, "The Club," Churchill named his "The Other." The nine members were a motley group, delighting in raucous banter and debate. In one of their charades, they called on a member and gave him a subject to talk about extemporaneously. When Churchill was called upon, the acting chairman held up a card with the subject, SEX. Churchill rose, looked at the card a minute, then said, "SEX . . . It gives me great pleasure," and sat down.

During World War II, when a bomb exploded on The Strand, throwing the Grill Room musicians onto the floor, Noel Coward casually moved to the piano to play and sing for his fellow countrymen until the flames were extinguished and the "disturbance" was over.

Since World War II, the American Bar has been a popular international rendezvous.[9] Benny Goodman, who played there in 1936, had the whole world "Stompin' at The Savoy"—"Savoy the home of sweet romance . . . My heart is singing while the band is swinging. Never tired of rompin' and stompin' with you at The Savoy."[10]

LONDON TO PARIS
With American Teenagers

Since it was one of those bomb scare years, and travel agents were leery, a friend and I joined a group of American teenagers who were not afraid of anything—thirty-five of them, with their teachers from New Jersey, Texas, and California. Everyone met at Heathrow Airport, and after touring London, Oxford, and Stratford-on-Avon, we headed for Paris via Canterbury, then ferried from Dover to Calais.

In Paris at our hotel near The Invalids, the California chaperone received a message to return home immediately—a family emergency. His

Here come the students

contingent of twenty-five, mostly boys, joined the pretty school teacher from Texas. This was her first trip to Paris, and she didn't waste a minute. As she raced from one landmark to another, there was no counting of heads. Keep up with her or else. The boys ran after her all over Paris. At the metro, one boy at the end of a long line said he always stayed at the end because she was usually on the wrong side of the track. This way, he would be first in line when they turned around. The tiny shops in the Forum des Halles reminded them of rabbit hutches, and Pompidou Centre looked like pictures in their anatomy book. They dutifully followed a guide through Notre Dame, but no one told them to climb to the top and pat the gargoyles. The entrance is around the corner to the left of the front portal.

2

Notre Dame

Prostitutes, a Hunchback, and Général de Gaulle

IT IS TRUE. Notre Dame in Paris[1] is on an island, Ile de la Cité, between two branches of the Seine River. Another little island, Ile Saint Louis, trails barge-like behind. State-owned Notre Dame Cathedral, truly a catholic church in the universal sense of the word, dominates Ile de la Cité.

On Sundays, colored sheets of paper are handed out at Mass[2] with the Epistle and Gospel in different languages: English-yellow, Italian-green, German-orange, and so on. People of all races, colors, and creeds come "to sit alone in the great dim, soothing refuge." As we waited for Mass to begin, we dreamed of kings and queens in velvet robes sweltering in July, priests shivering in January, Vikings, and armor-plated crusaders.

Three hundred years before the Crusades, Vikings in dragon-prowed ships sailed up the Seine, spreading terror and destruction. After the fourth siege Parisians, imploring Our Lady's protection, dedicated the city to her. The present cathedral was begun during the reign of Louis VII and his first queen, Eleanor of Aquitaine. At the dedication (1163), one of the delegates was Thomas à Becket, archbishop of Canterbury, whose quarrel with his old friend, Henry II of England over state control of the church, led to his murder some seven years later in 1170.

Soon after the dedication, the Patriarch of Jerusalem, Heraclius, came

2,000 miles from Constantinople to plead at Notre Dame for a third Crusade. No one was interested until Jerusalem was captured by the Moslem leader Saladin. Two years later, Louis IX bought from the Venetians three relics of Christ's Passion: the sword that pierced His side, the sponge soaked in bitter wine, and what was left of the crown of thorns. The son-in-law of the Emperor of Constantinople[3] had sold them to a Venetian trader. The relics were kept in the specially built Sainte-Chapelle, Paris' stained-glass sparkling jewel case. Today the relics are at Notre Dame.

War, plague, and vandals ravaged fourteenth-century France. For one hundred years, English and French fought over Eleanor of Aquitaine's land after her second marriage to the future English king, Henry II. When England won the Battle of Agincourt (1415), the French signed a treaty that disinherited the dauphin, made victorious King Henry V heir to the French throne, and gave him the king's daughter, Catherine,[4] in marriage. The English king died two years after the wedding, and his infant son became king of England.[5] After Joan of Arc's victory at Orléans, to protect England's claim to the French throne, the English quickly crowned the nine-year-old boy king of France at Notre Dame.

The French dauphin, now King Charles VII, ousted the English from Paris (1453), and at Notre Dame, a Mass of Thanksgiving and *Te Deum*[6] (Glory to God) was sung as bells pealed and clanged and did whatever else bells do on such a jubilant occasion.

In Rabelais' satire on French society, *Gargantua and Pantagruel*, (1534) Gargantua, from a family of giants, visits Paris and throws the city into panic when he steals the bells of Notre Dame and drapes them around his horse's neck. Rabelais' patron was King Francis I, whose frail fourteen-year-old son married sixteen-year-old Mary Queen of Scots at Notre Dame. Two years later he died, and Mary went to her fate in Scotland. The king's second son, Henri II, married fourteen-year-old Catherine de' Medici at Notre Dame, but when their daughter, Marguerite, married eighteen-year-old Huguenot Henri of Navarre, the ceremony was performed outside on the square. After exchanging vows, the wedding party attended Mass in the cathedral, while in the garden the irreverent bridegroom (bedecked in yellow satin embroidered with pearls and gems) and his raucous soldiers regaled themselves telling dirty jokes.

Ten years later, after three attempts to conquer Paris, Huguenot Henri of Navarre decided "Paris was worth a Mass." Three years later, he became a Catholic and king of France, as church bells rang throughout Ile de la

Cité. Seventeen years later, the bells tolled for his murder. He was stabbed twice by a religious fanatic, Ravaillac, as his coach was leaving rue Honoré toward narrow rue de la Ferronnerie.

His son, Louis XIII, and Anne of Austria (daughter of Spanish King Philip IV) married at Notre Dame, and twenty-three years later, the queen's prayers to the Blessed Virgin were answered with the birth of a son, future Louis XIV.[7] The entire kingdom was dedicated to Our Lady in gratitude.

Although Louis XIV lived in his father's old hunting lodge at Versailles—as far as possible from enemies in Paris—he donated a new high altar for the cathedral. The dauphin, before becoming Louis XVI, married fifteen-year-old Marie Antoinette of Austria at Notre Dame, and celebrated the birth of their daughter with one of the most unique parties in history; a wedding for one hundred starry-eyed young couples, which included a trousseau and dowry for the brides and a reception at the Louvre.

Those were the happy days. Later, during the Revolution, hunger and hate demanded action. Mobs of starving people destroyed all symbols of power, especially heads with crowns. First they executed King Louis XVI and Queen Marie Antoinette; then they smashed the sculpted crowned heads on the portal of Notre Dame including those of the Three Magi and the twenty-eight kings of Judea.[8] They also converted Notre Dame into a Temple of Reason where gauze-draped prostitutes danced on the altar and were worshiped as goddesses. Although priests and nuns were killed and churches and seminaries destroyed, God prevented Our Lady's cathedral from being demolished by converting it into a wine warehouse for military hospitals.

To gain popular support after the French Revolution, Napoléon returned religion to its former dignity and became a hero. Parisians celebrated the Concordat with Rome in a denuded, profaned cathedral Easter Sunday 1802. Napoléon, who knew the importance of pageantry, arrived from the Tuileries Palace along banner-lined streets in his ornate carriage, preceded by Egyptian Mamelukes[9] (sultans) in colorful costumes leading white Arabian horses. A retinue of stately servants followed, dressed in green, their red waistcoats trimmed with gold lace. Stepping from his carriage before the battered portal of Notre Dame, the little First Consul in his red uniform[10] acknowledged the wild applause as people hugged each other and wept.

Two years later, at his coronation in Notre Dame, he grabbed the crown from the pope's[11] hand to show who was boss and crowned himself Emperor. Then he crowned his wife, Josephine, Empress.[12] His mother, who disapproved of Josephine, was absent. Seven years later, however, after Napoléon divorced Josephine, she was there for his marriage to Marie Louise of Austria and, again, for their son's baptism.

After the three-day 1830 Revolution when King Louis XVIII's brother, King Charles X, was deposed, Victor Hugo wrote *The Hunchback of Notre Dame*. Although the novel was written in 1831, it takes place during medieval times. Humpback Quasimodo,[13] the deaf, lame, half-blind bell-ringer of Notre Dame, had been left as a baby in the cathedral and raised by one of the priests. The cathedral, with its leering monsters, grotesque birds, and medieval art, was Quasimodo's whole world. Hugo's Quasimodo, scampering from tower to tower, swinging on his beloved bells, will always be part of Notre Dame.

Victor Hugo, mourning the ravished cathedral of the 1830s in his *Notre Dame of Paris,* said, "but now the spirit has left it. The abode remains and that is like a skull; sockets of eyes still there but sight is gone." Declaring that "great edifices, like great mountains, are the work of ages," his book inspired, among others, a young architect, Viollet le Duc, and Prosper Mérimée (author of *Carmen*), to restore Notre Dame and other medieval monuments throughout France.

When Citizen King Louis Philippe had to flee, Napoléon III came to power as a Republican. But when he made himself emperor, exiled Victor Hugo lambasted the emperor's police state. Hugo returned to defeated Paris after the Franco-Prussian War to find boulevard St. Michel in shambles; the paving stones at place de Pantheon ripped up, and horse meat rationed at one pound per two people every three days. After the Prussians left the bombed city, Communards, incited by Karl Marx's *Das Capital* (1848), hoisted their red flag[14] over the Hôtel de Ville, proclaiming their Commune.[15] During the vicious civil war that followed, the Church of the Madeleine was shelled, and 20,000 Parisians killed each other. A black marble plaque at Notre Dame commemorates sixty-three hostages shot by the communards—including the archbishop and five priests.

When fighting ended after three months, Rodin, the sculptor and nature lover, wrote about the anemone "whose sad heart is encircled by a black crown. Its sisters in full bloom are designs for rose windows. The anemone—of the violet color I love in Notre Dame touches me like a memory, especially now that we are returning to God—this flower and I."[16]

Notre Dame

Forty years later[17] at Notre Dame, Joan of Arc, who had been burned at the stake as a heretic, was declared a saint and patroness of France.

During World War I, relics of Christ's Passion were brought from La Chapelle to Notre Dame and carried in procession down the aisles of the cathedral for four years. In World War II, the bells were silent, the rose windows removed, and the portals blocked with sandbags. In May 1940, the French government gathered for a High Mass, as priests called upon Saint Louis and Joan of Arc to deliver their country from Nazi Panzers. A lighted votive candle before a statue of Our Lady was kept burning night and day for four years until Paris was free.

> When prayers take flight
> Think they are lost,
> The gleam of a candle reassures them.
> —MARIE NOEL

Dynamite that the Nazis had placed under bridges and historical monuments, plus three tons of TNT in the crypt of Notre Dame, were ready to be ignited at a signal. Miraculously, Paris was spared destruction when German General Dietrich Von Choltitz surrendered[18]—ignoring Hitler's order to "rain rockets on Paris." On August 25, 1944, the Feast of the Assumption and the Feast Day of Saint Louis, Patron Saint of France, the Second Armored Division under Général Leclerc[19] and the Fourth U.S. Infantry liberated Paris. As French tanks with the Cross of Lorraine insignia rumbled through the streets, atop the Eiffel Tower Private Étienne Kraft unfurled the *tricolore,* made from three old army sheets; one dyed pink, another faded blue, and the third, tattletale gray. War correspondent Ernest Hemingway led a big Resistance contingent to the bar of the Ritz Hotel and ordered seventy-three dry martinis.

The next day, behind four French tanks, 6'5" Général de Gaulle marched down the Champs Elysées at the head of his heroic Resistance fighters[20] to place a wreath on the Tomb of the Unknown Soldier. Riding in an open car from the Arc de Triomphe to Notre Dame, he defied enemy air attack, snipers, and political enemies. As shots rang out, thousands took cover behind tanks. Arriving at Notre Dame rigidly erect and outwardly indifferent to gunfire, de Gaulle marched confidently toward the Cathedral of Our Lady. When firing swept across the square, Général Leclerc's officers desperately tried to restore order. As de Gaulle stalked through the portal of

Dr. Don Simoni-Godefroy from Marseille and the author outside Notre Dame, after a memorial Mass for Resistance fighters.

The Last Judgment to attend a Mass of Thanksgiving, firing began inside the cathedral. The congregation automatically ducked to the floor when hidden enemy snipers fired from above, but de Gaulle continued down the aisle of the half-darkened cathedral at a steady pace as his friend, Admiral Georges d'Argenlieu,[21] muttered, "I can see more rear-ends than faces." In his place of honor at the left of the main aisle, gunfire still sweeping the cathedral, de Gaulle, hymnal in hand, bellowed back each phrase of the "Magnificat."[22]

It was de Gaulle and his faith we remembered at Notre Dame, during a special anniversary Mass for the Second Armored Division of the French Army that liberated Paris. As the Free French heroes, veterans of incredible bravery and torture, moved down the right aisle of the cathedral carrying their regimental flags, the last flag, waving high above the procession, was an enormous American flag.[23] Outside the cathedral after Mass, I overheard a lady tell her friend, "Ah, de Gaulle—the only man I was ever faithful to."

3

The Louvre

A Shipwreck, Horses, and Nudes

EMPRESS EUGÉNIE AND GÉRICAULT

After their tour of Notre Dame and a quick view of the city from the Eiffel Tower, the revved-up teenagers gave themselves two hours to "see the Louvre." Wherever my friend LaDelle and I wandered, there they were—waving wildly and beaming as they flew on to the next gallery.

At a slower pace, my friend and I could appreciate why Napoléon III's Empress Eugénie had studied posture and poses from the sculpture and paintings at the Louvre. The great French actress, Rachel (1821–1858), taught the empress sweeping bows and majestic entrances. Rachel[1] was so skinny, "an empty carriage pulled up to the stage door and Rachel got out."

We could also imagine Empress Eugénie in 1870 during the Franco-Prussian War, fleeing through the Louvre to escape the victorious Prussians. Hurrying from the Tuileries Palace through a passageway to the Louvre,[2] she stopped long enough to tell her friends to turn back—that she would continue alone with her lady-in-waiting. The last picture she noticed was Géricault's *Raft of the Medusa*. Years later, exiled in England, she said, "How strange that that painting (a sinking raft) should have been the last one I saw in the Louvre."

Back to Europe with the BUSY BODY

Géricault's *Raft of the Medusa* (1819)

The *Medusa* was a real ship. The captain, an elderly, incompetent man, had not been to sea in twenty-five years. He had been appointed by a friend of a friend. The *Medusa,* with 400 people aboard, plowed into a sandbank seventy miles off the coast of Africa while the crew was celebrating the crossing of the equator. The ship could have been saved by throwing tons of flour overboard. Instead, the captain loaded the officers into four lifeboats and the gentry into barges. The rest, left on shore, were ordered to build themselves a raft. They were left in the ocean standing waist-deep in water, with one bag of sea-soaked biscuits, two casks of water, and six barrels of wine.

The lifeboats were supposed to tow the heavy overcrowded raft, but when they became a drag on the officers' boats, one boat after another dropped the towropes leaving 150 people adrift in the Atlantic Ocean. Two officers aboard the raft who had refused to leave their men survived to tell the story. Among those on board were veterans of Napoléon's wars and convicts sent to fever-ridden outposts in Africa. Also on board was a twelve-year-old cabin boy.

The first day at sea, half in and half out of the water and scorched by the sun, they ate all the biscuits. One of the survivors wrote, "Very heavy waves rolled upon us which often threw us down with great violence. Cries of the people mingled with the roaring of billows. The dreadful sea lifted us every moment from the raft and threatened to carry us away. Several men were swept overboard. Another dozen were crushed to death by the constant shifting timbers on the raft."

"Second day. Some threw themselves off the raft in despair—others from hallucinations. A new more violent storm that night. Dozens lost footing and drowned. Many soldiers and sailors mutinied. One group fell on the wine and drank until they lost reason . . . in their drunken fury they tried to kill the officers gathered near the center of the platform."

After twelve days without food or water, the men ate leather belts and sun-dried human flesh. On the thirteenth day, when a sail was sighted on the horizon, they "straightened some hoops from the wine casks and tied handkerchiefs to the ends. One man, assisted by us all, mounted to the top of the mast to wave these little flags." To their horror, the ship suddenly vanished from sight. Two hours later, they saw it again heading their way.

The Louvre

Of the fifteen survivors (out of 150), five were so weak they died before reaching France. Since news of the disaster had been suppressed, the two surviving officers published the story, and twenty-six-year-old Theodore Géricault painted it.

His painting required hundreds of decisions. The most important was which episode of the hideous tragedy to dramatize—the mutiny, the rescue, or what? And how to transform reality into art? He chose the moment when the ship was sighted; a moment of utter despair and desperate hope.

For sixteen months Géricault studied waves crashing against a raft at Le Havre and the effect of light on the waves. Then he locked himself in his studio to paint on an enormous canvas. To make sure he didn't leave the studio at night, he shaved off all his hair. The painting, exhibited at the Paris Salon in 1819, was called *Shipwreck,* but everyone knew it was the *Medusa*. The judges, embarrassed at the portrayal of such hideous suffering they knew to be true, called it ghastly and turned away. Depressed and discouraged, Géricault accepted an invitation to show the painting in London, where it was a huge success.

We could have admired the painting for hours. Géricault used two pyramids in the composition; one formed by the tilting raft, the guy lines, and the mast. The other pyramid is based on fallen bodies, topped by a man frantically signaling to the distant ship. The curve of the canvas sail forms a parallel line with the outstretched arms of the desperate men. Géricault's friend, Delacroix, modeled the figure whose arm dangles over the side. The contrast of despair and hope makes the painting one of the most wrenching dramatic pictures ever painted—an indictment against those who ignore human suffering.

EUGÈNE DELACROIX (1798–1863)

Géricault and fellow artist Eugène Delacroix were friends during their wild oats days. Géricault, seven years older, led the way until his early death at thirty-two, when he was thrown from a horse. Delacroix, who had followed every step of Géricault's *Raft of the Medusa,* went on to become France's outstanding intellectual painter, renowned especially for his dazzling colors.

Delacroix, George Sand (the female free-love novelist), and Chopin were buddies despite the fact that Chopin couldn't relate to anything but music—quiet music that is. George Sand wrote, "Chopin fears Michelangelo, and Rubens gives him gooseflesh." Delacroix's double portrait of Sand and Chopin was cut in half. Now only Chopin's portrait is in the Louvre.

Delacroix's other friends, Honoré Balzac, Alexandre Dumas, Franz Liszt, and Victor Hugo were approximately the same age; all intense utopian Romantics—associated with the nineteenth-century literary movement emphasizing imagination and emotions. Lord Byron, Sir Walter Scott, Shakespeare, and Goethe (*Faust*) had set the stage for them with stories of crumbling chapels, eerie moonlight, moaning wind, and bats.

After Géricault's tragic death, Delacroix followed his own path, guided by Raphael, Michelangelo, John Constable, and Peter Paul Rubens.

Delacroix's *The Massacre at Chios*

The story of Delacroix's *The Massacre at Chios* was authentic and current, like Géricault's *Raft of the Medusa*. Greeks on the little island of Chios had ignored the Turks' order to fight against their countrymen. In reprisal, the Turks slaughtered some of the Greeks, and the rest became slaves. Delacroix made the painting as large as possible—to "make a stir," which he did. The Greeks' desperate struggle for liberty evoked strong sympathy in France, especially among the Romantics, whose idol, Lord Byron, had died in Greece—a champion of freedom from tyranny.

A year after making a stir, Delacroix went to London, where he lived with a horse trainer on Edgeware Road and painted magnificent, unforgettable horses. He also studied John Constable's light in landscapes. He said, "Shakespeare's plays compensated for rainy weather and the concert music—which had too many horns." When he returned to France, he redid *The Massacre at Chios,* improvising on Constable's color techniques; for instance, to reflect the scorching sun on the arm of a forlorn, wrinkled woman, he made pink, orange, and yellow hatchings. To show the shadow of her elbow, he used light blue with flecks of green and red.

Delacroix's *Sardanapalus*

An Oriental man reclining on an enormous bed placidly watches his wives, slaves, and favorite horse being slaughtered by eunuchs and palace officers. The man, Sardanapalus, is oblivious to the mayhem. You would think he was patiently waiting for the next course at a Roman banquet.

Delacroix had read Byron's play, *Sardanapalus.* Rather than be killed by enemies, the Assyrian king ordered a huge funeral pyre, built and heaped with his worldly luxuries, where he was to be consumed with his possessions.

Alexander the Great discovered the tomb. The epitaph reads, "I have eaten, drunk, and amused myself, and I have always considered everything worth no more than a fillip." Aristotle, the Greek philosopher, was disgusted. He said it was an epitaph worthier of a pig than a man. The name, Sardanapalus, became synonymous with a weak, effeminate man whose self-indulgence led to a cowardly death.

In Delacroix's painting, instead of death by fire, Sardanapalus orders everyone killed, then drinks poison. Delacroix's style is similar to Géricault's *Raft of the Medusa*. Like Géricault's raft, Sardanapalus' bed tilts diagonally backward. Parallel lines, colors, and the repeated use of pearls tie the composition together. Instead of a dab of red paint, red tassels indicate blood where the sword plunges into the horse's chest. Other red tassels represent flames over the funeral pyre. Pearls, suggesting smoke, are used for the flow of continuity.

The secret of the action in this "scandalous" painting is the repeated pattern of writhing curves. The golden lyre matches the curve of the slave girl's hips, and the flowing drapery on the nude in the foreground repeats the curve of a shoulder and breast. Violence and clutter are coordinated in perfect unity.

Painters, like actors, strive for variety. Delacroix has positioned his nudes in wonderful poses. Wonderful but exhausting for the models—except for the one sprawled face down on the bed. If contorted bodies bother you, enjoy Delacroix's fabulous jewels. You will be more worried about the jewels being burned than the people.

Delacroix's *Liberty Leading the People*

The Revolution of 1830 (the battle of the rooftops) was fought practically on the doorstep of Delacroix's studio on quai Voltaire. As the king's troops stormed through the narrow streets, people threw everything they owned down on them—tool chests, benches, washtubs, and more.

After Louis Philippe (the Citizen King) was crowned, Delacroix's *Liberty Leading the People* was exhibited at the Paris Salon of 1831. Lady Liberty, with her torn dress falling off her shoulders—way off—seems to be marching straight out of the frame. Among the students and workmen rushing to follow her is Delacroix, dressed as a medical student in a top hat, and a young street urchin, brandishing pistols. Lying at her feet in the mud, a wounded man has died for her. Another man drags himself toward her as she strides straight ahead over corpses and torn-up paving stones. Half goddess, half woman, she holds aloft a musket in one hand and the *tricolore* in the other.

Delacroix modeled his *Liberty* after a seamstress who had shot nine Swiss guards to avenge her brother's death at the barricades. Although Delacroix was a witness ("We had all we could do to make our way through the massed guards"), he was not emotionally involved. He said all the political turmoil made his painter's hand shake.

After the 1830 conquest of Algeria, the new government under the Citizen King sent an ambassador, Count Charles de Morny, to the sultan of Morocco. Morny invited Delacroix to accompany him. From Toulon they landed in Spain where "all Goya is alive around me . . . the Spanish are dressed à la Figaro."

In Morocco, the natives' regal posture fascinated him. "The rascals who will mend your shoe have the dress and bearing of a Brutus or Cato." The horses were equally amazing. "They are absolute devils, even the gentlest. I saw two in the fiercest battle you can imagine. They plunged into a stream but continued to fight. It was hard to get them out."

As they entered the town of Meknes, 200 miles into the interior, they thought they were in a war zone. Either that or everyone had gone berserk—running, shouting, and shooting rifles in the air. Later they learned that the sultan had ordered everyone to close shop and make merry for their benefit.

Delacroix managed to get himself invited to a stag party for a Jewish wedding where, for the occasion, Jews and Moors mingled, squatting on the floor around the walls of a small, stifling room. Prominent Moors had paid musicians to play all day and all night for the stag party. The dancing girls scarcely moved their feet, but what they did with the rest of their bodies made up for it. Delacroix decided the room was so small they had to dance that way and that incense reduced the stench of oily, unwashed, sweaty bodies.

The highlight of the Moroccan adventure was the harem he bribed his way into. He was so excited he calmed his fever with cool sherbets.

Delacroix's *The Women of Algiers*

Delacroix named his harem masterpiece *The Women of Algiers*. Years later he still dreamed of the mysterious veiled women enveloped in silk and gold. He could still smell incense and the fragrance of roses and gardenias entwined in their hair.

The entire Moroccan experience was shock treatment. The encounter with the Arabs' manners and morals gave him a new outlook on life and himself. Good, evil, sin, purity—the poor man needed counseling. Observing the Arabs' repose and perfect dignity one minute and their wild frenzies the next made him realize that that's the way it is with humans. In some cultures the contrast is—shall we say—more extreme?

THE LIFE OF MARIE DE' MEDICI (1573–1642)
(Rubens' Version)

As publicity man for Marie de' Medici, Rubens rivaled P.T. Barnum. He had attended her proxy wedding in Florence to Henri IV of France and was later commissioned to commemorate her life in a series of paintings. The paintings are grandiose and majestic—a show of heroic bravado. Who wants to remember unhappiness? The truth was so embarrassing that the Flemish artist disguised reality under baroque allegory. Rubens' first four paintings represent her Destiny, Birth, Education, and The Presentation of Her Portrait (to her future husband, King Henri IV, former Huguenot Henri of Navarre).

The king's first marriage was to his cousin "Margot," Marguerite de Valois. Her mother, Catherine de' Medici, widow of King Henry II, had arranged the marriage, hoping for peace with the Huguenots. Five days after the wedding at Notre Dame, Catholics massacred 3,000 Protestants in Paris. Duc Henri de Guise, who had organized the plot, told the twenty-four-year-old king, Charles IX, that it was his mother who had authorized the slaughter. Reluctantly, the king gave the order. Two years later, haunted by the memory, he died. His effeminate brother became King Henri III.

Spared during the massacre, the Huguenot bridegroom was kept under guard. When he escaped, he rounded up 12,000 Protestant supporters to secure his right as next heir to the throne. For twenty years he galloped across France on horseback trying to conquer cities. The trouble was, he didn't know what to do after he conquered them.

In the meantime, Catherine de' Medici, sixty-seven and crippled with rheumatism, still journeyed throughout France in a litter trying to make peace. Her death and the assassination of her last son, King Henri III, left Henri of Navarre heir to the kingdom; but for ten years, France was without a king as the Huguenot Prince of Navarre tried to take cities by starvation (Calais, Rouen, Chârtres). After his third attempt to take Paris by starving the people failed, he gave up and promised to take instructions to become a Catholic. Three years later, in 1595, at Chârtres, Henri of Navarre became king of France.

His first wife, beautiful, witty Margot, had been a prisoner for eighteen years to prevent her from causing trouble between Catholics and Huguenots. Now that Henri was king and needed a legitimate heir, he made Margot consent to an annulment.

When his ministers chose Marie de' Medici, another Medici from Florence, as his future queen, the king was on the rebound. He had planned to marry his favorite mistress, Gabrielle d'Estrée, pregnant with their third child. During Holy Week, they separated for a few days as a Lenten sacrifice, since they were living in adultery. Gabrielle left Fountainebleau to stay with her aunt in Paris. On Holy Thursday after Mass at Saint Germaine d'Auxerrois, labor pains started, and on Good Friday, after severe hemorrhaging and convulsions, she and her mutilated baby were dead. The wedding was to have been Easter Sunday.

The king, now forty-six, found another mistress half his age, Henriette d'Entragues, a woman determined to be queen. He even signed a promissory note demanded by her parents that he would marry her if she produced an heir—which she did. A frightening thunderstorm caused a miscarriage.

During this trauma, the king had signed a marriage contract to wed Marie de' Medici, hoping her uncle, the Grand Duke of Tuscany, who had helped him finance wars, would cancel his enormous debt. While Shakespeare's *Hamlet* was playing in London (1600), twenty-six-year-old Marie de' Medici married Henri IV by proxy[3] in the cathedral in Florence, then sailed for France escorted by seventeen galleys, with her sister, aunt, papal legate, and entourage.

The rough sea voyage was a nightmare, but according to Rubens' painting, somehow aboard the lurching galley she struggled into a dress with a scratchy, ruffled collar that must have weighed fifty pounds. She draped millions of dollars of pearls around her neck, piled her hair up, and made a regal descent down the gangplank to meet her eager bridegroom—who

The Louvre

wasn't there. They waited a week. When no word arrived, the caravan left for Aix-en-Provence in a cold wind so strong it toppled the litters and wagons. Still no word from the king. En route to Avignon the swift current of the Durance River was another terrifying experience, but on their arrival, a messenger was waiting with word that the king would meet her in Lyon. Eight months later, when the king showed up in her bedroom in dirty, smelly clothes, she could only say she had come to obey his Majesty.

The next day, after their marriage, they headed for Paris in the coldest weather in thirty years, when wine and ink in inkwells froze (1600). The king's retinue departed first, stopping at Fountainebleau where his mistress, Henriette, was living in luxury with the king's two-year-old son, César, by his former mistress, Gabrielle. The new queen of France, from the lavish Florentine Court of the Medici, had to ride with the king's little bastard son from Fountainebleau to Paris, where she was installed in the cold, bare, rundown Louvre.

When the queen had a daughter, Henriette had a daughter. When the queen had a son, Henriette had one a month later. Henriette even named her children the same as the queen's.[4] So many females trooped in and out of the king's apartment increasing the population, that the Louvre was like a brothel. One of the king's favorites was a sixteen-year-old orphan. Another mad passion was the Prince of Condé's fifteen-year-old bride. When the prince discovered the rake's progress with his bride, he whisked her off to the Netherlands held by the Spanish Habsburgs. Furious, the fifty-six-year-old king declared war against them, something he had meant to do anyway. During his absence, his queen, Marie de' Medici, was to rule as regent.

The day after her coronation at Saint Denis, Henri IV wrote in his diary, "Back to Paris to put everything in order. Saturday I will run at the ring. Sunday my daughter will be married. Tuesday, the marriage feast and Wednesday to horse and away. I cannot convince myself I shall ever enter Germany." He didn't. On Friday, he was stabbed by a fanatic who thought he was doing God a favor. The assassin, Francis Ravaillac, was promptly "torn asunder by horses." Henri IV, the *Vert Galant*, was dead at fifty-seven—the king who said, "I cannot have a melancholy man in my service. If a man is not good for himself, how will he satisfy others?" His son, future Louis XIII, was nine.

The queen governed as regent for her son, who had been reared at Saint Germaine among the king's numerous illegitimate offspring. Since birth, the young dauphin had been under the care of appointed people—with no affection or relationship with his mother.

Surrounded by hate and intrigue at court, the queen, with no one to trust, had turned to her nursemaid, Leonora Galigai, her friend from childhood who had accompanied her to France. As queen, Marie heaped money, estates, and titles on conniving Leonora and her husband, whose comic-opera name was Concino Concini. They held the power. They were the ones who bestowed favors. What a funny script! They were originally the maid and butler.

The nobles whom the king had kept at bay, now like ravenous wolves encircling a campfire, prepared to attack. The more the foreign queen bribed them, the hungrier they became. The more they threatened, the more she conceded. Although her handsome eldest son had been crowned king at thirteen, she continued to rule as regent.

The pious, musically talented dauphin was a victim of child abuse, mental and physical.[5] Evidently Henri IV thought he was disciplining a horse by the frequent beatings he ordered. The sexually abused boy suffered a speech impediment and chronic stomach disorders. At fourteen, he married devout little fourteen-year-old Anne of Austria[6] from the Habsburg ruling family in Spain. Encouraged by Marie de' Medici's enemies, the adolescent boy was determined to rule. He had been ignored long enough by his mother, and even worse by the Italian, Concini, who had replaced his father's advisers with his own. Concini held the second highest position in France.[7] The sixteen-year-old king had Concini murdered[8] and held his mother captive in the Louvre with her friend, Leonora. The queen, in tears, was sent to the royal château in Blois under guard; Leonora was thrown into the Concièrgerie and beheaded. The new teenage king replaced Concini with big, good-natured duc de Luynes, a champion falcon hunter. The duke, twenty years older, had befriended the neglected, reticent boy. Ambitious Cardinal Richelieu (depicted in the novel *The Three Musketeers*), manipulated himself into the queen's favor and followed her to Blois, but the king sent him to Avignon—out of the way. However, when she discovered that Louie had arranged his sister Christine's wedding to the prince of Piedmont without consulting her (she wasn't even invited to the wedding!) she escaped.

On a cold February night the queen, with the help of a few nobles, squeezed (she was plump) through a window of her guarded château, climbed down a rope ladder, and escaped to Angoulême, where she led a

The Louvre

revolt against her son. The king sent troops, but Richelieu, as villainous as Shakespeare's Iago,[9] was back in favor and persuaded him to negotiate. Rubens painted their formal reconciliation.

When the king's friend duc de Luynes died, Richelieu (1585–1642) replaced him and extended the Thirty Years War. He persuaded the young king to destroy the enemy, the Catholic Habsburgs, by using Protestant mercenaries against them—despite the fact that the king's mother, wife, and sister were related to the Habsburgs. When the soldier-king (an expert swordsman) lay dying in Lyon of an abscess in the intestines, his mother and wife never left him. After a miraculous recovery, he begged their forgiveness. He reinstated the queen and was about to replace Richelieu when Richelieu sneaked into the queen's Luxembourg Palace, burst into the room weeping (he cried a lot), and demanded that the queen should go. The king dismissed him, and Marie de' Medici was ecstatic. The next day at Versailles, the king reversed his decision.[10] Richelieu had triumphed again—like the sinister Simon Legree in *Uncle Tom's Cabin*—with a whip in his hand. A psychiatrist might say the king's submissive behavior reverted to a subconscious memory of his father's whip. For the next eighteen years Richelieu dictated French policy.[11] He ruthlessly punished enemies and even persuaded the king to escort his mother, the queen, to Compiègne forty-five miles from Paris, where he left her a prisoner.

Richelieu's war against the Habsburgs followed. Throughout Europe, churches, homes, and farms were ravaged and burned.[12] Marie de' Medici escaped first to the Spanish Netherlands, where she was asked to leave, then to her daughter in England,[13] who had married King Charles I. Again she was unwelcome. Her pleading letters to Richelieu and her son, Louis XIII, were ignored. "I would be so happy if you would deign to grant me the great favor of my return to France." No answer. She died at sixty-nine in a house owned by Rubens in Cologne.[14]

Of Rubens' twenty-one paintings of Marie de' Medici's life, the best known is *Disembarkment at Marseille*. Her stately descent down the gangplank is idealized by Rubens' angel blowing a trumpet to announce her safe arrival. Rubens' swirly-bodied voluptuous nude, Fortune, with her husky arm around the helm, supposedly guides one through the voyage of life, but she looks as if she were clinging to the helm instead of guiding it.

Three paintings highlight the climax of Marie de' Medici's life, when she finally becomes ruler after years of humiliation. One, *The Assumption of the Regency,* is a masterpiece of turbulence. Rubens captures the crashing, churning waves of resentment, rivalry, and jealousy after the king's death when the queen triumphantly assumes power. From there on, her life story is all downhill, but you would never guess it from the paintings.

The Louvre ended the tour for the teenagers. The girls went back to the hotel to wash their hair and blew out all the fuses with their hair dryers. The next morning we waved goodbye to the happy busload as they headed for the airport and home, the girls clutching sixty-dollar-an-ounce perfume and the supercharged boys ready for the next adventure.

4

Café Procope and Mirabeau (1749–1791)

Ça Ira—"So It Goes"

DURING THE CENTENNIAL CELEBRATION in France, we missed Bastille Day, but a month later people were still celebrating. Across the Petit Pont on the Left Bank behind Notre Dame, we found the oldest restaurant in Paris, Café Procope, opposite the site of the old Comédie Française. Café Procope is named for the Sicilian who started it four years before Molière's theater troupe moved in across the street.[1] One customer was Molière's widow, Armand.

Since 1685 Café Procope has been a meeting place for writers, poets, philosophers, and revolutionaries. When we visited, Lafayette's "Declaration of the Rights of Man" was printed on the outside wall next to portraits of Benjamin Franklin, Marat, King Louis XVI, and others involved in the Revolution. A lady-in-waiting to Marie Antoinette described Louis XVI as a "stout man about 5' 7" tall, square-shouldered and with the worst imaginable bearing. He looked like some peasant waddling behind his plow . . . yet in his court attire he looked magnificent."

Inside Café Procope the gracious ambience suggests contentment and joy—joy at being a survivor. A special on the menu was *Lobster Thermidor*, invented to celebrate the end of the Terror during the month of *Thermi-*

Back to Europe with the BUSY BODY

dor,[2] (Greek word for heat) July 19 through August 17, 1794, on the new Revolutionary calendar.

From an upstairs window the manager, dressed as a revolutionary citizen, showed us the Liberty Tree at the end of the street, and the nearby building where Marat, the ex-doctor with the horrible skin disease from hiding in cellars and sewers, printed his radical newspaper. Other mementos were a 200–year-old coffee machine and Voltaire's desk with a green marble top. There should have been a reminder of Mme. Tussaud[3] and her uncle, Dr. Curtius (who made wax figures of decapitated heads), and Mirabeau,[4] the brilliant orator of the first National Assembly, whose voice held Mme. de Staël[5] spellbound for two hours.

If anyone could identify with tyranny and injustice, it was comte de Mirabeau[6] from Provence. From the age of three, when his face was disfigured by smallpox, his father's aim in life was to destroy him. The sadistic parent had him confined at twenty in one prison after another for fifteen years. One prison, described in Dumas' novel, *The Three Musketeers,* was the infamous Isle d'If outside the harbor of Marseille. Protests by Mirabeau's jailers of the inhuman treatment ordered by his father eventually secured his temporary release. Between escapes, releases, and love affairs, he visited England, Holland, Switzerland, and Belgium. In the barbaric prison of Vincennes outside Paris where Mirabeau spent three years in solitary confinement, his father's plan to exterminate him nearly succeeded.

During Mirabeau's ordeal, seventy-year-old Benjamin Franklin, in his homespun brown coat and outlandish but warm beaver hat, was in Paris hoping for French aid for the colonists. His face was imprinted on practically everything. He wrote to his daughter, "There were so many Franklin dolls, you might say that I am almost I-doll-ized." Always a cheerful optimist, the phrase he used throughout the American Revolution, *Ça Ira* (So It Goes)[7] was set to music and sung. During the French Revolution, however, it meant "Hang all the Aristocrats."

When France signed a treaty with the American colonies (1778), Mirabeau was nearly dead in a dark, filthy cell, and twenty-year-old Lafayette, wounded in the Battle of Brandywine, Pennsylvania, was shivering at Valley Forge. Five years later Mirabeau, finally released, went to Holland and wrote about prison reform. Bankrupt France had a $100 million deficit, and people were starving. The financial situation was so desperate the king summoned the Estates-General. On May 5, 1789, 1,200 representatives of nobles, clergy, and commoners met for the first time in more than 175 years in the town of Versailles. Swiss Guards in puffed sleeves and pantaloons, nobles in lace and glittering diamonds, bishops in bright vestments, and black-clad commoners marched to the Assembly Hall.[8] Comte de Mirabeau, head high and defiant, marched with the commoners. Publicly slandered by his father, he had been rejected by the king as a delegate to the Assembly of Notables (Nobles). Mirabeau's only comment was, "He has thrown away the lemon while it still has juice in it." (Later the king retrieved the lemon.)

Jacques Necker, the king's finance minister, the man the nation looked to for direction, opened the session by reading numbers and statistics for three hours. Everyone, including the king, fell asleep. It was Mirabeau, in a triumph of the human spirit, who emerged as the outstanding leader of the assembly.

The next day, when delegates arrived at the Assembly Hall, guards with bayonets blocked the entrance and locked them out in the rain. A notice informed the nation's deputies that sessions had been suspended—the hall was being remodeled. Dr. Guillotine, for whom the guillotine was named, was a delegate from Paris. He suggested using a friend's indoor tennis court nearby. On the floor of the tennis court surrounded by high walls, Mounier, a delegate from Grenoble, proposed the famous Oath of the Tennis Court: ". . . that all members of the assembly take a solemn oath never to separate; to meet wherever circumstances might dictate until the constitution of the kingdom is established on a solid foundation . . ."

The following day, when they assembled in the Church of Saint Louis at Versailles, three bishops, 150 clergymen and forty-eight nobles joined the Third Estate of the commoners. Abbé Siéyès, a delegate from Fréjus on the Riviera, announced that the Third Estate intended to write a constitution with or without the others. At a "Royal Session"[9] (which included spectators John Adams, his wife, Abigail, and Thomas Jefferson), the delegates presented their Bill of Rights, demanding an end to feudal laws and the end of tax exemption for clergymen and nobles—which the king rejected.

When the royal party left, with much fanfare, the king's master of ceremonies remained to order the assembly to disband and meet in some other town—preferably far away. Mirabeau broke the stunned silence. His powerful voice bellowing throughout the enormous hall informed the man that he was not qualified to tell them they must go. "If you have been asked to put us out, you will have to request another order that force be used, for the people will leave only by the force of bayonets"—words every

Back to Europe with the BUSY BODY

French child knows by heart—a French version of Patrick Henry's "Give me liberty or give me death." At the next session, the assembly made its deputies inviolable to arrest, and the clergy announced it would renounce all tax exemptions. July 9, 1789, the Third Estate declared itself the National Assembly. When the assembly began writing a constitution restricting the king's power, they also took over the country's finances. Money is power. Now they could influence and intimidate the government.

The king, horrified by their demands, said he needed time to consider. Instead, he fired Necker, the finance minister, and stationed troops around Paris and Versailles. When hungry Parisians learned that Necker, their hope for reform, had been fired, they went berserk looking for food and weapons, convinced there was a plot to starve them. Jefferson wrote, "The patience of the people, who have less of that quality than any other nation in the world, is worn threadbare. The Queen . . . is indignant at all obstacles to her will . . ."

Parisians had set up their own city government with a militia of 4,800 unarmed men. Their request for rifles stored in the Hôtel des Invalides, had been denied. On July 14, 1789, in the rain, an unarmed crowd accompanied by drums and three officers on horseback left from rue St. André des Arts for the Hôtel des Invalides. Guards outside the moat held their fire, but more than one hundred men were killed in the dark, underground corridors where weapons were stored. Now they had 28,000 muskets and twenty cannons—but no ammunition. Gunpowder was stored in the Bastille.

The mob surged on to the Bastille, where a delegation demanded that the Bastille be transferred to the new city government. The drawbridge was let down and the delegates invited to lunch. When they failed to return, a second delegation was sent. The governor of the Bastille, marquis de Launay, showed them guns and ammunition but said he regretted they could not have them. Then, like a scene from "The Three Stooges," the second delegation ran back to the Hôtel de Ville for further orders. Four hours later the mob attacked the walls with battering rams and blew up the gunpowder. When the king at Versailles was informed, he inquired incredulously, "You mean a revolt?" Jefferson's friend, duc de Liancourt,[10] replied, "No, your Majesty, a revolution." The next day the king told the assembly he would withdraw the troops.

A delegation from the National Assembly[11] arrived at the Hôtel de Ville to announce the good news. The crowd made Lafayette General of the

Café Procope and Mirabeau

Militia, and the astronomer Jean Sylvain Bailly,[12] mayor. By late July 1791, the assembly had endorsed Lafayette's "Declaration of the Rights of Man."[13] After sending the document to the king for his signature, they tackled the Constitution with 200 excitable Frenchmen talking at once and spectators in the gallery yelling their approval or hissing. The king suffered one shock after another, especially the assembly's attack on religion—beginning with the abolition of church tithes.

With freedom of the press, newspapers unleashed vitriolic lies against the royal family, nobles, and clergy. Marat, in his newspaper, called for all nobles to be killed. He said the nobleman comte de Mirabeau's success in the assembly was due only to his vast lungs, and he hoped Mirabeau would catch eternal whooping cough. A tide of rebellion rolled across the land and crashed back with violence and destruction.

When the king was presented with nineteen articles of the Constitution, he said he could agree with three of them but would have to study the rest. Mirabeau roared to the nation's delegates, "Let us dare to tell the king he is mistaken about the nature of our request. We have not asked him for advice. We simply want his signature. Justice and current circumstances make it necessary." Three months later when there was still no reply, Mirabeau exploded, "What are they thinking of? They will perish. People will stomp on their corpses."

In October, the French regiment attended a banquet at Versailles. Wine flowed, inhibitions vanished, and enticing court ladies replaced the new red, white, and blue cockade with those of the old regime, black and white. Parisians claimed that French guards had stomped on the red, white, and blue cockade, the new symbol of freedom. Indignation, fury, and desperation led to the Women's March on Versailles. Six thousand hungry women of all ages and classes swarmed to the Hôtel de Ville to seize cannons and muskets. Fishwives, artisans, and sympathetic aristocrats, accompanied by veterans of the Bastille, marched in a cold October rain twelve miles through the Bois de Boulogne to Versailles, demanding bread and punishment for the French guards.

The famished, exhausted women—many pregnant—some barely able to drag themselves, reached Versailles at 4:00 P.M. after a six-hour march. At the palace they were informed that the king was hunting,[14] and the queen was at the Petite Trianon. Why didn't they try the National Assembly down the street? Off they swarmed, shouting, "Bread!" and "We want our little mother, Mirabeau."

Back to Europe with the BUSY BODY

Fifteen were admitted into the hall, where they presented their demands: bread, punishment for the bodyguards who had insulted the cockade, the king's return to Paris, and his signature on the "Rights of Man." Jean Mounier from Grenoble, president of the Assembly, accompanied the bedraggled women to the palace in the rain, where he waited for hours with a few women delegates. When the king finally appeared, the girl chosen as spokesman fainted. Louis XVI revived her and assured the women he would personally provide Paris with bread. By 2:00 A.M., Mounier had talked the king into accepting their demands—except one. He refused to return to Paris. When Mounier returned to the National Assembly, the delegates had adjourned leaving the women in the hall. Mounier ordered bread for them before convening the assembly.

The returning delegates found themselves jammed among wet women carrying pikes and scythes and clamoring for Mirabeau. "Get our little Mirabeau to speak. We want to hear him." Suddenly, Mirabeau's voice thundered above the tumult, "I should like to know why it has been fit to come and disturb our sittings." In the sudden silence, he asked the president to preserve the dignity of the debate by ordering unauthorized members to return to the galleries. Mirabeau, their champion, had taken command. Not a word was heard out of them as he reprimanded them. "The representatives of a nation cannot carry on an intelligent discussion in the midst of a scandalous tumult. I hope the friends of liberty have not come here to interfere with the liberty of the assembly." This was language they understood. They burst into applause, and calm was restored.

Lafayette had arrived in Versailles from Paris after midnight with the National Guard. Assured by Lafayette of protection, the king retired, and Lafayette with no sleep for twenty hours, collapsed at his father-in-law's home, the Hôtel de Noailles in Versailles. Two hours later he awoke to pandemonium. Six men armed with knives had forced their way into the courtyard and stabbed several of the king's bodyguards. They were on their way to the queen's apartment before they were overtaken. Lafayette rescued seven more bodyguards.

Lafayette, the perfect director for a Cecil B. deMille mob scene, calmed thousands of crazed people. He persuaded the royal family to announce that they would gladly take up residence in Paris. He also told the king and queen (whom the Parisians blamed for all their woes) to stand on a balcony with their ten-year-old daughter and four-year-old son. Impulsively he went down on his knee and kissed the queen's hand. After a second of shocked silence, the unpredictable mob that minutes before was ready to kill them, roared, "*Vive le Roi, Vive la Reine!*" Lafayette had won another victory.

The triumphant women of Paris accomplished what the representatives of France had failed to do. With the royal family as their prize, they returned to Paris—the royal coach guarded by the National Guard and Parisian women riding in carts drawn by the king's horses. Sprawled over flour bags, waving loaves of bread and decapitated heads on pikes, they headed for Paris. The procession, splashing through the mud, took seven hours to reach Paris. At the Hôtel de Ville, lit by thousands of torches, Mayor Bailly pinned a red, white, and blue cockade on the king's hat while the mob cheered their victory. Many persuaded themselves the revolution was over. Mirabeau knew better.

The National Assembly, now in Paris,[15] continued to terrify the king, virtually a prisoner of the Parisians. Crippled comte de Talleyrand,[16] denied a military role and forced into a church career (without an ounce of faith), was finance general of the Church. Using Mirabeau in the assembly as his orator, Talleyrand succeeded in nationalizing all church property. The next step was control of the clergy by making them employees of the state. Forced to swear allegiance to the state, those refusing to obey were killed or jailed. So much for freedom of religion. Talleyrand's mentor, Voltaire, would have been pleased. Louis XVI, whose religion meant more to him than life, could not imagine confessing his sins to some improper and probably scandalous clergyman. He finally called on Mirabeau for advice.

At first Mirabeau, like Lafayette, had tried to persuade the king to lead the new reformed government, but Louis XVI had stubbornly refused. Now Mirabeau set about trying to save him—the king whose signature on a *cachet-de-lettre* had sentenced him to fifteen years in prison. A *cachet-de-lettre* was the means by which the king could arrest and jail people without a trial.

When the king's sisters set out for Rome during Holy Week with their entourage and millions of francs, Mirabeau prevented their arrest. For weeks they had been ordering black taffeta blouses, nightgowns, and capes with frills. Some wit wrote, "All that Mesdames take away belong to us, even their chemises. Personally, I do not like our chemises going to Rome."

When Mirabeau, after consulting with Jefferson, voted to give the king absolute veto power, all Paris furiously denounced him—including twenty-six-year-old journalist-orator, Camille Desmoulins, Mirabeau's admirer. At a chance meeting in the Tuileries garden, disillusioned Desmoulins called Mirabeau a traitor. Mirabeau turned on the charm and invited him to dinner. Afterwards, Desmoulins[17] wrote, "His table is too loaded with delicacies. I am being corrupted . . . I have all the trouble in the world to resume austerity and detest aristocrats whose crime is to go on having these excellent dinners."

While Mirabeau risked his life to save the royal family, the king was secretly making his own plans—to escape. The tragedy is that Mirabeau worked himself to death for a monarch who had no intention of following his advice. With no hope of saving the king, Mirabeau's body and iron will, which even prison could not conquer, collapsed. Before his death, however, God sent him one of the greatest gifts a man can have, a true friend. In Mirabeau's case, the friend was a rich one—comte La Marck, a wealthy landowner who paid Mirabeau's debts and gave him the little comfort he knew during his last tumultuous year.

Mirabeau, who had reasoned with rioters in Marseille and Aix, also brought order to the National Assembly. He worked closely with Benjamin Franklin and, alone, delayed the Reign of Terror. He was elected president of the Assembly in March, 1791, and died four months later at forty-two. The tarnished knight's quest for the Holy Grail—liberty—was over.

5

Saint Sulpice Church[1]

"The Three Musketeers," a Jewish Priest, and a Nun on Horseback

NEAR THE LUXEMBOURG GARDENS in tree-shaded Saint Sulpice Square, a young couple in blue jeans sat on a bench studying their guidebook as two ten-year-old boys zipped around on roller skates. The usual male newspaper reader was there, while another man paced the square checking his watch. Someone was late.

Parisians love the pretty park-like squares outside their churches. "The Fountain of the Four Cardinals"[2] in the center of Saint Sulpice Square splashes down on two huge lions guarding statues of four seated Sulpician priests.[3] The title is a joke and a play on words in French. The priests never made it to cardinal, especially Bossuet and Fénelon.[4] Originally they were the best of friends, but Bossuet, the most powerful archbishop in France, was jealous of Fénelon and became his vicious enemy.

We happened to wander by in time for a 6:45 P.M. Mass. Afterward, still intrigued by the huge shells used for holy water[5] and the pulpit with the double staircase, we found a little room where rosaries and postcards were sold. A thin, elderly man was talking faster than a machine gun to a lady at the desk. My friend was supposed to take a pill, so we politely asked, *Pardonnez-moi. Est-ce que possible avoir une verre de l'eau, s'il vous plaît?*

or something like that. The man, who turned out to be a Sulpician priest, went into the sacristy, got a milk bottle and a *very* small glass, kicked open a door that opened into a dried-up, neglected postage-stamp-size courtyard, turned on the hose, filled the bottle, and poured a drink into the *very* small glass.

The forlorn courtyard longed to tell of other days and times—like the time King Louis XIII's three musketeers fought their famous duel in nearby rue des Canettes.[6] Louis XIV's mother, Anne of Austria, laid the cornerstone for Saint Sulpice[7] in 1646, and Molière's wife, Armande, was buried here. When Napoléon returned from Egypt, he used the church as a banquet hall.

In the seventeenth century when Saint Vincent de Paul[8] (1580–1660) was convinced the Church was going to ruin due to the ignorance and evil lives of many priests, a few secular priests dedicated themselves to educating the clergy and keeping them as holy as possible. Another objective was to help the destitute throughout the world, especially blacks. The priests became known as the Holy Spirit Fathers or Sulpicians. The first pastor, Jean Olier,[9] a former aristocrat who sacrificed wealth for poverty, started a seminary[10] with courses in theology at the Sorbonne. Between 1600 and 1640, Paris became the missionary center of the world.[11]

The ninth superior general of the Sulpicians, Father Jacques André Emery (1782–1811), was threatened with death and imprisoned twice during the Revolution[12]—the second time for nearly a year. The seminary was closed and eight seminarians executed. After the Revolution, the only good to come from the madness was the end of class distinctions. There was no more separate housing for seminarians of noble birth attended by their valets. Spirituality took precedence over prejudices acquired from birth.

When the National Assembly required priests to swear allegiance to the government rather than to the pope,[13] those who refused were executed or exiled. Anticipating the Terror, Father Emery sent four priests and five seminarians to America (1791) to found a seminary in Baltimore, Maryland. Patrick Henry and James Monroe, who were on the same ship, taught them English.

In 1807, Sulpicians in Baltimore welcomed Elizabeth Ann Seton, whose father was the first professor of anatomy at Columbia University. Her stepmother was from the wealthy New York Barclay family. The ex-New York debutante was now a widowed, destitute schoolteacher with five children. The head of the Sulpician seminarians in Baltimore, Father Duboise, learned of her plight and asked her to start a school in Baltimore.[14] When she arrived with four companions, also teachers, Father Duboise gave them his two-room log cabin. Elizabeth Seton became a convert and a member of Saint Vincent de Paul's Daughters of Charity. She started the first parochial school in America. An expert horsewoman, she galloped down Maryland roads in her black cloak and bonnet in all kinds of weather helping the poor. Undernourished, she died at forty-seven and became the first American saint.

After the French Revolution,[15] Napoléon's relationship with Father Emery was a psychiatrist's dream—envy, respect, and jealousy. Napoléon, posing as peacemaker, planned to announce a Concordat[16] (1801) with the papacy. When seventy-year-old Father Emery suggested that Napoléon allow publication of peace overtures beforehand, Napoléon told him to beware of the consequences if there was any publicity. When the Sulpicians pressed for details and conditions, Napoléon jailed Father Emery with common criminals for three weeks.

The contest of wills continued. Napoléon appointed Father Emery counselor for life to the Imperial University—responsible for education throughout the empire. The next confrontation came with Napoléon's divorce from Josephine and marriage to Marie Louise of Austria.[17] Father Emery and thirteen cardinals refused to condone the marriage. Two months later Napoléon retaliated. His minister of public worship exiled the cardinals and expelled Father Emery as superior general. Continuing the power play with his opponent, Napoléon named Father Emery head of a committee to improve his relationship with Pope Pius VII—his prisoner at Fontainebleau.[18] During a tempestuous meeting at the Tuileries in 1811, Napoléon exploded: "What? Do you mean I don't have the right to tell the pope I can appoint bishops?" Father Emery replied, "Never." One month and eleven days later, Father Emery died at seventy-nine.

A seminarian during Napoléon's reign wrote that the Society of Saint Sulpice was rekindled from ashes through the devoted care of Father Emery at a time when religion in France was about to be banned throughout the country. "The soil of France is covered with lycées, military schools, and other institutions where godlessness is encouraged. Immorality is tolerated and materialism promoted and applauded. What Napoléon counts on most is the destruction of the moral fibre of the youth. His success so far . . . is frightening."

After Father Emery's death, Napoléon confiscated Father Emery's mail at the seminary and found more than a few derogatory remarks about himself, which he used as an excuse to demolish the seminary. He said the church façade would show up better.

The finale of the feud between Napoléon and the Church came after Waterloo. As the Allies headed for Paris, Napoléon sent the pope back to Savona in Italy to deprive the Allies the honor of freeing him. At the restoration of Bourbon king Louis XVIII, the Sulpicians returned.

FATHER FRANCIS LIBERMANN

The eleventh superior general, Father Francis Libermann,[19] was a Jewish convert to Catholicism. Father Libermann lived through two revolutions (in 1830 and 1848) and a seven-month cholera epidemic. This physical wreck of a man with epilepsy had a God-given talent for psychological analysis. "He knew a soul through and through in an instant. He went right to the basis of my character and the source of my trouble. Immediately he pointed out what I should do and how." So many people came to him seeking peace of mind, it's a wonder he accomplished anything.

As spiritual director for seminarians, Father Libermann worried about the clergy's loss of human sympathy and Christian charity. It wasn't just the clergy about whom he was concerned. "Psychologists, social workers, doctors and nurses need inspiration and encouragement if organized charity is not to become the great fiasco of our century."

He reminded the seminarians that most souls are lost through discouragement. "Mildness and persuasion reach the heart, but harshness and rigidity cause only an external change. If you treat people with consideration and real charity, you will help them overcome their faults." He also told them not to walk around looking like gloomy sad sacks. "At your age gaiety is a necessity. When you feel like laughing, go ahead, laugh. Be cheerful, laugh heartily."

His ideas were a hundred years ahead of his time. "Above all," he said, "you should respect individual personalities. Everyone has his own pathway—his own direction to follow in going to God." He advised students to develop their personalities not by repressing their nature, but by unfolding their individuality with the help of God's grace . . . and to be tolerant. For example, "If you were to try and force Father Arragon to conduct himself in a sedate, polite, and friendly fashion, you would be pursuing a will-o-the-

Saint Sulpice Church

Father Libermann

wisp. You would stand a better chance of stopping the sun in its course, but if you treat him kindly, let him act according to his character and the way he is built, you will certainly bring out the good in him. If we accord to everyone the freedom to follow his own ideas and to do good in his own way, in his own manner, a great deal of good will be achieved."

He told them not to talk too much. "A multiplicity of words drains your spirit like water and gives self-love a chance to grow unhampered . . . and don't parade your knowledge even when people obviously don't know what they are talking about."

He also told them to stop thinking about themselves and go help someone much worse off. I don't know if they took his advice, but it reminded me of the minister who told Effie, one of his flock, that she was grieving too much. Effie told him, "Preacher, I can't help it. When the Lord sends me tribulations, I got to tribulate."

Father Libermann was probably the first to hold a motivational behavior seminar . . . comparable to those held today for people to be "in sync." In the early 1800s, he advised spiritual directors to adjust their speech and behavior to the emotional make-up and interests of the people with whom they deal. "If you treat everybody identically alike, you will never succeed."

A century before families became addicted to television, he was saying, "Modern man easily loses his inner freedom in his constant agitation. Hyperactive, tense, anxious, he lives passively instead of actively, being influenced rather than influencing."

He even helped an unhappy, oversexed man who thought for sure he was going to hell. Father Libermann told the man to check with his doctor. Maybe bloodletting or a laxative might help. Research in endocrinology has confirmed his idea that often moral problems are the result of a physiological problem.

While sickly Father Libermann was being sent to different places to recuperate and was falling on the floor with epileptic seizures in the classroom, Eugène Delacroix was painting *Liberty Leading the People*, and young seminarians were arguing passionately about politics. Professors and students shivered as they hurried along drafty corridors while cold, cutting winds from the Seine howled through the ancient buildings.

Thirty years later, the Church of Saint Sulpice was just as cold when Delacroix (a year after the 1848 Revolution) began painting the Chapel of Angels, the first chapel inside the door on the right. *Saint Michael Slaying the Demon Dragon* is on the ceiling. On the right wall greedy Heliodorus, minister to the king of Syria, is stopped from looting Jehovah's Temple by three avenging angels. One angel's magnificent horse stomps on Heliodorus, whose henchmen cringe in a corner. Loot is spilled all over. Delacroix holds the swirling baroque action firmly in place with a colossal central column. Behind the column a rose-colored drapery billows in a brisk breeze. One angel resembles a purple-robed scuba diver. Another flexes his muscles like Popeye the Sailor Man.

On the opposite wall is Delacroix's painting *Jacob Wrestles with the Angel*. Jacob had tricked his blind old father, Isaac, into giving him the patriarchal blessing of the first born, which rightly belonged to his brother, Esau. When Esau and his father learned of Jacob's deceit, "furious" is a mild word. If you don't want to blame Jacob, you could blame his mother, Rebekah. It was all her idea. Jacob was her favorite. To prevent Esau from killing Jacob, she arranged for Jacob to stay with her brother, Laban, across the Jordan. On the way, he dreamed his "Jacob's Ladder" dream. At the top of a ladder reaching to heaven with angels ascending and descending, the Lord appeared and told Jacob that he and his descendants would be given the promised land of Canaan.

After living with his Uncle Laban for twenty years, Jacob had another dream in which God told him to return to Canaan. Several angels appeared to reassure him that everything would be fine—not to worry. Jacob was not so sure. To smooth the way, he sent a messenger, who was to inform Esau of everything that had happened and tell Esau that his brother was returning. Then Jacob implored God to save him from Esau. He thanked God for being so kind, even though he certainly didn't deserve it, and finally, he sent Esau some sheep. (Here's a present. Please don't kill me.)

During the night, an angel appeared as a man and proceeded to wrestle with Jacob all night. When the angel realized Jacob would not surrender, he lightly touched him on the thigh, dislocating the joint. Still Jacob would not give up. He told the "man," "I will not let go until you give me your blessing." The man asked his name. "Jacob." The man replied, "Your name shall no longer be Jacob but Israel, which means 'Prince of God'." The angel blessed him, then vanished. Jacob renamed the place where the angel had appeared *Phanuel,* meaning "the face of God." "Surely the Lord was in this place, and I did not know it." Through Jacob the promise God made to Abraham was fulfilled—that his descendants would inherit the promised land. Jacob didn't know who his opponent was, but in the end, he asked a blessing of him. He didn't realize he was an angel—a messenger of God.

In Delacroix's *Jacob Wrestles with the Angel,* the peaceful *Midsummer Night's Dream* setting contrasts with hand-to-hand combat. Jacob's muscles are as powerful as the wildly imaginative tree branches. One branch repeats the motif of horses' hooves.

The angel of God, determined to accomplish his mission, is Delacroix's typical combination of combat and spirituality. The story is interpreted as a symbol of the ordeals God sometimes sends His special people. It is also a reminder of God's mysterious ways: His long-term plan and strange choice of people.

Jacob's aloneness through trials and tribulations (to which Delacroix could relate) is represented by a flat still life in the foreground: a hat, scarf, spear, and arrow. It should have been Delacroix's brush, palette, and canvas.

Delacroix worked on the Chapel of Angels at Saint Sulpice for two years. When the government demanded to know when the painting would be finished, Delacroix told them he didn't know any more than they did. Ten months later, he died of tuberculosis.

6

Garnier's Opera House
Where the Whole World Meets to Get Off Their Feet

IN A SLIGHT DRIZZLE, we parked our little white Renault half on the street and half on the sidewalk at the back of the opera building—where architecture looks business-like contrasted with the rest of the lavishly decorated building. We walked around steps and steps and steps until we found an open door on the street level, then down more steps until we found ourselves wandering around in storage rooms for costumes, scenery, and props. Next to a cafeteria we spied an elevator that deposited us in the fabulously ornate white marble foyer designed by Charles Garnier for Napoléon III.

When Garnier showed the innovative plans to Empress Eugénie, she asked, "What on earth is this?" He told her it was a new style called Napoléon III. Unfortunately, the emperor and Eugénie were not around for opening night. By then, Napoléon III had been dead for two years after having been defeated and captured by the Prussians. Empress Eugénie was an exile in Chislehurst, England. Instead of the emperor and empress, it was the newly elected President of the Third Republic, Field Marshall MacMahon, with his wife and Garnier, who ascended the brilliantly gaslit white marble staircase for the gala occasion.

Garnier's Opera House is like a gorgeous woman. Fascinated by her beauty, one never suspects that hidden beneath the lovely features there might be suffering and pain. During the 1870 Franco-Prussian War, the ornate building was used as a gigantic storehouse and prison. Then, through the bloody days of the Commune, she watched Parisians slaughter each other on her doorstep.[1] Under dusty sheets during World War II, she endured the humiliation of Nazi boots demeaning her dignity.

The day we visited the Opera we were not knee-deep in tourists. There was time to enjoy the paintings, sculpture, mirrors, marble, and gold. There was time to think of that elegant evening in 1875 when Parisian elite, glittering with jewels, filled the crimson-carpeted halls with a hubbub of happy noise. Throughout the performance, they continued to inspect their glamorous new opera house, the largest in the world. (If they had checked the whole place out, they would have had to open 1,606 doors and peer into 334 dressing rooms.)

The program that cold January night included Delibes' ballet *La Source* and Rossini's *William Tell* Overture, but the singers could barely hear the orchestra. The sulking musicians played pianissimo throughout the entire performance. They were insulted at being buried in what they considered a hole. Now we call it an orchestra pit.

Seventeen years before the grand opening, in front of the old opera house on a narrow street,[2] an Italian terrorist had thrown a bomb at the emperor's carriage.[3] One hundred and fifty people were injured, the carriage blown up, and the coachman killed. Neither the emperor nor his wife, Eugénie, was touched. They calmly walked in and took their seats, and amid cheers, the performance began. That is *savoir faire*! The shakes came later.

To avoid a repeat performance, the emperor ordered a new opera house surrounded by wide-open space.[4] The site selected was north of place de la Concorde. There was one slight problem for the architect, Garnier. The selected spot was on a swamp which took eight months to drain. Today water is still beneath the opera house, and—who knows?—maybe the bones of the Phantom of the Opera.

Garnier thought of everything: Apollo, the Greek god of music, located on the roof, separate entrances for pedestrians and those arriving by carriage; and rehearsal rooms for the singers, dancers, and orchestra. Before elevators were installed, it took the orchestra and singers more than an hour to reach the rehearsal room.

What Garnier never could have envisioned was Marc Chagall's new

Carpeaux's *La Danse*

ceiling, *Bouquet of Dreams,* a swirly, whimsical world of color floating above the crimson-cushioned seats. The whirling, circular *Bouquet* represents music, ballets, and stage sets. Chagall chose the color red in the *Bouquet* to represent composers Ravel and Stravinsky; white streaked with yellow is Debussy and Rameau (court composer for Louis XV); green is for Berlioz and Wagner; blue for Mozart and Mussorgsky; yellow for Tchaikovsky and the French troubadour Adam de la Halle. Scattered stage sets suggest Verdi's *Aida,* Meyerbeer's *Les Huguenots,* and Stravinsky's *Rake's Progress.*

In Chagall's fantasy world, objects merge and change form as they do in fairy tales, where swans change into people and frogs turn into princes. In *The Bouquet of Dreams* a chicken plays a flute, two legs dance a *pas de deux,* a winged eagle has the body of a cello—but that's all right. This is Chagall, dreaming of all creatures great and small; man and nature united in one big, beautiful creation. Animals, people, plants, sun, moon, wind, weather are all part of God's beautiful and wondrous creation. God used Chagall as His spokesman. Earlier, it was Saint Francis of Assisi.

Chagall wrote: "Up there I wanted to reflect, like in a mirror, a bouquet of dreams and creations; of actors and musicians up there remembering the color of the audiences' clothes moving about below. To sing like a bird without themes or any method." Now, "up there," in heaven Garnier and Chagall are getting acquainted. A friend told me that during the renovations that took place under President de Gaulle, he and other Parisian boys played Tarzan on the ropes backstage.

As we left the beautiful opera house, pigeons were flying around the foyer, where busts of Gounod, Lulli, Debussy, Gluck, Rameau, and Handel greet visitors and audiences who enter the traditional way. Outside the door we found the replica of Carpeaux's famous sculpture, *La Danse.*[5] When the statue was unveiled in 1868, an indignant journalist wrote, "Is opera meant to become a brothel? When the dancer on the right is arrested for drunkenness, the whole group will collapse."

Of all the congratulations and bravos Garnier received for his magnificent achievement, the one he treasured most was a medal from his workmen commemorating their happy relationship.

7

Opéra Comique and Bizet's *Carmen*
A Girl's Picture and a Recipe for Gazpacho Soup

NEAR GARNIER'S OPERA HOUSE, tucked away off boulevard des Italians on rue Favart, is the beautiful Opéra Comique or Salle Favart. Charles Favart (1710–1792), the son of a pastry cook, was such a talented playwright and successful director of the Opéra Comique that jealous Comédie des Italians forced him to close. Favart took his company to entertain French troops fighting the Austrians in Flanders. The enemy troops wanted to be entertained too, so between battles, Favart's vaudeville troupe performed for both sides. When the head of the French army, Marshal Saxe, made advances to Favart's wife, the star of the show, she escaped to Paris. Favart, after being served with a *lettre de cachet* sentencing him to prison, fled to Strasbourg. Although the Marshal made Favart's wife his mistress, she was so fickle that he stashed her in a convent. After he died in 1750, she returned to her husband and performed for the next twenty years during the time of King Louis XV.

Until gaslights were introduced in 1820 (under Louis XVIII), theater audiences choked from smoky candles and sooty oil lamps. "We suffocate, can see little, and hear even less." But the duchesse d'Abrantes raved about the magnificent opera scenery: "A cloudy world surrounded by mist . . .

Back to Europe with the BUSY BODY

golden palaces suspended in the air."[1] Also suspended in the air were dancers who flew across the stage attached to wires. One critic wrote, "They were as nimble as hams hung in the butcher's shop." Another observed in Rossini's opera *Moses,* "The Red Sea which had been happy to let the Israelites cross, did not want to engulf the Egyptians. Precautions have been made to ensure that the next time, the Red Sea knows its rôle better."

In Baroque operas, gods and goddesses flying to Mount Olympus in the god machine often dangled in midair, begging stage hands to rescue them. In the casual Théâtre des Italiens, the leading man blew his nose, greeted friends, and ate spaghetti in the middle of a performance. One time when Desdemona fell down after being murdered, she got up to die more comfortably on a bed.

Today the Opéra Comique is the second auditorium of the French Opera Company. The sculptured facade is lighted by Art Nouveau globes atop swirly wrought-iron lamp posts. Here on opening night 1875, Bizet's *Carmen* was a dismal failure. Bizet rewrote it, and two nights later the audience applauded and cheered. However, critics had already condemned it. After Bizet's death, his friend Ernest Guiraud changed the spoken dialogue into music, and when it opened as an opera at the Grand Opera House, *Carmen* conquered the world. If the short story writer Prosper Mérimée had not been so thirsty and insisted on stopping at a Spanish inn, he never would have met Carmencita, and there never would have been a *Carmen.*

Unfortunately, Bizet's flamboyant Spanish opera, based on Mérimée's quiet, brooding story, opened at a family theater where everything ended happily. *Carmen* did not end happily. The producer even begged, "Please try not to have her die. Death on the stage of the Opéra Comique? Never! Don't make her die. I beg of you, don't." But Carmen died, and her fate became Bizet's personal tragedy.

Bizet was named for three emperors: Alexander the Great, Caesar, and the Holy Roman Emperor Leopold I. He settled for Georges. Even people who cannot carry a tune know songs and snatches from his opera *Carmen.*

Both his parents were musical, especially on his mother's side. At nineteen he was the youngest composer[2] to win the Prix de Rome, the highest award of the Music Conservatory. After three idyllic years of study at the Villa Medici, the brilliant, good-natured genius returned to Paris ready to prove himself. His first opera, *The Pearl Fishers,* set in Ceylon, was produced at the Théâtre Lyrique (today's Odéon),[3] and the audience actually applauded. But exuberant Bizet ran up on stage to take a bow, and from then on, the press hated him. "This sort of exhibitionism is admissible only for a most extraordinary success. Even then we prefer to have the composer dragged on stage in spite of himself or at least pretending to be."

Despondent, Bizet took refuge at le Vesinet, twelve miles from Paris, where his father had recently built two cottages. On the train he met a neighbor he could at least talk to—the incredible Celeste Magador, reformed prostitute, actress, singer, dancer, circus rider, writer, producer, countess, and now landowner. She bought a piano for him, and once more he regrouped and tried again, this time with *The Fair Maid of Perth*, which was set in a Scottish locale. It closed after eighteen performances.

Other musicians in Paris, who were coping with their own problems at the time, were Offenbach, Berlioz, Gounod, and Saint-Saëns. Emperor Napoléon III and Empress Eugénie ruled, Impressionists were painting and Jules Verne[4] was writing, but Thomas Edison and the Statue of Liberty were more popular.

In 1869 Bizet, at thirty-one, married the twenty-year-old daughter of his renowned piano teacher at the Music Conservatory, Fromental Halévy. What Bizet didn't know was that the whole family worshipped money, his mother-in-law was emotionally unstable, and his pretty bride was not the ideal helpmate. They made his personal life hell.

A year after the marriage, France declared war on Prussia. The writer Théophile Gautier, left safety in Switzerland. "When I heard they were beating up my Mama, I came home." Emperor Napoléon III was captured, Paris was encircled by Prussians, and Bizet joined the wholly disorganized National Guard. "Our guns weigh fourteen pounds. That's heavy for a musician. These weapons kick back, spit, do everything possible to be more disagreeable to those who fire them than to the enemy." He relieved the monotony of standing guard by noting the key in which the cannon shells screamed.

For three weeks Paris was bombarded, people starved, and the only way out was by balloon. "One-hundred or more scoundrels and agitators proclaim to be republicans. . . . They will start an insurrection, that is clear." The Prussians recognized revolution in the air. They stayed in the city one day then retreated to the outskirts to watch the French destroy themselves. The artist Pissarro fled from Louveciennes outside Paris. He left 1,500 canvases, which the Prussians used as aprons and ruined with the blood of slaughtered animals. A neighbor wrote to tell him his house had been confiscated. "There are a few pictures which these gentlemen, for fear of dirtying their feet, put on the ground in the garden to serve as a carpet." During the infamous civil war, newly married Bizet fled with his wife to Compiègne. When the Communards were defeated, Bizet returned to Paris.

A year later, in 1872, his moody opera *l'Arlésienne* opened with no publicity while the usual fashionable audience was on holiday. The bourgeois, who came to the theater to show off their marriageable daughters, talked, laughed, went in and out banging doors, and by the end of the first act the house was three-quarters empty. Shaking a fist at the vacant theater, a bitterly disappointed Bizet kept repeating, "They did not understand me. They did not understand me." Alphonse Daudet, the playwright from Nîmes who wrote the story of *l'Arlésienne,* said, "I am sunk in my arm chair and 250 years old. And to think I have to start work again. It was a most glorious fall in the midst of the nicest music." One cranky critic wrote that music is rarely welcome in a drama, but Daudet told a friend, "When we have dark weather here in Paris, I ask my wife to play it and instantly my heart swells like a sponge." He also said, "The zigzag violin bowing of the gypsies kept me from seeing the Exposition. Each time those cursed violins caught me as I went by, it was impossible to go farther. I had to stay there until evening, a glass of Hungarian wine on the table, a lump in my throat, madness in my eye. My whole body quivering to the nervous beat of the tympani."

L'Arlésienne, set on the edge of a swamp in the Camargue where bulls are bred and wild horses still roam, is the true story of a young farmer in love with a city girl from Arles. When the hero learns from the girl's former lover that she is a "vile jade" who has been his mistress for two years, the boy commits suicide.

The timing for the tense tragedy was terrible. Parisians had just survived a year of starvation, bombing, and slaughter. Who needed more tragedy? There wasn't even a pretty girl to look at. The city girl never appears on stage.

Fortunately for Bizet's morale, when his *l'Arlésienne* music was presented without the libretto, it became popular in the concert halls. Glowing embers buried under ashes of despair burned a little brighter, and he tried again, this time with Prosper Mérimée's short story "Carmen." While orchestrating 1,200 pages (each note blotted with special powder), he also gave piano lessons to pay for a new baby boy. One piano student remembered Bizet jumping up in the middle of a lesson, running into another

Opéra Comique and Bizet's Carmen

room to play a melody in his head. "I remember particularly, 'The Toreador Song.'"

Mérimée died in Cannes five years before Bizet's opera opened. While traveling in Spain, he usually carried on his saddle a big pot, oil, pimentos, and a live rooster for his supper. One night, however, he stopped at an inn where he sketched a dark, pretty girl who gave him her recipe for gazpacho. His nervous guide insisted on leaving. He said the girl was a witch: "First a whore, then a procuress, then a witch." When Empress Eugénie's mother told Mérimée a true story of a girl believed to be a witch, he remembered the gypsy girl, Carmencita, at the inn.

Mérimée knew his gypsies. He had studied the girls leaving the cigar factory in Seville with their "impudent glances and swaying hips like fillies." He loved their passionate, exaggerated expressions, such as "I would stab the sun if I were not afraid of leaving the world in darkness."

The opera *Carmen* is a fascinating combination of Mérimée and Bizet. In Celeste Magador's *Memoires,* Bizet recalls, "Moderation is not part of my nature. My life has been one long excess. The defects in my character have protected me. I have always been capricious and proud. The men to whom I have given the most are those who asked the least." He rewrote "If You Love Me, I Don't Love You" thirteen times before using it in the Spanish dance, *Habanera,* in Act I.

For years Bizet had maintained the farce of appearing optimistic. Like a gambler down to his last hope, *Carmen* would be his winner. The director hated it. He did everything possible to undermine the production. He said Bizet's music was cochin, Chinese . . . utterly incomprehensible. When *Carmen* opened, journalists had already judged it in print as immoral (Carmen and her friends smoked on stage) saying "Mlle. Carmen should temper her passions." One critic called Bizet a musical anti-Christ who dreamed of destroying melody, rhythm, and tonality.

In his fatalistic *Carmen,* Bizet sees himself. When Carmen tries to seduce Don José from his duty, enticing him with visions of a free, wandering gypsy life, Bizet sadly remembers his happy times in Italy. When Carmen sings of her determination to be free, it is Bizet's desperate cry. His marriage was miserable. His self-confidence as a man and musician was shattered. If only he were free—maybe. Carmen was as destructive to herself as she was to her lover. In the card scene when she draws the ace of spades, she foresees her own death. ("Death! I've read it well. First I, then he.") Three months after opening night, Bizet was dead at thirty-seven.

The critics literally broke his heart. The terror of believing them took its toll. His response was a French shrug; "Perhaps they are right." The critics' judgment of "guilty" and "failure" brought on another anxiety attack of flaming tonsillitis and muscular rheumatism. A suicidal swim in cold water caused paralysis, a heart attack, and death—the death Carmen had read in the cards. His last concern was for his father. "How are you going to tell my poor father?" Bizet never knew he had produced the greatest French opera of the nineteenth century.

The funeral was marvelous! Four thousand people crowded into the Church of the Trinity in Paris. All the singers from the Opéra Comique were there. After Chopin's "Funeral March," during Mass the actor who played Don José in *Carmen* sang the *Agnus Dei* (Lamb of God). After Mass, the organist improvised on themes from Bizet's music. When antisocial Saint-Saëns heard of Bizet's death, he was in the organ loft in the Church of the Madeleine. He sat at the top of the winding staircase, head buried in his hands.[5]

8

Napoléon III (1808–1873)

A Matter of Pride[1]

ALSO NEAR GARNIER'S OPERA is the church of Saint Augustin, named for Saint Augustin from Algiers. Part Renaissance, part Byzantine, Saint Augustin is one of the most fascinating churches in Paris. Buried on either side of the steps are Philippe Égalité and twenty-four-year-old Charlotte Corday from Saint Saturnin in Normandy, who stabbed the revolutionist Jean-Paul Marat (in his bathtub) for his role in the murder of moderate Girondists in the National Assembly. Inside the church, high, arched windows encircle the dome like Saint Sophia's in Istanbul. In a little park on one side, roses bloomed, and Parisians basked in the sun, reading their books and newspapers. The church was built during Napoléon III's Second Empire.

Napoléon III (Louis Napoléon), is associated with today's beautiful Paris, the Suez Canal,[2] Empress Eugénie's dresses by Charles Frederick Worth, and the fall of the Second Empire. Louis Napoléon, Empress Josephine's favorite grandson, was a quiet, sensitive little boy who wanted to sell violets when he grew up. He should have done that. Instead, he listened to stories about his godlike uncle, Napoléon I.

Louis was seven and his brother eleven when Napoléon I was sent to Saint Helena. Under the new Bourbon regime of Louis XVIII, both boys were exiled with their parents—who were separated. Louis Napoléon accompanied his mother, beautiful Hortense (Josephine's daughter), to Arenenberg, Switzerland,[3] while his brother went to Italy with his father, Louis Bonaparte, Napoléon's brother. At school in Augsburg, Austria, Louis' tutor extolled the Napoléonic legend, convincing his obedient student that it was his duty to continue the work of the great conqueror. Against his nature, the compassionate boy (who probably inherited Josephine's genes) prepared himself for his assigned role as a soldier.

During their exile, both boys, now teenagers, had joined Italian revolutionaries fighting to oust the Austrians. Their knight-errant endeavor for this cause was Louis Napoléon's first attempt to carry on the Napoléonic tradition. After his brother died of pneumonia and measles during a retreat from the Austrians, Louis Napoléon embarked on a series of comic-opera escapades. His cousin, Princess Mathilde, remembered him as "gay, unruly, a bit of a story teller, and a little given to banter."

In order to visit France, his mother, Hortense, now forty-seven, met him at Pesaro, Italy, and managed to obtain a passport under a false name. With Louis disguised as her footman, they traveled undetected and landed on the Citizen King's doorstep. The king of the French was not amused. He had been capitalizing on Napoléon's name to win votes by bringing Napoléon's body back from Saint Helena and remounting his statue on the Vendôme Column. Again Louis and his mother packed their bags—this time for England.

When it became obvious that the Citizen King would not restore their fortune, they had to return to Switzerland. Still in disguise, they stopped at Fontainebleau in France, where Louis had been christened twenty-three years before. They also visited Josephine's tomb outside Paris in Rueil Malmaison. Nearby at Château Malmaison,[4] however, where Hortense had lived with her mother, her brother Eugène, and Napoléon, they were told by new owners that visitors were not allowed. Back they went, still incognito, to Switzerland.

Four years after Napoléon's only son and heir died at twenty-one of tuberculosis,[5] Louis Napoléon decided it was time to unseat Citizen King Louis Philippe and carry on the Napoléonic dynasty. He chose Strasbourg as the first city to be liberated. In the middle of the night he arrived at the fort with a few followers to announce the good news that the city was free.

At twenty-eight, sensitive Louis Napoléon, who was still unable to hurt anyone, naïvely thought he could conquer by persuasion. It doesn't work

Napoléon III

that way. As the French say, "You cannot make an omelette without breaking eggs." When the little group marched into a cul-de-sac, they were surrounded by soldiers with bayonets. Later he wrote, "I realized our plan had gone wrong." They were arrested and marched off to prison. French king Louis Philippe muttered something like "I was afraid of that," and ordered him off to America, where he visited New York, Niagara Falls, and had a picnic in the Adirondacks with his uncle Joseph Bonaparte, also in exile.

When word arrived that Louis' mother was dying, he left for Switzerland (in disguise) and fortunately arrived in time. Hortense was buried[6] next to her mother six years after she had visited Josephine's tomb.

Louis joined other exiled Frenchmen in London while his agents in France kept the Napoléonic cult alive. By 1840, Louis had waited long enough. He would give France a second chance for glory. This time the target was Boulogne in Normandy. With a live eagle chained to the deck of a steamboat, the would-be king, with fifty-six friends, set off on his mission down the Thames and across the channel. Landing at Boulogne, they trooped into the Old Town barracks but were promptly shoved out. Then they headed for the High Town to storm the fort, but the gates of the medieval walls were locked. When the National Guard appeared, the liberators ran to the shore, threw themselves into the water, and swam, dodging bullets, toward their steamer.[7] Port officials hauled them out of the water. In their soggy new uniforms, with teeth chattering and pride shattered, they were corralled into the castle. It was another failure for the softhearted young man. He was sentenced to life imprisonment at Ham on the Somme River (between Amiens and Laon), where he lived in two rooms on the first floor of a medieval donjon.

Compared with Lafayette's ordeal, his confinement was paradise—cold and damp, yes, but the benefits were great: friends, games, books,[8] a mistress, and his personal valet. However, he constantly planned his day of conquest. After six years his father's illness provided an excuse for another slapstick escape. Dr. Conneau, Louis Napoléon's friend and doctor, pretended his patient had taken an overdose of castor oil and could not possibly be up and about. (The doctor mixed chemicals to make an unpleasant odor to prove it.) That night at bed check guards found a dummy in the prisoner's bed.

Louis Napoléon walked out of the fortress dressed as a carpenter and smoking a pipe, his face shielded by the wooden plank he carried over his shoulder. His valet distracted the workmen by offering them a bottle of wine. Two hours later, Louis and his valet caught a train for Brussels and from there returned to England. He never did get to his father's deathbed in Italy.[9]

He was living on King Street off Saint James' Square when news arrived of the 1848 Revolution. It was King Louis Philippe's turn to flee. Surely now the French would call for him. When they didn't, he returned anyway, to run for deputy of the Seine. His campaign workers in France had been distributing pamphlets promoting him as champion of the oppressed and upholder of law and order. They stuck little *tricolores* in people's lapels and sold matches with his picture on them. After thirty years of exile, prison, and plotting, he did something right. The advertising campaign paid off. First he was elected deputy for the Seine by 4,420 votes, and in the next election, for president of the Second Republic, he won in five departments over his only opponent. When he entered Paris in triumph,[10] Parisians were shocked. They thought they had elected another heroic Napoléon. Instead, their new leader looked exhausted. He was little, skinny, stooped, and shy. However, his famous name and quiet strength were reassuring. Instead of making speeches, he listened. "Words directed toward him are like stones thrown into a well; one hears the noise, but one does not know what has become of them," said de Tocqueville.

When he was elected president, he made the mistake of swearing to uphold the Constitution—which limited him to a four-year term. He assumed the National Assembly would release him from his oath, but they didn't. To them his idealism and concern for the poor indicated weakness.[11] It made them nervous. As emperor, he could make things happen. He was especially interested in Louis Pasteur's studies. (It wasn't until he asked Pasteur why so much wine went bad on the way to the consumer that the negative role of oxygen was understood.)[12] Socialists and radicals were determined to defeat him, and investors were not investing until after the election. To carry out his dream, his alternative was a *coup d'état*.

The *coup* was accomplished with comparatively little violence. The soldiers had been wined and dined at supper parties—with emphasis on the wine. Officers chummily lit enlisted men's cigars, and everyone helped each other stagger home. Overnight, opposition politicians and representatives were hauled out of bed to jail.[13] The assembly was dissolved and the right to vote restored. Awaiting the outcome at the Élysée Palace, President Louis Napoléon wore his bathrobe over his boots and spurs, not knowing whether to go to bed or jump on a horse.

Napoléon III

The third day of the coup, Victor Hugo, the ferocious watchdog of human rights, gave him some trouble. Hugo had formed a resistance committee, urging Parisians to build barricades. He also signed a poster labeling Louis Napoléon an outlaw. When 30,000 soldiers fired on 1,200 pathetically armed civilians, resistance collapsed. In an election three weeks later, eight million Frenchmen voted for Louis Napoléon and his Constitution—giving him unlimited power for the next ten years. The Senate named him emperor, and at forty-four, Louis Napoléon became ruler of France. Karl Marx complained he was too much like his uncle. Others said he was too much like Karl Marx. Now that there was "law and order," the emperor could move into his dream castle, the Tuileries, and fulfill all his dreams. "I want to be a second Augustus, he declared,"because Augustus . . . made Rome a city of marble."

Continuing the work of his uncle, Napoléon III made Paris so beautiful his plans were copied by cities throughout the world. Georges Haussmann,[14] probably the most honest public administrator in France, made the emperor's dream on paper come true. Louis Napoléon had drawn up blueprints in four colors—red was priority number one. The Bois de Boulogne (designed after Hyde Park in London), the Opera, and the Hôtel Dieu were marked red and completed in five years for the 1855 Exposition—as well as The Louvre, place de l'Hôtel de Ville, Napoléon's barracks, rue de Rivoli, and boulevard de Strasbourg. The whole city was torn up and filled with dirt, dust, mud and noise. His seventeen-year public works project gave employment to thousands who came to Paris on the new railroads. Paris under glittering gaslights became the prosperous capital of the world.

In France a thin line separated opposition and revolution. If the emperor's plans for the benefit of his people were to be accomplished, there must be peace. And there was—peace with no liberty. All dissension was silenced after an Italian terrorist bombed the emperor's carriage as he and Eugénie arrived at the Opera on rue Peletier for a performance of Rossini's *William Tell*. Immediately, the assembly passed the infamous Law of Public Security, which allowed the government to fine, jail, or deport anyone holding inconvenient opinions.

In 1860 Louis Napoléon lifted the lid off the boiling kettle to let a little steam escape. He allowed opponents in the assembly to disagree with his policies and permitted debates to be published. He formed a new liberal government, but it was too late. "The Empire is Peace," he once said. If he had followed that policy, the story might have been different. As it happened, the drama became a tragedy.

Like Napoléon I, he had married[15] to produce an heir, flaunted mistresses, and assumed the role of liberator. He had married blonde, twenty-six-year-old Eugénie de Montijo from Granada—seventeen years younger and famous for saying, "The only way to my room, Monsieur, is through the castle chapel." Their licentious, immoral court contaminated all Paris. De Tocqueville wrote, "We are marching toward universal prostitution. The empire is given over to the pursuit of sexual gratification. Spirituality and grace have yielded to flesh triumphant and the worship of banknotes."

Loquacious, excitable Eugénie, pushy and power hungry, embroiled her husband in disastrous foreign policies. Twice she had acted as regent when he led troops into the Crimea[16] and Italy. During the Italian War, an Englishman, Lord Houghton, wrote that he was going to Oberammergau to see the Passion Play, but Jesus was taken off to serve in the artillery with Judas Iscariot as his superior officer.[17]

Eugénie also met with the National Assembly when her husband was incapacitated with agonizing pain from gallstones. Doped to relieve the pain and indecisive, his whole character changed. Under his wife's influence he governed with endless maneuvering and temporizing. Those who opposed the empress were fired.

After attempting for twenty years to sway the destiny of Europe in the Napoléonic tradition, Louis Napoléon's life ended like that of his hero, Napoléon—in defeat on the battlefield and exile. Goaded on by Empress Eugénie,[18] the fiasco in Mexico[19] was as disastrous as Napoléon's Egyptian and Russian campaigns. Through intricate details of power politics in foreign relations, Louis Napoléon's story reaches its climax in Spain.

In the 1860s the Spanish throne was empty, and the name of a Prussian prince[20] had been submitted as a substitute. Louis Napoléon vehemently objected, and Eugénie, unfortunately influenced by war-hungry Otto von Bismark, demanded an apology from affable Prussian king William I. The king wrote to his wife, "They want me to sit on the stool of repentance." A matter of pride led to war between France and Prussia, with Eugénie and Bismark, the Prussian Premier, mainly responsible.

Bismark's plot to expand his empire and provoke France into war succeeded. While France disarmed, he mapped his strategy. The French Assembly that voted to disarm had also voted for war. Louis Napoléon, knowing the odds, wept. Eugénie bundled her fourteen-year-old son and sick

Napoléon III

husband off to war with makeup to hide his pallor[21] and dyed hair which had turned completely white. Then she formed a cabinet of world imperialists. The emperor, trapped at Sedan with General MacMahon, sent his wife a revealing, pathetic note: "The army is shut in on all sides. No troops, no ammunition, no food . . . I feel sad when I see how heavy your heart is . . . If only I could find a small place there." Rather than sacrifice 130,000 men, the emperor surrendered. After six months' imprisonment in Belgium,[22] he joined his wife and son, who had escaped separately. Their son had been sent alone to Chislehurst, England, where Eugénie had joined him with the help of her American dentist, Dr. Evans, who had made a fortune in gold fillings.

With stoic dignity, calm, soft-spoken Louis Napoléon suffered public abuse for two years. He died after two operations two days apart for gallstones. In the eyes of the world he was a failure, but the inscription on his tombstone might have been the tribute of a friend. "His remarkable smile, which could light up his dark countenance, his quiet, calm dignity and absence of irritability were the grandest example of human moral courage." Six years later, their twenty-three-year-old son died fighting with the English in South Africa against the Zulus. He was found naked in a ditch with seventeen spear wounds. Eugénie died at ninety-four.

9

Chopin (1810–1849)

The brooks murmur. A bell is ringing.

*My flock lingers on the steep slope and I watch them—singing carefree—
The hedge is blooming. The lark sings and my heart sighs.
I say to the bird, Go little psalmist.
Carry the song of our earth to the Heavenly Spheres.*
—STEFAN WITWICKI, Polish poet

PARIS TOUR GUIDES point out #12 place Vendôme, where Chopin died, but his residence at Square d'Orléans is more fun. A covered cobblestone driveway leads into a large courtyard. Today, the apartments are painted a bright cheery yellow.

When Franz Liszt heard Chopin play for the first time, he went home to practice six hours a day for four years to equal Chopin's technique. He never did. No one could imitate Chopin's disciplined left hand as his right hand rippled over the keyboard. Captivated audiences, waiting in suspense, never knew where the next wavy, undecided chord would fall.

Chopin's music was the song of his Polish earth, the gaiety of youth, and grief for his beloved homeland.[1] No one hearing his happy waltzes and galloping mazurkas would guess he weighed less than one hundred pounds, had to be carried upstairs, and was in such pain from tuberculosis he gave piano lessons from a couch.

When Chopin arrived alone in the Paris of Citizen King Louis Philippe, he had a few letters of introduction, not much money, and no country. His native Poland had fallen to the Russians. Warsaw, after heroic resistance, was in ruins, but there a mother's prayers for her only son, Frédéric Chopin, were answered.

Chopin

Homesick, discouraged, his money dwindling, Chopin met in the boulevards Prince Radziwill, for whom he had performed in Warsaw. The prince arranged a concert at Baron Rothschild's, where a committee was set up to launch Chopin's career. Society women adored him. They all wanted to protect the thin, blond genius whose offbeat music, whether wistful or rollicking, left them spellbound. The one who snared him was George Sand, the celebrated female writer who wore men's clothing,[2] smoked cigars, and wrote about free love for women and what went on in their heads (mostly hers). Chopin, the new darling of the salons, intrigued her. He even looked like his music—mysterious, fragile, and aloof. Always on the lookout for a new lover to analyze, Sand planned her strategy for the conquest. She asked Liszt and his mistress, comtesse Marie d'Agôult, to introduce her to Chopin at their next soirée. Reserved, well-bred Chopin was not impressed. It didn't take a Freud to figure out that this liberated woman had a problem. Sand had staged herself leaning against a mantelpiece puffing a black cigar and dressed in a Turkish outfit: wide purple pantaloons with a red scarf wound around her black hair. On the way home Chopin asked his friend, the artist Delacroix, "Is she really a woman? She didn't please me at all." But she did get his attention. A month later she was on the guest list at one of Chopin's intimate concerts, given mostly for his Polish friends. This time she came dressed in a red and white Polish costume. No matter what she wore, she was dumpy—with large, masculine features, a double chin, and protruding lower lip. Conversation-wise, she was a parasite—enjoying others' conversation but never contributing. If she hadn't been famous, she would have been called a bore. Still stalking her prey, she wrote to the banker Grymala, "Get Chopin to come to Nohant [her country home in Berry]. Notify me first so I can send Mallefille [her current lover, her son's tutor] to Paris or Geneva."

Chopin had no idea what he was in for—or maybe he did. Even after she sent him a note saying "I adore you," he dragged his feet about going to Nohant. Sand's campaign continued in Paris. By the following spring, he had taken an apartment near hers in the neighborhood of Notre Dame de Lorette,[3] and they were lovers.

Meanwhile at Nohant, Mallefille, the tutor, was getting suspicious of his frequent field trip assignments. He cut short a trip to Le Havre and went to Paris instead, where he stationed himself outside Chopin's apartment. When Sand arrived for her nightly rendezvous, the hot-blooded Creole charged in after his two-timing mistress waving a gun, yelling, and threatening to kill them both. Fortunately, one of Chopin's Polish friends was there to disarm the furious man.

Obviously a change was imperative. The Spanish island of Majorca sounded romantic—and far away. Sand, with her two children, Maurice, fifteen, and daughter Solonge, ten, arranged to meet Chopin in Perpignan[4] (seven miles from the Mediterranean) in deference to Chopin's guilty conscience. He was having trouble rationalizing adultery and conforming to her contempt for marriage.

The romantic free-love honeymooners and the children—Maurice, resembling a girl with long blond hair, and Solonge, with short dark hair and dressed as a boy—boarded a paddle-wheel steamer for Barcelona. The weather was gorgeous, the scenery exotic, and at last Chopin was hers—another conquest for Sand. Now she could be mistress, mother, and nursemaid. They needed her. And that was the truth! The three-month sojourn was a nightmare, although Chopin composed some of his most beautiful music there.[5]

In Palma, the capital of Majorca, the only lodging available was upstairs over a noisy barrel maker's workshop. After four days, they found a house with two rooms outside town in an olive grove. When the cold rains came, the roof leaked and the charcoal brazier smoked. Sheets, pillows, and clothes were clammy and mildewed. Chopin was coughing so badly three doctors declared him practically dead of a contagious disease, and the landlord evicted them. Now what?

Fortunately, or unfortunately, the French Consul found them an abandoned Carthusian monastery big enough to house a small army, perched on a hill where the wind howled through damp, chilly corridors and deserted chapels—a perfect setting for a ghost story. Chopin wrote, "My cell is like an immense coffin. I certainly write you from a strange place."

On a trip to Palma for food, Sand and Maurice were caught in a torrential rainstorm that washed out the roads. For six hours in the dark, they sloshed through water up to their knees. Frantic Chopin, alone with Solonge, decided Sand and Maurice were dead and that he was nearly dead too. He went into a trance, during which he composed Opus 15 in D-flat. Severe hemorrhaging ended the Majorca sojourn. Chopin was lifted into a rickety two-wheeled cart without springs and jolted into Palma. There they boarded a boat loaded with pigs for Barcelona, where a doctor stopped the bleeding.

By the time they returned to Nohant, friends in Paris knew Chopin was

Chopin

Sand's latest catch. What surprised them was that she had kept him so long. In 1842 they moved from their Paris residences to place d'Orléans. Sand's apartment was #5 with the two windows over the arch. Solonge, now fifteen, had her own room, and Maurice, nineteen, had an apartment and art studio. Chopin was across the court on the first floor in #9, where he gave piano lessons. Flamboyant Alexandre Dumas père, the most celebrated playwright in France,[6] was one of five other tenants. Sometimes they all brought food and ate together. Chopin wrote to Sand at Nohant, "Yesterday I dined at the Franchommes by the fire-place in my frock coat. He was pink, warm, and barelegged. I was yellow, faded, and cold with three layers of flannel under my trousers. Your little garden is all snowballs, sugar swans, cream cheese, Solonge's hand, and Maurice's teeth."

Those were the happy days, but Sand, who wrote one book after another, also wrote a friend that she was tired of sleeping with a corpse. "For seven years I have lived like a virgin."

At Nohant, Maurice (her favorite, who could do no wrong) was sleeping with Sand's young niece, whom she had befriended. When Chopin protested, Sand's attitude was "How dare you criticize my son?" To get rid of unloved Solonge, Sand arranged her marriage to the sculptor August Clisinger, whom everyone knew was a monster. When Chopin warned Sand against the depraved, dissolute man, her response was "How dare you interfere!"

Her next novel, *Lucrezia Floriani,* made Chopin look like an idiot.[7] Then came her "I'm tired of you" letter: "Farewell, my friend. May you recover from your ills. I will thank God for this bizarre conclusion to nine years close friendship. Let me know how things are from time to time."

The next year when the 1848 Revolution erupted in Paris, a wealthy Scottish spinster, Jane Stirling, his student for seven years, bundled Chopin off on a tragic concert tour of foggy England and Scotland. Queen Victoria, after attending one of his concerts, wrote, "After dinner there was some pretty music." Chopin wrote, "I am out of my element, like a violin string on a bass viol." The damp, cold climate was much worse than Majorca. Jostled from one cold mansion to another, half dead from coughing and hemorrhaging, he returned to Paris after seven months.

A former schoolmate, now a priest,[8] visited him, but like that of his whole generation, Chopin's early faith had been perverted by Voltaire's scoffing skepticism. He told the priest he wouldn't want to die without receiving the sacraments but "I don't understand things as you do." Several weeks later when Chopin was dying, the priest remembered and gave him the last rites. The funeral, held in the recently completed Church of the Madeleine, was paid for by Jane Stirling. The cost included 3,000 invitations (a custom of the times) and the orchestra and chorus for Mozart's *Requiem*.[9]

Chopin's courageous suffering was over—both the physical pain and Sand's public humiliation and ridicule of him. He endured all with the same gentle smile. The mischievous youth whose hilarious caricatures and gift for comic imitations had left his friends doubled up with laughter left the world his most precious gift—his music.[10]

He was buried in Père Lachaise Cemetery, where a handful of Polish dirt he had been carrying around for twenty years was scattered over the grave; and guess who sculpted his monument—Solonge's horrible husband.

10

The Palais Royal
Bawdy Letters, Orgies, and the Can-Can

THE PALAIS ROYAL, at the end of rue de l'Opéra, once housed a theater for the seventeenth-century genius Molière. Before the Revolution, the gardens swarmed with military officers, priests, and pickpockets. Noblewomen with hairdos swirled up like Dairy Queen ice cream cones glided in hoop skirts among red-rouged prostitutes. Political pamphlets were sold, orators harangued, rumors flew, and reputations were ruined. The little toy cannon[1] built by Louis XIII boomed at noon when the sun was hot.

During the Belle Epoque in the late 1800s, the Palais Royal was a private little village. Before World War II, one patron at the neighborhood restaurant, the Grand Véfour,[2] was Colette[3]—gifted author of *Gigi*—Colette, the beloved little girl who did not grow up in the most delightful way.

As we strolled through the deserted tree-lined park, a composed, sixtyish woman was sitting on a bench near the pool with her shoes off, reading a book. The Parisienne was at home in her tranquil, cloistered garden. Like the garden, she seemed to have had her day.

The original Palais Royal was built by conniving Cardinal Richelieu, who starved Protestant Huguenots at La Rochelle and wiped out Catholics throughout Europe in his wars against the powerful Catholic Habsburg family. Richelieu left the palace to his king, Louis XIII. When the king died, his widow, Queen Anne of Austria,[4] moved from the run-down Louvre into the elegant palace with her two young sons and renamed it Palais Royal. They were driven out during the Fronde, a five-year uprising against the monarchy.[5] The queen's eldest son, Louis XIV, moved to the Louvre when he became king, and the Palais Royal became the residence of his talented brother Philippe, duc d'Orléans, known as Monsieur (1640–1701). King Louis XIV, jealous of his brother's military victories in Holland, dismissed him from command and prevented him from holding office—any office. Philippe became another dissolute at court influenced by degenerates. His second wife,[6] Liselotte, a blunt Bavarian princess, spent her time writing letters and hunting on horseback. An Annie Oakley with a deadly accurate pen, the princess called the king's bastard children "mouse droppings in the pepper." As we strolled through the palace garden, we imagined her in her apartment writing letters at an open window surrounded by her French spaniels, parrots, and flocks of canaries. Effeminate Monsieur's apartment was cluttered with crystal chandeliers, clocks, candy, mirrors, and paintings. Liselotte, brought up in *The Sound of Music* scenery, hated the dirty, smelly, overcrowded Palais Royal. She said it was impossible to enjoy even the garden. She couldn't take a step without being watched from a hundred windows. After her fourth child was born, she wrote, "Monsieur made *lit* [bed] apart very soon after. I never enjoyed the business sufficiently to ask him to return to my bed." She had to sleep on the edge of the bed and kept falling on the floor "like a sack of corn." If she stretched out her foot and accidentally touched Monsieur, he woke her up and yelled at her. Monsieur died after an emotional quarrel with his brother, Louis XIV.

THE REGENT, PHILIPPE (1674–1723)

Monsieur's brilliant son, Philippe II, who was interested in science and the arts, was another victim of Louis XIV, who feared him as a potential rival. The kind, modest youth was deliberately corrupted by depraved tutors. His military heroism, like his father's, was rewarded by loss of command. The final degradation came when he was ordered to marry the king's bastard daughter by Mme. de Montespan.[7]

With self-respect gone, Philippe II proceeded to play the role of "worthless." Hiding hurt and frustration with a smile and shrug, he deliberately shocked and scandalized the establishment with his after-hours parties. His friends "swapped impieties as hard as they could . . . made tremendous

The Palais Royal

noise and would fall drunk as could be, then went off to bed and began all over again the next day."

When Louis XIV died, Philippe II ruled France as regent for the five-year-old orphaned heir, Louis XV. As regent, Philippe worked fourteen hours a day (with a hangover) trying to pay off the Sun King's debts after fifty years of warfare. The regent was one of the first nobles sincerely sympathetic toward the people, but his attempt to give them a more democratic form of government was blocked by enemies. His mother, Liselotte, wrote, "Good Lord, he forgives everything undertaken against him and merely laughs at it." In the end, there remained only bitter cynicism. His character had been so undermined that there was no right, no wrong, no God. Louis XIV had been successful. The tree was bent as intended.

CITIZEN ÉGALITÉ (1747–1793)

The regent's son, known as Philippe Égalité (equality), served in the Navy, but King Louis XVI and Marie Antoinette, who hated his ideas, eliminated his job and left him in an empty honorary position. Heavily in debt, he remodeled the Palais Royal, built stately galleries with shops, restaurants, and cafés, and collected rent on sixty apartments. The garden, with straight rows of linden trees, was opened to the public, and since this was private property, police were prohibited. Gamblers could cheat and trollops could trollop. Here in 1789 before the Revolution, Camille Désmoulins climbed on a table shouting his call "to arms."

Égalité, a Republican who flaunted his liberalism, hoped to replace his cousin, Louis XVI, as king. Twice he was exiled to his country estate in Villers Cotterets. Two days after the storming of the Bastille, Lafayette, who was in charge of law and order, accused him of inciting riots and ordered him out of the country. A year later, he returned—to the Terror—and risked his life saving fugitives. Égalité, who voted for the king's execution, was in turn executed by those he had championed. His eldest son, Louis Philippe, born at the Palais Royal, became king of the French in 1830 after Napoléon and two Bourbon kings had been deposed.

LOUIS PHILIPPE, THE CITIZEN KING (1830–1848)
A Refugee Who Slept with a Squaw—Two of Them

Louis Philippe, Égalité's son, who became the Citizen King, was educated at the Palais Royal by his father's mistress—his mother's lady-in-waiting, comtesse de Genlis. When she became governess for Louis Philippe and his two younger brothers and sister, Louis Philippe was eight. Mme. de Genlis ruled their lives. The boys wore lead soles attached to their boots to make their legs strong. They slept in cold rooms with only one blanket and were forbidden to eat sweets or play with other children. At each meal they spoke a different language. Their father, Philippe Égalité, and Mme. de Genlis shared with the children Lafayette's dream of liberty.

When the French Revolution erupted, Louis Philippe was with the army in Vendôme, but his father was executed, his mother sent to the Luxembourg prison, and his brothers, thirteen and seventeen, were imprisoned in Marseille. His sister Adelaide and Mme. de Genlis escaped to Belgium, where Louis Philippe and his valet joined them. Forced to flee again from revolutionaries, Adelaide and Mme. de Genlis eventually found refuge in a convent in Switzerland. Louis Philippe, with his valet, roamed the mountains on foot for months—cold, hungry, sleeping in fields and under hedges. Eventually, a friend[8] found him a position teaching math at a school in Reichenau, Switzerland.

After Robespierre was killed, the Directoire permitted their mother to remain in Paris provided that her sons leave France—get out of Europe—cross an ocean! Louis Philippe, twenty-three, landed in Philadelphia on October 24, 1796. Four months later his brothers arrived from Marseille. With Louis Philippe's servant, Beaudoin, the three brothers toured America on horseback with a knapsack, a rough map, and a compass. A watercolor of Niagara Falls by his brother, duc de Pensier, still hangs in the Palais Royal.

At Mt. Vernon, they were welcomed by their hero, George Washington, whose letters of introduction were a blessing as they headed west through the sparsely settled frontier—lucky to find a roof over their heads and a piece of cornbread. At an Indian village when the chief was sick, Louis Philippe cured him with a "bleeding" that Mme. de Genlis had taught him. As a thank-you present, the Indian chief invited Louis Philippe to spend the night on a straw mat between his grandmother and his great-aunt. Before their survival tour ended, they had visited practically every Indian tribe in America.[9]

After the French Revolution and Napoléon, the next Bourbon king, liberal sixty-three-year-old Louis XVIII, returned from exile in Ghent and pardoned his cousin, Louis Philippe, and his family. Louis Philippe was so happy to be home after twenty-two years that he kissed the bottom step of the Grand Staircase in the palace, which had been wrecked by the mob.

The Palais Royal

When Louis XVIII died in 1824, his brother, sixty-seven-year-old Charles X, succeeded him and suspended all liberties. During the 1830 revolution, King Charles fled to Scotland. France was in a quandary trying to unite Monarchists and Republicans. The people wanted Lafayette, now seventy-one, as president of a republic. Instead, Lafayette endorsed Louis Philippe as king of the French—told him he was the best Republican and pinned a *tricolore* on him. *Tricolore* flags went up, and everyone tried to sing the *Marseillaise,* but they couldn't remember the words. It hadn't been sung in sixteen years. Lafayette thought everyone, including Louis Philippe, had agreed upon a government like England's. Wrong.

During a three-day uprising in July, Alexandre Dumas, author of *The Three Musketeers,* stood guard shouldering a gun near the Palais Royal dressed in the gaudiest uniform he could find:[10] a blue-and-yellow uniform dripping with colored ribbons, huge silver buttons, and dozens of medals, with a black hat topped with a red horsehair plume. He even had medals pinned on the seat of his pants, "For the kings who have been dethroned." A friend took one look and said, "Why a man could get sunstroke just walking past all this glitter."[11]

A staunch Republican, Dumas worked at the Palais Royal as a clerk for Louis Philippe, duc d'Orléans. When he heard that his friendly employer was now a terrible king, he wrote his mistress, "Rest assured my angel, all is well. Yesterday the duc d'Orléans was proclaimed king. I spent the evening at Court. The whole family is as nice and simple as before." Victor Hugo also spent an evening with the duc d'Orlèans. He wrote, "I shuddered as I watched him hack that beautiful roast. I hope he reigns better than he carves."

Intelligent, good-natured Louis Philippe, a fascinating conversationalist, tried to be popular as an ordinary citizen. He walked around Paris wearing a round felt hat, carried an umbrella, laughed, and gossiped. His wife, Queen Marie Amelie, an early Bess Truman, was as bourgeois as Louis Philippe. Louis Philippe wanted to be known as the Citizen King, but power-hungry, self-centered men controlled the government, and promised reforms were never made. Balzac was writing about corruption and what poverty does to a man's soul. George Sand, the people's literary champion, disagreed with her communist friends who wanted to abolish private property, prohibit religion, and destroy the family. In *Lelia,* her heroine says, "The error of Socialism is that it overlooks the importance of the individual. It hopes to impose the happiness of all on each. We cannot hand

Back to Europe with the BUSY BODY

out happiness to others. The individual must win his own." She also had her heroine demand the same sexual satisfaction her husband enjoyed and the right to leave him if she didn't get it. No wonder so many people visit Nohant, her home in the province of Berry.

When Louis Philippe came to the throne, Charles Gounod, composer of *Ave Maria,* was twenty-seven. He wrote wistfully, "Liberty is . . . a true land of promise. . . . To enter it we must become God's own people. Liberty is as real as heaven but must be earned and conquered by . . . generosity—not by taking life but by bestowing it in the moral as well as the material sense."

Under the Citizen King, the Palais Royal was a fashionable rendezvous for the wealthy, who patronized exclusive shops in the arcades. George Catlin, the American Indian artist, came to town with his show-biz troupe of buffalo-robed, red-painted Indians who danced, yelled, and cavorted for the king and his family. (The king had a true friendship with the Indians after living with them in America.)[12] Alexandre Dumas and Victor Hugo had box-office hits, and noisy cabarets, packed with rollicking polka dancers, featured the frenzied can-can imported from Algiers. When Mark Twain first saw the can-can in Paris, he covered his eyes with his hands but admitted later that he peeked and "was astounded at what he saw." Liszt drove the ladies wild at concerts tossing his long, blond hair, while Chopin's ladies wanted to take him home. Composer Hector Berlioz fell in love with a Shakespearean actress, and Gounod had nervous breakdowns. Offenbach furnished the comedy. In a burlesque on a Victor Hugo play, actors spoofed the long-winded monologues by constantly looking at their watches and imploring the audience to have patience—it wasn't over yet.

Also in Paris were 4,000 hungry men from all over France looking for work. The return of Napoléon's body from Saint Helena to recall the glory of France did not feed their families. When they revolted in 1848, the Palais Royal was destroyed, and Louis Philippe with his wife fled to Claremont, England, disguised as Mr. and Mrs. Smith. Louis Philippe declared, "I shall never abdicate—at least not until I have consulted my wife."

Napoléon III used the Palais Royal for offices. In 1872 the palace was burned by the Commune, but it was later restored. During World War II, those hunted by Nazis hid in the attics. Today the Palais Royal houses the State Council, but the once-elegant entrance to the garden, despite protests, is littered with dirty, faded black-and-white pedestals used in circuses. A fountain is filled with shiny silver balls. Parisians say they look like boils on one's bottom.

11

In Memory of Molière (1622–1673)
"I'll Have to Get Myself a Clown's Disguise"

TWO STREETS FROM the Palais Royal, a statue of Molière (genius actor, playwright, and producer) stands opposite his home at 40 rue de Richelieu. For 300 years, visitors throughout the world have stared up at the second-floor windows of his home, imagining the dying actor, costumed as Argan in *Le Malade Imaginaire*, being carried up the stairs after collapsing during a performance at the Palais Royal Théâtre. Molière, Jean Baptiste Pouquelin III, who masked his personal sorrows under the role of a comic actor: Molière, *Buffon trop serieux*, the very serious clown.

His mother died when he was nine. His father, a prosperous furniture maker for Louis XIII, gave his son an excellent education, then purchased a royal position for him; that of valet *tappissier* (hand me my shirt and fix the footstool sort of thing); but after meeting Madeleine Béjart,[1] his first love and lifelong friend, Jean Baptiste joined her raggle-taggle family of actors and became Molière the actor.

When their first theater (on a tennis court) failed they moved to another, where they played tragedy after tragedy for two years. Molière, assuming responsibility for everyone, was arrested for debts and imprisoned in the Châtelet. After Papa Monsieur Poquelin paid the debts (although he knew his son as an actor would be condemned by the Church as a "non-person"),[2] Molière left Paris with Béjart's troupe of Bohemians and toured the provinces for thirteen years. Their caravan, carrying costumes, candles, props, make-up, long curly wigs, scenery, and so on, jolted them thousands of miles from one city to another through dirt, heat, cold, wind, rain, and ruts. It was the happiest time of Molière's life. When they returned to Paris, he was thirty-six and highly regarded as an actor and playwright by powerful friends. One was an old schoolmate, Prince de Conti.[3]

Young King Louis XIV gave them a new theater in the Palais Royal and eventually his patronage, making them the *Troupe du Roi.* Molière's comedy, *Les Précieuses Ridicules,* ridiculing the silly, affected manners of the elite in their literary salons, was such a hit they doubled the price of admission. Until then, no one had dreamed of laughing at the aristocrats' ridiculous behavior. Now all Paris was laughing.

Molière, producer of spectacular extravaganzas for King Louis XIV, was a quiet man—an observer—kind, tolerant, and highly intelligent. But Molière, the serious man, is revealed in his plays.

When he wrote *l'École des Maris* (*School for Husbands*) he was about to be married—and he was terrified! He was forty years old, madly in love, and about to marry the baby of the troupe:[4] tall, talented, vivacious Armande, whom he had helped raise and spoil. She was twenty. As a husband, how should he treat her? Although in the play Sganarelle is the strict disciplinarian, Molière's personal ideas are those of wise, gentle Ariste; treat her with understanding and indulgence—which he did, and almost lost her. The loose reins he gave his wife were too loose.

Ten months after the marriage, his *l'École des Femmes (School for Wives)* was another triumph. Molière's worst fears about his marriage had happened. His wife was unfaithful, and he was consumed with jealousy. In the role of Arnolphe he makes fun of himself for being the male chauvinist husband who expects his wife to be dependent on him—and faithful. In the play, his wife Armande, in the role of Agnes, has no conscience, has never heard the word "abstinence," and has no idea what jealousy is. She cannot understand why Heaven should be offended. "'Tis so sweet and so pleasant." When Molière, as Arnolphe, realizes he has nothing to appeal to, he falls at her feet begging. She can go anywhere, do anything. Just don't leave him. His stage wife thinks he is crazy. As Arnolphe, Molière made his audience laugh and shout. Offstage, Molière was the man *qui n'est pas rieur*—who does not smile. This play made many enemies. At a time when

In Memory of Molière

husbands could banish their wives for life, lock them in a castle, or confine them in a convent, Molière's views of women's rights were shocking.

In 1670 the Turkish sultan sent an envoy to Versailles. To impress the Turks with his magnificence, Louis XIV ordered a coat made of diamonds. When the Turks showed up in dirty turbans and ignored the Sun King's glitter, the king was furious. He ordered Molière to write a comedy portraying them as fools.

Le Bourgeois Gentilhomme (The Would-Be Gentleman),[5] a song and dance play, supposedly ridicules middle-class Monsieur Jourdain, who has the impudence to want to improve his station in life. He has the audacity of aspiring to be one of them! In a burlesque Turkish ceremony, Louis XIV gets even with the disrespectful Turks and Monsieur Jourdain is made "noble."

Actually Molière has made Louis XIV as conceited as *The Emperor and His New Clothes.* The satire is on the king and nobles, but their superiority complexes have blinded them to the truth, like the ludicrous emperor who, falling for flattery, walks around naked while being complimented on his new clothes. Only Molière, the trapeze artist, could walk that high-wire, balancing his parody between *Le Bourgeoise Gentilhomme* and the court. One false move would have been fatal.

His play, *Le Tartuffe,* was banned twice. Moliére ridiculed hypocrites in the Church who had no concern for their fellow man—"who show uncommon zeal for the next world in order to make their fortunes in this." Furious Church officials denounced the play, claiming, "It is not for comic theater to get itself involved with the preaching of the gospel." The hilarious seduction scene when Tartuffe, the religious hypocrite, tries to seduce Orgon's wife, and the funny reverse psychology scene "playing games that lovers play" help lighten the heavy satire.

When he wrote *Le Malade Imaginaire* (one of his funniest plays) ridiculing the barbarous[6] seventeenth-century medical profession, Molière was a very sick man. He had tuberculosis and ulcers and had been on a milk diet for years. For six years he lived in the suburb, Auteil, where there were cows.[7] When friends begged him to rest he replied, "What am I to do? There are some fifty poor workers who have only their wage. What is to become of them if we do not play?" Like Michelangelo, he was abused and overworked by a tyrant. However, unlike Michelangelo, Molière had lost his faith. Descartes' theory of "Questioning" poisoned seeds of faith already on rocky soil. Molière had hoped by exposing men's faults he might change their ways . . . if they could only see themselves, as they are . . . No way! Any parish preacher will tell you. Once in a while . . . maybe.

Le Malade Imaginaire (The Hypochondriac) was written with seventeenth-century doctors dressed as sorcerers in wigs, gowns, and witches' hats. They rode on mules and jabbered in Latin and Greek. In the third act of *Le Malade Imaginaire,* when Argan is inducted into the medical faculty, the President sounds like the comedian Danny Kaye; "Do you swear to medicade, purgandi, bleedoni, prick and cuttandi, slashandi?" While the audience roared with laughter, Molière was seized with a violent coughing spell. He covered by fake laughter, and when the curtain came down he said, "I have a murderous chill," and asked to be taken home. One half hour later he was dead.[9] Although priests from Saint Eustache refused to administer the last rites, God had already sent two angels of mercy to console His servant in the last agonizing moments; two Sisters of Charity, who had come to Paris during Lent to collect money were boarding at Molière's home.

12

Place de la Bastille and Beaumarchais (1732–1799)

Welcomed in One Town. Imprisoned in Another.

IN A WARM, GENTLE RAIN, with feet happily ensconced in plastic rain shoes, we took Metro Bastille to place de la Bastille. Again in Paris, it's off with the old image of mobs, violence, peasants, and kings and on with the new. Across from place de la Bastille a new opera house spirals upward. Jagged angles of reflecting glass are superimposed on a curve, as dissonant as a wrong chord—maybe to mirror the turbulent history of the place. Whatever—the location of the opera house is a perfect setting for Beaumarchais' *The Barber of Seville* and *The Marriage of Figaro*. If anyone understood the political and financial intrigue during its construction, it was Beaumarchais. His handsome statue is around the corner on rue St. Antoinne, where he built an enormous mansion—during the Revolution!

Before the French Revolution, Pierre Caron de Beaumarchais (1732–1799) was the most exciting man in France, with his witty, upbeat "Figaro" personality—"everywhere rising above circumstances . . . mocking the foolish, braving the wicked. . . ." As a secret agent for the French government, he was the man most responsible for the French money, arms, and equipment that brought victory to Washington's starving American troops.[1] How does the son of a watchmaker become a secret agent for two kings? First, you make a watch for Mme. du Barry, then you buy an ap-

Back to Europe with the BUSY BODY

pointment to get one foot into court life. Beaumarchais' appointment entitled him to carry a sword in a privileged parade serving the king's meat. Handsome, witty, and well educated (albeit self-educated), he was soon teaching King Louis XV's four daughters to play the harp. His first court appointment was a springboard that catapulted the watchmaker's son into the air for the rest of his life.

When a wealthy financier[2] made him a business partner, he bought a mansion in rue de Conde and two more court offices. One office required him to sentence violators of game laws:

> Here in the Louvre I sit in state
> Through tedious mornings occupied
> As stern as Minos, I decide
> The doom of pallid rabbits and the
> Pain reserved for wretched poachers
> in the plain.

When in Spain on business, he stored in his head scenes of fashionable Spanish society and characters for his plays. He should have stayed in Spain. From then on, he needed all the wits of Figaro to keep his head on his shoulders.

In Paris, while trying to collect a debt, he was arrested for forgery and fraud. Another time he was nearly killed by a nobleman[3] who was acquitted, while Beaumarchais was found guilty and jailed. Twice, the wife of his court-appointed lawyer[4] demanded money to obtain an interview for him with her husband. Beaumarchais paid the extortion money, and still the lawyer refused to see him. Beaumarchais' brilliant indignant letters against the counselor set all Europe laughing. "Those remarkable writings were at once a plea, a satire, a drama, a comedy, a gallery of pictures."

Finally Parliament fired the counselor and declared that Beaumarchais and the counselor's wife, Mme. Göezman, were both guilty. Both were shamed by the infamous label *blamé,* which deprived them of all civil rights and prevented them from holding public office. Financially, Beaumarchais was ruined. Socially, he was the hero of the hour.

Since the counselor represented the king's Parliament, Beaumarchais was not exactly the king's favorite, but after receiving one of Beaumarchais' ingenious letters suggesting that the king and state use his talents, Louis XV sent him secretly to London to stop blackmail against Mme. du Barry.

His mission accomplished, Beaumarchais returned to Paris, only to learn that the king, who never could find anything "divine" about himself, had died of smallpox. If Louis XV had lived eight days more, Beaumarchais would have been cleared of all charges. He wrote, "I am amazed at the fate that follows me."

The next king, Louis XVI, also gave Beaumarchais secret missions: to retrieve secret papers from a London agent and stop slander against Queen Marie Antoinette. Beaumarchais' adventures make Cellini's escapades tame. In Vienna, Marie Antoinette's mother, Empress Maria Theresa, confined him to house arrest for thirty-one days.

In his spare time he had written *The Barber of Seville*. Beneath the bubbly comedy are all his misfortunes caused by slander.[5] Gaining permission to stage the play took four years. Twice it was cancelled two days before the performance. When it opened in 1775, Beaumarchais had added so much it was a flop. He rewrote it, and three months later everyone loved it. Even the critics apologized. Under light-hearted dialogue, jokes, and music, Beaumarchais buried scornful remarks about the privileged aristocracy, the despotism of authorities, censorship, and slander. Beaumarchais, as Figaro, says, "I hasten to laugh at everything for fear of being obliged to weep."

Soon the play became a gold mine for the Comédie Française and the actors, but not for the playwright, who received nothing. Through Beaumarchais' efforts the National Assembly, after fifteen years, decreed that the works of living authors could not be produced in France without consent of the authors, and that the Society of Dramatic Authors should never meet without saluting the bust of Beaumarchais.

Still under the dread stigma *blamé*, Beaumarchais was sent secretly to London to retrieve French plans to invade England if war broke out again. Beaumarchais, a convicted forger without civil rights, was dictating foreign policy to young King Louis XVI. "Give the Americans sufficient help to put their forces on an equal footing with those of England." The king even filled out a question and answer sheet Beaumarchais sent him. French Minister Vergennes told Beaumarchais to set up an export-import business as a cover to send supplies, but to do it secretly.[6]

Under an assumed name, Beaumarchais traveled to the West Indies, Marseille, Le Havre, and Nantes organizing shipments of arms, food, ammunition, and equipment, but in Nantes he blew his cover. He couldn't resist supervising a rehearsal of *The Barber of Seville*. When English spies protested, the French government forbade the ships to sail. However,

Back to Europe with the BUSY BODY

Beaumarchais sneaked them through the English blockade, and they arrived safely in Portsmouth, New Hampshire, in time to help win the Battle of Saratoga (1777), the turning point in the colonists' war for independence.

He was in Passy outside Paris at Benjamin Franklin's headquarters[7] when word arrived that the colonists had retaken Philadelphia (1778). As he drove furiously to bring the news to Paris, his carriage tipped over. "My right arm is cut, the bones of my neck are nearly crushed, but the charming news from America is a balm to my wounds." Less charming was the fact that he had received no payment for his efforts.

The following year, when France officially recognized America's independence, the French Navy could legally escort Beaumarchais' ships. During a sea battle with the British in the West Indies, Beaumarchais lost ten ships bound for America loaded with guns, cannons, powder, brass mortars, clothing, and tents for 25,000 men. The good news—after eight years—was the verdict from the Court of Appeals in Aix en Provence: "not guilty of forgery."

The Marriage of Figaro (Le Mariage), his next play, is a whirlwind masterpiece.[8] Disguised characters running on and off stage, in and out of hiding places, mirror his own frantic life. The play mocked the government so boldly it was banned for five years—but it made Marie Antoinette laugh. "Drinking without thirst and making love at any time, Madame, is all that distinguishes us from other animals." Her friends arranged a performance at the Comédie Française and invited all the leading aristocrats. On opening day, a half hour before curtain time, police arrived with orders to cancel the performance. Blood vessels nearly burst with fury. The cast had rehearsed for two years and more than 2,000 tickets had been sold. The words *oppression* and *tyranny* were heard everywhere. Undeterred by the order, the queen's friends arranged another performance. Beaumarchais agreed only on condition that after the performance, it would be performed publicly. When the king's brother[9] told the king the play was only a bunch of [censored], Louis XVI gave his approval. Beaumarchais was ecstatic! *Le Mariage*[10] could now be performed by the Comédie Française in their new theater (today's Odéon).[11] On opening night 700 carriages vied for position. The ticket line stretched to the Luxembourg gates. Three hundred women came early and invaded the actresses' dressing rooms to be near the box office when it opened. Beaumarchais crouched down in one of the box seats.

Place de la Bastille and Beaumarchais

For four years he had fought for this night to even the score with the jealous nobles, lawyers, and churchmen who had made him suffer. He did have to delete some passages, such as Marceline's tirade against men when she is revealed as Figaro's mother: "You're worse than ungrateful men . . . Your victims are playthings of your passions." Another cut was Figaro's funny line "Good day oh doctor of my heart, soul and other viscera." The theme of *Le Mariage* is embodied in the peasants' celebration scene, contrasting the gaiety and courage of hard-working commoners with the cynicism of unscrupulous courtiers. The bigger that joyous picnic table on stage, the better.

Le Mariage was a wild success. Beaumarchais, the watchmaker, had triumphed over a king! Behind the light-hearted wit of Figaro, one aristocrat observed, "It appears to me that the nobility showed a great want of tact in applauding it. . . . They laughed at their own expense, and what was worse, they made others laugh too. . . . The jokes that amused them were directed against themselves, and they do not see it. What inexplicable blindness." She added that she was enraged with herself for having been amused. Even Beaumarchais said, "There is something more outrageous than my piece and that is its success." Five years later people who had laughed at jokes against themselves were trundled to the guillotine. *Le Mariage* was performed in practically every theater in Europe. The jokes ignited flames of revolution.

At the height of Beaumarchais' success, the king decided Beaumarchais was crowing too loudly and needed a lesson in humility. In the middle of a card game, he wrote on the back of the seven of spades an order for Beaumarchais' arrest. Fifty-three-year-old Beaumarchais was carted off to Saint Lazare prison, a reform school for juvenile delinquents. The next day he was freed, but he refused to leave until he knew the reason for his arrest. Five days later his family made him leave—unshaven, disgraced, and humiliated. The king had promised to make reparation, but on the way home when Beaumarchais saw a caricature of himself—naked and being thrashed like a naughty boy—he hid for weeks, with time to think about arrogance and pride. The king was astounded at the change in flippant, high-spirited Figaro and promptly forgave him.

Beaumarchais was one of those "still serenely unaware of how near they were to edge of the precipice."[12] In the middle of the Revolution he built an enormous mansion opposite the Bastille and moved in with his family and dog, an English greyhound whose collar noted, "I am Mlle. Follette. Beaumarchais belongs to me. We live on the Boulevard." The day after the attack on the Tuileries, a mob of 30,000 swarmed into his new home looking for weapons while Beaumarchais hid in a friend's closet. Although he was denounced by Marat and imprisoned, his life was miraculously saved by a woman he had once befriended.

When revolutionaries forced a war with Marie Antoinette's nephew, Francis II of Austria, France needed weapons. There were 60,000 in Holland. Beaumarchais, now sixty-two, was sent secretly, and again with no pay, to procure the muskets. He spent three miserable years huddled in cold attics in poverty and despair.[13] While he was gone, he was declared a political exile. His property was seized, his money frozen, and his family imprisoned.

When Robespierre had fallen and Napoléon was on the rise, Beaumarchais returned to his ruined mansion. He died peacefully in his sleep a few years later—one of the first to help American colonists in their fight for freedom. Cheery, optimistic Figaro changed the course of history. A friend wrote that under an exterior of lightness and gaiety, Beaumarchais had severe principles. He never spoke ill of his enemies, even those intent on ruining him. "Eh, my friend. Should I lose the time which I pass with you in recalling things which would only afflict your spirit and mine? I try to forget the follies of those about me and think only of what is good and useful."

13

Passy: Maison de Balzac and Honoré Balzac (1799–1850)

If I Were Noble, Someone Would Love Me

FINDING OUR WAY to Balzac's home in the suburb of Passy was no problem. Leave from Metro Trocadero. Get off at Passy and ask, "*Où est Balzac? à droit* [right] *ou* [or] *à gauche* [left]?" No matter which way they pointed, we couldn't find our way out of the station. Then Maurice showed up. Wonderful Maurice from Brittany—in his mid-twenties. Not only did he escort us to Maison de Balzac, he spent the afternoon with us. We followed him, and there we were at 47 rue Raynouard in about ten minutes.

Since all Paris was on holiday, the streets were practically deserted—as was Balzac's ivy-covered cottage. The cool, green oasis is a tranquil memory of Paris. But something was wrong. The place was too serene. Balzac never had a tranquil moment in his life. (Maurice and I ran down the back steps and out the door he used to escape from bill collectors.)

Balzac is usually remembered from the musical comedy *The Music Man*, in which horrified mothers discover their children have been reading Balzac in the school library! He should be remembered as the literary giant captured in Rodin's statue of Balzac in Paris.

"His constant good humor became infectious. His magnetic black eyes shone with kindness . . . good nature radiated from him." How could that be? From the day he was born until he was fourteen, he was boarded out.

Back to Europe with the BUSY BODY

All the poverty, loneliness, and despair his characters suffered, he had experienced. Success finally came after ten years of failure. After success came the difficult part—how to keep it (and the money) without messing up. Balzac was too involved in juggling 2,000 characters[1] in his head to be sensible. He wrote seventy-four novels in twenty years. Those in *The Human Comedy* depict every aspect of his society and every type of human being ("She had a mind like an unruffled pond over which no wind ever stirred"). Bouncy 5'2" Balzac, full of gaiety and charm, wrote about some of the most sordid characters in literature.

One of the most famous stories in *The Human Comedy* is *Père Goriot,* about a father who sacrifices everything for his two ungrateful daughters. When Balzac was living at rue Cassini[2] near the Observatory, he found the boarding house where Père Goriot would live. In Balzac's time, it was an unsavory neighborhood where people existed on small fixed incomes; widows of Napoléon's ruined army, thousands of prisoners of war, people wiped out by get-rich schemes, and students from the Latin Quarter. Balzac describes exactly what pension life was like. He checked out the cobblestone streets and alleys, the entire neighborhood from rue St. Jacques to Jardin des Plantes. When Père Goriot left the Pension Vauquer to visit his selfish daughters, Balzac blocked his route like an actor during rehearsal. He'll turn here, cross the street, then down three blocks, and so on.

Once he noticed a woman selling old clothes in the neighborhood and started a conversation with her to note how her voice reflected her personality. He modeled the proprietor of the boarding house after her. He also found an ex-criminal, invited him to dinner, and learned that prison life, for one thing, dries up the vocal chords. In *Père Goriot,* Vautrin[3] is the ex-criminal whose insight into a man's character is spooky.

Balzac wrote *Père Goriot* in forty days (1834), drinking coffee constantly to keep awake. Like a muleteer cracking a whip over his plodding mules, he drove himself daily for sixteen hours straight, writing under pressure to meet deadlines and pay debts. To relieve anxiety, he went on buying binges, which drove him further into debt. His business ventures were disastrous no matter what he tried—law, printing, publishing, a pineapple plantation in Paris, and a silver mine in Sardinia. From his traumatic failures, he learned practical details that went into his novels: how banks and money lenders operate, how trade is financed, how speculation works, and so on. His mind became a data bank.

He also became an "Artful Dodger," running from bill collectors and dodging the National Guard. When he was summoned for duty as a sentry at the Paris Arsenal, he was living at his secret hideout on rue Cassini. (Three small rooms were decorated more for a sultan than for a fat little writer wearing a monk's comfortable black cassock.) When guards caught up with him, they hauled him off in a green paddy wagon to a prison nicknamed Hôtel des Haricots (beans). The only food was cold beans.

Balzac was not happy. Worse than the cold beans, he had been arrested by a dentist!—a sergeant in the guard. When his publisher visited, he brought dinner and champagne and arranged to have it served in the dining hall. He also secured a private cell where the now-happy genius wrote for two weeks in peace and quiet.

Balzac's next hideout, *Les Jardies* in Sèvres,[4] (another suburb), was atop a hill, where he could see his creditors coming. At a given signal, servants hid everything valuable in his mistress'[5] cottage behind thick bushes on the property.[6] On cue, Balzac would hide in a gully.

Les Jardies, the first house he owned, was built on clay soil—another disaster. During grandiose remodeling, the garden walls collapsed, and when they were rebuilt, an avalanche of stones descended on his neighbor's property.

Already labeled a laughing stock by jealous journalists,[7] Balzac's *Les Jardies* furnished more copy for their ridicule. His friends were heartbroken to see the kind genius satirized as a bungling fool. To mask the hurt, Balzac responded with bravado, the typical pattern, playing the role of buffoon already painted by the press. His table manners were terrible— he waved his knife around like a baton. No matter how brilliant and compelling his conversation, it was loud! His boisterous laughter jiggled pictures on the walls. (Delacroix, a fastidious dandy, literally cringed.)

In his attempt to crash society, he could spare only an hour from his sixteen-hour-a-day writing schedule to be one of "them." It was a tremendous effort to even make the scene. When he did arrive at a salon, huffing and puffing, his trousers didn't match his jacket, his buttons were buttoned wrong, and there wasn't time to tie his shoelaces. He tried to be foppish, but he was too fat. He even bought a pince-nez and six pairs of yellow gloves.

He never did conquer a pathetic compulsion to belong and to be accepted in the best society. To the genius whose grandfather was a peasant, "best" meant nobility—synonymous with money and power. On his first trip to Russia, he traveled first class with six horses, a carriage engraved with a coat of arms he had created, liveried servants, and tons of luggage. He even bought a title for himself, which everyone ignored.

At *Les Jardies* he wrote for three years like a madman—seven or eight books at once. The writing routine was interrupted by a National Guardsman who trotted him off to jail again for seventy-two hours. He was supposed to help harvest grapes.

Still fleeing creditors, he packed his candle holder, special paper, and raven-feathered quills and moved from *Les Jardies* to a split-level house in Passy, where he lived for seven years under an assumed name.[8] At that time, the house was above a laundry. The neighborhood was filled with noisy children and smelled of soap suds. "Above my head in summer, there was a corrugated iron roof. Below me, a laundry keeping up all day long a fire lit for a railroad engine."

Today his home in Passy has books, letters, cartoons, and pictures on display—also his famous walking stick encrusted with turquoises. In one room of the cold, dark, empty house is Balzac's sturdy little writing table with heavy, knobby legs and his high-backed chair that had to be constantly replaced. He said the chairs kept dying on him. The table and chair stand like monuments in a mausoleum.

When Balzac lived here, he still wrote like one obsessed—five books simultaneously.[9] While others slept, he pulled the curtains tight to shut out early morning sun and slipped into his other world. Occasionally he had to replace dripping candles in the candelabra, and when his nerves screamed for rest, he fought back with caffeine in coffee made from the strongest coffee beans. At midnight, he had a light snack, then back to his imaginary friends and acquaintances. His pen flew along the paper—light blue to cut the glare and very smooth. The only pause was the quill being dipped into an inkwell left from his miserable school days in Vendôme—no reference books. All the research, descriptions, and characters were in his head—characters whose behavior Balzac scrutinizes under a glaring spotlight. From the ridiculously small table, his characters paraded on to immortality.

> It has seen all my wretchedness,
> knows all my plans, overheard my
> thoughts . . . .

Balzac considered *Cousine Bette,* written at Passy, his best work. Her home in rue du Doyenne was near place du Carrousel. Balzac modeled *Cou-*

sine Bette, the hysterical, elderly spinster, after the Swiss governess[10] who helped bring Russian Mme. de Hanska and Balzac together. To atone for her role in an affair that led to adultery, the pious accomplice entered a convent.[11]

All Balzac's characters are complex psychological studies; "subtext," directors call it. Even for his most corrupt characters, Balzac shows enormous compassion for humanity, especially women, "who need more than meaningless affairs of all sorts," and for all lost souls consumed by envy, greed, selfishness, or whatever deadly sin. As he tells their story, what emerges from his heart and pen is understanding and pity. Balzac named his tableau of society *The Human Comedy,* in contrast to Dante's *Divine Comedy.*

At forty-two, he had written one hundred books with 2,000 characters, but now every system in his body was collapsing: digestive, respiratory—well, not quite all. There was one system still functioning. Until that broke down, he had a succession of mistresses. His first mistress, Mme. de Berny, was older than his mother and had seven children. "I never had a mother. As soon as I was born I was sent to a policeman's house until I was four. From four to six they boarded me out. At six and a half, I was in school at Vendôme until the age of fourteen. In all, I have seen my mother twice."

Mme. de Berny had an excellent influence over him. Balzac said, "She sustained me by word, deed, and her devotion through great storms." At one time, he had three motherly mistresses, along with a few nonmotherly types. The woman he intended to marry was twenty-seven-year-old Polish-Russian Evelina de Hanska, from the highest Polish aristocracy, five years younger than he. When they finally married, Balzac had achieved his goals in life: to be rich and famous and marry a woman of noble birth. No general ever fought a battle with more persistence and determination to win than Balzac. To win Mme. de Hanska, he fought with charm, sex, and words—millions of words. He wrote her letters every week for eighteen years. When he received orders to meet her, he jumped to attention, traipsing all over Europe, sometimes under horrible conditions. Twice when victory seemed certain, he received "Let's call the whole thing off" letters that plunged him into such despair that he was unable to speak or write. But never did he accept defeat. He regrouped and launched a new offensive. March 14, 1850, after an eighteen-year campaign, Balzac and Mme. de Hanska (whose wealth was staggering) were married in the church of Saint Barbara in the Ukrainian town of Berdichev.[12] Five months later in his new

Back to Europe with the BUSY BODY

mansion in Paris, after years of excruciating pain[13] ("My head weighs more than the dome of Saint Peter's"), his abused body gave up. Hector Berlioz and Victor Hugo were the last friends to see him.

God has many ways of rewarding His people. Mme. de Hanska, a Russian countess, bored and isolated in a palace in the middle of the Ukrainian cornfields, had written a letter to Balzac, the famous new novelist. Thanks to her, his reputation grew rapidly after his death. Balzac and his hard-to-get bride are buried together in Père Lachaise Cemetery.

Maurice Bonny and the author checking out the back stairway down which Balzac fled from creditors

14

Rueil Malmaison: Château Malmaison
The Haunted House of Napoléon and Josephine

AN EARLY MORNING ten-minute train ride from Gare d'Austerlitz with other rise-and-shine passengers brought us to Château Malmaison, a "retreat" home for Napoléon and Josephine. At one time, it was used as a prison and named "bad house" (malmaison). Usually we came, we saw, and it was closed. This time we checked and went on a Wednesday, when admission is free. Don't go on Tuesday; it's closed.

When vicomtesse Rose de Beauharnais met Napoléon Bonaparte in society, he was commander in chief of the Army of the Interior and had a new uniform. Accustomed to army barracks and poverty, the artillery genius, suddenly transplanted into a gaudy ballroom setting, was edgy, uneasy, and completely out of his element. The viscountess was a widow, Marie Josephe Rose Tacher de la Pagerie de Beauharnais, whose quiet Creole charm captivated him. Looking directly into his eyes, sincerely interested, she complimented him on his military talent and asked specific questions about the capture of Toulon. He fell passionately in love with his "incomparable Josephine."

Paul de Barras, a powerful member of the Convention, let Napoléon know he would do well to marry her (one woman less for him to keep). Napoléon proposed and Josephine refused. He scared her. After a word from

Barras, Josephine changed her mind. The day of their wedding the little parvenu started his ego trip by making everyone in the wedding party defer to the great Napoléon. He kept everyone waiting two hours. The wedding night was a losing battle with Josephine's jealous pug dog, who refused to leave his place on Josephine's bed and sank his teeth into the bridegroom's leg. Forty-eight hours later the groom galloped off to conquer Italy. Josephine was exhausted! The Corsican's frenzied lovemaking was not what she was used to. Frenchmen made much better lovers.

From Italy came a barrage of passionate love letters begging her to join him. (King Henri IV's love letters are masterpieces, but Napoléon's are steamier.) By campfires and candlelight in his tent, he scrawled a torrent of uninhibited emotions: "On my heart, at my lips. Come by easy stages. Come gently. A kiss on your ear, then a kiss lower, then much lower." Prosper Mérimée, who edited the letters for Napoléon III, said, "There were kisses everywhere upon portions of her anatomy not to be found in any Academie Française Dictionary."

The more she stalled, the more frustrated he became. She even pretended she was pregnant, with three doctors constantly at her side. When he learned she was going to parties, he ordered her to be in Milan on a certain date. When he threatened to resign his commission and get her, Barras ordered her to go.

Of course she was forgiven. Between embraces—and battles—Josephine was forced to follow him all over Italy. When the Austrians killed two of her horses, she fled on foot with her dog and hitched a ride to Milan in a wagon—and Napoléon wondered why she couldn't be more ardent!

At Mombello Castle near Milan, the victorious master of Italy entertained in kingly splendor. First, he made himself president of the Italian Republic, later, king of Italy (1805). He sent cargoes of loot to fill the empty treasury in Paris, which was the original idea for the Italian campaign. No one suspected Napoléon was hooked on power. Talleyrand, the new minister of foreign affairs, was the first. To Frenchmen still in shock from the Revolution, Napoléon was a long-awaited hero bringing glory and prestige.

Now that Italy was defeated, the would-be world conqueror sailed off to seize Egypt. Imitating Alexander the Great, he brought aboard scientists and scholars. Before leaving, he had told Josephine to buy a country estate. She knew the perfect place: Malmaison in Rueil, near her daughter's boarding school ten miles west of Paris.

Château Malmaison

There was another man in Josephine's life, Lt. Hippolyte Charles, who made her happy at Malmaison. When Napoléon heard about it, he left his army (and mistress) to their fate in Egypt and stormed back to France determined to divorce her. Josephine cried all night outside his locked door. When her children, Hortense and Eugène (fourteen and sixteen), added their pleas, he opened the door. "I couldn't bear the sobs of those children."

Napoléon stayed at Malmaison on weekends in the summer when he was first consul, between 1800 and 1803. Tour guides say, "It was here that Josephine and Napoléon were the happiest." Napoléon maybe, but Josephine? He brought all his women to Malmaison for command performances—not only when Josephine was there but also while she was away taking cures to get pregnant. One favorite, who had beautiful hands but big feet, was said to have the hands of a queen and the feet of a king. Another one wouldn't leave. He ordered Josephine to make her go away. "She wants me under her thumb. I won't have it. Tell her." Josephine's aristocratic education did not include the roll of bouncer.

At Malmaison and other homes, Josephine was a serene peacemaker between conservative aristocrats and liberals. "His wife's bright, gentle eyes and her silvery caressing tones were so enchanting that one stood still simply for the pleasure of hearing her."

Malmaison is full of pictures, but the mental ones are the best. Each time Napoléon and Josephine visited, fifty mounted soldiers escorted them. Sometimes dinner was served outdoors on the lawn in front of the château. In the dining room, the rose in the startling black-and-white checkered marble floor marks Josephine's place at the table. Napoléon didn't waste time on food. He ate breakfast alone and downed his dinner in twenty minutes. No one was supposed to tell him what time dinner would be served. Once, the cook prepared twenty-six chickens in succession to have a perfect one available when he was ready.

The game room on the ground floor was Josephine's favorite room. Napoléon was an early-to-bed person, while Josephine stayed up until eleven—shooting pool or playing chess and whist by candlelight. No one wanted to play games with Napoléon. He cheated.

When Hortense, Josephine's daughter, brought her young friends from boarding school to Malmaison, there were happy times. Talented Hortense sang, composed, and played the piano while lovely Josephine strummed the harp. (She only knew one piece.) When they performed Beaumarchais' *Marriage of Figaro,* Hortense's brother, Eugène, was Don Basilio, the music teacher. Besides being handsome and a great dancer, cheerful Eugène was devoted to his single-parent mother. He became her protector when he was a boy, even before his father, vicomte Alexandre de Beauharnais, was guillotined. A room on the second floor of Malmaison is dedicated to Hortense and Eugène.

On the first floor, the tastefully decorated council chamber suggests a military field tent. Napoléon conferred there with Paris officials[1] responsible for beautifying the city or with lawyers composing the Napoléonic code (which made the personal lives of citizens a state concern) or trying to sell Louisiana.[2] Beyond the council chamber, the library is just as Napoléon left it—with a history book opened on the desk, a world map, and a globe marked with a blue pencil. A lot of pacing went on in this room, as well as temper tantrums. One time Napoléon was so furious with his foreign minister, Talleyrand, he threw his hat on the floor and stomped on it. Other times in fits of rage, he kicked the logs out of the fireplace or jabbed his penknife into a leather chair. The slashed chair is still there. Today, people pay money for managing stress.

What I remember about his beige bedroom is the tables designed like military drums, the tiny bed, and his clothes thrown over the back of the chairs. Not much time was spent in bed. He couldn't sleep. Josephine would read him to sleep, soothing his racing brain with her soft, musical voice. If he woke up at 3:00 A.M. or whenever, his sleepy valet was ordered to have hot water ready for a two-hour bath. While he soaked, he dictated.

Josephine's bedroom resembles the inside of a desert chieftain's tent. The circular ceiling is propped up with gold lances against crimson-draped walls. Sphinxes support her wash stand, and swans and cornucopias adorn the gilt sleigh-shaped bed enveloped in draperies. Woven into the middle of an Aubusson red and gold carpet are two white swans, Josephine's emblem, symbolizing eternal love. This bizarre bedroom was no place for Napoléon. He moved into a room over his study at the other end of the château. Once, poor jealous Josephine and her lady in waiting crept through the long, dark corridors and staircases, attempting to catch him with one of his conquests.

If there were happy memories for Josephine at Malmaison, they would be of her grandchildren and her garden. Hortense wrote, "The First Consul always took my mother's arm to lead her away from the others for a long stroll through the garden." Sea captains roaming the world brought her all the roses available at the time. Two varieties, "Josephine" and "Malmaison," are still around but susceptible to mildew. People throughout the world sent flowers and plants to Malmaison: purple magnolias from Charleston, South Carolina, lilacs from Kew Gardens in London, blue lotus from the Nile, a sacred fig tree from India, eucalyptus from Australia, and many more. Alexander von Humboldt sent her hundreds of bulbs and seeds (cactus, dahlias, gladioli). Napoléon confiscated 800 bulbs from the Schöenbrunn Palace in Vienna.

At Malmaison, Josephine guided guests through her greenhouses, reciting hundreds of botanical names. She gave tours in the art gallery, spent money, and posed for portraits. Her real happiness was her beloved daughter, Hortense, who visited with her sons. At Malmaison, the little boys had their own enormous zoo and aviary. They could mess around in the mud, suck sugar cane, and play with an orangutan dressed in a chemise, who fed himself with a knife and fork.

After Napoléon crowned himself and Josephine Emperor and Empress, he set out to conquer Europe. In Poland, he took Countess Marie Walewska as his mistress. He also sent Josephine a letter telling her how much he loved her but that she couldn't come there—and to be happy with her lot. She tried, but Josephine was feminine: warm, loving, clinging, dependent. Although she had been ordered to marry the intense little soldier, she had grown to love him during their thirteen-year marriage despite his adultery. Napoléon scolded her for her enormous debts, but her quiet nature was pleasing to him.

When Josephine learned Marie Walewska was pregnant, she knew she would soon be discarded. After the dreaded divorce, Josephine was sent to the dilapidated château of Navarre, sixty miles from Paris near Evreaux in Normandy. "Go take possession of your new domain. You may leave March 5. Spend the month of April there." She was permitted to visit Malmaison at tulip time, but that summer, she wandered around Switzerland terrified she wouldn't be allowed back into France. Permission to return to Navarre and, eventually, Malmaison, was finally granted.

At Malmaison, she learned that Napoléon had married the defeated Habsburg Emperor's daughter, eighteen-year-old Marie Louise, and that Marie Walewska of Poland had a son fathered by Napoléon. The final blow was the news that the new empress, Marie Louise, had delivered an heir to the throne.

After Napoléon's Russian fiasco, he escaped to Fountainebleau as the Russians swarmed into France. When Paris fell, Josephine fled from

Back to Europe with the BUSY BODY

Napoléon's Farewell to Josephine.
Reproduced from an antique glass slide, courtesy of Michael Urbanek

Château Malmaison

Malmaison to Navarre where Hortense and her sons joined her. Miraculously, they made it safely from Chârtres through Cossack-infested woods. Thirty-eight-year-old Tsar Alexander I of Russia treated both Napoléon and France with incredible generosity. After Napoléon was exiled to Elba, Tsar Alexander allowed Josephine to return to Malmaison, where her treasures remained intact. Thanks to him, her life was spared. When he called on her, he fell under her spell like everyone who met her. But rejection, divorce, and worry about Napoléon and her children had taken its toll. Hortense wrote, "So deeply affected by our recent disasters, her health had been affected." Josephine died at fifty-one in her ornate bed at Malmaison a few days after catching a cold. No more migraines and stomach spasms. No more heartache. She was spared the trauma of Napoléon's escape from Elba, his defeat at Waterloo, and final exile to Saint Helena.

For three days, the large entrance hall at Malmaison, with its stately columns, was draped in black as friends from all walks of life paid their respects. Both the Russian Imperial Guardsmen and the French National Guard escorted her coffin to the parish church of Saint Peter-Saint Paul in Rueil.

After Waterloo, with nowhere to go, Napoléon asked Hortense to open Malmaison for him—which she did. "I never would have abandoned the man whom I called my father in the hour of his misfortune. This was the one way for me to show my gratitude to him." Napoléon knew the consequences for her would be exile, but he was oblivious to the fate of others: it was always "My will be done." "I am not like other men. The laws of mortality and society are not applicable to me. I have the right to answer all your objections with an eternal 'I'."

Hortense, too, knew she would be branded by the returning Bourbons. After living in exile for seventeen years, in 1831, still a fugitive, she visited her mother's tomb. With her was her twenty-three-year-old son, Louis Napoléon. When he became emperor twenty years later, he restored Malmaison, making sure the pictures were hung exactly as he remembered them.

15

Normandy

For Those in Peril on the Sea[1]

MONT SAINT MICHEL

From the train at Saint Malo, a former Corsair city,[2] we took a bus to Mont Saint Michel, the mysterious, medieval monastery that rises from the sea and sand.[3] The bus was packed, but before the twenty-eight-mile ride was over, we were the only ones left. We drove across a long causeway and, since the tide was out, over the sand to the gate of the old city at the foot of the rock. A group of English mothers and their beautifully mannered children were feeding long loaves of bread to mallard ducks and dainty grey-and-white seabirds. When the ducks stole a piece intended for the little birds, they were properly reprimanded, "Naughty, naughty." Soon a tour bus arrived, and the delightful group climbed aboard waving good-bye to the "darling little souls," wishing them bon appetit.

Our hotel room was opposite steep steps that led up to the abbey church. When the hotel boy turned a key in the lock of a narrow, wooden door in the rock, surprise! We were expecting to sleep in a cave like The Three Bears. Instead, it was a good-sized room with twin beds. In the bathroom, an arrogant white bathtub, big as a boat, defied the intruder to fill it up. All that plumbing, all that electricity, all that rock was brought from the mainland and lifted by pulley or dragged up the single steep cobblestone

Normandy

Mont Saint Michel

path. That night we dreamed of knights and monks who might have slept here. The next day outside our door, perched on a wall above us, we saw a funny statue of Saint Anthony with a bewildered "Where am I?" look on his face. A tinkling church bell was calling people to Mass, and as others centuries before had climbed to the church, we followed in their footsteps.

In the fifteenth-century parish church, Benedictine monks in sandals and plain white robes celebrated Mass as they have since the eighth century. Perhaps even then gladioli adorned the altar as they did on this day. Ironically, the tour does not include the church, which is the whole reason—*le raison d'être*—for this wonder of the world.

No danger of offending a Calvinist here. The beauty of art has been minimized: bare walls, a plain stone table, a Bible, two brass candlesticks, a chalice, and a pewter plate to celebrate the Last Supper. Saint Michael's[4] magnificent silver statue stands in a side chapel. Sword raised high, he is about to slay Satan, represented as a dragon at his feet. His other hand holds a shield emblazoned with a cross, thrust toward the dragon—lest we forget the true purpose of the miracle monastery.

After Mass, we ate breakfast on a terrace overlooking the bay, and at nine o'clock in the morning, instead of coffee, I ordered *calvados*, which I thought was the name for cider. It wasn't cider. It was one big gulp of apple brandy—what New Englanders call apple jack! An American writer, Irving Cobb, called it essence of lockjaw: "A sudden violent jolt has been known to stop the victim's watch, snap his suspenders, and crack his glass eye right across."

When the fire in my stomach burned down, we toured the monastery, cloister, gardens, ramparts, and the fourteenth-century house of a young bride,[5] whose husband, Bertrand du Guesclin, went off to fight the English and left her locked in a chastity belt. The heavy, ugly metal contraption belongs in a torture chamber.

There are two versions of Mont Saint Michel: the magical silhouette against the sky and the noisy reality of the village below the awesome abbey. In 708 A.D., God is said to have sent his militant archangel, Saint Michael, to the Bishop of Avranches twenty miles away, instructing him to build a shrine in the nearby forest on a cone-shaped rock. The shrine was to be dedicated to Saint Michael. Twice the angel delivered the message, and twice the bishop decided he was hallucinating. The third time, Saint Michael muttered something about "Some people have to be hit over the head" and clobbered him. (The bishop's skull actually has a dent in it.)

After a little wooden chapel was built on the rock, a tidal wave swept away the surrounding forest. When fire destroyed the shrine, a small granite church replaced it. Charlemagne came to pray, and in 966 A.D., William the Conqueror's grandfather, Norman duke Richard I, sent for Benedictine monks to build a three-story monastery.

From the ninth to the eleventh century, fearless Northmen, "tall as date palms," had been ravaging the coasts of Europe. People prayed, "From the fury of the Northmen, good Lord deliver us"—and He did. Not only did He send Saint Michael, but in 991 French king Charles III gave the Northmen a permanent home on French soil—Normandy. The once fierce warriors settled down on their farms, deserted their Druids, and became French-speaking Christians, while their leaders became nobles like William the Conqueror.

There was a time when William, Duke of Normandy (later the Conqueror), and his rival for the English throne, Harold the Saxon, were friends. When they came to Mont Saint Michel together in the eleventh century, it was Harold who rescued William's soldiers from the quicksand. By using the Norman's long, narrow shields as life rafts, he dragged the men from the sinking sand.

Normandy

During the Middle Ages, thousands of pilgrims in grey hooded robes and broad-brimmed hats, carrying staffs to lean on, walked to the shrine over the mile-long salt marshes and waited for the tide to go out. "In the leafy woods, tents were set up with bread, pastries, fruit, fish, birds, cake and venison." In the days of great faith and chivalry, minstrels sang and strummed their lutes as kings and commoners came to seek Saint Michael's blessing and protection.

Eleventh-century pilgrims scooped up cockleshells for souvenirs. Today, tourists swarm into shops jostling for ashtrays and thimbles. In restaurant doorways lining the steep path up the mount, tuxedoed waiters smile a welcome.

This is no place for invalids. The straight-up-the-mount trudge is one challenge, then begins the climb to the monastery balanced on the flattened peak of the rock. The group we joined must have graduated from a physical fitness class. Young mothers carried infants and dragged strollers effortlessly up ninety steps. At the top of the mount, two monasteries clinging to the sides of the rock rise into the sky, each three stories high.

The tour starts on the top level in the graceful, airy thirteenth-century refectory. A few curious men in the group examined long, narrow, recessed windows with plain glass. Once, soft light from stained glass filtered through the elegant hall that is now stripped and empty, and monks cooked over flaming logs in the two adjacent fireplaces. A reader's throne carved into a granite wall was used by monks who read scripture during meals, since conversation was forbidden. Empty stone shelves on another wall held basins of water for sticky, greasy hands.

Below the refectory are two enormous gothic halls. One, a guest hall of the original monastery, was completed in 1058. Three rows of massive round columns support beautifully carved Roman arches. The masculine, militant hall, lighted on two sides by small round windows, has a quiet strength—as solid as the faith of those who built it. Between 1050 and 1122, Norman VIPs slept and dined here. Once it was the scriptorium where monks copied manuscripts, painted miniatures, and tried to keep warm in front of the hearth.

When William the Conqueror and Harold the Saxon stayed here with their soldiers, where did they park their clanking suits of armor, and how could they tell them apart? The enormous, empty room once resounded with the roar and clamor of 200 rowdy, smelly soldiers. Sixty black-robed monks waited on them, laying straw on the floor at bedtime and preparing meals over a blazing fire. At each long table, forty men with ravenous appetites gulped wine from cups or bowls and ate with their hands from huge serving platters.

After-dinner entertainment was provided by William the Conqueror's minstrel, Taillifer, who sang and acted out graphic, gory songs called *chansons des gestes,* describing bloody hand-to-hand battles. The most popular was *The Song of Roland,* an epic poem dramatizing the defeat of Charlemagne and his nephew, Roland, by the Saracens of Spain. Forced to retreat into the narrow pass of Roncesvalles in the Pyrenees, twelve knights, including Roland, were slashed to pieces by the enemy. Although the event had happened three hundred years before, practically every Frenchman knew the poem by heart. *The Song of Roland* must have been sung hundreds of times at Mont Saint Michel. The men gathered in the guest hall listened spellbound as they relived the slaying and hacking of battle when "eyes flew out and brains dropped to the ground."

They never tired of hearing about Roland, who, though mortally wounded, killed the pagan who tried to steal his Christian sword. Determined that it should never fall into heathen hands, he lay on top of it and prayed, "Oh God, the Father who never lied, who raised up Lazarus from the dead and Daniel from the lions saved, save my soul from all perils for the sins in my life I did."

One hundred years after William the Conqueror came to Mont Saint Michel, twenty-year-old King Henry II of England came with his thirty-year-old wife, Eleanor of Aquitaine. Henry II, originally from France, was the son of the Count of Anjou, nicknamed "Plantagenet" for his habit of wearing a yellow broom flower *(planta genestra)* in his hat when he hunted. The count had recently turned his Norman duchy over to his son, Henry. When Henry invaded England (a year after he married Eleanor), he became the first Plantagenet king of England.

Henry II and Eleanor of Aquitaine came to Mont Saint Michel in 1158, five years after their coronation in Westminster Abbey—long before the king's character slid downhill. His insistence that *his* will be done led to the murder of his friend,[6] Thomas à Becket, archbishop of Canterbury. The king's marriage wasn't going too well, either. Eleanor's dreams of courtly love had faded years ago. Humiliated by her husband's unfaithfulness, she took revenge by turning their five sons against him. The king kept her a prisoner in different castles throughout England for fifteen years.[7] Headstrong, haughty Eleanor, whose life had started with fun and games, flutes and troubadours, died defeated in her schemes for her sons against her husband and against French king Philippe Augustus,[8] son of her first husband (by another queen).[9] When an ally of King Philippe's burned the village at Mont Saint Michel, the king, in reparation, financed a new monastery that clung to the other side of the rock—a marvel of the world, Le Marveille.

Like the first abbey, it is three stories high, with one building piled atop the other; the almonry on the first level (where money was given to the poor), guest hall on the second, and refectory at the top level, where the tour starts. On the level below the eleventh-century guest hall, the thirteenth-century hall is divided in half by slender columns. One guest was King Louis IX, patron saint of France, who came on a pilgrimage before his first crusade.

Saint Louis wasn't always a saint. For thirty years he had been bossed around by his widowed mother, Queen Blanche of Castile, who was accustomed to cracking the whip over wild barons in her realm. When Louis' fourteen-year-old bride-to-be, Margaret of Provence, stayed at Pontoise, near Paris, Queen Blanche arranged for them to sleep on different floors. Margaret's room was located where the queen could keep an eye on them if they tried to sneak into each other's rooms. Louis and his fiancée had to meet on a back staircase. Servants warned them when the imperious Queen Mother headed their way. Even after their marriage, Blanche continued her role as ringmaster.

When the tall, thirty-year-old adolescent king finally had a chance to lead an army against rebellious barons, Satan gave the orders. After diabolically crushing the revolt, Louis became so ill he should have died. His mother, Blanche, promised God if He allowed her son to live, he would make a crusade to Christ's sepulchre. After Louis' miraculous recovery, she hated herself for making that stupid vow. Her husband, Louis' father, had died during a crusade. Louis was delighted. Now he could be his own man. God would be proud of him, and he would return victorious in God's service.

He built a harbor at Aigues Mortes near Nîmes, then sailed for Cyprus, where 1,800 vessels from different countries waited, sails billowing, as far as one could see. When they reached Damietta in Egypt (125 miles north of Cairo), Louis jumped from the ship into water up to his shoulders. Sword held high, lance around his neck, he led the charge against the infidel. Tragically, he took the worst possible route to find the enemy—through a maze of canals in the Nile Delta. At Mansura, fifty miles away, his brave crusaders were annihilated. The king and his two brothers were captured and another brother killed. The Moslems, determined to kill everyone, refused the peace terms.

How could God have allowed this to happen? Why had God forsaken him? To comfort the miserable king, on the feast of Pentecost[10] God sent the Holy Spirit, who brought him the gift of healing, a prayer book, and the seven gifts given to the Apostles (wisdom, understanding, knowledge, piety, fortitude, counsel, and fear of the Lord). King Louis threw himself prostrate on the ground and told the Moslems to kill him—torture him—whatever they intended. The Moslems were so impressed with his courage that they accepted the peace terms, but they held him prisoner for a month, until half the ransom was paid.

King Louis became a different person. He decided his soul was not exactly pure and humble and pleasing to God, so he changed and became like Mother Teresa. He buried the putrid, mutilated corpses of his fallen crusaders and cared for lepers and those with the most revolting diseases.

As king of France for the next forty-four years, he practiced Christian charity, combining the manners of a king with the habits of a monk. On a second crusade he watched his son, Tristan, die of the plague in Tunis, and a few days later he, too, died.

King Louis provided the necessary funds to fortify Mont Saint Michel just in time. The impregnable fortress was repeatedly attacked during the Hundred Years' War with England and again in the sixteenth century when Huguenots besieged it. During the French Revolution, 300 priests who refused to conform to the atheistic government were imprisoned here.

Napoléon I converted the monastery into workshops where prisoners made straw hats and boots. In 1863 his nephew, Napoléon III, prohibited the monastery from being used as a prison, and when his Second Empire collapsed, Marshal MacMahon, president of the new Republic, placed the abbey under the Department of Public Monuments.

During World War II, although the shrine was occupied by Nazis, Saint Michael, his sword raised against evil, was still on guard. On June 30, 1944, the thundering tanks of General George Patton's Third U.S. Army burst through enemy lines to liberate Avranches—Avranches, where God's great avenger, Saint Michael, first appeared to Bishop Aubert in the eighth century. Today in Avranches, a monument to General Patton stands on a patch of U.S. territory with trees and soil from different states. The memorial reads, "Making the Avranches breakthrough in the roar of its tanks while marching toward victory and the liberation of France, General Patton's glorious American army passed over this crossroad."

16

Aquitaine

Troubadours, Wine, and Some Dead People

CHIVALRY AND THE COURTS OF LOVE

Aquitane, in twelfth-century France, included land from the Loire to the Pyrenees. During the Crusades, when the Tower of Pisa in Italy was being built (1173) and glorious cathedrals in France were zooming heavenward, an amazing phenomena occurred.

Chivalry, like Merlin's magic potion, cast its spell over brutal men who previously had sworn loyalty to feudal lords. Now they pledged their allegiance to ladies—usually someone's wife. After Chrétien of Troyes (ninety miles from Paris) wrote for the first time the tales of chivalrous knights at King Arthur's court, suddenly foppish troubadours in Italy and southern France strummed lutes under windows and sang passionate love songs to lady loves.[1] In his youth, Saint Francis of Assisi, with his lute, was one of the midnight serenaders. Dante in Florence worshiped his Beatrice; in Avignon, the poet, Petrarch, adored from afar his Laura. He wrote to his brother, reminiscing about their youthful days: "And what of our curling irons and our artful locks which cost us labor and pain and robbed us of our sleep! What pirate could have tortured us more than we did ourselves? How often in the morning we saw red wounds on our foreheads so that when we wanted to show off our beautiful hair, we had to hide our faces."

Aquitaine

Landless nobles,[2] needing food and lodging, journeyed to castles commanded by women. Bored, unhappily married females languished all over southern France. Many a fourteen-year-old girl, married to a much older man she hadn't seen in years, welcomed any man who showed up. But the troubadours sang of love—good, wholesome, platonic love. Saint Bernard's reaction was, "Yeah, right!"

One lady of the castle was Eleanor of Aquitaine. After divorcing her husband, King Louis VII, she established her magnificent court at Poitiers and welcomed the troubadours singing of devotion to highborn ladies beyond their reach. Eleanor's fierce grandfather, Duke William IX, wrote wonderful poems, but no way were they platonic.

I'll make a new ditty before the wind, the ice, and the rains come. My Lady tests me and puts me on trial to discover how, in what manner I love her . . . I surrender and yield myself up to her . . . without her I cannot live, I have such a great hunger for her love. For she is whiter than ivory . . . If I do not have help soon to make my fair lady love, I will die . . . if she does not kiss me in her bedroom or outdoors.

Poems, set to music, followed set rules. Medieval people loved rules. They had lists and guides for every occasion, including table manners. "When you are through gnawing a bone, do not put it back in the dish. The correct place is on the floor." Fleas and lice were a major problem, and one courtesy book requested men not to scratch that part of the male anatomy that the Middle Ages called the codware. Ladies were advised, "If you cannot help scratching, then take a portion of your dress and scratch with that."

Andreas Capellanus, author of the *Rule Book,* warns that "love easily obtained is of little value and that a great excess of lust prevents love. Such men are like a shameless dog. In fact, I believe they should be compared to asses."

Rules for *Behavior for Lovers* declared that love must be at first sight. First you see your beloved; you turn pale, you are smitten—you can't eat, you can't sleep, and you are compelled to make your love known. You must be completely at her will. The main theme of *Behavior for Lovers* is the "exquisite pain and mental anguish of the lover."

Not all troubadours were men. There were twenty known women troubadours who wrote exactly what they thought; "Elias Cairel, you're a phony if I ever saw one, like a man who says he's sick when he hasn't got the slightest pain." Male troubadours were ambiguous and cautious, but not the women. "Handsome friend, as a lover true I loved you for you pleased me, but now I see I was a fool for I've barely seen you since."

Besides the troubadours' flattering songs and feasting, another pasttime was the "Courts of Love" modeled after the rules and high standards of King Arthur's Round Table. At the Courts of Love, one troubadour would sing a stanza about his love problem, and another would sing a second verse giving advice. Since neither could agree, they appealed to a great lady for her decision.

Most knights in the Middle Ages were as illiterate as their peasants, and as wild with their wives as they were with the enemy. The purpose of a wife was to breed sons—period. Suddenly the Church, which previously had regarded women nearly as evil as the devil, reversed itself, and used King Arthur's code of chivalry to teach and promote Christian virtues. In songs and sermons, the lady on the pedestal was the Virgin Mary, and King Arthur represented God the Father, whose rule is gentle but firm.

In Chrétien de Troyes' hilarious *The Grail*, the hero, Perceval, has never heard of a knight. When he meets one and learns that knights gallop about the countryside on horses, sleep in castles, right wrongs, and specialize in "prowess," he wants to do that.

Before leaving for King Arthur's court to become a knight, his mother gives him all kinds of advice. "Darling son [he thought that was his name], Charity is the greatest virtue. Believe in God, adore Him. Go toward worthy men. Help widows and orphans, and if you find a disconsolate maiden, be ready to assist her."

After being knighted at King Arthur's court, Perceval's path seemed strewn with disconsolate maidens. One maiden on a weary palfrey was the most wretched he had ever seen. As he galloped toward her, "She pulled her clothing round her to cover herself better. More holes then began to open, for when she covered herself further, every hole she closed, opened a hundred more." After righting the wrong (an innocent maiden falsely accused of unfaithfulness) that had left her in this plight, Perceval continued onward.

In a beautiful stretch of meadow . . . he saw a pavilion, and on a bed covered with silk brocade, a maiden lay sleeping. His mother had told him, "Darling son, he who wins a maiden's kiss has a great deal. . . . And if she has a ring on her finger or a purse on her belt . . . I grant you permission to accept the ring and purse." Now he told the fair maid in the pavilion, "Maiden I greet you as my mother instructed me." Then he kissed her twenty times, took her ring and left. "Maiden, I wish you every blessing... You are much better to kiss than any chambermaid in my mother's entire household."

Needing lodging for the night, he banged at a town gate until a gaunt and pale maiden hurried to the windows of the hall and asked him to accept such lodging as there was. "That evening the knight had all the comfort and all the delight possible in a bed with the exception of a maiden... but of this pleasure he is ignorant. And therefore I delight in telling you that he fell asleep quite quickly, free of all care."

Not so with his hostess. "She resolved to go to her guest and tell him something of her situation." She left her room, went to his bed, knelt down, threw her arms around his neck and wept so much she woke him up. "He behaved with such courtesy that at once he took her in his arms and drew her toward him..." "Oh noble knight... there is no creature alive so sad or so wretched..." After hearing her sad story, he comforted her. "Dear friend, weep no more... Lie down beside me in this bed." She allowed him to kiss her, and I do not think he was displeased. Thus all night long... they lay beside each other. That night she knew this much consolation, arm clasped in arm, their mouths touching, they slept till daybreak.

So continues Chrétien de Troyes' story, *The Grail*, loaded with Christian doctrine and written according to the "Rules," i.e., honor, prowess, humility, righting wrongs, and comforting maidens.

SAINT ÉMILION (THE FAMOUS WINE TOWN)
A Texan and an Art History Pottery Museum

The highlight of a thirty-minute bus ride from Bordeaux to Saint Émilion was the little first-graders who clamored aboard with their pretty teacher. School was out, and they had been eating chocolate ice cream cones. Some looked like Bozo the Clown. Others had mustaches. All the way to the next stop, they sang happy songs in their innocent young voices. Before they came, we had to listen to "Bad, bad boy. You make me feel so good."[3]

We drove past the lovely town of Libourne, where two rivers meet.[4] Before the railroads, it was the shipping port for Saint Émilion wines. In the hilly countryside, an elderly lady walked her bike up a hill, and grapevines grew in different stages; some with clusters of purple grapes, others only two feet high, propped up on stakes. Drab little villages, like Cleopatra's

Back to Europe with the BUSY BODY

early morning face without makeup, came alive and beautiful with geraniums, roses, and crepe myrtles. On every tiny town square, sobering war memorials recall *les enfants de France*. At Saint Jean de Blaignac, we turned left and followed the river.

The bus driver deposited us in Saint Émilion at the bottom of a steep hill in this medieval town, perched on top of a cliff. Ancient limestone houses and buildings the color of *café au lait* are jumbled together, and some of the up and down streets are narrow alleyways. Underground caves are used for storing wine. The town, once surrounded by a wall, is now surrounded by grapevines. When Julius Caesar conquered Gaul (55–54 B.C.), the Romans brought their own grapevines and grafted them to the vines of Saint Émilion.

Saint Émilion is named for an eighth-century hermit monk from Brittany. Returning from a pilgrimage to the shrine of Saint James in Compostella, Spain, he chose to live in one of the limestone caves, where he carved out niches for a bed and a seat. During the next three centuries, Benedictine monks excavated more rooms and a chapel with fifty-foot columns—known as "monolithic," since each pillar is carved from a solid slab of limestone. Dominican and Franciscan monks built monasteries here, and the Knights Templar built a Commanderie or hostel for pilgrims en route to Spain. However, invading Norsemen and Saracens destroyed them. When twenty-nine-year-old Eleanor of Aquitaine married eighteen-year-old French Henry Plantagenet (who became King Henry II of England two years later), English kings became dukes of Aquitaine for 300 years.[5]

King Henry's son, Richard the Lion-Heart, granted Saint Émilion privileges, free customs, and appointed judges, or "Jurats" to govern the provinces. King Henry's youngest son, John, known as "Lackland," officially established the Jurade, a municipal governing body. His Magna Carta (1215) made Saint Émilion a commune. Men of property were allowed to elect judges and govern the town and its wine. King John's son, Henry III, increased the Jurade's power (1312) to administer a hospital and tax the nobility and clergy. In return, he required that regular wine shipments be sent to England. The British called the light-colored wine "claret." (They mixed red and white grapes together.) The wine "that whispers and doesn't shout" had to be labeled with the seal of the Jurade (the town's coat of arms), depicting a grape-like cluster of *fleurs-de-lys* and three heraldic lions.[6]

The French Revolution ended the Jurade, but Saint Émilion wines continued to gain fame. Then disaster! During the period of America's Civil

Aquitaine

The monolithic church at Saint Émilion

Back to Europe with the BUSY BODY

War, nearly all the grapevines in Europe were dying from a disease called phylloxera, caused by an insect that destroyed the roots. France had imported grapevines from America, and with the vines came the deadly insect. No grapes, no wine. France without wine? Like Ireland without shamrocks. Thousands were unemployed. To give them work, Napoléon III kept changing army uniforms, with dozens of buttons to be sewn on.

In desperation, France appealed to America for help. Officials in Washington told the French delegates they didn't know anything about grapes, but someone in Texas did—Thomas Volney Munson, from Denison, Texas.

For years T. V. Munson had been experimenting with vines throughout the country. Searching for them, he had traveled 40,000 miles by wagon three weeks at a time, always in danger of floods and hostile Indians. The deep-rooted, disease-resistant grapes of the Southwest were his bonanza. Texans called them "post oak" grapes since they grew on oak trees used for posts.

A representative from Cognac, France, Pierre Viala, spent eighteen months with Munson, loading thousands of root stocks of different disease-resistant species, especially the post oak, onto mule carts to be sent to France. The plague was halted after three to four million acres of vineyards were completely uprooted and replanted with the American rootstocks. Twenty years later, after the vineyards of France and Europe were saved, France awarded Munson the *Chevalier du Merité Agricole*.[7] Before he died at seventy, Mr. Munson, a true vintner, told his friends to "Plant a vine above my grave and see it clasp its hands with joy." All Europe clasped their hands with joy.

CHÂTEAU MONBOUSQUET

Château Monbousquet, in the commune of Saint Sulpice Faleyrens, is one of seven communes outside Saint Émilion allowed to be classified as Saint Émilion. Of all the châteaux whose wine is comparable with that of the Grand Cru Classé properties, one of the most famous is Château Monbousquet, made from 60% Merlot grapes, 30% Franc Cabernet, and 10% Sauvignon Cabernet grapes.

Château Monbousquet, on the outskirts of Libourne, dates back to 1540. The white stone château stands sheltered among beautiful old trees, serenely overlooking a large pond—exactly the same since 1584 when it was remodeled. Today, Monbousquet is owned by Mr. and Mrs. Gérard

Perse, but when we visited, Alain Querre was the proprietor.[8] After World War II his father, Daniel Querre, with a friend,[9] refounded the Jurade and took over Château Monbousquet, almost completely replanting the vineyard. Thanks to his son, Alain Querre, who showed us around Saint Émilion, we learned that Aquitaine is divided into five departments and that both Saint Émilion and Bordeaux are in the Department of the Gironde. Wine areas are divided into districts according to the soil, and districts are divided into parishes (villages), estates, and châteaux. Twice a year, a panel[10] meets to determine by blind tasting which wines are qualified to be labeled "Saint Émilion." If, after a second tasting, they fail the high standards, the wines are denied the appellation Saint Émilion.

Each proprietor of Saint Émilion makes his own wine. The vintner's vines are part of his family. No unions here. "Look at these tender young grapes. You have to baby them. A mother cannot go on strike and neither can we." Parenting these babies requires dedication, patience, and sacrifice. The stubborn ones are the most trying, but with patience, eventually they turn out very well. Harvest time is family reunion time. The babies have matured with all their individual characteristics: the proud, the sensitive—some are genial and courteous, some courageous. Others are positively stylish, like the 1983 Grand Cru Château Puy-Razac[11] that we sampled at lunch. (Sorry. It wasn't a sample. We drank the whole bottle.) With Alain's gracious wife and brother, we drank to the vine, the "negociant" that makes strangers friends and celebrates *la joie de vivre*. We celebrated with a 1983 La Tour Blanche, which, like most Bordeaux sweet wines,[12] is made from grapes hand-picked one at a time as each grape reaches perfection. Some rows are picked ten times within two or three months. The secret of the smooth flavor is a white mold on the dried-up grape. One vine makes only one glassful. I suspect La Tour Blanche is one of Alain's favorites because it recalls so many happy times. As he shared *souvenirs* with us, I thought of all the wine stories I have heard; some hilarious, some wistful, associated with different occasions: a sunny picnic in a field of flowers, soft candlelight, joyous celebrations. French people always remember exactly which wine they had and where.

We should have come to Saint Émilion during one of the Celebration days. Twice a year, following a medieval ritual, the twenty-four Jurats[13] parade through the ancient streets in scarlet robes, long white capes, and red hats. In June, they celebrate the flowering of the vine at a Mass of Thanks-

Back to Europe with the BUSY BODY

Jurats at King's Tower overlooking monolithic Benedictine Collegiate church

giving in the fifteenth-century Benedictine Collegiate church. In the fall, they walk in procession to La Tour du Roi (The King's Tower) above the town to the ruins of the king's castle to announce the result of the harvest. Once, when someone inquired, "What if the harvest is bad?" he was told in that case, they pronounce it "insufficiently fine."

We climbed up to the ruins of the old castle to get a painter's paradise view of the ancient town with its rust-colored tile roofs. At night we ate outdoors under ancient lime trees. A couple opposite us who were leaving, stopped by to congratulate us on how well we had handled the menu. (We didn't order eel.) The girl said they were from California, and in one French town she had made the mistake of ordering eggs for dinner. The waiter stood with his hands on his hips and glared. She said she no longer orders eggs for dinner, but she does look for a balcony where she can dry her laundry. When the sun went down, it was so chilly my friend draped herself with the tablecloth, canceled her ice-cream order, and asked the waiter to please bring a hot plate to warm her hands. As a souvenir of Saint Émilion, we bought a poster of the brightly-robed Jurats in procession, and there among them was our host. Thanks to him, Saint Émilion was not just another bus stop.

Aquitaine

HOSPICE DE LA MADELEINE

Today, Alain Querre has created the largest pottery museum in France, showcasing the history of Southwest France with ancient vessels unearthed throughout Aquitaine. The underground museum, located in the oldest stone quarry of Saint Émilion, has been hollowed out over eight centuries.

In 1199 the Jurades of Saint Émilion signed a contract with English king John II (Richard the Lion-Heart's brother), giving them the right to govern the town and its jurisdiction. To protect their new liberties, they excavated the Madeleine stone quarry to build ramparts and a Town Hall, later called The King's Castle (Château du Roi) or King's Tower (Tour du Roi). The museum is named Hospice de la Madeleine.

The entrance to the courtyard is a bright, cheery, enclosed garden, where you are greeted by young wine gods swinging merrily among bushes and by wildly imaginative animals made from broken bicycles. The first exhibit is a laundry or wash-house with more than 500 iron and pottery vessels from the Charente and Périgord regions. Three times a year women washed clothes in these huge pottery vessels, using wood ash as a detergent.

Other exhibits include iron pots, *peyrols,* for cooking the family pig, a 200–year-old chamber pot, *porte déjeuner,* that was used to carry food to field workers, colanders for filtering cooking oil before being used for lamps, a pestle and mortar for crushing sea salt, and roof ornaments that contained holy water, medicinal herbs, or stone axeheads (protection from lightning). Also from the Charente River region are cheese strainers and a seventeenth-century decanter for cognac, and from the Auvergne, jugs for lard and hazelnut oil. Big, round iron cauldrons were used in Aquitaine to boil crushed chestnuts. Tiles protected women's legs from the heat as they stirred the mixture for hours. Speaking of heat, a small warming pan, once filled with hot embers, was placed under a little wooden stool to warm women's bottoms. When they sat on the stool, their long skirts made them look like hens sitting on their eggs. Consequently, the warming pans were called *couvets* from the French word *couver* (to sit on eggs). A little waterfall and a spring provide the setting for water jugs called *cruches de tête* (pitchers-on-the-head), since the women carried the pitchers on their heads.

The museum's *pièce de résistance* is the Potters Workshop, with a sign that says "Who has not, cannot." Men laugh at this, but it really means, "Without real knowledge of the virtues and vices of clay, a student potter can do little." Fifty fascinating ceramic plaques by Daniel Piron, inspired by medieval engravings and commentaries, depict the ancient civilization of wine growers south of the Loire River.

During the Middle Ages, people lived in fear of hell, corrupt judges, and bad barons. Piron's pictures illustrate translations by the contemporary poet, André Berry:

> However, you must earn your living and that of your family. Prune your vine, catch fish, take the fish to market and pay a Toll every time you go under or over a bridge.

One traveler wrote, "May boatmen be damned. The fact is that though this river is very narrow, these men demand payment from everyone rich or poor . . . and four times as much for a horse, but their boat is small, made from a single tree trunk, and can barely carry a horse."

The exhibit is a medieval comic strip, much more fun than the Bayeux tapestries. A version of Adam and Eve is hysterical. "The Unfortunate Wedding Night" shows the bride, duchess Eleanor of Aquitaine, waiting in her curtained bed while her pious bridegroom, the future French king, spends the night praying in a chapel.

A troubadour on guard outside a window complains to his friend inside about not having had any sleep all night. Exhausted, he says, "The dawn will soon be here." The troubadour lover inside replies, "Sweet gentle friend, I am in such a sweet place that I wish that day will never come. I am embracing the most charming lady of the whole world and do not care for dawn or jealous husbands."

My favorite picture is the wine fleet formally anchored in Libourne on Saint Martin's day, November 11. The tall-masted ships seem made of fishnets. Another favorite shows French soldiers arriving from Saintes, Angoulême, Limoges, and Périgueux to oust the English. I wish I had known the artist who drew such funny expressions on their faces. The only thing missing from Alain Querre's "This Was Our Life" museum is a chapel to thank God that it was their life—not mine.

Aquitaine

THE ABBEY OF FONTEVRAUD

Here, at Last, You Will Find Peace.
—POPE JOHN PAUL II to the Gypsies, 1988[14]

At the Royal Abbey of Fontevraud near Chinon in the Loire Valley, women ordered men around for more than 700 years. The abbey was one of the wealthiest and most important in France. Over the years, thirty-six ab-

Abbey Fontevraud and the tombs of the Plantagenets

besses of high nobility ran the monastery under the Rule of Saint Benedict. The founder of the abbey, a Breton monk,[15] established Fontevraud in 1099 for his crowd of disciples. Near a fountain (*fonte*) in a remote, forested valley, he started the little settlement, with a chapel and huts for the old, the sick, "fallen women," lepers, monks, and nuns. Fontevraud also provided a refuge where battered women could recover self-respect and dignity.

The great Romanesque abbey was built thanks to benefactors such as Eleanor of Aquitaine and her husband, King Henry II. After the king's death at his castle in Chinon, he was buried at Fontevraud. Then his son, Richard the Lion-Heart, released his mother, Queen Eleanor, from Winchester Castle in England. Eleanor was impressed by the piety of the order—Fontevraud became her favorite retreat and eventually her home.[16] She died there, old and frail at eighty, dressed in the nuns' black and white habit. She is buried in the chapel with the king, their son Richard, and Isabella of Angoulême, wife of their youngest son, John. Effigies of the king, queen, and Richard are mottled, cracked, and faded red, grey, and blue the way they should be; but Isabella's dark green and gold robe looks as if she had recently ordered a new one. There they are—flat on their backs—one of the most dysfunctional families in history. When Henry died, his wife, his four sons, and King Philip II[17] were all plotting against him.

Today, Fontevraud is famous for its turrets and the kitchen with six enormous fireplaces and twenty flues shooting through the roof, as well as for the Plantagenets buried there. A pretty, dark-haired girl with a beautifully trained voice gave us a tour in English, but an Irish accent sneaked in with delightful, subtle humor. She told us the first abbess, Louise de Bourbon, had her picture painted on top of Christ's Crucifixion. "Naughty." Her well-written script was easy to follow, thanks to phrases such as "As we have just said . . ." Today the vast, empty stone rooms with lovely gothic arches have the same lingering sense of peace the cloistered Benedictines sought 800 years ago.

17

Brittany

*A Duke Who Flew Too High,
A Duchess and Her Printing Press,
and Jules Verne and His Naughty Son*

BRITTANY, A CRAGGY PENINSULA south of England, is the land of King Arthur and his Round Table, Wagner's *Tristan und Isolde,* The Edict of Nantes,[1] artists, explorers, sailors, and saints, saints, saints. Celtic inhabitants of the British Isles crossed the channel in 500 A.D., fleeing the Angles and Saxons. Missionaries from Britain and Ireland converted the country, naming towns and villages for their saints, such as Saint Malo, Saint Yves, Saint Pool, Saint Tugual, Saint Breiuc—a litany that goes on and on. A line of Breton dukes ruled at Rennes until Anne of Brittany inherited the province. To save her inheritance, pious fifteen-year-old Anne married French king Charles VIII in 1491.[2] The archbishop of Nantes told her it was either marry "the enemy" or lose Brittany. After her husband Charles banged his head on a door and died, the king's cousin (who became King Louis XII) came to offer his condolences. Then he divorced his wife[3] and married the newly widowed queen of France and Brittany. When their daughter married frivolous Francis I, according to the marriage contract, Brittany became part of France (1532).

NANTES

On the train to Nantes, there must have been something wrong with the lady in front of us. For more than an hour, her hand moved back and forth over her husband's shirt, smoothing out invisible wrinkles. It wasn't a caressing massage; her hand just couldn't stop. The view from the window was much better: ponds, streams, ancient bridges, purple and white lilacs, and men in heavy rubber boots riding bicycles.

We stayed at a hotel near the train station down the street from the castle of the dukes of Brittany. The castle looms right on the street—which is not where castles are supposed to loom. During medieval times, the river lapped against the walls. Now cars rumble by.

Of the three museums in the castle, Musée des Arts is the most fun, especially the Breton closed beds (*lits clos*)—cozy but claustrophobic, especially for a family of four. When the carved panels of the built-in bed are closed, the wall becomes a beautiful work of art.

Germans occupied the castle from 1939 to 1945, and after they left, fragile ceramics hidden in the castle were found unharmed. The ecstatic curator said he dreamed that a Breton bagpipe melody arose, and all the little people painted in their festive costumes on the plates started to dance for joy.

The spacious courtyard is the best place to dream of the jousting tournaments and religious plays once held here. We also imagined richly clad duc de Fouquet descending the outside staircase, walking unsuspectingly to his doom.

NICOLAS FOUQUET

Handsome, powerful, popular Fouquet was Louis XIV's finance minister, recommended by Cardinal Mazarin,[4] chief regent for the king's mother. To meet the king's exorbitant expenses, Fouquet followed Mazarin's practice of taxing starving people while pocketing enormous sums for himself. His other position, attorney general, protected him from investigation.

Alarmed at the extent to which Fouquet was diverting the nation's taxes, Mazarin nonetheless let Fouquet off with a warning—which Fouquet ignored. He never should have underestimated Louis XIV and never should have built himself the most glorious palace in France: Vaux le Comte. The dying Mazarin told his twenty-two-year-old king about Fouquet's financial manipulations and recommended another minister, young Colbert, as watchdog. Colbert found six million livres that Mazarin himself had squirreled away and turned the money over to the king, who promptly appointed him Fouquet's "assistant." Every morning, Fouquet went over the accounts with the king, and every evening Colbert showed how Fouquet had altered them.

Fouquet, whose motto was "How High Can I Fly," proceeded to fly higher and higher. He bought Belle Ile off the coast of Brittany, repaired the ramparts to make it a fortress, and then, under the pretext of starting a sardine industry, created his own fleet with whaling boats and armed vessels purchased from Holland.

When Fouquet learned Colbert had turned the king's mother against him, he tried to bribe the king's mistress to put in a good word for him. The indignant mistress told the king, who tricked Fouquet into selling his position as attorney general. Now he could be prosecuted. Nineteen days after Fouquet had flaunted his fabulous palace at the king and court, Louis XIV arranged his arrest.

Under the pretext of a royal hunt near Nantes, D'Artagnan, the king's most trusted Musketeer, was instructed to have the royal carriage and troops ready to seize Fouquet. After a meeting in the palace, Fouquet left by way of the outside staircase in the courtyard and strolled out the main gate into the street, where he summoned porters to carry him in a sedan chair toward the cathedral. In Cathedral Square, D'Artagnan, on horseback, accompanied by fifteen Musketeers, met up with him and showed him the king's orders. The royal carriage pulled up, and Fouquet had to climb in. D'Artagnan became Fouquet's bodyguard for the next four years, while the king's prisoner was transferred from one jail to another. The trial lasted three years. Although most of the judges voted for exile, Louis XIV, in revenge, illegally intervened and sentenced the likeable high-and-mighty duke to life imprisonment in Pignerol, a cold, bleak dungeon at the foot of the Alps, where he died fifteen years later. Then Louis XIV summoned to Versailles the artists who had created Fouquet's palace and gardens. He also took the orange trees.

DAUNTLESS DUCHESSE DE BERRY (1833–1870)
A Lady with a Mission

Down the street from the château in Nantes is the house[5] where the duchesse de Berry, a thirty-five-year-old widow, hid with her printing press—flooding the courts of Europe with letters, seeking help to put her son on the French throne instead of the Citizen King, Louis Philippe. Her husband had been murdered outside the Opera House in Paris, leaving her with a daughter and one son next in line for the Bourbon monarchy.

The uprisings she had instigated in Marseille and the Vendée had failed, and now she and a Breton lady, disguised as peasants, made their way toward Nantes. They walked for two days, ate black bread and cabbage soup, and spent the night in a shepherd's hut. In Nantes, she set up headquarters in the home of two faithful Royalist sisters[6] at #3 rue Mathlin Rodier, where for five months she and a few others carried on an opposition government from their attic room, before they were betrayed by a man[7] pretending to be a friend. Even Louis Philippe's *Journal Le Breton* said that "the man who betrayed her is a miserable man. Shame on him. Fortunately he is not French." (He was from Cologne.) When soldiers burst into the house, there was barely time to rush to the attic and squeeze into a hiding hole behind the fireplace. All night, two women and two men[8] squashed together, standing upright trying to breathe through cracks in the tile roof. Police ordered the walls demolished with pickaxes. Soldiers posted overnight lighted a fire to keep warm, and when it died down, they lit it again. The chimney bricks became so hot, the duchess's long brown skirt caught fire. She "put out the flames in what under the circumstances was the only way possible." After sixteen hours of hell, covered with dust and ashes, half asphyxiated, they surrendered. The heroine of the drama was the maid, Charlotte Moreau. Although questioned, threatened, and bribed, she refused to talk. Her only reply was "To betray is not a French word." One who had shared the ordeal was Achille Guibourg, the duchess's handsome lawyer—and lover.

The duchess was imprisoned for eight months in the castle of Blaye, high above the Gironde River—the pregnant duchess. How awful! She was a noble! She could never be plain Madame Guibourg! She smuggled a note out in an altar boy's scapular to an ex-mistress of King Louis XVIII,[9] asking her to find a "suitable" husband. The suitable husband was Count Hector Lucchesi-Palli, who was in the diplomatic service of the duchesse Caroline's brother, the king of Naples. Records were changed to make it appear that the marriage had taken place during her stay in Italy before embarking on her crusade.

When her baby, a girl, was born, it was announced to the world that the former duchess was the wife of Count Lucchesi of Sicily. Since she was now a foreigner, she could no longer claim to be regent, and a month after the

Brittany

baby was born, the former duchesse de Berry was released and escorted to Palermo, Sicily. The obscure and not-too-busy saints[10] she had prayed to answered her prayers in a strange way. She and her polite, gentle husband settled in Austria[11] and had four children: three girls and one boy.

JULES VERNE (1828–1905)

The man with the wild imagination, whose characters lived years ahead of their time, was blessed with pious parents who had a sense of humor. The whole family played the piano and sang. He and his younger brother, Paul, were buddies, and his three sisters provided inspiration for the genteel, brave women in his novels. Unfortunately, Verne was the quiet type in matters of the heart and couldn't express his feelings. He did have one confidant to whom he could pour out his woes—Jules Pierre Hetzel, his editor and publisher. In a letter to Hetzel he wrote, "You ask me to throw in a few words of feeling, yet those words just won't come. Love is an all absorbing passion and leaves room for little else in the human breast. My heroes need all their wits about them."

He studied law in Paris and worked as a stockbroker, but he had to write home for money. His father didn't think that was a good idea, character-wise. Verne wrote back, "I have reached the age when one needs above all a tender companionship and a stable union. At present my heart is a desolate void . . . In short, what I need is to be happy. Neither more nor less." That did it. His father relented.

He became friends with Alexandre Dumas and his son, who introduced him to the theater world where he wrote plays and learned to construct plots. Verne was in Paris (age twenty) during the Revolution of 1848 when the Citizen King, Louis Philippe, fled to England, and Louis Napoléon finally rode into Paris on his white horse to proclaim the Second Republic. Verne was also there during Louis Napoléon's *coup d'état,* when shopkeepers' signs had to be changed every few years (e.g., "Shoemaker to the King," then under the Republic an *Égalité* sign, and finally "Shoemaker to the Emperor").

Verne's first novel, *Journey to the Center of the Earth,* was a bestseller, but his love life in Paris was disastrous. Twice this handsome man fell madly in love, and twice his beloved married another, until in 1857 he wrote his father, "I think I am in love with a young widow of twenty-six from Amiens. Oh why does she have to have two children?" His bride's quick wit matched his own, but intellectually her brain was confined to the home and hearth. Their one child, Michel, drove his father crazy. Verne, trying to meet his publisher's deadlines, wrote day and night behind closed doors in his imaginary world, while the little boy, deprived of his father's attention, kicked and screamed and got blue in the face with tantrums. Anything he wanted, he got. Even at four, he batted his eyes and flattered his mother, who thought he was adorable. As a teenager, he was so incorrigible Verne arranged to have him put in jail until the first ship docked to take him to sea—for eighteen months.

Jules Verne was more successful with his books[12] than with his son. His cousin, a teacher at École Polytechnique, helped with the geography, physics, and math. Verne's stories are so real, you are there—at the center of the earth, in a balloon, under the sea—wherever he wants to take you. Unlike his contemporary, Edgar Allan Poe, who wrote science fiction,[13] there is no fantasy in Verne's stories. His intrepid heroes are real; indomitable, determined, with never a doubt about their success, despite seemingly hopeless situations. In *Journey to the Center of the Earth*, he writes, "As long as there is a breath of life, I will not allow a creature endowed with a will to give way to despair. We call on an unspeaking God to whom we abandon ourselves."

Jules Verne inspired hundreds of inventors and explorers. When Admiral Richard Byrd took off on the first airplane flight over the North Pole in 1926, he said, "It was Jules Verne who launched me on this trip." Apollo 9 American astronaut Frank Borman told Verne's grandson, "Our space vehicle launched from Florida, like Barbicane's in *From the Earth to the Moon*. It had the same weight, the same height, and splashed down in the Pacific two and a half miles from the point mentioned in the novel."

Jules Verne received the Legion of Honor medal a few days before the Prussians invaded France (1870). He wrote his father from Paris, "There is one huge question. Have we any weapons? Unfortunately, it seems we have no arms at all." After sending his wife, Honorine, and children (their son and Honorine's two daughters) to Amiens, he joined the Home Guard. He mounted a little cannon on his fishing boat and patrolled the estuary of the Somme. His wife, who had four Prussian soldiers billeted in her house, fed them rice to make them constipated.

In the meantime, Michel, home from his "cruise," had run off with a touring operetta singer, Thérèse, who was four years older. Eventually they married in Nîmes, but again he ran off—with another woman, seventeen-year-old Jeanne Reboul, a talented pianist. When a son was born, they moved to Paris, then to Dinard on the coast, and charged the bills to his father—including the cost of a divorce from Thérèse and marriage to Jeanne. Then one of those accidents in life happened. On March 9, 1886, a mentally deranged nephew shot Verne, and the bullet lodged in his shinbone. Five and one-half months later, he wrote to Alexandre Dumas' son, "They've perforated the tibia. It takes months and months to heal." Michel, the prodigal son, took over as his father's secretary. After months of pain, but still writing,[14] sixty-year-old Jules Verne spent a happy summer in 1888 with his son and family at Dinard.[15]

Michel's beautiful wife, Jeanne, or "Maja," brought the aging writer pure joy. At last, he could share his love for music and conversation with this highly intelligent girl. Michel still didn't have a job, and now he had a wife and two little boys to support. During the 1897 Paris Exposition, while working on the exhibits, he finally found his calling in the business world: nickel mines, paper mills, banking, and a film company to make movies of his father's books. Michel's son, Jean, credits his mother, Maja, "who, by keeping a tight rein, had succeeded in restraining his violence and bringing him round the course without mishap. No mean feat."

Before Jules Verne died at seventy-eight, he and his problem child, Michel, had become fast friends. Everything turned out fine—just like in his stories.

A SEVENTY-NINE-YEAR-OLD PILOT
Auray

Our next stop in Brittany was Auray, where we were greeted by a seventy-nine-year-old friend, Père Abel le Bourhis. He reminded me of a small Winston Churchill—the same determined face with a bulldog chin and piercing blue eyes. Père le Bourhis taught English in Brittany for seventeen years and knows everyone for miles around. His love for Americans goes back to World War I. When he was seven, he learned to play baseball by watching American sailors, on shore leave from a mine sweeper, playing ball on his native island, Hoëdic. He drove us to the Auray River channel and harbor, where Benjamin Franklin landed in 1776 with his two grandsons, ages seven and sixteen.[16] The inn where they stayed is still there.

Père le Bourhis, left for dead by the Nazis and who always wears his black cassock, is also an airplane pilot. Each time we climbed into his car, he checked the instruments: "Cabin door closed, seat belts fastened, fuel

Back to Europe with the BUSY BODY

Père le Bourhis

okay, engine on, all clear," and then off we flew at seventy miles an hour. Since he is bald, to prevent catching cold, he wears his pilot's helmet. When someone told him his zodiac sign is the Lion, our Père replied, "Yes, I am a lion—but a lion without a mane."

He took us to beautiful inlets in the Morbihan Gulf, where the sea spills into the land. One place, Locmariaquer, with its many oyster beds or *parcs*, reminded me of Elizabeth Clark's book, *The Oyster Beds of Locmariaquer.* The eleventh-century church in Locmariaquer, like other churches in Brittany, has small model boats hanging from the ceiling, in memory of men lost at sea. To demonstrate the marvelous acoustics in the little medieval stone churches, our Père would reverently burst into Gregorian chants.

Père le Bourhis, whose father was a lighthouse keeper, remembers as a boy (born 1910) seeing only the lighthouse, the sea, the flat horizon, and ever-changing light. His intellect is that of a Renaissance man, and his enthusiastic *joie de vivre* makes everyone's heart happy. Strangers in the street stop to ask if he will bless their babies. In Pleyben, our little Père showed us one of the many *calvaries* in Brittany—those strange monuments hewn from great rustic granite rocks. The sculptures represent episodes from Christ's Passion.

Brittany

In Carnac, Le Menec, and Kermario, 2,935 astonishing standing stones or *menhirs* are lined up for two and one-half miles over the long flat plains. In Menec, the prehistoric stones form eleven parallel rows with a semicircle of seventy stones at the end. At Kermario, some stones, twenty feet high and weighing 400 tons, stand apart. Others are in groups or rows. The gigantic monuments have been there more than 40,000 years, and archaeologists are still guessing why.

Our *bon chauffeur* pulled off a dirt road into a small low complex of whitewashed stone homes dwarfed by giant menhirs. The next surprise was around a corner—where in a cozy Breton restaurant, we met the owner and his wife. While our Père chatted with everyone, and while the owner's wife flipped paper-thin crêpes, we inspected an old cider press.

During our visit with the little priest, we stayed in the town of Saint Anne d'Auray, the most famous pilgrimage place in Brittany, five minutes from Auray. Our hotel,[17] opposite the basilica, was next to a diorama where wax figures in period costumes depict the story of Saint Anne's only appearance on earth. The figure of the humble peasant, Yves Nicolazic, to whom Saint Anne appeared in 1623, seems as inspired as Michelangelo's sculpture.

SAINT ANNE D'AURAY AND HER MESSENGER

The story of Saint Anne d'Auray is the seventeenth-century story of Yves Nicolazic, a highly respected farmer born near Auray, France. The people of his town, Ker Ana (village of Saint Anne), had had a special devotion to Saint Anne, the mother of the Virgin, since the sixth century. They believed that an old chapel dedicated to Saint Anne had at one time been built there. They also believed that the only remains of the chapel, a few rocks, were on the site of Nicolazic's father's barn.

In August 1623[18] when Nicolazic was praying to Saint Anne in the barn, supposedly the site of the old chapel, a hand appeared in the dark holding a lighted torch. Six weeks later and for several months, the light alone would appear while Nicolazic was praying.

One summer evening while Nicolazic was leading a cow to another pasture, he saw Saint Anne dressed in white, standing near a spring and holding the lighted torch. A year later, on July 25, 1624, Saint Anne appeared to him again—this time during the day. She called him by name, then vanished. The same evening she reappeared, lighting the whole barn with her presence. She said, "Yves Nicolazic, do not be frightened." Then Saint Anne told him that once a chapel there was dedicated to her. "It has been 924 years and six months since it was destroyed. I want it built again, and I want you to do it. God wants me to be honored here."

Since no one believed his story, Saint Anne appeared daily to encourage him. One night, he invited witnesses to accompany him. They followed the light, which led toward the spring. Suddenly the light stopped and disappeared into the ground. When they started to dig, they found a wooden statue of Saint Anne. The parish rector, who had scoffed at the story, was suddenly paralyzed. Every evening for a week, he dragged himself to the spring where the statue had been found. Soon he was miraculously cured. With his blessing the next year, 1625, a church dedicated to Saint Anne was completed where Saint Anne had indicated. Three years later, a tower was built as a beacon for thousands of pilgrims, including King Louis XIII's wife, Queen Anne of Austria, Marie de' Medici's daughter, and Queen Henrietta of England. Mme. de Sévigné noted that, from the official book of miracles, Saint Anne was concentrating on children and sailors.

During the Revolution, the church was closed. When Emperor Napoléon III came to power, he and Empress Eugénie visited the shrine, as well as the president of the new Republic, Patrice MacMahon. A new basilica on the same site was erected in 1877. Yves Nicolazic, the devout peasant, is buried there.

In Brittany, there are many "Pardons"—religious processions to various churches for the purpose of seeking pardon for sins. The Pardon at Saint Anne d'Auray is the largest. On July 25, thousands of deeply religious pilgrims come to honor Saint Anne. In front of the basilica, a large park is enclosed by three walls. Each wall, a city block long, is inscribed with the names of 240,000 area men killed during World War I.[19] Saint Anne's statue, silhouetted against the sky, proclaims Brittany's centuries-old dedication to Mary's mother, who has performed so many miracles for the seafaring Bretons.

GAUGUIN, MONET, AND FLAUBERT
Pont-Aven

From Saint Anne d'Auray we went to Concarneau on the Atlantic—where we climbed the ramparts of the old walled city and visited the Marine Museum. We even got up at 5:45 A.M. to watch fish being unloaded from the ships, like it said in the guide book. We wondered why there wasn't more action! Can you believe? Wrong season. An eighteen-mile bus ride

Brittany

Pont-Aven

brought us to Pont-Aven, where Paul Gauguin and other nineteenth-century artists[20] congregated in the summer. Pont-Aven, twelve miles from the sea, was cold and rainy even in June. In winter, the whistling wind tears straight across the Atlantic. The tiny town is charming but claustrophobic, with a picturesque harbor and pretty stream, strewn with boulders, that flows through town, mostly behind houses. The regional coifs in shop windows are the only reminder of Gauguin's famous paintings. Don't expect to come home with reproductions. To see paintings of Pont-Aven, you have to take a bus from Concarneau to the Beaux Arts Museum in Quimper.

Pension Gloanec, where Gauguin stayed in Pont-Aven, is now a shop with newspapers, magazines, and postcards. From his window upstairs, he painted the little town square on market days, when it was crowded with country folk in colorful local costumes—usually under umbrellas.

American artists were the first to discover the little beauty spot in Brittany. Soon other painters came—from France, Scotland, and Australia. Thirty-eight-year-old Paul Gauguin arrived in 1886, penniless.[21] When he heard that the owner of Pension Gloanec encouraged and sympathized with artists, he left his wife and five children to "do his thing." Thanks to kind Marie Jeanne Gloanec, who stood for no nonsense and boarded him on credit, Gauguin was able to paint his Breton masterpieces.[22] She fed him hearty soup and fish, and with her two helpers, she cared for him when he broke his ankle in a brawl in Concarneau. He got into a fight with sailors who laughed at his Javanese mistress and her monkey.

While Gauguin, the ex-sailor and ex-stockbroker, was tramping around Pont-Aven in a greasy fisherman's jacket and wooden shoes, Claude Monet was bundled up in oilskins and a Breton beret, battling the elements at Belle Ile. A local porter helped carry his canvases, which had to be anchored with stones and rope against the wind and spray. He wrote to his wife, "There was so much hail, I was afraid it would make holes in my canvases." He spent hours in the cold rain. Sometimes the wind blew the palette and brushes from his hands. "By evening I sleep like a log and am not bothered too much by the racket the rats make. The wind never stops. The house trembles. It is like being at sea. I am in a country of superb wilderness, an accumulation of terrible rocks, and a sea of incredible color. In a word, I am thrilled."

Forty years before artists discovered Pont-Aven, thirty-year-old Gustave Flaubert hiked through Brittany with a friend.[23] One night they slept in a prison, another time in a convent, and at Vitre, in a shoemaker's hut in the woods. His worried mother followed in a carriage and caught up with them in big towns. Ten years later, he wrote *Madame Bovary*.

18

Auvergne

Le Puy en Velay and Lafayette's Motto, "Why Not?"

LE PUY EN VELAY

On the way to Le Puy en Velay in the Haute Loire, well-behaved children returning from vacation, weighted down with backpacks, struggled through the aisles of the train. Across from us, a young couple in their mid-twenties, with sheet music spread out, were engrossed in music talk en route to a performance. As we approached the city following the Borne River, tents, campers, colorful umbrellas, and patient fishermen lined the river bank. Children splashed in clear, sparkling water, and trout ran for cover.

You may travel from India to Labrador, but you will never see needle-like peaks (*puys*) sticking straight into the sky like the ones at Le Puy en Velay in the Auvergne region in central France, where Robert Louis Stevenson traveled on his reluctant donkey. The peaks were formed by flaming volcanoes. Atop the highest one, an enormous statue of Our Lady of France[1] is silhouetted against the sky for miles. The Virgin is crowned with stars and holds the Baby Jesus on her arm. He is supposed to be giving the city His blessing, but He seems to be waving hello to His friends. In the ancient town, on rue des Tables, where merchants once displayed merchandise on tables, mesmerized tourists watched the flying fingers of two beautiful young girls making the renowned Le Puy lace. Dozens of small spindles zoomed back and forth. Behind the girls, a stone staircase of 134

Le Puy en Velay

steps leads to the twelfth-century Romanesque cathedral of Notre Dame, one of the most original in France. The gaudy facade with yellow, black, and reddish stones reflects Moorish influence from Spain. The cathedral is on the site of one of the earliest visions of the Virgin (432 A.D.).[2] Here in the eleventh century, *Salve Regina*[3] *(Hail, Holy Queen)* was sung for the first

Auvergne

time—composed as a processional chant by the spiritual leader of the First Crusade, Adhemar, Bishop of Le Puy.[4] Sculptures in the cathedral depict him with pilgrims en route to the Holy Land.[5] In the northern gallery, an enormous Byzantine fresco of Saint Michael the Archangel stares straight through you. It is the largest painted figure in France.

Standing next to me in the gift shop, one of those young, irresistible Frenchmen confided something to his friends in way-too-fast French. I asked the sales clerk to tell me what he said. His answer was "I think he is in love with you. How rude." I didn't think so. He made my day.

During the Middle Ages, hundreds of thousands came to Le Puy to honor Our Lady. Saint Louis donated a Black Virgin statue,[6] and Joan of Arc's mother came with her two sons in 1429, as Joan began her mission. Pilgrims and tourists throughout the world continue to honor Mary at Le Puy en Velay—also Saint Michael the Archangel. A tiny, very tiny church, Saint Michel d'Aiguilhe (needle), has perched for 1,000 years on a soaring pinnacle. Near the altar, which was made from a Roman column,[7] part of the needle-like spire pokes through the stone floor. The ancient chapel blends perfectly into the rocky *puy*. The only modern note is a stained glass window, and whoever produced the perfect harmony of old and new should be hired in Paris, where cold, impersonal contemporary buildings clash with classical beauty. Among the crowd spiraling up the 269 rocky steps,[8] worn into grooves by medieval pilgrims, were servicemen from different countries with their wives and little children.

CHAVANIAC
A Little Boy and a Big House

Thirty miles from Le Puy en Velay, on the highest part of an old Roman road, is Lafayette's birthplace: Château Chavaniac, near the village of Chavaniac. The interpreter during our visit was fun, black-eyed Carolyn Allan. As we crossed a street, she laughed, "I run and scoot. It is good for my body."

People strolling through the château's informal English garden resembled figures from an Impressionist painting. At the garden entrance, the American flag and French *tricolore* fly side by side. The director of the Memorial, Monsieur Michel Chambon, and President Monsieur François Gilbert (pronounced "Jeebare"), showed us a young tree they call "The Moon Tree," which was planted from a seed sent to the moon with America's first astronauts. Etched on a large volcanic stone in the garden are twin profiles of Lafayette and President George Washington.

Back to Europe with the BUSY BODY

Lafayette's home "Chavaniac"

Inside the château, the updated library is filled with rows of books in English, including the *Katzenjammer Kids* and *Life with Father*. One enormous book is filled with pictures of Americans who died in France during World War I. Our escort, Monsieur Gilbert, said one guest pointed to a picture and shouted, "That's my grandfather."

In Lafayette's bedroom, the red-and-white toile wallpaper is designed with schooners and Indians. A special friend of the Indians, Lafayette visited practically every Indian nation in America. His presence in this room where ambassadors stay overnight is overwhelming.

In the reception room, copies of the U.S. Constitution and Lafayette's "Declaration of the Rights of Man" hang side by side. Two crossed swords on the wall, however, are the most significant mementos at Chavaniac. Benjamin Franklin's little twelve-year-old grandson presented one of the swords to Lafayette when he landed at Le Havre after his role in the colonists' victory. The Continental Congress ordered the sword, with a gold hilt set in diamonds, from the best jewelers in Paris. Franklin himself engraved scenes of America breaking her chains and the main battles in which Lafayette fought. He also engraved the Latin words, *Cur Non,* Lafayette's motto, "Why Not?" The other sword, made from locks of the Bastille, was given to him by the French National Assembly.

Auvergne

At the end of our tour, hundreds of people were waiting in line to visit the home of the eighteenth-century hero.[9]

LAFAYETTE AND CHAVANIAC
Marquis Marie-Gilbert du Motier de Lafayette (1757–1834)

> *Look at me, a funny looking little man*
> *A foreigner. But see, I crack jokes,*
> *I wear clothes. I am a human being*
> *Endowed with the dignity of the human soul.*
> —CARLOS ROMULO[10]

Unfortunately, Lafayette's personality never quite comes across. He is always seen on a horse—either quelling mobs, commanding armies, or upholding law, order, and honor. But of all the unlikely people, God chose Lafayette, a wealthy noble (and skeptic at that) to bring His "Golden Rule" to the French. He also used a few Americans as role models, for example, Benjamin Franklin, George Washington, and Thomas Jefferson.

Lafayette was two when his father, an officer in the king's army, was killed.[11] His mother left Chavaniac to live in Paris with her father, leaving the little boy with his grandmother, two elderly aunts, and the local priest, Abbé Fayon. Chavaniac is where Lafayette's character was formed, especially by his tutor, Jean Frestel. "Cruelty or kindness, hatred or love, can take root in anybody anywhere but is largely a matter of what kind of person each individual, man or woman, chooses to become." The elderly ladies regaled the little boy with stories of his noble ancestors who fought for the French kings, especially the one who served under Joan of Arc. Most importantly, Lafayette learned at an early age the meaning of compassion. At a time when commoners were considered inferior, Abbé Fayon and the ladies taught him that commoners were also people entitled to respect and sympathy, and as head of his vast estates, he was the benefactor of his people. For nine years, the little marquis, in a silk suit, three-cornered hat, and buckled shoes, traveled throughout the countryside, master of his peasants and estates—his mind filled with dreams of glory when he, too, would be an officer in the king's army.

At eleven, he was influenced by Rousseau, Diderot, and Voltaire at the Jesuit boarding school, College du Plessis, on rue St. Jacques in Paris.[12] Two years later, his mother died, followed in a few weeks by her father, marquis de La Rivière. The thirteen-year-old orphan inherited the marquis' estates and immense fortune, making him one of the wealthiest nobles in France. After serving as a cadet with the king's bodyguards, the Musketeers,[13] the tall, red-headed teenager entered the military academy at Versailles. Then a marriage was arranged with Adrienne d'Ayen, granddaughter of the duc de Noailles, whose family, after the Bourbons, was the wealthiest in France. Four hundred guests attended the reception for the sixteen-year-old bride at Hôtel de Noailles, her grandfather's palatial residence in Paris, 202 rue de Rivoli.[14] That night, according to custom, the guests, after too many toasts, crowded around the newlyweds' four-poster bed. To stop the lewd jokes, the six-foot, eighteen-year-old bridegroom threw himself on top of his little bride. His shocked father-in-law quickly closed the curtains and shooed everyone out.

Although presented at court and invited to balls, Lafayette was never meant for court life. He was so awkward dancing quadrilles and minuets, Marie Antoinette laughed at him. He tried drinking all night with the courtiers but suffered such a hangover, he never did that again. Sex? He could do that.

While stationed at Metz with his regiment, he learned about the American colonists' Declaration of Independence. Rushing to the aid of the underdog, he obtained a commission as major-general in the American army from a representative to France, Silas Dean of Connecticut. The rest of the story is heroism, incredible bravery, and dogged dedication to the ideal that all men are created equal and should have a voice in their government.

Getting himself to America was his first victory. The only ones who approved were his mother-in-law and his wife—who had just had a baby girl. The baby lived only one year. Against Louis XVI's[15] orders, after many complications, Lafayette outfitted his own ship[16] and sailed[17] with eleven others for America. During the two-month voyage, he memorized the Preamble[18] to America's new Constitution and practiced English with the German major, Baron de Kalb. The only thing Lafayette knew about military strategy was what he read on the way over—Julius Caesar's *Gaelic Wars*.

The ship's captain missed the port of Charleston, South Carolina, and landed fifty-five miles away at Georgetown Bay. Again after serious setbacks, the little group in their impressive military uniforms, plumed hats, and white silk stockings set off for Philadelphia in grand style; servants on horseback, a big open baroque, two coaches, and a baggage wagon. When the wheels broke, they continued on horseback and finally on foot,

Auvergne

through forests and swamps with snakes and mosquitoes. They walked for thirty-two days—600 miles.

In Philadelphia there were more obstacles, but Lafayette finally met his hero, forty-five-year-old George Washington,[19] who practically adopted the orphan. On August 20, 1777, the nineteen-year-old youth from Auvergne became an official member of General Washington's military family.

The always fearless Lafayette fought in the Battle of Brandywine. At a bridge near Chester, Pennsylvania, bullets flew through his hat, jacket, and leg. Washington sent his personal doctor and told him to "treat 'the Boy' as if he were my son." While recuperating, with his leg propped up and cared for by the pacifist Order of Moravian Brothers, he learned that his teenage wife had given birth to a second daughter, Anastasie.

Still using a cane, he spent the winter thirty miles from Philadelphia, in snow and freezing temperatures at Valley Forge[20] with Washington's troops, who were dying of starvation and the cold. The Americans marveled at the wealthy French noble willing to suffer with them. Washington wrote,[21] "We have this day no less than 2,873 men in camp unfit for duty because they are bare-footed and otherwise naked." Thomas Paine declared, "These are the times that try men's souls."[22] Lafayette and Washington, however, were optimists. During one of the darkest moments of defeat, Washington told Lafayette, "We must not . . . expect to meet with nothing but sunshine. I have no doubt everything happens for the best. That we shall triumph over all our misfortunes and in the end be happy."

The American War for Independence was one miracle after another. When Benedict Arnold won the Battle of Saratoga for General Gates,[23] Washington delayed crossing the Delaware River for a day of prayer to thank God, and Samuel Adams, a delegate to Congress, declared the day of victory the first official Thanksgiving Day. A devout Congregationalist, Samuel Adams proposed that an Anglican clergyman from Philadelphia read prayers before their meeting,[24] after fasting the day before. When news arrived that both Holland and France had signed an alliance with the colonists, ecstatic young Lafayette impulsively kissed dignified General Washington on both cheeks.

With the formal alliance against Britain, the French fleet arrived at Newport, Rhode Island, with more men and supplies. However, cooperation between the French and Americans seemed impossible. French Ad-

Back to Europe with the BUSY BODY

miral d'Estaing and Irish-American General Sullivan snarled and hissed like alley cats. Lafayette was caught in the middle. Tactful General Washington suggested he take a leave of absence and visit France to further the American cause at Versailles. On the voyage home, he learned that British deserters on board planned to capture him.[25] While the leaders slept, Lafayette ordered their hammock ropes cut. Snared and entangled, the conspirators were captured and chained.

In France, a frenzied hero's welcome awaited him. Even the king and queen forgave him for leaving without their permission.[26] At twenty-one, he was the hero of two worlds—and to his nineteen-year-old wife, Adrienne.

At Versailles, he convinced French leaders that the cost of one ball would equip the whole ragged American army. To aid the colonists, Louis XVI's cabinet ordered French Général Rochambeau to sail with 4,000 troops. On Christmas Eve (1778), Adrienne had a boy they named George Washington. A few weeks later Lafayette informed Adrienne he had to return to the colonies. She asked, "When?" The reply was, "Tonight."

When he landed in Boston wearing his blue and buff Continental army uniform, church bells rang, guns roared, and fireworks blazed. In Morristown, New Jersey, he joined General Washington, who sent him to Richmond, Virginia, to stop two English armies from joining forces. Lafayette, reinforced by generals Anthony Wayne and Baron von Stuben, forced Cornwallis to leave Richmond[27] and flee to Yorktown,[28] on the Virginia coast. French troops under Général Rochambeau joined Washington's army and headed for Virginia. Miraculously, French Admiral de Grasse arrived at Yorktown in time, with twenty-nine ships and 3,000 troops. Below Yorktown, Washington and Général Rochambeau joined the Americans and Frenchmen under Lafayette's command.

Three days later, on October 9, 1781, Cornwallis surrendered. For six years, ragged colonists had fought British regulars and German mercenaries. During the solemn handing-over-of-the-sword ceremony, when defeated British troops marched past Lafayette's division, his band broke the dignified silence with a blaring rendition of *Yankee Doodle,* a song the British wrote to mock the Americans.[29] The American adventure was over.[30]

In France, young Lafayette was the toast of the nation. Adrienne had another daughter, Virginie,[31] and they bought a house in Paris, near place de Saint Sulpice. While it was being decorated, Adrienne, for the first time,

Auvergne

visited Chavaniac, where hundreds of peasants waited on the broad terrace to greet them.

One day, Lafayette received a letter from General Washington, informing him that he had retired. "I am solacing myself with . . . tranquil enjoyments. . . . Envious of none, I am determined to be pleased with all . . . I will move gently down the stream of life until I sleep with my fathers." Lafayette wrote back that he was coming to have a cup of tea with him—and he did. He left Adrienne at Chavaniac with the three children and sailed for New York City[32]—which he had never seen. (It had been occupied by the English.) In New York, he rode in an open carriage and was fêted with flowers, crowds, and banquets. From there he traveled to Philadelphia, where he received another wild reception. At Mount Vernon, he stayed eleven days with Washington, whom he idolized as the father he had never known. Then he toured all twelve states, including the old battlefields. When he visited the Mohawks in upstate New York, at Fort Schuyler, he squatted around a fire, smoked a peace pipe, and ate with his fingers. While he was there, his friend "Grasshopper," the official orator of the Six Nations, signed a peace treaty with the new republic. Lafayette returned to Virginia for one last rendezvous with Washington, knowing it was their last meeting. At Annapolis, Washington and "the Boy" parted with an emotional *au revoir.*

The rest of Lafayette's life was one long battle to bring the same rights the colonists had won to his own countrymen. His friend Thomas Jefferson, now an envoy to France, wrote to James Monroe, "My God how little do my countrymen know what precious blessings they are in possession of which no other people on earth enjoy. I confess I had no idea of it myself." Another friend in Paris, Abigail Adams, wife of John Adams, wrote, "To be out of fashion is more criminal than to be seen in a state of nature to which Parisiens are not averse."

France was bankrupt. Throughout the country people were starving, and practically no one in power cared. At an Assembly of Notables (nobles), called to solve the money problem, Lafayette shocked the delegates by denouncing the greed of highly placed scoundrels at the price "of the sweat, the tears and it may be, the blood of the people." He and his friends called for a meeting of the Estates-General, representing the three "states": nobles, clergy, and commoners. At the meeting, Lafayette presented his revolutionary *Rights of Man,* and while it was being debated, a starving mob stormed the Bastille and beheaded marquis Bernard de

Back to Europe with the BUSY BODY

Launay, the officer-in-charge. The terrified assembly appointed Lafayette commander of the nation's militia (1789). He was the only one with any influence over the madmen. His citizen-soldiers became the National Guard, sworn to keep order and protect the king. Lafayette ordered the Bastille, a symbol of tyranny, destroyed and sent one of the keys to General Washington.

The highlight of his see-saw career was the first anniversary of the storming of the Bastille. As Commander of the National Guard, he was master-of-ceremony over 300,000 people gathered at the Champs de Mars. Fourteen thousand "federates," representatives of the Army, Navy, and National Guard from eighty-three Departments[33] throughout France, came to celebrate the new constitution. Even the king took the oath—with his fingers crossed.

Duchesse de Tourzel, governess of Louis XVI and Marie Antoinette's children, wrote that, for months, people "wielded picks and pushed wheelbarrows so as to transform the ground of the Champs de Mars into a huge amphitheater. There were workers, bourgeois men and women, Carthusian monks, and others from different orders, military men, beautiful ladies, men and women from every class and all stations of society. . . ."

The sense of solidarity didn't last long. A year later on the same site, Lafayette, forced to stop a riot, ordered the National Guard to fire into the crowd. Twelve people were killed, and suddenly, thirty-four-year-old Lafayette became an enemy. He resigned, went to Chavaniac, and two months later, was called back. Royal émigrés were about to invade France, and Lafayette was sent to command one of three French armies against them. While he was gone, law and order collapsed. A drunken mob invaded the Tuileries, put a revolutionary red[34] hat on the king, drank his wine, and blew smoke in his face. Incensed, Lafayette charged back to Paris on his white horse. He strode into the assembly, demanded punishment for the invaders, then galloped to the Tuileries to check on the king. Marie Antoinette, who hated him, muttered "Better perish utterly than be saved by Lafayette." Austria and Prussia threatened to invade[35] if there was another attack on the Tuileries or if the king was threatened again. That did it! The French Revolutionary army declared war on Austria, and patriotic Frenchmen throughout the country rushed to enlist. Troops from Marseille marched to Paris with arms, baggage, and two cannons. They marched to the tune of a new song, *La Marseillaise*.[36] By the time they reached Paris, 415 miles away, they should have been hoarse, thirsty, and

Auvergne

ready to bury the song. A mob invaded the Tuileries and burned it, "an eerie vision of Paris at night lit by the Tuileries in flames." The royal family fled to the assembly for protection and were taken prisoners[37] as the National Guard joined the rioters.

The assembly, led by Robespierre, Danton, and Marat, ordered Lafayette to turn his command over to their man and return to Paris—where he had already been denounced as a traitor. With seventeen others, he fled to Belgium, where he was recognized,[38] arrested, and sent under guard from one prison to another. In Olmutz, Austria, Lafayette was sentenced to five years solitary confinement.

Meanwhile Adrienne at Chavaniac sent their youngest daughter, Virginie, into hiding. She buried her husband's awards and swords and arranged for their fourteen-year-old son to stay in England. While making plans for her own escape, she was arrested. The embarrassed leaders who worked on the estate gave Lafayette's eighty-four-year-old Aunt Louise Charlotte permission to remain at Chavaniac under guard. The château was saved, but a band of terrorists stripped it bare and burned the furniture in a bonfire to the Goddess of Reason. In Le Puy, they auctioned off the rest of Lafayette's possessions. Adrienne and fifteen-year-old Anastasie were imprisoned in nearby Brioude, then transferred to a crowded jail in Paris, where Adrienne's mother, grandmother, and older sister were guillotined.

Irate letters from America protesting their treatment poured into France. The American minister in Paris, Gouverneur Morris (not a governor),[39] reminded Robespierre that the United States was France's only friend. "Was one life too much to spare?" Adrienne probably survived the Terror because of the thousands of letters from America and the efforts of James Monroe,[40] the new American minister to France. She was given better quarters but was still kept a prisoner. Finally freed on January 22, 1795, she was nursed back to health by James Monroe[41] and his wife, Elizabeth.

As the madness continued, the king and queen were executed, as well as Robespierre. A five-man Directoire took over the government and released Adrienne and her daughter, Anastasie; they returned to Chavaniac, where Virginie emerged from hiding to join her mother and sister, but their governess died of a heart attack from fright. Their brother, George, was safe in New York with Alexander Hamilton (who spoke French).

Adrienne knew nothing of her husband's fate. When she learned he was alive,[42] she set out to join him. Abbé Durif drove her and the girls in the one leftover horse-drawn cart to Le Puy to persuade the new revolutionary commissioner for permission to be imprisoned with her husband. When the pretty young girls, twelve and eighteen, also begged to stay with their father in jail, the astounded commissioner agreed. James Monroe arranged passports for Adrienne to travel with her daughters, supposedly to the United States, but at Dunkirk a pre-arranged ship, ostensibly bound for New York, took them to Hamburg where the American consulate gave them passports under assumed names, transportation (a carriage, horses, and coachman), and money. In Vienna, Adrienne received permission from Austrian emperor Joseph II to share her husband's imprisonment. On October 24, 1795, a guard unlocked Lafayette's cell door. The half-dead, ragged man on the cold stone floor looked up to see his beautiful wife and lovely teenaged daughters. They shared his suffering for two years; no light or air, the smell of latrines, a starvation diet, and screams of tortured prisoners.[43] Adrienne nearly died of scurvy.

As part of a treaty with Austria, the five-man Directoire ordered Général Napoléon Bonaparte to free them (September 19, 1797). Adrienne and the girls were allowed into France, but not Lafayette. The little family stayed with Adrienne's aunt[44] at Wittmold near Hamburg, where their son George, now nineteen, joined them after six years in America. Adrienne returned to Paris, where she obtained permission for Lafayette to stay in Utrecht, Holland, at that time under French rule. After Napoléon fled from Egypt,[45] Adrienne had a two-hour visit with the little Général, who issued a passport for her husband. Napoléon secretly planned to become emperor and figured Lafayette's popularity might be useful. Free after seven years, Lafayette returned to France.

At first Napoléon and Lafayette got on well enough. Napoléon, like Mephistopheles, tempted Lafayette with power—a seat in his hand-picked Senate. Honest as ever, regardless of the consequences, Lafayette refused. "I should be obliged the next day to denounce the government and its chief." The final break came when Napoléon crowned himself emperor.[46] "Everyone has fallen in line except Lafayette. . . . He is all ready to start trouble again." Lafayette retired for twelve years to his wife's enormous estate, Château de la Grange at Rozoy-en-Brie, forty miles east of Paris.[47] One reason he had retired at forty-six was that he had slipped on ice and broken his left thigh bone. Primitive surgery[48] left his hip permanently stiff. The once vain hero walked the rest of his life with a limp.

If Lafayette were a hero, Adrienne, an amazing businesswoman, was the heroine. Thanks to her, debts were collected and confiscated properties returned. She died at thirty-seven on her son's birthday, Christmas Eve,[49] from complications caused by her imprisonment. No longer would she have to share her husband with Diane de Simiane, his mistress since his first return from America.

After Waterloo, the Bourbons, émigrés, and allies swarmed back to Paris, and a divine-right king ruled again—right where we were before the guillotine and Napoléon's manslaughter.

For awhile, obese, gouty,[50] sixty-one-year-old Louis XVIII gave the people a constitutional government with many reforms, but as he became incapacitated, his reactionary brother ruled behind the scene. All liberties were repealed, despite protests from Lafayette and his friends.[51] When the king died (1824), his brother became King Charles X, and Lafayette's dream of liberty became a nightmare. But then, one of those "not to worry" rainbows appeared in the sky. President Monroe invited him to visit the United States (1824).

In America, he was hailed again by cheering crowds—just what the sixty-seven-year-old "Boy" needed. This time his son, his secretary, and his valet[52] accompanied him as they met his old friends[53] and toured twenty-four states. President Monroe greeted them at the new capital in Washington,[54] where Lafayette addressed a joint session of Congress before continuing a cross-country tour. He celebrated his sixty-ninth birthday at the White House,[55] then reluctantly returned to France. He had dragged out the visit as long as possible—fourteen months.

During the July 1830 Revolution, he commanded the National Guard that drove Charles X from France. No one knew what to do next, except Lafayette. This was his third revolution. He formed a provisional government that put the ex-king's cousin, Louis Philippe, on the throne as a constitutional monarch. He also remembered his successful balcony scene at Versailles, when he forced the royal family out on the balcony, and the fickle mob cheered. Now he staged another balcony scene at the Hôtel de Ville, when he thrust a *tricolore* flag in the Citizen King's hand and kissed him on both cheeks. Again, thousands cheered, and again, he was appointed commander-in-chief of the National Guard—at seventy-three. Too late he realized the government was not "of the people." Money-men ruled.

Drenched in a rainstorm, he literally caught his death of cold. Even after he died,[56] the Bourbons feared him. Although they forbid cheering and

Back to Europe with the BUSY BODY

funeral orations, thousands lined the streets, as 3,000 National Guardsmen[57] from all over France accompanied his coffin, covered with the Stars and Stripes and the French *tricolore*.[58] The silent funeral procession marched from the Church of Notre Dame de l'Assumption[59] to the cemetery of Picpus, described by Victor Hugo in *Les Miserables,* near the destroyed Bastille. Lafayette's stubborn fight to end tyranny was over. He was buried beside Adrienne and her family in a secluded walled garden on the grounds of a convent.[60]

His own country denied him a funeral with military honors, but the Americans made up for it. French and American flags flew at half-mast in the black-draped Capitol in Washington. Lafayette's friend, Andrew Jackson, "Old Hickory," was president, and ex-president John Quincy Adams, also a friend,[61] delivered a eulogy, as Congress stood in silence to pay homage to "the Boy;" the wealthy aristocrat who had helped Americans win their independence.[62] The American ship, *Brandywine,* brought dirt from Bunker Hill and Virginia to surround his casket.

And so it goes; *Ça ira.* Lafayette's lifelong crusade for truth, justice, and tolerance continues throughout the world. But freedom from oppression once achieved, how to keep it? How to distinguish lust for power disguised as compassion? Easy—look for truth and honor—attributes of George Washington and the marquis de Lafayette.

19

Berry

Two Hours and Two Different Worlds

GETTING THERE was half the fun—watching people, especially the men, as confused as we were checking train schedules and platforms. The laid-back "no problem" ones were either girl-watching, chewing on something, or combing their hair. The Paris train to the province of Berry, two hours away, leaves from Gare de l'Australitz. My little white ticket was #184. You sit in a designated place (for thirty minutes) and watch a board under a clock until your number comes up. Then you go to another place to make a reservation. After the train arrives, the tricky part is finding the right car. When you are finally seated, it is another of life's great achievements.

A burly Englishman opposite us on the train recognized us as Americans and proceeded to quote his favorite limericks:

> There was a young lady from France
> Who thought she'd take just one chance.
> In the arms of her beau, she let herself go
> And now all her sisters are aunts.

> There was a young woman from Kent
> Who said that she knew what it meant
> When men asked her to dine, with cocktails and wine
> She knew what it meant, but she went.

THE JACQUES COEUR TOUR

Our destination was Saint Amand Montrond, a little town in the former duchy of Berry—the beginning of our long-anticipated Jacques Coeur Tour. Berry was part of Eleanor of Aquitaine's land. In the ninth century, Charlemagne created the kingdom of Berry for his son, Louis, with Bourges the main town. When Eleanor of Aquitaine divorced French king Louis VII and married future King Henry II of England, their sons inherited her French territory. Wars between the two kings and their sons continued for one hundred years. In the fourteenth century, French king Jean II gave the duchy to his youngest son, twenty-year-old duc Jean de Berry.

During centuries of warfare, Berry has been miraculously spared. On the Jacques Coeur Route[1] alone, there are more than ten beautiful feudal castles and privately owned Renaissance châteaux hidden among forests, rivers, and lakes. We were met at the railroad station by our charming tour director and hostess, Marie-France de Peyronnet, whose mother's twelfth-century feudal home, Ainay le Vieil, is often called Le Petit Carçasonne. We headed for Gien, the first stop on the tour, to see the first château built in the Loire Valley.

GUTSY GIEN

During World War II, Gien was an important escape route for the French. It was bombed by the Germans, then four years later by the Allies to prevent the Germans from escaping. Gien, with its historic castle, bridge, and church, has been patiently and beautifully rebuilt.

Anne of Beaujeu, favorite daughter of Louis XI, the Spider King,[2] lived in Gien. At twenty-two, she ruled as regent with her husband, Pierre de Beaujeu, for her twelve-year-old brother, future King Charles VIII. She arranged his marriage to Anne of Brittany and negotiated treaties, which eventually added Brittany and Orléans to France. Anne of Beaujeu, whose husband's estates in Burgundy included Beaujeu, was the most respected lady in France. Her church in Gien, dedicated to Joan of Arc, although bombed during World War II, has been restored. The Stations of the Cross, mounted on colored ceramic plaques, not only depict Christ's Passion, they also advertise Gien's famous *faience* (earthenware pottery). Colored ceramic capitals on the pillars illustrate episodes in Joan of Arc's life.

Sixteen-year-old Joan of Arc, dressed as a page, prayed in the old church

March 1, 1429, after she rode into Gien from the cold, wet countryside en route to Chinon to meet the dauphin. Four months later, she returned with him on their way to Rheims to accomplish her mission. The spineless dauphin, however, suddenly balked. Jealous court favorites had persuaded him it could be dangerous. Furious, frustrated Joan galloped into the country, leaving him behind. Five days later, he joined her. Seventeen days later, he was crowned king of France. Joan came again to Gien to pray, but this time in despair. In a battle nearby at La Charité, her army had been defeated by the Burgundians. It was the beginning of the end of her earthly mission.

GIEN'S LA MUSÉE DE LA CHASSE
The Big Bad Wolves

Gien's Hunting Museum is a man's reward for being dragged to places his wife wants to visit. Even if he doesn't hunt, the museum will be a favorite memory. Housed in a fifteenth-century château on the site of one of Charlemagne's fortresses, it was the first château on the Loire built for Anne of Beaujeu during her regency. Demolished during World War II, it is now restored with the original pepperpot towers. Typical of the area are the black and red bricks in geometric patterns.

Fathers and sons touring the museum were fascinated by Robin Hood crossbows, a dog jacket with iron spikes, and a wolf trap made from an old carriage spring. At one time, wolves running in packs caused many deaths. A handsome museum guide, dressed in dark olive green, told us that wolf hunters belonged to an honorary society created by Charlemagne, which still exists, with two members from each of the 150 French counties. Uniforms of Napoléon's wolf hunters cover an entire wall.

La Musée de la Chasse captivates the whole family. Women peered at the falconers' hoods, gauntlets, and bags, reminiscent of romantic days when ladylike ladies in long velvet gowns rode sidesaddle, with a falcon perched on their arm. Since hooded hawks were trained at night, the ancient art of falconry (before the gun) required skilled professionals who could work in the dark. Other exhibits include a collection of 4,000 uniform buttons,[3] Gien porcelain, tapestries, and horns: powder horns, hunting horns to call wolves, automobile horns, and others. The grand finale is the stained glass window of Saint Hubert, patron saint of hunters, and paintings by François Deportes, Louis XIV's "Painter of the Hunt."

Back to Europe with the BUSY BODY

CHÂTEAU LE VERRERIE AND THE SCOTCH GUARD

A Sea of Waving Plumes and Shining Helmets
Forests of Tall Gleaming Lances...
—SIR WALTER SCOTT, *Ivanhoe*

Château Le Verrerie (seventeen miles from Gien) was once the home of the Scottish Stuarts in France, the French kings' army commanders, and bodyguards. The château, overlooking a mysterious lake, is nestled in the Solonge forest, a perfect setting for a romance novel of love, peace, and chiffon dresses.

The Scottish-French connection began when the Normans conquered England. Questionable claims of William the Conqueror's successors over Scottish kings caused years of warfare. In the thirteenth century, soldiers of English king Edward I conquered Scotland, but were driven out by Robert the Bruce. His daughter married a Stuart, and their son became the first in a long line of Stuart kings.

The French and Scots allied themselves (1346) against England,[4] their mutual enemy. During the Hundred Years War (1337–1453), the English captured most of France north of the Loire, while the sixteen-year-old French dauphin cowered in a castle at Bourges, 150 miles from Paris. When he asked the Scots for help by honoring their old alliance with France, Sir John Stuart of Darnley, Constable of the Scottish army, and his brother, William, marched with 6,000 kilted soldiers and their bagpipes to the rescue. When they won a battle near Tours (1423), the dauphin added the French *fleur-de-lys*[5] to the Stuart coat of arms, and gave them the duchy of Aubigny sur Nère[6] in Berry, which included a hunting lodge, later called Le Verrerie. The dauphin also gave the Stuarts the title *Seigneur* or Lord of the Manor. The constable and his brother were killed fighting at Orléans. French and Scottish troops attacked as the English were bringing in provisions for Lent (wine and herring).

For the next 600 years, France used the brave Scots in their wars. In return, France received and pensioned Scottish exiles fleeing English political and religious persecution.[7] Beraud Stuart, Captain of the Scotch Guards (grandson of the Scottish constable who died at Orléans), grew up at Le Verrerie and started a glass (*verre*) factory. He also made sacks for grapes and feed. Like his ancestors, Beraud went to Scotland to confirm the old French-Scottish alliance, but two trips in two years and malaria from an Italian campaign were too much. Beraud died at fifty near Edinburgh.

Berry

Le Verrerie in Beraud Stuart's time was a simple lodge with a fifteenth-century chapel. When Beraud's son-in-law and heir, Robert Stuart, saw French king Francis I building a magnificent château[8] on the Loire, he wanted a more elegant home. Between 1517 and 1520, Robert Stuart added today's beautiful pale pink Italian loggia. Since he had no heirs to inherit the château, or ensure the Stuart line at Aubigny, he was allowed to adopt a nephew.

In Scotland, James V,[9] a Stuart king, married French Catholic Mary of Guise, mother of future Mary, Queen of Scots. James V died at thirty, "worn out by amorous excesses," leaving his six-day-old daughter, Mary, heir to the throne. Protestants and Catholics killed each other, and when Mary, Queen of Scots was executed, her orphaned son James I, brainwashed and seduced by politicians, was crowned king of England, Scotland, and Ireland. His son, another Stuart king, devout Charles I, was executed. His crime? Not only had he ruled as a Divine Monarch,[10] under the impression that he had been "divinely" chosen to rule without consulting others, he had also married a Catholic, eleven-year-old Henriette-Marie, daughter of French king Henri IV. Defeated by Oliver Cromwell in a Civil War, on a cold January day, 1647, he was beheaded by a Puritain Parliament. On the way to the execution, as he crossed the park from Saint James' Palace, he asked to wear an extra shirt so he wouldn't shiver from the cold. People might think he was frightened. "No man so good was ever so bad a king."

His son Charles II, the "Merry Monarch" of the Restoration Period, inherited Le Verrerie and the Aubigny sur Nère duchy. After the English king's death, Louis XIV gave the land and a title to the Frenchwoman Louise de Keroualle, one of the Merry Monarch's many mistresses,[11] for "services rendered." Louis XIV paid her to persuade the English king to sign a secret treaty with France in his third war against the Dutch.[12] She spent her remaining fifty years in Aubigny, where she was loved as much by the French as she was hated by the English. Her son by the Merry Monarch was the first Duke of Richmond. He was made a French citizen in order to inherit the duchy. In 1842, Le Verrerie was acquired by marquis de Vogüé, whose descendant is the present owner and host; warm, genial comte Antoine Vogüé.

Views from the château windows are as priceless as the art treasures. Carved into the wooden balcony of the chapel are the Vogüé coat of arms; a cock and the Stuart coat of arms—three shoe buckles with the French *fleur-de-lys*. Many Stuart weddings were held in the chapel, but few baptisms. Although some *seigneurs* of Aubigny dutifully produced heirs, most of the French Stuarts preferred male companions.

Le Verrerie, one of the few châteaux on the Jacques Coeur Route with dining and overnight accommodations, is supervised by comtesse Françoise de Vogüé. The countess has found her niche. By sharing the peace and beauty of Le Verrerie, she makes herself happy, as well as others. Who needs a therapist to relieve tension when there's a château waiting in Berry?

Thanks to the Vogüé family, Château Le Verrerie remains a tribute to brave men from Scotland who fought for France and managed to speak French with a Scottish brogue.

SANCERRE
Too Late for the Party

Poplar trees line the road from Gien to the ancient town of Sancerre, set atop a beehive-shaped hill. The countryside seemed waiting for photographers, artists, and film directors to call, "Action!" Silly billy goats[13] teased each other, windmills whirled, and apple pickers were in place on ladders.

Approaching Sancerre, we drove past wrought iron fences festooned with artificial pink blossoms and trees spruced up with flowers in their leaves. The flowers were left-over decorations from a recent wine fair. In town, a huge wine bottle, dangling on a wire above the main square, jiggled happily if a bit unsteadily. Clusters of fake purple and white wisteria resembling grapes were draped everywhere. The town ladies had made them from "packing-popcorn." A green telephone booth sprouted red crêpe-paper geraniums, and the Town Hall boasted liberty, equality, and fraternity with blue, white, and red streamers. Over the door, a shaft of wheat represented prosperity. The cheerful homemade decorations made a festive setting for lunch outdoors at La Tour Restaurant on the square.[14] The waiter, with one plate piled atop another, brought paté, omelet, Sancerre's celebrated *chèvre* (goat cheese),[15] and bread—in the other hand, a pitcher of dry, white, spicy wine—Sancerre, of course. Inside the restaurant, Maurice Chevalier's umbrella and jaunty black high silk hat hung on the wall behind the door. How disappointing. He should have been dining in a cozy corner with a beautiful woman, captivating her with his debonair French charm. He may be dead, but we'll never forget his merry, mischievous smile.

Berry

CASTLE MAUPAS AND THE DAUNTLESS DUCHESS

Down the road from Sancerre there's an old fortress-castle, Maupas, which has been in the Maupas family since 1725—home of Antoine, marquis de Maupas and his wife. The first marquis de Maupas tutored the duc de Berry, grandson of King Charles X, who fled to Scotland during the 1830 Revolution.

A dark-haired girl, seventeenish, greeted us at the door in her black and white maid's uniform and ushered us into the large entrance hall. One wall is covered solid with plates. Eight hundred-eighty-seven plates in different patterns from different countries fill the wall space up the staircase to the second floor. Those plates[16] are very impressive. (My grandfather lined his entrance hall with losing horse race tickets.)

More impressive than plates was the young country girl who greeted us at the door and gave us a tour in perfect English. Her quiet air of goodness and dignity was as welcome as Edith Wharton's *Age of Innocence*. Among the many treasures[17] she showed us was a little boy doll dressed in a suit of armor, and a crucifix carried by members of the Maupas family as they were carted to the guillotine.

Entranced by priceless Aubusson tapestries and opulent decor, we were brought back to reality in the kitchen, with the hand pump for water and tin jugs used to heat water in bedroom fireplaces. Tall riding boots beside the huge fourteenth-century fireplace belonged to the driver of the coach in which Louis XVI fled to Varennes.

One bedroom in the castle was occasionally used by Marie-Caroline, the duchesse de Berry,[18] the same adventurous duchess whose husband had been murdered[19] and who plotted with her printing press in Nantes to gain the throne for her son, the heir, rather than Louis Philippe, the Citizen King.[20] She left her harp and gold canopied bed at Maupas for the wilds of Brittany. Her cloak-and-dagger escapades to regain the throne for her son make those of Bonnie Prince Charlie seem boring.

BOURGES AND SAINT ÉTIENNE'S CATHÉDRALE

He who bears in his heart a cathedral to be built, is already victorious.
—ANTOINE DE SAINT EXUPÉRY, *Flight to Arras*

On the road from Castle Maupas to Bourges, capital of the province of Berry, we passed families picking blackberries. In Bourges, we stayed near the cathedral at the small Angleterre Hôtel, which has an excellent restaurant.[21] As usual, we were impressed by the quiet, well-behaved families—especially the one with a baby in a high chair. Throughout the meal, the mother kept dipping the baby's pacifier in wine.

From our hotel we walked through narrow, ancient, cobbled streets to the nearby cathedral, and there it was—perched on its platform, queen of the hill. "You could see it, enormous and indifferent, at the end of every street."[22] Propped up by giant angel wings (flying buttresses), Saint Étienne's (Stephen's) magnificent cathedral[23] continued to rise majestically through three centuries of war, finally rivaling the beauty of Chârtres.

The sculpture over the center portal recalls Saint Stephen and Saint Paul (when he was Saul the Roman centurian, who stood guard as his fellow soldiers stoned Saint Stephen to death). The upper row portrays Saint Stephen's vision: "Behold I see the heavens at the right hand of God" (Acts 7:54).

Buried beneath the cathedral in a twelfth-century crypt is Jean, duc de Berry, remembered for his illuminated prayer book, *Les Trés Riches Heures*.[24] On the right of the main altar, a sign on a pillar points to an audiovisual presentation of the cathedral's art. We gazed spellbound at the awesome beauty of the film, like pirates staring at a jewel chest. Next to Chârtres, Bourges Cathedral has the most magnificent collection of stained glass in the world. Every guild[25] in town donated windows: the Butchers, the Bakers, the Candlestick Makers, Coopers, Stonecutters, Masons, and Furriers. The figures are so large you don't break your neck looking at them. A guidebook tells the stories in the windows. A few favorites are:

1. Chapel of Our Lady of Lourdes

Saint Dionysius of Athens becomes a convert after hearing Saint Paul speak to the Athenians. He later becomes a bishop, martyr, and patron saint of Athens, Greece.

2. Chapel of Saint Francis de Sales[26]

Fresco of Saint Solonge, patron saint of Berry. Born in Ville Mont near Bourges where her father worked in the vineyards, she had the gift of healing, and a special power over animals. As a young girl she had taken a vow of chastity, and when the Count of Poitiers' son, a rejected suitor, kidnapped her, she jumped from the horse, severely injuring herself before her kidnapper "dispatched her with a hunting knife."

Saint Thomas, the Doubter, and How He Went to India. Gondoforus, a king of the East Indies, wanted the most beautiful palace in the world. He had heard of Thomas the Builder (a carpenter) and sent his messenger, Abbanes, to bring Thomas to India. Thomas was willing to bring Christ's message anywhere in the world, but "Please God don't send me to India"—with its millions of people. Maybe he had a premonition he would be martyred, and he was. When he realized God was arranging it, he said, "Thy will be done," and went.

In India, the king explained the palace plans to Thomas, gave him money for building materials, and left to tour his kingdom. Thomas was so busy preaching the gospel, he forgot what he came for. He gave money to the poor in the king's name, and soon the entire city was converted. When the king returned, he sentenced Saint Thomas to prison. Before the king could decide how to torture and kill him, his brother, Gad, died. Angels brought Gad to heaven, where he saw the palace sparkling with jewels and gold and silver that Saint Thomas had described—the palace God was preparing for the king.

Gad was given a chance to return to earth to tell his brother, the king, what Thomas meant when he talked about "my Father's house has many mansions," and the heavenly mansion being far better than an earthly one. The king was so fascinated that he released Thomas, and both he and his brother Gad were baptized.

3. Chapel of Saint Ursin

Saint Stephen. How his relics were brought from Jerusalem to Constantinople, then to Rome.

Saint James. Associated with the pilgrim church of Santiago de Compostela in Spain, where the saint's relics are preserved. He is also associated with the pilgrims' emblem, the cockleshell. In the story depicted in the stained glass window we see Saint James, who converts Philetus, an apprentice to the magician Hermogenes. Hermogenes is being attacked by demons and rescued by both James and Philetus. Hermogenes is converted and burns his magic books. We also see James on his way to his execution, healing a cripple. One guard is so impressed that he, too, is converted, but James and the guard are beheaded.

JACQUES COEUR (1395–1456)
I Never Promised You a Feather Bed

Jacques Coeur, from Bourges, was born at a special time for a special reason. He paid Joan of Arc's soldiers, and after her death, financed supplies and an army necessary to oust the English from Normandy. Jacques Coeur became the greatest ship owner and trader possibly in the world, with headquarters at Montpellier and, later, Marseille. His ships shuttled pilgrims to and from the Holy Land, where he traded silk, paper, and lead for spices, perfume, and luxuries from the East. Jacques Coeur was in Florence buying silk when Cosimo de' Medici and other Florentine bankers controlled the European banking world.

When Jacques Coeur started his career, the disinherited, destitute[27] dauphin of France was holed up in a castle at Bourges.[28] He should have stayed hiding behind the curtains, as in George Bernard Shaw's play *Saint Joan*. Kings can ruin a man's life.

After the dauphin was crowned King Charles VII, and Joan of Arc was burned at the stake, the king's troops freed Paris, which had been occupied by the English for sixteen years. Jacques Coeur became head of the Mint and later finance secretary, or *Argentier*. As *Argentier*, he financed the king's wars and accounted for everything the king and his extravagant court confiscated. He served on diplomatic[29] missions and accompanied the king on his travels.

When English ambassadors came for peace talks at the court in Tours (1435),[30] the occasion called for a great celebration. The month-long *fête* was eventually fateful for three leading characters: Jacques Coeur, the king, and Agnes Sorel, lady-in-waiting to the queen. The young girl's beauty included attributes such as kindness, sympathy, and consideration, but when a king in the fierce fifteenth century said, "I want you," what was a girl to do? For that matter, what was a wife to do? More than one wife was imprisoned for life. Agnes Sorel bore the king four daughters. The twenty-eight year-old Agnes died during the birth of her last child.[31]

Eight years later, Jacques Coeur was blamed for her death. Jealous enemies[32] accused him of poisoning her, and the king went along with the farce. That way the king could renege on money he owed him. Originally, the king, with his tragic background, evoked sympathy, but the matter of money can change a man's character.

King Charles VII, heavily in debt to Jacques Coeur, had recently learned that Jacques Coeur had borrowed money from Pope Nicholas V to help finance the conquest of Normandy. Now, the king was also in debt to the pope, his rival, who wanted the money repaid to fight the Turks.

Jacques Coeur was arrested at Poitiers, stripped, hands and feet chained, and threatened with torture. For two years he was dragged from dungeon to dungeon. Despite a court ruling that Agnes Sorel had not been poisoned, the king seized Jacques Coeur's property and tried to poison him.

One of Jacques Coeur's former ship captains, his nephew Jean de Village, had sent word to him from Marseille to call whenever he was needed. He wrote, "I have the courage with the help of God." Now the captain received an SOS from Jacques Coeur, imprisoned at Taillebourg near Poitiers, saying he had pretended to swallow poisoned food and wine, but in five days, when he should be dead, they would know he had faked it and would kill him.

A Franciscan monk helped Jacques Coeur escape. Under the right of asylum he made his way from one church to another, until he reached Beaucaire in Languedoc. Across the Rhône at Tarasçon, he would be safe in King René's domain. Three ship captains with twenty armed friends came from Marseille to Beaucaire, knocked a hole in the city wall and rescued Jacques Coeur, waiting outside the Church of the Cordelliers. Arriving safely in Rome,[33] he was welcomed by old Pope Nicholas V.[34]

Rome was swarming with bearded oriental scholars and artists seeking refuge from the Turks, who were advancing on Constantinople. The aging pope was busy expanding the Vatican library to preserve scholarly Byzantine books, but before he died, he made sure the world knew the truth about Jacques Coeur. "They had calumniated him because of the things he had done for the Church. He had procured for us some other things contrary to the wishes of the said Majesty on account of which he has suffered unjustly very grave and prolonged persecutions."

When the new pope, Calixtus III (1455–1458), pleaded in vain for Christians to unite against the Turks, Jacques Coeur, at the head of a fleet, sailed to the island of Chios off the Greek coast to liberate the Greek Isles. After a sea battle, when his ships were bombarded day and night, he died of wounds on Chios, in the Aegean Sea, three years after the fall of Constantinople.[35] The king condescended to give Jacques Coeur's children whatever was left from a public auction of his property. The king's son, however, Louis XI, the Spider King, reversed the decision against Jacques Coeur, took the family under his special protection, and restored their lands.

Jacques Coeur was buried in the Church of the Cordelliers in Beaucaire. In Bourges Cathedral a plaque reads, "Lord Jacques Coeur, a Soldier-Captain of the Church Against the Infidel"—few words for a man who gave his fortune to his king—a king whose thanks was a dose of poison.

At least Jacques Coeur died nobly defending his faith. The king's death was not noble. As his next mistress, he had taken Agnes Sorel's cousin as madam of his harem. Syphilis showed up on one leg in a festering, swollen ulcer. Ulcers in his mouth were so excruciating he couldn't eat. The man who tried to poison Jacques Coeur died of starvation.

JACQUES COEUR'S PALACE
The Party's Over

Jacques Coeur's fifteenth-century home in Bourges[36] reflects both the times and his lifestyle, but not the man. His house seems to belong more to ship carpenters, stone masons, and artists. You begin to get the idea when you see two hooded house-servants carved in stone peering from fake

Jacques Coeur's home

windows on either side of the front entrance. "Be constantly on the watch. Stay awake. You do not know when the appointed time will come. It is like a man traveling abroad. He leaves home, places his servants in charge. . . . You do not know when the master of the house is coming."[37]

The fortified side of the palace, with its massive towers and delicate turrets, was a warehouse—an early department store—where merchandise was sold. Carrier pigeons flew from ship to shore bringing messages, especially, the current rate of exchange.

From a narrow street, we stepped through a dollhouse doorway into a vast stone room—melancholy, empty, and bare—the way it should be. Everyone is gone. The house is deserted. When you gradually notice the comic relief, the fun begins.

In the Merchant's Gallery where spices were stored, the ceiling is shaped like an inverted ship's hull, built with chestnut wood to prevent termites and cobwebs. The only thing in the cold, barren room is a coffin, a memorial to Jean, duc de Berry, patron of Jacques Coeur's father, a fur merchant. Jacques Coeur's emblems, hearts and shells, are carved everywhere; *coeur* (heart) and cockleshells, the symbol of Saint James, his patron saint. Stars were his wife's family emblem. The only remaining stained glass window from Jacques Coeur's time is in this room. His schooner, *Le Galée,* etched in silver and gold on stained glass, resembles one of Columbus' little ships, sails full-blown and packed with people.

Over the kitchen door, stone rabbits, snails, and monkeys frolic among foliage. In the fireplace near the kitchen, stones were heated for the sauna. A complicated engineering system provided hot water and plumbing for the latrines in the wall.

Throughout the house, stone people peer down from everywhere. All sorts of people talk with each other: spinners, sweepers, peddlars, and wine-growers. The women are the most interesting, in their low-cut Renaissance fashions, exposing bosoms that range in size from small to extra large. Carved over doors and walls are proverbs and maxims, such as "Keep Silent and Listen. Do What You Can." "A Closed Mouth Catches No Flies," "Say It, Do It, Shut up" (*Dire, Faire, Taire*).

The Festival Hall was the party room where people had fun, especially the stone sculptors. At one end of the hall, a monumental fireplace resembles a miniature castle. Carved on it are stories and parodies ridiculing the wealthy upper class and nobles. One panel is a spoof on jousting tournaments. Serious-faced shepherds and swineherds sit astride donkeys, with ropes for stirrups, jousting with brooms. Another panel shows gluttonous people stuffing themselves and playing silly games.

The last room was the 500–year-old chapel. Above the arched entrance, sculptured ladies laugh and chat on their way to Mass. A little boy with his finger over his mouth signals for them to be quiet. Angels floating over the painted chapel ceiling hold long, swirling scrolls with words from the "Gloria" and "The Song of Songs"—a perfect ending for the tour. Jacques Coeur may have been born a commoner, but he was truly noble in the role destined for him in uniting France. His motto was, "To the Valiant Heart, Nothing is Impossible."

MEILLANT
Fit for a King

Meillant, twenty-one miles south of Bourges, is another fairyland castle—an enormous one. There is no hint of warfare here, only serene, idyllic beauty. Once past the moat, green forests and birch trees surround a spacious courtyard. The enchanting scene is reflected in a lake, where stately swans glide leisurely by. Meillant's owner, tall, elegant marquise Jeanne de Mortemart, is a descendent of King Louis XIV's finance minister, Jean Baptiste Colbert. Colbert's third daughter, Marie Anne, married the duc de Mortemart. Before the wedding, Colbert sent the duke to Italy and instructed him to write an account of the journey. "To avoid depression, pass the time taking delight in what you must do. You shall see that all you do on my advice will turn to our greatest satisfaction." The duke wanted to pass the time with his Marie Anne.

Meillant evolved from a twelfth-century medieval fortress into a sixteenth-century French Renaissance castle. One distinguished guest was King Louis XII.[38] The cupola of the many-sided Lion Tower, with a balcony for astrologers, was designed by Leonardo da Vinci, and the ornate sculpture of arms and emblems was carved by Jacondo, who worked with Michelangelo. A separate chapel resembling a tiny cathedral was also designed by Jacondo.

Inside the seventy-five-room château, the Grand Salon, with its exquisitely decorated beamed ceiling, has an enormous Renaissance fireplace with a musicians' balcony above the chimneypiece. The library, lined with books to the ceiling, resembles a small town public library. In one bedroom, the marquise has rigged up an old tin bathtub with a shower-capped mannequin immersed in styrofoam bubbles. In another, a mannequin is snuggled under the covers, sound asleep. Gracious, queenly marquise de Mortemart was too shy to practice her English, and my French vocabulary was definitely limited. How sad, but we could laugh together. Sadder is the fact that her son (and only heir) does not share her interest in the home, which has been in the family for more than 500 years.

LA COMMANDERIE AND THE CRUSADES
Desert Warfare in a Suit of Armor

Berry is full of surprises. This time it was La Commanderie, home of the delightful comte and comtesse Bernard de Jouffroy-Gonsans and their three lovely daughters, Aloutte, Constance, and Sophia. La Commanderie is another château where you can dine, stay overnight in beautifully decorated rooms, fish, golf, and, if you ride horseback, the count, a descendent of Jacques Coeur's son, Geoffrey,[39] will accompany you through 300 acres in the Tronçais forest. If you like to sing, beautiful comtesse Michèlle is a great accompanist. She told us funny stories about guests on bicycles and foreigners coping with the language problem.

Surrounded by forests and meadows, the small castle, twenty-two miles from Bourges, was built in the 1600s by the count's ancestors on the ruins of a Knights Templar's commandery. Commanderies were fortified distribution centers for supplies sent from Great Britain and Europe to crusaders in the Holy Land in the Byzantine Empire—separate from the Roman Empire. The Commanderies were maintained by three orders of knights. The first order was the Knights Templar. The others were the Knights Hospitallers and the Teutonic Knights. For 450 years, tolerant Moslems had allowed Benedictine monks to manage hostels for pilgrims traveling to the Holy Land. In the eleventh century, two great powers, the Fatimids[40] from Egypt and the Byzantines, were getting along fine. Trade was great and prosperity had never been better. Then came the Seldjuk Turks, who had been converted to Islam by a group of princes called "Seldjuk." Although Christians were massacred and churches destroyed, appeals for help from the West were rejected. After the Turks defeated Byzantine armies and seized Jerusalem (1071), Byzantine emperor Alexius Comnenus persuaded Pope Urban II to send troops. Urban II, from France, who knew Western knights killed each other for fun and for something to do, decided that now they could kill for a cause. He traveled throughout Europe preaching a Holy War,[41] promising the remittance of sins. The following year (1096), four official armies headed for the Holy Land.[42]

Back to Europe with the BUSY BODY

Survivors of an unofficial army recruited by a monk named Peter[43] had swarmed into Byzantium in May, and in December, the first of four armies headed by knights arrived. The horrified Byzantine emperor had only asked for one thousand mercenary troops, not hordes of plunderers to be fed. On July 15 of the following year the crusading armies captured Jerusalem, but the slaughter was so horrible, the Moslems vowed to drive the Christians into the sea. During the siege, one hostel, dedicated to Saint John of Jerusalem, was used as a hospital. The enlarged Order of Hospitallers adopted the monastic rules of Saint Augustine and became known as "Hospitallers of Saint John of Jerusalem." Donations of money and land poured in, and commanderies and infirmaries were built throughout Europe. When the Hospitallers came under the protection of the Church, the knights became a military order, escorting pilgrims and defending the Holy Land.

Nineteen years later (1118), nine pious warrior-knights from France dedicated themselves to protect pilgrims and guard the Church of the Holy Sepulchre built over Christ's tomb. Like the Hospitallers, they professed vows of poverty, chastity, and obedience. Since their headquarters was in a building on the supposed site of the Temple of Solomon, the order was called "Knights of the Temple of Solomon," or Knights Templar.

Fanatical fighting against the Turks continued, and the crusader king of Jerusalem, Baldwin II,[44] (from today's Belgium) needed help. He sent two Knights Templar to Abbot Bernard of Clairvaux, the most influential churchman of the time. The Templars, traveling from Syria, showed up at Clairvaux near Troyes[45] in filthy, tattered robes, short hair, and thick, bushy beards. They described their way of life—prayer and battle—and asked for men, money, a rule to govern their daily lives, and recognition by the Church. Eventually they received their request—and more. Unfortunately, the "more" became a big problem. Like the Knights Hospitallers, the Templars became an international order with special privileges and dispensations, responsible only to their grand master and the pope. Their uniform, a white mantle emblazoned with a splayed red cross on the left breast, was worn over heavy, padded chain mail; a long, steel-knit sweater. The Templars adopted the austere rule of Saint Bernard's Cistercians: "If you wish to sleep you will be awakened. . . . We promise you bread and water, hardship and work, and the poor robe of the House."

The Templars' lay brothers, the "sergeants," were similar to the support group of the Hospitallers and the Cistercians, outnumbering the fighting monks nine to one. They were up at 4:00 A.M. in the summer and 6:00 A.M. in winter. The most overworked were those knocking dents out of armor. They ate meals in silence while the Bible was read to them and talked with their hands in a kind of medieval sign language. If they wanted more fish, they made a swimming motion. They could leave only if they had a nosebleed. A few were excused from afternoon prayer; for example, "brother baker," if he had his hands in the dough; "brother blacksmith," if he had an iron hot in the fire; "brother squire," if he was paring or shoeing horses' hooves—and any brother who was washing his hair. Chess and cards were forbidden, but hopscotch was okay.

The Templars' grand master, Hugh de Payens, recruited throughout France, Normandy, England,[46] and Scotland. As the order grew, commanderies were needed throughout Europe. Pope Innocent III granted more privileges in order to administer their farflung gifts of estates, farms, and castles. Despite promises to the Byzantine emperor, the knights kept the lands they had captured and established feudal kingdoms. For the next fifty years, pilgrims trooped back and forth to the Holy Land, taking time out to pick fleas. "Clothes and hair became nesting places of every sort of vermin, lice, and fleas. In fields and woods we take off clothes, sit naked, and carefully pick out every bug. Hours might pass." One pilgrim warned first-timers they must not laugh at thieves. "If you laughed, they thought you were making fun of them. Keep a straight face no matter what. Their touchiness is beyond belief." Venetian guide books gave the rate of exchange and useful phrases such as "Woman, shall I sleep with you?" If that didn't work, they appealed to flattery. "Beautiful maiden, come and sleep with me." If the maiden was still reluctant, "Woman, I am already in your bed." An Englishman's travel guide recommended a berth in the highest part of the ship. Those in the lowest are "ryght smolde to ryng hote and stynkynge." He also advised pilgrims "to get quickly off at Jaffa in order to get the best donkey to ride on."

The 2,000–mile treks came to a halt when Mohammedan leader Saladin united his people, in 1268, and captured Antioch, Saint Paul's home base. Pope Eugene III (1145–1153) assigned thirty-six-year-old Saint Bernard to stir up enthusiasm for a second crusade to recapture Antioch. Saint Bernard, the tall, tonsured monk, emaciated by austerities, respected the pious, serious Templars, but had little sympathy for the ordinary egotistical knights. When he was ordered to promote the crusade, he obeyed but wrote, "Villages and towns are empty . . . scarcely is it possible now to find one man among seven women . . . everywhere there are widows whose husbands are alive."

Fifty years after the First Crusade, King Louis VII of France left on the Second Crusade (1145),[47] carrying the traditional flag of French kings, the Oriflame; a red banner with yellow flames, originally made from Saint Denis' cloak. The twenty-six-year-old king was accompanied by his beautiful, opinionated wife, Eleanor of Aquitaine,[48] in doublet and hose, leading her knights from Aquitaine.

About the same time, German king Conrad III left from Germany. With two kings leading thousands into battle, the Second Crusade should have been a glorious victory. It was one of the most badly botched campaigns in history.

Another fiasco was Eleanor of Aquitaine's marriage to King Louis VII. When she left for the Holy Land, she had been married eleven years to her devout but boring husband. When they arrived in Antioch and Constantinople, satin sheets and lemon pies compensated for Turkish spears and the terror of raging seas. Her uncle, Raymond of Poitiers, whose light-hearted personality matched her own, was Prince of Antioch. Jealous King Louis disagreed with the prince about war strategy[49] and abruptly left Antioch for Jerusalem with his furious wife, who threatened to divorce him. The decision to attack the friendly city of Damascus, where Saint Paul was baptized, ended in a humiliating retreat and thousands of casualties. Saint Bernard, who had preached the disastrous crusade—who slept on straw, who had reproved kings, and founded at least sixty-eight monasteries, died in disgrace ill, alone, and humiliated—like the One he had sought to imitate.

When the French king returned to France with his still-fuming wife, he had changed from Attila the Hun to a monk—a monk still trying to produce an heir. When a third daughter was born, the king appealed to the pope for a divorce, using as an excuse that they were cousins in the fourth degree. According to church law, they should not have married. The divorce was granted and caused a war for one hundred years.[50]

After the disastrous Second Crusade, Saladin, sultan of Egypt and Syria, captured the entire Latin kingdom.[51] After the crusaders (under a Roman, or "Latin" pope) had defeated the Holy Land invaders, they set up their own Latin kingdom in the Byzantine Empire.[52] The French-speaking Latin kingdom, intact for sixteen years, was inhabited by Oriental grandchildren of the first crusaders—laymen who had married Christian Syrians,

Lebanese, and Armenians. Saladin captured Jerusalem in 1187, and two years later, the Third Crusade was organized to retake it. Sixty-four-year-old King Frederick I (Barbarossa) of Germany left from Regensburg, while King Richard I (the Lion-Heart of England), and King Philip Augustus[53] of France met at Lyons. To protect Paris while he was gone, King Philip built the Louvre as a fortress against invading Normans and wolves (louves). Richard I and King Philip Augustus took separate routes but met in Sicily for the winter. The rendezvous was touchy to say the least. King Philip was the quiet type—Richard the Lion-Heart was boisterous and volatile. Richard I had allied himself with French king Philip II (Augustus) against his own father, English king Henry II, for possession of French land. After his father's death, King Richard the Lion-Heart could drop the farce of friendship with the French king. An alliance was no longer needed. However, they continued the pretense of friendship long enough to honor their crusader's vow.[54] Philip Augustus left Sicily in March—as soon as possible—but Richard needed action along the way. First he attacked Messina in Italy and gave it to his widowed sister, Joanna, who lived in Sicily. Then he conquered Cyprus, (which he later sold to the Templars), found a husband for his sister, and despite being a homosexual, sent for his fiancée and got married.[55]

When energetic, enthusiastic German king Barbarossa drowned in Turkey, the remnants of his army met the English and French kings at the port of Acre. During the two-year siege, a third order of knights with privileges and property was founded in Germany: the Teutonic Knights.

King Richard the Lion-Heart ended the siege of Acre in a little more than a month. While taking bows and waving his banner, Leopold, Duke of Austria, behind him, also waved his banner. Incensed that the Austrian was stealing his scene, King Richard struck the duke's banner to the ground in a fit of fury that he paid for later—in prison.

Instead of staying to fight a hopeless war, King Richard signed a three-year truce with Saladin (1192), murdered 2,700 hostages who were supposed to have been exchanged, and left without waiting for his army and fleet.[56] The truce included safe passage for pilgrims to the holy places in Jerusalem, leaving the situation right where we were one hundred years and thousand of lives before.

Now that power had shifted to Saladin's Egypt, and Moslems controlled the land routes to Jerusalem, the only way to the Holy Land was through Egypt. The Knights Hospitallers, who had switched to sea power, captured the Egyptian port of Damietta at the mouth of the Nile. They also patrolled the seas protecting pilgrims and traders on the three-week voyage from Venice to Jaffa, the port of Jerusalem (today's Tel Aviv). Their light galleys, with 300 rowers, held between sixty and one hundred bodies herded into the hold. Reserved space was designated by chalk marks around mattresses. Jesuit founder Saint Francis of Loyola's pilgrimage in 1523 lasted 342 days; sixteen days in Jerusalem, 140 days in harbors, thirty-two days waiting for ships, and fifty-four days aboard ship.

Saladin died in 1193; his brother, who succeeded him, granted a series of truces to the Christians. He told Saint Francis Assisi, who came on a pilgrimage, that if the crusaders would leave Damietta he would return Galilee, Central Palestine, Jerusalem, and the true cross. The Knights Templars and Hospitallers turned him down. Peace? What would they do then?

When the port of Damietta was recaptured by the Moslems, Pope Innocent III called for the Fourth Crusade (1198) to retrieve it. Since the crusaders couldn't raise the exorbitant fees for transportation on Venetian war galleys, wily Doge Enrico Dandolo made a deal with them to the effect that, "If you get me the port of Zara on the Dalmatian coast and sack Constantinople, the wealthiest place in the world, I'll postpone the bill. Look what's in it for us!" The deal was made, the Egyptian campaign cancelled, and 480 vessels took off with men, horses, and provisions to kill and loot Christian Constantinople. The pride of Byzantium was ravished and a Latin kingdom established there for nearly fifty years. They forgot all about rescuing the Holy Land.

Horrified, Pope Innocent III excommunicated everyone responsible. Then he turned his attention to the Cathars, the Albigensian heretics[57] in southern France, who believed that the Devil created the world, and that sex and procreation were evil. Ten years of preaching had been useless. When they murdered a papal legate, the pope sent 6,000 French Knights Templars to wipe them out.

For forty years, there was peace in the Holy Land, but Pope Innocent III was determined to take Jerusalem. The first objective was the port of Damietta in Egypt, then Cairo. The expedition might have succeeded if the exotic semi-Oriental king of Sicily, Frederick II,[58] had shown up. Although he had taken the vow, there were a few problems (revolts) preventing his departure. The pope threatened to excommunicate him for breaking his vow.

Twelve years later, Frederick II finally set sail. When a fever forced him to land in Italy, the new pope, Gregory IX, did excommunicate him. Eventually Frederick II left his harem in Sicily, and with his Frankish knights and faithful Saracens, the excommunicated king embarked on the Sixth Crusade. During friendly talks, the sultan of Egypt signed a treaty giving him Jerusalem, Nazareth, Bethlehem, and more. Diplomacy succeeded after years of bloodshed. When Frederick's treaty expired (1244), the Egyptians captured Jerusalem, and trade became the new religion. "In Syria once there dwelt a company of wealthy merchants . . . that had a far-flung trade in spicery and cloth of gold and satins of rich dyes . . . and business was a pleasure."

When Mongols swept into Palestine two years later, wiping out both Saracens and Christians, saintly French king Louis IX charged to the rescue of Jerusalem like Don Quixote attacking the windmills. Both were defeated but undaunted. The only one we can relate to in this wild drama is Jean de Joinville from Marseille, the king's friend and historian, who was scared half out of his wits and convinced he was mad to be there. King Louis IX died[59] at fifty-six in Jaffa, during his second attempt to regain Jerusalem.

With the capture of Acre in 1291 by the Mamelukes, eight crusades to the Holy Land came to an end. The Knights Templars shifted their center from Palestine to Paris. King Saint Louis' grandson, Philip IV, delivered the death blow to the Templars.

King Philip IV had inherited wars and debts. He owed money to the Jews, the Lombards in Italy, and, worst of all, to the Knights Templars, who had refused his request for membership. Their enormous walled Temple occupied a third of Paris and had become the international bank of Europe. Philip envied and hated the Templars. He also hated Pope Boniface VIII. During the Crusades, before the fall of Palestine, the clergy had been taxed by the pope to help cover expenses. Philip continued to tax the clergy. He was not supposed to do that. Philip IV and the pope fought for years.

What to do? The king's legal adviser initiated a hate campaign against the pope, then drew up twenty-nine charges against him. The charges were so diabolical and ludicrous that people thought the lawyer was mad. With the help of the Roman Colonna family, the king's intoxicated soldiers roared off to the pope's summer residence at Agnani, set the church on fire, and seized the sixty-eight-year-old pope in bed before dawn. Three days later, the townspeople, who had cooperated, sobered up and rescued him. A month later the pope died in Rome, a prisoner of the rival Orsini family. The next pope, Benedict XI, died of poison eight months later. French king

Back to Europe with the BUSY BODY

Philip IV appointed as the new pope Clement V, a man he could manipulate, whose residence would be in Avignon. That took care of the pope problem. Next he arrested in one night every Jew in France, confiscating their money and property. Fifteen months later, again overnight, 5,000 Knights Templars in France were arrested, mostly the brown-robed sergeants of the order: the tanners, tailors, shoemakers, farmers, vintners, and servants, who had manned the hostels and had kept supplies going to the Holy Land. They were accused of 127 fiendish atrocities and for seven years were kept chained in solitary confinement. Hundreds died of starvation and torture. One hundred twenty were burned alive.

When Pope Clement V told the king his action was illegal, King Philip IV called a meeting of the Estates General to condemn the Templars. (Six out of eight delegates were his appointees.) Now that everything was legal, the king could confiscate their wealth—but not yet. The pope declared it was the responsibility of the Church to condemn them. Using the same tactics the king had used to avoid responsibility, Clement V in Avignon called a Church Council to approve his decision to arrest and abolish the order.

In Paris, there was still unfinished business. The Templars' grand master, Jacques de Molay, and the preceptor of the commanderie in Normandy, Geoffrey de Charney, had to be eliminated. On an islet in the Seine in the shadow of Notre Dame, two bearded skeletons, tortured for seven years, were dragged before King Philip IV, who gave the order "Burn them." Thirty-three days later Clement V died. King Philip IV died within the year (1314). Dante, in his *Divine Comedy* put them both in Hell. The Templars' property, money, and 3,000 commanderies throughout Europe went eventually to the Knights Hospitallers and kings and princes in various lands.

The Knights Hospitallers survived persecution because their navy had defended Cyprus, Rhodes, and Malta against repeated Ottoman advances toward southern Europe. Today, known as the Knights of Malta, they still care for the sick and needy throughout the world.

What is left to say about the crusaders? That they finally took a bath; they brought about a renaissance to medieval narrow minds; they believed in God; they were not indifferent to Him? According to Our Lady of La Salette near Grenoble, who appeared to two children in 1846, her Son is most hurt by man's indifference to His sacrifice—his "hardening into habit of not rendering Him honor—not giving Him even a crumb of His due."

Berry

CASTLE AINAY LE VIEIL
Cowboys and Indians in France

"Yes, Virginia, there is a Santa Claus," and real people do live in castles—Marie-France de Peyronnet, director of the Jacques Coeur Tour, for one. As a child she played in dungeons and towers and paddled a boat in the moat of her twelfth-century castle. She and her sister, Marie-Sol, with their boy cousins, played Richard the Lion-Heart and Philip Augustus instead of Cowboys and Indians. In the courtyard the boy cousins rode bicycles, instead of horses, in jousting tournaments. Rows of raked leaves represented advancing armies. Over the entrance in the inner court, a statue of Saint Michael guards the feudal castle encircled by high, forbidding walls. Ainay le Vieil (old) was inherited through Marie-France's mother, Baronne Géraud d'Aligny, whose ancestor[60] was master of the king's horses for Louis XII (1498–1515).

Moats, these days, are usually filled in. Not this one. As we cautiously made our way along the edge of the underground moat surrounding the castle, I wished there were a troop of Cub Scouts trooping behind me, especially when we came to an emaciated head staring from the top of a dungeon. Marie-France's son had made it with *papier-mâché*.

Château Ainay le Vieil

Back to Europe with the BUSY BODY

Among the many mementos that have survived at Ainay le Vieil are a tiny music box and a pendant containing a good luck spider, gifts from Marie Antoinette to her children's governess during their imprisonment. Period furniture in the Grand Salon is intimately arranged before a massive fireplace. Above it, the deep blue chimneypiece, covered with gold *fleurs-des-lys*, was built especially for a visit from King Louis XII[61] and his second queen, Anne of Brittany, in 1187. A beautiful small chapel with a stained glass scene of the Virgin is tucked among grandiose rooms. The chapel with religious paintings and sculptures has provided solace throughout wars, death, and tragedy.[62]

While Marie-France shares decorative arts and mementos of kings and queens with visitors, her sister, Marie-Sol, shares the beauty and fragrance of the castle's rose garden with its 200 varieties—in French, a *rosarie*. With ancient trees and medieval towers in the background, the garden celebrates the joy of life; God's booster shot for the soul. His rainbows come in pastels, but His roses shout for joy in riotous colors. One rose commemorates the one hundredth anniversary of the Virgin's first appearance at Lourdes (1858). Another is named for Jean Baptiste Colbert, King Louis XIV's finance minister, whose direct descendant is Baronne d'Aligny, our tour director's mother.

JEAN BAPTISTE COLBERT (1619–1683)

Colbert, from a family of international traders and bankers, originally served under King Louis XIII's minister, Cardinal Richelieu—also under Cardinal Mazarin, regent for young King Louis XIV. Horrified at the astronomical deficit and dishonest practices of Mazarin and his officials, Colbert proceeded to correct the abuses. When Mazarin died, he left his home to Colbert and recommended him to Louis XIV, who appointed him minister of domestic affairs and superintendent of buildings. Colbert signed every decree issued by his master: taxes, anti-papal edicts, whatever—but to the king, Colbert's job description was simply "purveyor of money."

After Nicholas Fouquet, the attorney general and chief of finance under Mazarin, was convicted of embezzling and sentenced to life imprisonment, Colbert[63] began financial reforms. A compulsive workaholic, up at 5:00 A.M., he worked fifteen hours a day with time out to have ten children. Charles Perrault, (famous for his fairy tales), was Colbert's assistant and advisor in cultural affairs. He said Colbert "entered the office content; rubbing his hands with joy."

Colbert's two goals were to make Paris the most beautiful city in Europe and to establish a fiscally sound treasury. Louis XIV had different ideas. To maintain his image of grandeur, his father's hunting lodge at Versailles was to be transformed into the most spectacular palace in Europe. In his temple (Versailles), surrounded by worshipful servants, the Sun King intended to be another Caesar. He told the Academy of Medals and Inscriptions, "I confide to you the one thing in the world which is most precious to me, my glory."

To avoid deficit spending, Colbert taxed everything he could think of to finance Versailles, 3,000 courtiers, and the king's mistresses.[64] He also had to make secret arrangements for the king's illegitimate children. To encourage manufacturing, he established the Gobelin tapestry works, imported skilled weavers from Holland and Flanders, metalworkers from Germany, and laceworkers from Italy. To transport goods, he improved roads and ordered the 175–mile Canal du Midi built. Colbert constantly complained about the appalling expense of Versailles, but Louis XIV changed the subject by complaining about blueprints. "The doorway from my small apartment to my large one has to be opened in the room where I sometimes go during meetings when it is necessary. I mean the place where the commode is."

To create commercial trade for profit and taxes, Colbert established French trading companies. The English and Dutch had been trading in the Spice Islands above Australia since the early 1600s. Why not compete with a *French* East Indies Company? In the Caribbean, the Dutch were reaping profits from sugar and tobacco on the French islands of Martinique and Guadalupe. They practically monopolized the wine trade in France from Bayonne, Bordeaux, and La Rochelle. To capture these markets, Colbert organized three French trading companies.

France also needed a navy. There were 6,000 French sailors in the service of foreigners. France had only twenty-two leaky old galleys. To help create a powerful fleet, Colbert built the Royal Observatory, where stars were charted and maps made of coastal areas. Under an Academy of Science, schools were set up in every port. He sent his eldest son[65] to Italy, the Netherlands, and England to study the layout of ports, dockyards, and duties of officers. Colbert, the most conscientious, exacting, overzealous father imaginable, wrote to his son, "Your reports are not handsome enough. What I mean is you are galloping through them." But he also knew when to praise. "Nothing could be done better, my dear son, than this report. Do not slacken. Soon you will be as competent as I wish."

The nine-year commercial war (1663–1672) against the Dutch was a failure despite advertising to recruit colonists. Madagascar was touted as a "terrestrial paradise with gold mines that one can see when rain washes the soil. . . . Spring weather to be enjoyed year round. Enjoy watching Christians at work." Neither the king nor Colbert had any concept of free enterprise—only government dictatorship, controls, edicts, force, and pressure. The winners in the costly war were the owners of private trading vessels.

An attempt to colonize Canada fared no better. After La Salle discovered the Great Lakes and the Gulf of Mexico, colonists were sent to exploit fisheries and forests for Colbert's taxes. Instead, they followed the Indians into the wilderness to trap furs—for themselves. One trapper was the governor, Comte de Frontinac, with his partner, La Salle. Colbert even recruited the bishop of Rouen to encourage priests to find one or two girls in each parish willing to go to Canada. The bishop found 1,500. "When word came, all those disposed toward multiplication, hastened off toward the market place to sign up."

Now that the renovation of Versailles was under way (with as many as 30,000 workers), the Sun King invaded the Netherlands (1672). Colbert's chronic stomach pains worsened. People were starving. When they revolted, the king ordered them hung and their land pillaged. Colbert carried out his orders.

Six years of brutal warfare left French nobles impoverished and common people grubbing for cabbage stalks. When Colbert wrote the king, "There is much misery among the people," the king's reply was a concern about the setting for valves and the volume of water in the fountains at Versailles. When Colbert complained of the horrendous cost, the king replied, "It is enough that I desire it for you to find the means." Colbert's assistant, Charles Perrault, noted, "The Dutch war cast a pall over him. Now he enters his study with a downcast air, even a sigh." Colbert's goal of a fiscally sound monarchy was shattered. He was forced to use the same deplorable practices Fouquet had used—shady deals and financial juggling.

The dream of beautifying Paris had ended years ago. When the king repealed the Edict of Nantes (1685), thousands of Protestant skilled craftsmen fled to America. A few streets had been widened, paved, and lighted, and horses no longer slipped on garbage. Place Dauphine and the Triumphal Arches of Saint Denis and Saint Martin were built, as well as quays on each bank of the Seine. Colbert expanded the royal library and moved it from rue de la Harpe next to his home on today's rue Colbert. The beautiful façade of the Louvre was completed,[66] but before the roof was on, Colbert died—defeated in his economic war.

A few hours before Colbert's death (in excruciating pain from nephritis and gallstones), the king sent a note saying, "Take care of your health." When there was no response, Colbert's wife asked if he wasn't going to reply. He answered, "It is to the King of Kings I must respond." When she asked him again, he told her, "Madame, when I was in this room at work on the king's business, neither you nor others dared to enter. Now that I must work on the business of my salvation, you do not leave me in peace."

He was buried from Saint Eustache at night to prevent riots. Colbert, the king's tax collector, was the villain. It wasn't until the Revolution, seventy-four years later, that the king was blamed.

GEORGE SAND'S NOHANT
Home of a Nineteenth-Century Novelist
People and Puppets

Near Ainay le Vieil is "Nohant," home of Chopin's mistress, George Sand.[67] Tourists throughout the world shuffle through homes, palaces, and châteaux admiring furniture, chandeliers, and art objects, but the rooms have no warmth or real "people presence." At Nohant, however, George Sand's guests seem to have come to dinner and stayed forever—artists, musicians, radical politicians, illicit lovers, writers, and teenagers. Today her home, forty-three miles from Bourges, still teems with visitors.

People from everywhere filed through the château, paying tribute to the nineteenth-century woman's-lib freedom fighter. We were taken first to the large but far from energy-efficient kitchen, where an enormous wood-burning stove still rules the room. Sauce pans, their little copper bottoms on display, hang in two long rows across one wall. The only thing the kitchen lacked was a smell—cinnamon, turnips, chocolate—something.

In the drawing room, light blue upholstered chairs are pulled up to an oval table before the fireplace. Crooked pictures of all shapes and sizes clutter the blue-papered walls. One painting (circa 1836) shows twenty-five-year-old Franz Liszt playing the piano for Alexandre Dumas *père* (before he got fat) and Sand with her idol, Victor Hugo, author of *Les Misérables*.[68] Dumas and Hugo were both thirty-fourish. Standing with his arm

Back to Europe with the BUSY BODY

around the great violinist Pagannini is Rossini, the Italian composer (*The Marriage of Figaro*).

Before Sand wrangled an introduction to Frédéric Chopin,[69] Franz Liszt and his mistress, comtesse Marie d'Agôult, were guests at Nohant. Marie had left her husband and two little girls to fly away with Liszt and "live." An excellent pianist herself, she and Sand listened to Liszt banging and crashing away on the small spinet piano in the drawing room by the hour.

In the subdued, tranquil dining room, I looked for the silver punch bowl. "Romantics" got high sniffing brandy fumes burned in a bowl. Liszt smoked Sand's big cigars, while Marie had to watch Sand make passes at her lover. Sand, supposedly, was Marie's great and good friend. She even gave Marie her own bedroom with the Empire bedstead. To protect Marie from draughts, she made curtains for the bed. Too bad she goofed. She made them three feet too short. In the narrow, claustrophobic bathroom, there's barely room in the little four-footed tub for a bare body.

In the corner of Sand's bedroom, the little curtained bed is draped with material that matches the wallpaper—blue with hundreds of white dinner plate designs. Benjamin Franklin's picture was supposed to be hanging over her bed, but it wasn't. She loved his *Poor Richard's Almanac*[70] and never knew that the author of "early to bed and early to rise" stayed up half the night.

Another writer, Théophile Gautier,[71] gave a wonderful account of his visit to Nohant: "Breakfast at 10:00 A.M. Everyone sits down without waiting for Mme. Sand who arrives like a sleepwalker and stays asleep throughout the meal. After breakfast you go into the garden to bowl. That wakes her up. She sits down and begins to talk. At the moment the only thing of interest is mineralogy. Everyone has his little hammer. . . . Mme. Sand looks like a ghostly automaton. She talks in a mechanical monotonous voice dead level. In her attitude there is an almost elephantine gravity and dignity. . . . Her slow gestures are that of a somnambulist. Every now and then a wax match is struck, a little flame appears and her cigarette lights up. Always with the same mechanical movements. Not a gleam of light either in the sound of her voice or in the color of her speech. She writes from 1:00 A.M. until 4:00 A.M. Up at 11:00 A.M. Then another two hours during the day. It's as if you had a tap running. Somebody comes in and you turn it off. . . . Mme. Sand can't sit down in a room without pens appearing in front of her. Together with blue ink, cigarette paper, Turkish tobacco and striped note paper. It simply pours out of her. . . . You know what happened to her once?

Something absolutely monstrous. One day she finished a novel at 1:00 o'clock in the morning. 'Good heavens,' she said, 'I've finished and it's only one o'clock!' So she promptly started another." Delacroix said she wrote all night and used full-strength ether to relieve her headaches. She sent Chopin to bed with the children.

After Sand brought Chopin to live with her at Nohant, following their disastrous trip to Majorca, she discarded men's pants for voluminous, matronly black skirts. Now her role was that of mother hen. The painter, Delacroix, was their best friend, and for years they were a happy threesome. Delacroix said Chopin was such a delightful companion, "When I was with him, I felt one's own shortcomings no longer existed." On picnics, Sand trooped ahead of Delacroix and her children, Solonge and Maurice, while fragile Chopin, in white gloves, meticulously dressed, trailed behind on a donkey. In the evening they dined under the trees. Solonge and Chopin played duets, and everyone played charades. However, things change.

Sand's children, her daughter Solonge and son Maurice, became teenagers. Sand's boisterous Bohemian friends arrived en masse, and as Chopin's tuberculosis worsened, Sand took more lovers. The children were used to that, but Maurice wanted to be head of the house. He should make the decisions, not the musician who had moved in. When Sand's "farewell, I don't want to see you any more" note came, Chopin was in Paris giving piano lessons during the concert season. A few days before the 1848 Revolution, he had written a note consoling pathetic, neglected Solonge,[72] now nineteen. Chopin was her only friend. The following year he died.

The last room we visited at Nohant was the Marionette Theatre room, where Maurice's puppets are lined up behind glass on shelves along the wall. They seem to be waiting for *The Nutcracker's* old professor to bring them to life on their little stage.

Here, Maurice and his friend, Eugène Lambert, started their famous Literary Puppet Theatre. In the beginning it was just for fun. The teenagers, with a big towel over their heads, hid behind a piece of cardboard propped up against the back of a chair, and manipulated two sticks wrapped in colored cloth. After their first performance, the audience (Mamma Sand and a friend) applauded so enthusiastically the proud, happy boys built a stage with a frame. They also made four little painted puppets. Sand was the costumer. It was her idea to make a Green Monster with a huge mouth so he could swallow Pierrot. She made the monster's mouth from two old red slippers and his body from the sleeve of a blue satin dress. The Green Mon-

Maurice's puppet show

ster was really blue, but the audience never noticed. Maurice and Eugène dreamed up the wild fairy stories the puppets performed.

Their next theater, twice as large, resembled a little castle. By now, their Marionette Theatre was famous. Puppet devotées from the literary world gathered at Nohant contributing ideas and brilliant dialogue. The church bells at Nohant rang to announce performance days.

By 1847, they had eight characters. To have more than two puppets on stage, Maurice invented a rake with long teeth on which the puppets could move. Now they were able to have fun with special effects. To set the mood for murder shows, they dressed the puppets in ghostly white and lined them up as if they had all been hanged, with drooping heads and limp, dangling arms.

Maurice sculpted the puppets' heads, while Sand supervised. "If the puppets are too thin they will seem insignificant. They must be painted with oil paint without varnish and have real hair and beards. The eyes can be enamel like dolls, but we prefer a round black nail, curved like a pupil. This varnished nail receives the light with every movement of the head and produces the complete illusion of a glance." On performance day, if the varnish had worn off, they filed the nails to make them shine again.

With only two operators, if the show had five characters, one puppet had to be seated. The head, held up by a hook over the seat, was attached to an eyebolt hidden in the puppet's hair. Since it was difficult to get the eyebolt attached to the hook, sometimes the puppet, unable to sit down, jiggled hysterically above the chair. However, Maurice and Eugène, with their gift for improvisation, came to the rescue: "What's the matter with you? Are you ill?" "Yes, it's a serious disease called *piton*" (the eyebolt). "Alas, I know that too. We've all had that at some time." With the rake, they could now fill dead time on stage if something went wrong.

The 1848 Revolution disrupted everyone's life, but the next year Maurice (now twenty-four) and Eugène made up for lost time with bloody dramas like *The Crimson and Blood, A Woman and a Bag of Night,* and *The Rebellious Cadaver.* More than 120 plays were presented from 1854 to 1872. Some were parodies on hits such as Verdi's opera *La Traviatta,* adapted from *The Lady of the Camillias* by Alexandre Dumas *fils* (son), who had seen the marionette version at Nohant.

In addition to the rake, Maurice also invented a holder for the puppets awaiting their entrance. An iron wire in a spring held the puppets and allowed them to have the same movements as real people. Maurice wrote, "My Burattimo [puppet] turns his head, crosses his arms, knocks the wall with joy or despair. . . ."[73] Later Maurice decided to carry the puppets' heads, not by their costumes, but by cardboard in the shoulders and chest. Now the women puppets could have adjustable corsages and low necklines.

The Theatre of Nohant in 1872 had 125 characters and a huge inventory of accessories, thanks to Maurice's rod. The only problem was the costumes. George Sand had made them all, and now she had to remake them—boxes of them. "For thirty years I have spent many evenings and sometimes nights on this miniature work." Not only did she design and sew shirts, jackets, collars, and petticoats, but also authentic military costumes and the court costumes of Louis XV and Louis XVI, made of silk and velvet, embroidered with silver and gold thread.

After Sand's death in 1876, Maurice moved the marionettes to his home in Passy.[74] He died thirteen years later, but today his friends, the puppets, are back at Nohant, awaiting another opportunity to entertain George Sand's guests.

Back to Europe with the BUSY BODY

Our tour ended in a large entry hall, a room in itself—stately and formally impressive. At the bottom of an elegant marble staircase, a box containing two compartments was used for letters "to be mailed" and for "internal correspondence." If you needed anything, you wrote your name and room number on a note and put it in the second compartment. Gautier said, "I needed a comb. I wrote: Théophile Gautier, such and such a room and what I wanted. The next morning at six o'clock I had thirty combs to choose from."

Rooftops of the fourteenth-century village church on the estate slant at four different levels to make one beautiful composition. Inside the tiny church hangs a copy of Delacroix's *Sainte Anne Reading to the Virgin*, a reproduction painted by Maurice. When Delacroix was suddenly inspired (as painters are), he realized he had forgotten to bring his canvases. Mme. Sand, a born homemaker, poked around in an old wardrobe and found some white duck material she used for making corsets, which Delacroix nailed to a frame. One of the household maids posed as Saint Anne, and Sand's goddaughter posed as the "child." While Delacroix worked, with Maurice sketching along with him, Sand read to them. After dinner, Chopin's soothing music rippled through the dark, quiet night.[75]

Behind the château, a long tree-lined lawn resembles Rip Van Winkle's bowling alley where the dwarfs played nine pins. Between the house and lawn, under old trees, George Sand is buried near her father and grandmother. Two marble slabs in the soggy grass mark her final resting place, one for her, the other for her dog.

From the time of Louis Philippe, the Citizen King, until Sand's death in 1876, George Sand fought with her pen against tyranny—defying the threat of death, prison, and exile. "Her religion was political and social action." In *Leila* she implored readers to "Harden not your hearts. Help those less fortunate and devote your God-given gifts to mankind." Oscar Wilde wrote, "She felt everyone's misfortune." No heroine in her novels experienced such growth of character.

20

Touraine

Tours and Two Châteaux:
A Saint, Sleeping Beauty, *and a Photographer*
from Vogue

TOURS

In Tours on a Saturday night, we stood in the dark outside the train station with luggage at our feet, playing eenie-meenie-minie-mo with the hotels nearby, but not for long. A young man in his mid-twenties noticed our dilemma, took us across the square, checked us into a hotel, and led us to a restaurant. Not only did he speak English, he had received his master's degree in agronomy in North Dakota, and was now working in Angers. At his suggestion we ordered fresh trout, salmon, chasselas grapes, and wine. The Vouvray wine,[1] cold and tingly, was just as Molière had described, "saucy but not too impertinent." Our dinner deserved candles and crystal instead of noise and red-and-white checkered napkins. Our rescuer, Jean Luc, was a perfect host, whose conversation was as delightful as our dinner. After seeing us safely back to the hotel, the Guardian Angel disappeared into the night.

 The next morning, at 9:00 A.M., finding the Basilica of Saint Martin of Tours was not that easy. It should have been, except for the taxi drivers who offered directions. Three of them spread maps over the top of a cab while they argued among themselves about cathedrals and basilicas. We thanked them and waved goodbye, but if we had kept veering left, we would have been there in four long blocks (rue Descartes).

Back to Europe with the BUSY BODY

We arrived at the basilica in time to hear a concelebrated Mass with lovely, lilting French music. About fifty people were there, very devout and serene. A young father and his two little girls wore the same colored sweaters—red. I was glad the mother wasn't there. Four red sweaters would have been too much.

SAINT MARTIN OF TOURS
"Thank You for Coming"

Saint Martin, a fourth-century bishop of Tours, was born in Hungary but raised in Italy. His father was an officer in the Roman army. At fifteen, Martin was recruited into the army and sent to Gaul. Outside Amiens, he cut his own warm cloak in half to share with a shivering beggar, and that evening, when he saw Christ in a vision wearing the torn cloak, he promptly became a Christian.

His baptism occurred when barbarians were invading Gaul. Before a big battle, he refused to participate, saying he was now a soldier of Christ. When Caesar called him a coward, Martin volunteered to go unarmed into the battle protected only by the sign of the cross. Off he went, but instead of a battle, the enemy surrendered before the fighting began. The astounded emperor accepted Martin's resignation.

He returned to Italy, where he converted his mother, among others, then lived for a while as a recluse. Returning to Gaul, he joined the Bishop of Poitiers—again living as a hermit. When other monks joined him, the hermitage near Portiers became the first monastic community in Gaul. As Bishop of Tours (370), he built another monastery outside the city walls.[2]

Martin lived during the reign of two Roman emperors—Maximilian and Valentinian; the latter a fierce, haughty, man less lenient than Caesar. Valentinian's empress hated Martin. When he called on the emperor, she gave orders never to allow Martin to enter the palace. After fasting for seven days, an angel appeared, telling him to return, and this time the gates would be open. And they were! Suddenly, Martin was in the presence of the furious emperor, who demanded, "Who let you in?" To show his contempt for the bishop, Valentinian had remained seated. Suddenly the seat of the throne caught fire, burning the emperor's you-know-what. Leaping to his feet, the emperor found himself standing in front of the bishop in spite of himself. The stunned (and scorched) emperor granted all of Martin's requests.

His missionary work took him into the most remote parts of Gaul—by water, on foot, or on a donkey. Once, as he traveled through Burgundy on his little donkey, he was beaten by robbers on horseback. When the fun was over, the robbers mounted their horses, but they were rooted to the ground. The terrified thieves ran back to crumpled-up Martin, begging forgiveness. After he blessed them, the still shook-up robbers were able to gallop away.

Word of Martin's work with the poor, his miraculous healing powers, and his charity spread throughout Europe. One of those who received his blessing was Saint Patrick, returning to Ireland from Rome. When Saint Martin died in Candes (397), the people of Tours snatched his body and rowed it down the river. As they reached their city (in November), a miracle occurred: trees turned green, flowers bloomed, and the birds sang. The miracle is still referred to as "Saint Martin's Summer."

Seventy-three years later, a basilica[3] was built over his tomb in the monastery where Clovis, king of the Franks, came to pray after rescuing Tours from the Visigoths. The basilica became the most celebrated pilgrimage place in Gaul. During Charlemagne's time, the abbey or monastery was renowned for calligraphy and illuminated manuscripts. Burned by Norman pirates, it was replaced in the twelfth century by a new, enormous basilica, but the Huguenots sacked it (1562), and during the French Revolution it was destroyed.

Today, Saint Martin's tomb is in a nineteenth-century monolithic church, part of the ancient basilica. The crypt is surrounded by twinkling candles and a silver grill donated by Spider King Louis XI.[4] It occupies the same spot where it has been since the fifth century, and is still a world-renowned pilgrimage shrine, especially on November 11, the anniversary of his burial. Of the 4,000 churches dedicated to him, the most famous is Saint Martin-in-the-Fields in London.

Saint Martin is one powerful saint; whether in Martinville, Louisiana, or Tours, France—wherever. After our visit to his basilica, he thanked us by performing three miracles in one day; a tour of the city and visits to two châteaux.

CHÂTEAU USSÉ
Sleeping Beauty's Castle

From the basilica, we found the tourist office to inquire about visiting two places: Ussé, the *Sleeping Beauty* castle, and Château Saché, home of Balzac's friends and his refuge from bill collectors. The tourist office was open,

Ussé, Sleeping Beauty's Castle

but since it was Sunday, there was no transportation; no buses, no taxis, no way—except for another Guardian Angel who noticed us trying to comprehend why tourists couldn't tour.

Michel was in his early thirties, tall, blond, handsome—and had traveled in many countries. Sympathetic with our frustration, he spent more than an hour badgering every tour agent in Tours—to no avail. Finally he took us himself. We zoomed away in his little yellow car through the beautiful warm August countryside to Ussé, where people were shuffling through a guided tour of the castle;[5] but Michel knew how to do everything. He charmed the souvenir lady, explaining our plight, bought tickets, and showed us a shortcut to the Sleeping Beauty rooms—high in the enormous castle, with its towers, turrets, lookouts, moats, gables, and pinnacles overlooking the Chinon forest. We followed Michel through a narrow passageway forever. Suddenly he stopped, pointed, and said, *Voilà!* There, protected from the real world by glass, we saw three mannequins. A sweet prune-faced old lady was sitting at her spinning wheel, and standing in red shoes, face front toward her audience, was the princess with long, yellow, woolen braids. The prince stands by with a baffled "What have I done?" expression on his face.

Touraine

CHARLES PERRAULT
His Fairy Tales

In his fairy tale, *Sleeping Beauty*, when a beautiful baby princess was christened, all the fairies were invited to a party except one, who was so old everyone thought she was dead. When she showed up and there was no present for her, she was furious. All the fairies gave the little princess wonderful gifts; she would be the most beautiful person in the world, she would sing like a nightingale, and so forth. But the furious old fairy put a curse on her and prophesied she would prick her finger with a spindle and die. Fortunately, a good fairy changed the curse. Instead of dying, she would fall asleep for one hundred years—then she would be awakened by a handsome prince; and that is what happened. When she was fifteen and her parents were away, she explored the castle, climbing higher and higher. In a little room at the very top, a sweet old lady was spinning. As the bad fairy had foretold, when the princess tried to spin, she pricked her finger and fell asleep.

The forest grew dense, with only the top of the castle visible in the distance. Everyone in the castle slept too—except her parents, who had died. One hundred years later, the prince appeared, and the trees magically made a path for him. When he approached the lovely princess, she awoke.

The story says everyone in the castle awoke, but since they were "not in love" they began to die of hunger. It also says the prince and princess were married that day by the castle chaplain, but "they slept little."

They lived together without telling the prince's parents, and had a little boy and girl. After the king died, the prince publicly announced his marriage. When he left for war, his mother, the queen, ruled, but unfortunately she came from a family of ogres who liked to eat children. When she tried to eat her grandchildren (and their mother), the steward foiled her plans—so she ordered them thrown into a vat of vipers. The prince showed up in time to save them, and the enraged ogre queen jumped into the vat herself.

Perrault cleaned up all his fairy tales. Usually the beauty who fell asleep was raped and had one or two children before she woke up.

A Single Parent

Charles Perrault (1628–1703) lived during the time of Racine, Corneille, Molière, and La Fontaine. Colbert was Louis XIV's finance minister, and Perrault was Colbert's secretary. For twenty years he was one of the busiest men in France, keeping account of the Sun King's cultural affairs. One of his duties was to pay thousands of artists and workers at the Louvre and Versailles. He was a lawyer with a talent for getting the job done. At forty-four, he married a beautiful, nineteen-year-old girl who died of smallpox seven years later, leaving Perrault with three little boys.

Perrault was a "joiner" who thrived on committee meetings. He also wrote poems—mostly praising Louis XIV. You would think he was worshiping a Sun God. Then again, as Molière (and later Beaumarchais) knew, life was precarious if one were not noble. Referring to one titled woman, Perrault wrote, "I dared to propose to her that we both go to an attorney-at-law and recognize in all humility, once and for all that she was indeed a noble lady and myself, but a bourgeois."

Perrault was either an apple polisher or emotionally blind. Louis XIV's overblown ego and greed resulted in the first European world war, foreshadowing Napoléon. His conquest of the Spanish Netherlands was the beginning of more and more. "Everyone weeps for their sons, brothers, and husbands."

One does have to keep one's head above water in a sea of despair. One lifesaver is escape. Today, Gothic novels help. With Perrault, it was fairy tales. His youngest son, Pierre, at nineteen had accidentally killed a friend while fencing. (The friend was the only son of a widow.) After many court trials and a huge settlement, the youth joined the army and was killed—at age twenty-two.

Before the tragedy, Pierre and his father had worked together on *Sleeping Beauty*. At a time when no one would admit writing children's stories or fairy tales, Perrault acknowledged being the author of *Contes de Ma Mère l'Oye,* or Teller of Tales. (In the seventeenth century, it was common practice to refer to fairy tales as *Contes de Mère l'Oye.*) As an excuse for writing them, he said he wrote the fairy tales to amuse and instruct his children. Included at the end of each story was a moral. Wise Perrault realized the importance of parents communicating with their children. Together they could cheer the heroes and heroines and boo the villains. No matter how scary the story, children and adults knew everything would end happily for the good guys. In real life, one needs to be constantly reassured.

In English, *Contes de Mère l'Oye* means *Tales of Mother Goose.* In 1729 the tales were translated into English. French cakes became custard pies, woodcutters were faggot makers, the enchanted forest was guarded by Beefeaters instead of the Swiss Guard, and the Hall of Mirrors became a Hall of Looking Glasses. After the English translation, *Mother Goose* was published in German, Dutch, Italian, and Russian. Stories similar to those of Perrault existed in many languages before his *Tales* were published in 1697, but he was the first to make fairy tales literature.

By the time the Grimm Brothers published their tales in 1812, Perrault's had already been translated into German. Before that, French governesses in Germany had been telling the stories for years.

Charles Perrault writes like a lawyer; especially his *Christian Thoughts* and *Illustrious Men*. Every detail is worked out—no loose ends—logical, formal, concise. He still has a list of people indebted to him for his tales, including tourists to the fairy tale castle at Ussé.

CHÂTEAU SACHÉ
The Little Yellow Car That Could—and Did

Our whirlwind tour continued as we hopped into Michel's little yellow car and sped through the valley of the Indre. We flew along a narrow road between high, thick, green bushes, where signs are so misplaced you have to drive past the intersection to see which way to go, then back up to turn left or right.

Château Saché, where Balzac stayed so often with family friends,[6] was half an hour away. Surrounded by trees and rolling lawns that roll on and on, it is every city-dweller's dream. Lucky Balzac! Not really. He kept the same demonic discipline; the same grueling hours, caffeine, no sleep, and no exercise. Balzac's life at Saché is interwoven with his hectic life in Paris[7]—hiding from bailiffs, affairs with mistresses, and rendezvous all over Europe with Countess de Hanska and her retinue, which included her husband, Baron Wenceslav (twenty-five-years older than she), her daughter, Anna, and the governess. Later, Anna's husband was included.

At Saché the last of a tour group was disappearing through the front door of the château. Michel talked to the gruff lady concièrge, and this time it looked as if there might be a problem. Michel disappeared into the house, then came out to converse in rapid French with the no-nonsense woman in charge. He disappeared into the house again and *voilà!* He emerged with a key in his hand. We were permitted to unlock the door and join the tour already in progress. The tour was in French, but that didn't matter. Nothing could detract from Balzac's presence in this house.[8]

We merged with the tourists trooping upstairs to the second floor. In the center of the main room a huge glass-covered display table contains pages from Balzac's manuscripts. The walls are covered with caricatures and pictures. One picture shows Eve (Mme. de Hanska) with her husband and daughter at Neuchâtel, Switzerland, where Balzac met her for the first time after their letters had escalated to undying love and admiration. Other pictures include Eve's enormous home where she was born and her husband's palatial estate in Volhynia, set above a lawn sloping down to a river. She had sent Balzac a picture of it, but it was too large for his little three-room apartment on rue Cassini. He had a smaller copy made. The portrait of a beautiful girl and her baby is that of Zulma Carroud, a friend of Balzac's sister, whose sensible advice he never took. A collection of dolls costumed to help him remember his character's clothes is in an adjoining room.

As the gray-haired, matronly guide talked to her attentive audience (which included children of all ages), occasionally another woman wearing rubber gloves would slip through the group and quietly unlock the table. She gingerly lifted a page at a time from under the glass and disappeared with it.

I followed her to a back room, where an art director from *Vogue* magazine was photographing the pages. To see one page of Balzac's manuscripts is worth the trip to Saché. Hundreds of hen-scratched words fill the top, bottom, and side margins of each page.[9] Proofreaders could work on a page only two hours at a time. How they ever deciphered the minute hieroglyphics is mystifying. There are more corrections in the margins than words on the page.

The room the photographer was using had a back staircase by which we escaped the tour group. Michel returned the key to the concièrge, and we were off again in the little yellow car. Soon we were in Tours, crossing the Loire over Pont Wilson, a bridge[10] generations of soldiers have marched across—most recently in 1940, when the Germans bombed it and the whole center of town. On rue Nationale, Michel pointed to a row of flat little buildings and said that the one in the middle was Balzac's birthplace. Now it is a drugstore. He drove east to boulevard Herteloup, then north to show us the thirteenth-century Cathedral of Saint Gatien where Balzac was baptized. An old gabled house (once an armorer's shop) on rue Colbert is where Joan of Arc was fitted for her armor. An iron sign depicts a girl in armor, with the words *La Pucelle Armée* (The Maid's Army).

Suddenly we were passing Saint Martin's Basilica, where we had been the morning of that astonishing day. We screeched to a stop in front of our hotel, where Michel grabbed our bags, pushed them into the back of the car, and whizzed us to the railroad station in time to catch the last train to Nancy by seconds.

In Villandry Gardens with Michel Boudon,
who rescued us when we were "tourless" in Tours

21

Lorraine

Nancy:
General Patton, Art Nouveau, Two Cousins, and the Maid of Orléans

NANCY WHO? The city was named for a Roman castle, *Castrum Nanceium*, and the village that huddled around it. Streets in Nancy still have names from old inn signs, such as, Street of the Trumpeting Moor. We stayed at a hotel near the elegant place Stanislaus, built by the Polish king whose daughter married Louis XV in 1725, and had all those girls Beaumarchais taught to play the harp.

GENERAL GEORGE S. PATTON, JR.
Deja-vu

During World War II, General Patton made his headquarters at the Grand Hôtel in place Stanislaus.[1] Patton's Third Army faced the strongest German army on the Allied front. As his army and French Général Le Clerc's Second Armored Division stormed toward occupied Nancy twenty miles away,[2] German troops began clearing out. But the Allied drive came to a halt when their tanks ran out of gas.[3] Two thousand jubilant Germans raced back to Nancy to plant mines around the city and in the nearby forest. Three French Resistance fighters[4] risked their lives to warn Patton. A month later fuel arrived, and the drive toward Nancy resumed. Before leaving the city again the Germans bombed the post office, gas and electric utilities, and barges and bridges on the Meurthe River;[5] with loot piled on bicycles, wheelbarrows, and baby carriages, they left.

On September 15, Patton's Twelfth Corps, despite bombs still exploding, roared into the city, restoring freedom for the first time in five years. One mansion the Germans tried to destroy, and missed, was the magnificent home of M. Paul Cavalier, 4 rue d' Auxonne: The bombs fell on a neighbor's home, burying the owners M. and Mme. Lallement under debris. General Patton, inspecting the damage, heard a weak voice under the rubble crying for help. It was M. Lallement, pinned under an enormous table. Since it was impossible to pull him out, they used a crane to lift bricks, wooden planks, and the massive piece of furniture. They also unearthed M. Lallement, still alive. Crawling from his hellhole, M. Lallement noticed the three stars on his rescuer's shoulder. Looking up, he inquired, "Are you perhaps a general? Perhaps even General Patton?" The answer was *"Oui,"* and the two men shook hands. M. Lallement told the General he had been in three wars. Patton replied, *"Et moi deux."* He didn't mention being wounded during World War I in the Battle of the Meuse[6] (which left a huge hole in his hip). Mme. Lallement smiled. She was from Thiaucourt, the first village liberated by Americans in that battle.

ART NOUVEAU: ÉMILE GALLÉ

Nancy is an Art Nouveau showplace, with wild facades, exuberant stained glass windows, and *joie de vivre* everywhere. Louis Majorelle's wooden balconies look like porches with open-air attics on top—an open invitation to pigeons. One balcony is supported by wrought iron vine tendrils clinging to it. We crossed the street to stare more comfortably. Everywhere, we gazed at balconies and windows; light, airy, and graceful, or elegantly sturdy. A house on rue Charles III features a tulip tree window. A Cross of Lorraine decorates a window at 1 boulevard Charles V, and the window of Credit Lyonnais Bank is a solid mass of yellow clematis flowers. Thistles, symbol of Lorraine, decorate everything from façades to underwear.

We headed straight for the Musée de l'École de Nancy,[7] former home of Émile Gallé (1846–1904), genius glassmaker and furniture designer. Swirling designs in lamps, stained glass, wrought iron, and furniture flow from room to room—the only museum of its kind in the world.[8]

Gallé inherited the house and glassmaking business from his father.[9] He knew all the leading craftsmen in the city, and in 1901 founded the School of Nancy (workshops). With his knowledge of chemistry, he produced amazing varieties of colors and tints in glass, and his skill as an etcher-engraver made some of his glassware appear to be sculptured. Gallé's works are not exactly Shakespeare's "sermons in stone,"[10] but they show his awe of God in nature. A beetle adorns a green-tinted vase representing a forest; on another vase, a pine branch curves around it, with the pine cone draped over the side. Butterflies decorate a music holder, and carved cucumber vines twist among cabbages and rhubarb.

Wood, with its variety of patterns and color shadings, fascinated Gallé. He used more than 600 different veneers. A double bed he made as a wedding present for a friend fills a whole room. The headboard, shaped like a huge moth with outspread wings, is a collage of veneers. With lustrous bands of mother-of-pearl, Gallé emphasized the intricate beauty of God's design in this bothersome insect. Never has a lowly moth enjoyed such an appreciative audience. Visitors from everywhere file past the bed, admiring its beauty.

After Gallé's death, his wife wrote, "If Émile Gallé has renewed the decorative arts, it is from having studied plants, trees and flowers both as an artist and scholar." She might have added geology,[11] microbiology, and oceanography.[12] He etched a goblet for Louis Pasteur's seventieth birthday, with a myriad of microbes and medicinal plants. The new science of oceanography and the discovery of exotic sea creatures inspired a cup resembling a seahorse. The tail is a handle. During this same time Jules Verne,[13] fascinated by the underwater world, wrote *Twenty Thousand Leagues Under the Sea.*

Gallé never forgot nor forgave the German takeover of Alsace-Lorraine after the Franco-Prussian War. Although Nancy remained in French territory, the rest of Lorraine now belonged to Germany. He used Lorraine's national flower, the thistle, in a defiant gesture of patriotism. The Joan of Arc vase, created for the 1889 Paris Exposition, flaunts a thistle, his signature, and Joan in armor on horseback. The inscription reads "The peace we need is that they go back home."

Gallé died of leukemia at fifty-eight. His wife continued the school until 1931 for the benefit of 450 workers, including, at one time, Louis Majorelle, who designed the beautiful iron stair rail in Galleries Lafayette in Paris; René Lalique, the jeweler; Antonin and Auguste Daum, glassmakers; Alphonse Mucha, famous for his Paris posters, especially those of Sarah Bernhardt; and Hector Guimard, known for his *style modèrne* staircase for the first Paris metro. René Lalique, fourteen years younger than Gallé,

Lorraine

moved on from jewelry to glassmaking. His name became synomous with Art Nouveau. Unfortunately, Art Nouveau was so adaptable, within a few years the public tired of it. Victor Hugo complained, "You can't go out in the street anymore without banging your head on an Art Nouveau candelabrum."

THE BATTLE OF NANCY AND TWO COUSINS
"Spider" and "Rash"

Delacroix's famous painting *The Battle of Nancy* is also at place Stanislaus in the Musée des Beaux Arts. The painting represents a battle that occurred on the outskirts of Nancy, January 5, 1477, when Duke René II of Lorraine defeated Charles the Rash, last Duke of Burgundy. It sounds simple. Someone wins, someone loses—but not when the Spider King, Louis XI, is involved. He said he was like a woman. "When anyone tells me anything in an obscure manner, I must know at once what it is all about."

Louis XI, born in Bourges[14] (1423) and baptized at Saint Étienne, was the most feared, respected, and brilliant of all French kings. From his father, whom Joan of Arc pushed to Rheims to be crowned, he inherited his spindly legs, but mercifully not his character. Thanks to his tutor, his excellent education at Loches and Tours[15] emphasized humility, clemency, and a reminder that all men are equal in the sight of God. From the time he nearly drowned in the Loire on Good Friday and was miraculously saved, he relied on the Blessed Mother for her intercession. He rode in freezing weather to the neighboring shrine of Our Lady of Béhuard on an island near Angers to give thanks: "In memory of the bitter grief and anguish she had endured when she beheld her beloved Child, the Author of Life, hanging from the Cross." Louis spent hours praying before battles and walked miles on pilgrimages all over France to thank "the Virgin who so often was indulgent to the wicked and who had saved a bad son." Her statue and chapel at Béhuard are on top of an enormous rock. Our memorable visit was in the moonlight.

Like most dauphins, Louis couldn't wait until his father died so he could rule. At thirteen he married[16] frail, eleven-year-old Margaret of Scotland, daughter of James I. When she arrived with her escort of more than a thousand Scotsmen, the children hugged each other and went off to play, but because his father chose her and both parents adored her, Louis hated her.

At sixteen he accompanied his father, Charles VII, on a tour of the realm, and observed the king's indifference to his starving subjects. When he demanded something be done, the king rode off, leaving him to solve problems. With no money or troops, the teenage Lieutenant-General became his father's best commander.[17] He succeeded so well in various assignments that the king became not only jealous, but very uneasy. When spies told the king rebellious nobles had persuaded the dauphin to take over the government, the king packed his son off to govern a little state left to the heir of France, the Dauphiné (1447), whose capital was Grenoble.[18] Before leaving for the Dauphiné[19] at twenty-three, he was so indignant and disgusted with his father's unfaithfulness[20] and infatuation with Agnès Sorel, a lady-in-waiting at his mother's court, he cut the tails off all his father's horses. They never saw each other again.

What was to have been a four-month banishment turned into ten years—the happiest time of his life. He made war, secured treaties, established a bank system, created a parliament at Grenoble, and continued to plot against his father. He even arranged his own second marriage to Charlotte of Savoy,[21] after his first wife died at twenty-one. His furious, insulted father, who was supposed to arrange marriages, sent an army against him.

Terrified, Louis sent a note to his father saying he was going on a crusade with his uncle, Philip the Good, Duke of Burgundy. He wrote another note to his uncle asking for asylum—explaining that he was an innocent victim of injustice. With the marshall of Burgundy, he galloped as fast as possible for two weeks through Lorraine and Luxembourg to safety in Louvain, fifteen miles from Brussels. His uncle was off fighting, but his son Charles, eleven years younger than his cousin, escorted the shabby, penniless refugee to his father's brilliant court in Brussels. When sixty-year-old Philip the Good returned to Brussels, the vain, haughty duke, more powerful than the king of France, gulped, managed a smile, and welcomed him.

Unlike Louis' lonesome childhood, spent always in danger of being kidnapped, the duke's only son, Charles, had been petted and pampered. But he, too, schemed for the day he would rule. In contrast to his homely cousin, Charles was handsome—with beautiful black eyes—intelligent, excelling in everything he attempted. The difference was, Louis had mastered the virtue of patience. Charles never learned. Eventually he became known as Charles the Rash.

After the dauphin moved in with his uncle,[22] he found himself involved in a father-son relationship as stormy as his own. He played the role of

Lorraine

peacemaker and stayed five years under the duke's protection, until his father died, on July 22, 1461.[23]

During those years, Louis was the godfather when cousin Charles had a daughter[24] by his second wife, Isabella. When Louis' father-in-law reminded the runaway dauphin that he still had a wife (now sixteen) in the Dauphiné, he sent for her. Two years later they had a son, who died at four months. Louis decided God was punishing him for his extramarital affairs and swore to be faithful. Two years later a daughter[25] was born. His cousin Charles had always been faithful—probably because his father had thirty "known" mistresses and twenty-five bastards. Louis studied at the University of Louvain,[26] traveled throughout Flanders with his uncle, and hunted with his cousin Charles.

When Louis finally became king of France, at thirty-eight, from then on the cousins competed in a land-grab. At his coronation he swore to regain his lands—even those "sold, alienated, or pledged by his predecessors." This was bad news for cousin Charles. That's how the dukes of Burgundy had acquired their land. As king, Louis XI began to spin a web of international intrigue and became known as "the Universal Spider King."

First he took back all the towns along the Somme River in northern France that his uncle, Philip the Good, had claimed.[27] Next he broke up the insurrection of powerful nobles, which included his brother, brother-in-law, and Philip the Good.[28]

Charles the Rash and the Spider King knew what they wanted. The Spider King wanted to forge a nation, if possible, without war. Charles the Rash wanted to be Charlemagne, but first he needed the provinces of Champagne and Lorraine, to unite his territories into an independent state where he could be king—with Nancy as the capital.

The Spider King was a most unpretentious king. Except for special occasions, he dressed in a coarse gray robe, and wore a broad-rimmed hat covered with medals of the Virgin and saints. When dignified ambassadors from Lorenzo de' Medici's lavish court in Florence arrived in Tours, they wrote home that they had been received in a miserable hut, had to lodge like dogs, and eat in a tavern. They said the Spider King's dogs with their gold and jeweled collars were better dressed than the king. When the Count of Maine visited, the Spider King camped in the woods and gave the count his castle. Rash, like all the dukes of Burgundy, loved pomp and spectacle, elegant clothes, and jewels, but Louis knew from history that all that glitters does not guarantee lasting power. Spider chose his staff[29] mostly from the middle class and took advice from councilors and ambassadors throughout Europe.[30] One of his best informers was his barber-surgeon. Charles the Rash wouldn't listen to anyone.

When Charles' father, Philip the Good, became senile, Charles gathered an army to take Paris. The first battle, at Montlhéury near Paris, was a draw, although Louis reached Paris first—keeping it for France. When Rash, with armies of nearly all the nobles, laid siege to the city, Spider asked his cousin for a meeting. That way, instead of being hunted down and killed, he had an escort. In a treaty signed at Vincennes, a suburb of Paris, the Spider politely returned to Rash all the towns on the Somme River. He had to give Normandy to his own brother and all the fiefs in central France to his brother-in-law.[31] He also promised Rash his ten-year-old sister, Catherine, in marriage, with the province of Champagne as her dowry. The princes had won the first round.

Philip the Good died at seventy-one in 1467,[32] and his son Charles, no longer a rebellious teenager, wept. The following year, Charles married English king Edward IV's vivacious sister, Margaret of York, in Damme. During the festivities that followed in Bruge, as the Burgundians celebrated the wedding and truce with England, the Spider marched into Brittany and forced Rash's ally, the Duke of Brittany, to sign a peace agreement. Then Spider invaded Normandy. He told Rash he had to rescue his brother.[33] Besides taking Normandy, he also reclaimed two towns along the Somme.[34] Charles retaliated by sacking Dinant and Liège.

While Rash slaughtered innocent people, the Universal Spider pardoned his worst enemies, who then deserted Rash and became the Spider's most loyal servants. He ruined Rash's Fair at Geneva by establishing a Silk Fair at Lyon, and befriended the international banker, Lorenzo de' Medici, who cut off Rash's credit. To ensure peace, Louis hired 12,000 soldiers.

A year after his uncle, Philip the Good, died, Spider went to Péronne, northeast of Paris, to negotiate a treaty with Rash, now the new Duke of Burgundy. When the Spider arrived, Charles had just learned that Liège, a town he had recently subdued,[35] was rebelling. Rash decided the Spider was responsible, and now here he was at his doorstep. The Spider found himself in solitary confinement for three nights, sure that any minute he would be killed. He signed a treaty and every paper thrust at him. He gave away everything he had accomplished in eight years. He also had to accompany Charles to Liège and watch his merciless revenge on people who had dared defy him.

The Spider escaped by claiming he had to have the treaty ratified by Parliament in Paris. Off he scampered to safety, like Brer Fox. Then he left for Mont Saint Michel to thank the Virgin and Saint Michael for delivering him from the enemy. A year later, after the treaty expired, he accused Charles of treason.

From Liège, vengeful Rash destroyed Nestle in northern France, but failed to take Beauvais, where he was defeated by women whose terrified husbands were ready to surrender.[36] The heroine, twenty-six-year-old Jeanne Laisné, known as Jeanne de la Hachette, killed with an axe (hachette) a Burgundian trying to plant the Burgundian standard. She and the heroic women were responsible for the victory.

Charles the Rash, once a good-natured youth, seemed possessed by a demon. He quarreled with his allies,[37] who deserted him for twenty-five-year-old Duke René II of Lorraine (backed by the Spider). "He had a talent for alienating absolutely everyone." He renewed an alliance with England (1474) which his father had ended forty years before, as Joan of Arc had asked, then he persuaded his brother-in-law, King Edward IV of England, to invade France. But when Charles arrived at Picquigny near Dieppe to greet him, the Spider had gotten there first. He fed the starving English army with all the venison pies they could eat and enough wine to make them friends. Then he bribed the English king to go home. An Englishman wrote, "Blessed God for thousands of French wives whose soldier-husbands whom King Louis year after year sent home safe and whole. Another season of bloodless campaigning." When the seven-year truce with England was announced at Notre Dame de la Victoire near Senlis, Spider donated a silver lamp for the Virgin's altar, in "thanks to the glorious and blessed mother of God who has turned the king of England and his army out of France." He signed a nine-year truce with Rash and decreed that throughout France the Angelus be prayed three times a day, at the ringing of the Angelus bell, "for the gift of peace."[38]

Outwitted by the Spider and betrayed by his brother-in-law, Rash broke the truce and in a rage, seized Nancy, the Duke of Lorraine's capital. Still on a rampage, although he had completed his conquest of Lorraine, he massacred the Swiss garrison at Granson near Lake Neuchâtel. Swiss soldiers, paid by the Spider, surprised the Burgundians and forced them to flee, leaving everything behind, including 900 tents and Rash's jeweled hat. In revenge, Rash marched to punish the city of Bern, leader of the Swiss revolt. But first he needed the fortified town of Morat[39] that blocked the way. This time, he lost one third of his army. When the Spider refused Rash's request for a meeting,[40] Rash rounded up more troops to put down a rebellion in Nancy instigated by Duke René II of Lorraine. When Rash's army stormed the city, Duke René, for the first time, ordered the Cross of Lorraine, with its double bar, embroidered on all standards and pennants. The Swiss Confederacy under René won the battle. Rash, now totally out of control, ordered another senseless attack on Nancy.

Ignoring advice against campaigning in winter, just before Christmas, with 5,000 troops against nearly 20,000, he sent an advance guard into a narrow pass, and when the Swiss attacked, he was trapped. Three days later, forty-four-year-old Rash's naked body was found on a frozen lake, mutilated by wolves. The duke, once head of the most magnificent court in Western Europe, "remained dead on a field of battle stretched out like the poorest man in the world, a miserable human fragment." Spider went to thank Our Lady of France at Le Puy en Velay.[41]

JOAN OF ARC (*JEANNE D'ARC*)
Domrémy to Orléans

From Nancy in the province of Lorraine, we took a train to Neufchâteau (three miles), then a taxi (one mile) to Domrémy, where Joan of Arc was born. Outside the town, the small two-story stone house, like a shrine, stands at the edge of open space above panoramic scenery. Behind the house, a grassy hill climbs to a dark forest. A church, a stone's throw away, completes the setting for angels and saints.

Mark Twain in America was fifteen when he learned about her. Years later, he wrote *Personal Memoirs of Joan of Arc,* and cried as he read the manuscript to his family. He modeled Joan after his beloved daughter Susy, who died of meningitis at twenty-four, the same year the book was published (1896). Although Twain wrote the book under a pseudonym, he probably didn't fool anyone, especially when his pen galloped off in typical glee as it did when describing La Hire; "that military hurricane, godless swashbuckler, lurid conflagration of blasphemy, that Vesuvius of profanity forever in eruption," and so on.

Twain's gusto sounds Rabelais-ish, but Winston Churchill's lyrical admiration for Joan echoes a litany by Saint Bernard: "Her unconquerable courage, infinite compassion, virtue of the simple, wisdom of the just," and more. Crusty George Bernard Shaw, stirred by the heroic girl, saw her as brave, frank, sensible, and highly intelligent. No matter how Joan of Arc is portrayed, the documented story of her life and death is fact.

The peasant girl was born in 1412, while Fra Angelico was painting angels in Florence, and Burgundians and Orléanists were playing tug-of-war for possession of France. Joan's birthplace, Domrémy, was loyal to French king Charles VI, while the village of Maxey across the river sided with the Burgundians[42] and the English.

Joan was thirteen when the Archangel Michael,[43] surrounded by light, appeared in her father's garden. Three times he called her name, then announced, "I am Michael, Protector of France." He told her about the great *pitié* (misery) in the kingdom, and said, "It is you whom God has chosen to deliver Orléans and have the dauphin crowned at Rheims. He has chosen you to drive the English from France." She asked, "How is that possible?" She couldn't even ride a horse. He replied, "Take everything willingly. From heaven I will send you two councilors who will advise you." One saint was Catherine of Alexandria,[44] a fourth-century virgin-martyr who had converted pagan philosophers and 200 soldiers assigned to guard her. The other was Saint Margaret of Antioch,[45] another young Christian martyr whose pagan father tortured and imprisoned her. Thousands who witnessed her ordeal were converted.

During the next five years, the saints talked to Joan as often as three times a week. Enveloped in light, wearing dazzling gold crowns, they addressed her in French. Joan said, "They spoke most excellently and beautifully."

At sixteen, her Voices told her to go from Lorraine to France to raise the siege of Orléans, now in its fourth month. "Go, young girl of God (*fille de Dieu*) to Vaucouleurs. Robert de Baudricourt will bring you to the king."

Unaware of Joan's command, her parents permitted her to visit a cousin twelve miles away, near the fortified town of Vaucouleurs, where Robert de Baudricourt was Commander. Joan's cousin by marriage, Durand Lassois, without hesitation brought the teenage girl to the gruff, tough warrior. When Baudricourt heard her story, he roared with laughter and told Lassois to box her ears and take her home.

In January, Joan returned to her cousin's home (in Burey le Petite) and again was taken to the formidable Baudricourt, who still laughed. Two young squires,[46] however, believed her. They taught her to ride and outfitted her in suitable clothes. The enthusiastic people of Vaucouleurs donated a horse. They knew Merlin's prophecy that France would be ruined by a woman[47] and saved by a maid from Lorraine. Joan stayed with friends in Vaucouleurs three days, waiting for Baudricourt to make up his mind. Finally, in exasperation, she burst into the Great Hall of the fortress. "In God's name you have done ill in delaying me. This very day near Orléans there has been a great disaster. If you don't send me to Orléans, Orléans will suffer." Baudricourt still thought she was crazy. He knew the situation was desperate, but he hadn't heard of any battle. Later he learned of the disastrous French defeat at Vouvray, which had occurred on the day Joan had told him. Dumbfounded, he authorized her departure for Chinon and ordered a sword made for her small hand. On March 23, 1429, at 11:00 P.M., seventeen-year-old Joan of Arc, dressed as a page, with her friends, the two young squires and their attendants, galloped through the gate (still there) of the walled fort—to change the fate of France.

For safety, the little group traveled through enemy territory at night, double file, their horses' hooves muffled in cloth. To evade sentries, they forded icy rivers and slept during the day on the ground or in stables, stopping only at Auxerre and Gien to hear Mass, then continued in the cold rain and mud to the shrine of Saint Catherine de Fierbois.[48] The 350–mile journey took eleven days. At Fierbois, Joan stayed overnight at the almonry and spent most of the time praying in the chapel. From here, she dictated a letter to the dauphin at Chinon, asking permission to relate information which she alone possessed.

In Chinon, after the dauphin had kept them waiting three days at a local inn,[49] Joan, with Jean de Metz and Bertrand de Poulengy (the two squires who had befriended her), mounted the winding path to the castle on a ridge above the Vienne River. There they were ushered into a huge, torchlit medieval hall, crowded with noisy courtiers and ladies-in-waiting with towering headdresses and trailing gowns. The dauphin tried to hide, but Joan went straight to the spineless twenty-six-year-old and respectfully addressed him. "Most noble Dauphin, I have come from God to help you and your kingdom. I am God's messenger sent to tell you that you are the king's son and true heir of France."[50] According to reports they talked for two hours. Later Joan's confessor, Frère Jean Pasquerel,[51] said that the king told those present no one but God knew or could know what Joan had told him.[52] Jealous favorites at court advised the dauphin to have Joan questioned by church officials at Poitiers. After three weeks' interrogation, Joan

Lorraine

had had it. To one doubting Thomas who demanded a sign, she replied, "I have not come to Poitiers to show signs and do miracles. Send me to Orléans, and you shall have a sign. Give me men-at-arms, a few or many—and let me go." Their verdict that she was a child of God "made a dead France suddenly come to life like a corpse sitting up in a coffin" (Mark Twain).

Still counseled by her Voices, Joan and the saints had another surprise for skeptics. When the dauphin ordered a new sword made for her, Joan requested, instead, a sword buried behind the altar at Saint Catherine de Fierbois. She said it would be identified by five crosses cut into the blade. Buried in a niche behind the altar, they found the rusty sword in a forgotten chest.[53] Rust fell off like magic, revealing the five crosses.

The dauphin did not exactly say "I can't believe this is happening," but he did proclaim Joan "Commander of the French Army." He also appointed his most honest, trustworthy officer, Jean d'Aulon, head of her household, and a fourteen-year-old page, Louis de Coutes, her secretary. Another faithful convert was the king's cousin, duc d'Alençon, who gave her a huge war-horse.

From Chinon Joan rode to Tours, to be outfitted for a suit of armor. Leading 1,000 raucous French troops, the Maid on her armored horse headed for Blois, where the main army was being assembled and where her brothers Pierre and Jean, with two neighbors[54] and her chaplain, joined her. Duc d'Alençon, who became her best friend, supervised troops and supplies, and the famous Général La Hire, the French boys' hero, came to assist with the thousands gathering there. La Hire, a huge, burly, professional warrior, was one of the first to believe in Joan. Their relationship, based on respect, was *simpatico* from the beginning. Both were plainspoken, commonsense people. Joan told him the camp followers had to go—no loose women, no drunkenness, and no swearing. No swearing? Poor La Hire. He said he wouldn't be able to talk! Swearing was his native language. They compromised. It would be all right to swear by his baton, the symbol of his generalship, but not "by God." She also told him every soldier fighting for France must be free from sin. They all had to go to confession.[55] La Hire said he would rather go through fire. The third day in Blois, before leaving for Orléans, Joan said, "Just make up something"—and he did—the famous La Hire prayer: "Fair Sir God, I pray you to do by La Hire as he would do by you if you were La Hire and he were God."

Back to Europe with the BUSY BODY

With that, he put on his helmet and marched out of the tent practically purring—so pleased he was with himself. Inside the tent, Joan laughed so hard she cried.

The next day, April 27, 1429, the convoy left Blois for Orléans, with *La Pucelle* (the young maid) leading more than 4,000 armored soldiers carrying shields, swords, and lances. Waving above their heads was her white war banner[56] depicting the King of Heaven. Priests with banners of the Annunciation sang the Latin hymn *Veni Creator Sanctus* ("Come Creator Spirit.") The army marched two days through the marshy Solonge region, followed by 425 pack animals and sixty carts loaded with powder, cannons, food, and battle equipment. On April 29, Joan of Arc arrived on the bank of the Loire opposite Orléans. Opposite Orléans? Why had she been led across the river from Orléans instead of directly into the city, as she had ordered? "The Bastard" Dunois,[57] the dauphin's relative, head of the Orléans defense, welcomed her and admitted he had changed the route. Her plan would have brought the convoy directly past English fortifications. He intended to float food and equipment safely across the river to avoid enemy fire. She asked, "Has the army any value on this side of the river?" "No." "And yet knowing this, you disobeyed my orders. Please explain how the army is supposed to get to the side where the enemy is?" Twenty-six-year-old Dunois, a brave, professional soldier, sincerely believed God had chosen the Maid to rescue France. He had acted with the best of intentions, but soon learned to obey her orders, no matter what. There was a slight snag in his sensible plan. The river was too low for the barges to budge, and the wind was from the wrong direction. Joan was not happy. "I bring you better help than any knight or city—the help of the King of Heaven." At that moment, the wind changed, the water rose, and the sailboats floated. Dunois, as others before him, was left speechless by the dramatic timing of the miracle.

Since more supplies were needed, another convoy had to be escorted to Orléans. La Hire was sent back to Blois with the army and ordered to return on the other side of the river, according to Joan's original plan. Joan's chaplain, carrying a banner of the crucifixion, accompanied him. After dark, with Dunois, Joan's two brothers, and a few others, the "Maid of Orléans," her banner streaming, entered the besieged city of Orléans ringed with nine enemy fortresses.[58]

Mobbed by the frenzied crowd, the little group rode through torchlit cobblestone streets to the Cathedral of the Holy Cross (*Saint Croix*),[59] to

Lorraine

thank God for their safe arrival—then they went to the home of Jacques Boucher, where Joan would stay with his wife and teenage daughter, Catherine. (Boucher was treasurer for duc Charles d'Orléans, a prisoner of the English.) On Sunday, Joan's Voices told her to send Dunois to bring the army in Blois to Orléans—fast. Enemies were trying to disperse the troops. Her Voices also warned that the English would attack when the convoy (without Joan) reached Orléans. As the army neared Orléans, Joan met them outside the Burgundian gate. Riding at the head of her army, she marched them defiantly past enemy-occupied Fort Saint Loup. The stunned English could only stare. The "witch" had appeared from nowhere. Trying to avoid bloodshed, twice she sent messages[60] to the English, demanding surrender. Their commander, William Glasdale, called her a whore, and told her to go home and tend her cows.

Now that Joan was actually in Orléans, the people went wild. Without orders, a few hundred charged out through the Burgundian Gate, to storm Fort Saint Loup, built around an abandoned church. Warned by her Voices, with Jean de Metz and La Hire, she rushed to join them. Encouraged by her presence, the French army won their first victory in seven months—on the Vigil of the Feast of the Ascension. However, jealous captains were making their own plans. They told her they intended to attack an observation post the next day. Instead, their objective was Les Augustines, a strongly fortified monastery across the river, where French prisoners were being held. Discovering their deception, she joined them. As usual, the generals were amazed at her military ability, especially the placing of artillery. Although during the fierce fighting she had stepped on a spiked iron ball, her presence inspired the soldiers to win an all-day battle. The English abandoned the fort and retreated to the heavily fortified Bastille des Tourelles.

When Joan returned to the Boucher home to have her wound treated, the captains informed her they had decided to postpone an attack on Les Tourelles. She told them to get up early. "You have your council and I mine—like it or not, the soldiers will go out, and they will win as they have won before." She told her confessor: "Keep close to me at all times for tomorrow blood will spurt from my body above the breast."

During the night, Orléaners had ferried oats for the horses and bread and wine for soldiers stationed across the river at the ruined Les Augustine fort near Les Tourelles. Early next morning, she and La Hire arrived at the Burgundian Gate with an army ready to cross the river. When the guard refused to let them pass, he was lucky he wasn't crushed, as the Orléaners

Maid of Orléans

rushed past. Boats ferried them across the Loire. At 7:00 A.M. the assault on the massive fort began, with "The Gentle Bastard," Dunois, in command. Soldiers with axes and pikes mounted scaling ladders amid smoke, fire, the noise of cannons, and screams of dying men. While climbing a wall, an iron-tipped arrow pierced the muscle above her collarbone and shot through her shoulder—as her Voices had predicted. Although she had expected to be wounded, she was not prepared for the pain. She was taken off the field in tears by her confessor and John de Gamoche, a knight who had once sworn he would rather give up his banner than serve under a woman. Her brothers and Squire d'Aulon helped remove the armor and extract the iron bolt. Joan, herself, pulled the shaft out. To stop the bleeding they dressed the wound with olive oil, pig's grease, and bread soaked in wine diluted with water. The attack continued, but as Dunois later wrote, "There was hardly any hope of victory." The troops had been fighting for thirteen hours, and he was about to call a halt "when the Maid (back on her horse) came up to me and asked me to wait a little longer. She said, 'Let the soldiers rest, eat and drink. There will be a sign. When you see my standard fluttering out pointing toward the fort, resume your arms again, and the fortress shall be yours.'" Then she went off to a vineyard to pray.

The buglers, however, never received the message. When she heard them sound retreat, she ordered five shots fired in quick succession, the signal for La Hire's soldiers on the Orléans side of the river to make a counterattack on a broken bridge they had patched up as a catwalk from old guttering and planks. Duc d'Alençon later called this feat God's greatest miracle.

Joan mounted her horse and rode to the spot where she had been wounded. She ordered Paladin, her standard-bearer, to let her standard blow free. When the fringes touched the fortress, Dunois, in command, should sound the assault. When the army saw her banner, they surged toward the fort, now being assaulted from two directions. The English and Burgundians fled from the fort onto a drawbridge joining Les Tourelles to the bank. But the French had soaked an old boat in tar, placed it under the drawbridge, and set it on fire. The charred timber of the drawbridge collapsed, drowning the enemy in their heavy armor—and Joan burst into tears.

The last fort had fallen. The following day, the English in the remaining six forts marched away. In five days, the seventeen-year-old Maid of Orléans had raised an eight-month siege. Today, a simple cross on the quai wall at the end of Pont George V,[61] across the river from Orléans at Olivet, marks the site of Les Tourelles.

ORLÉANS
Joan of Arc's Mother, Wichita, Kansas, and an American Indian

The tourist office in Orléans, down a few steps from the train station, is one of the most helpful in France. Tiered steps and splashing fountains nearby provide a pleasant place to regroup from tired feet, indecision, or time out to people-watch. The town was filled with teenagers and college students sauntering in the sunshine. Orléans has been a university town since the sixth century. Our first stop was the cathedral. [62]

CATHEDRAL OF SAINT CROIX (HOLY CROSS)

Some places belong to dead people. The cathedral in Orléans is one. The church seemed packed with Joan of Arc's armored soldiers, who came first to pray for victory and, five days later, returned to give thanks. In the left aisle, a plaque commemorates the dauphin's cousin, who came from Scotland with his warriors to aid the French and was killed during the "Battle of the Herrings," the French defeat at Vouvray that Joan knew about. The plaque reads: "William Douglas for the defense of France versus the English."

The tomb in Joan of Arc's chapel shows Cardinal Touchet, a bishop of Orléans, kneeling before the Saint. His persistent efforts resulted in her canonization, in 1920—after 500 years of Vatican paperwork. The chapel's beautiful stained glass windows depict her life, and her statue is dedicated "To the glory of God and to the memory of one million of the British Empire who fell in the Great War 1914–1918 and who, for the greater part, rest in France."

THE BISHOP'S PALACE

Near the cathedral, the former bishop's palace is now the public library. Napoléon's second wife, Marie Louise of Austria, stayed here on her return to Austria after Napoléon's defeat at Waterloo. No way was she going to stick around. She pouted and complained for four days. Her hairdresser had deserted her, and her bedraggled hair itched. There was no warm water for her bath, and the jewels and gold plates she was taking out of the country had been confiscated.

Accompanying Queen Marie Louise was her blond three-year-old son. Napoléon had written to discarded Josephine, "He has my chest, my mouth, and my eyes. I hope he will fulfill his destiny." Three weeks later Napoléon was exiled, and his son was en route to Austria. When the little boy left Orléans, a lady stopped to kiss his hand, but he burst into tears: *"Je veux aller voir mon papa."* ("I want to see my father.")

Lorraine

HÔTEL DE VILLE

Also near the cathedral is a beautiful pink-brick mansion, with a magnificent wrought iron fence, once the home of Jacques Groslot, a wealthy merchant. Today it is the Hôtel de Ville, but posters advertise it as "Maison Jacques Groslot." One visitor in 1560 was Catherine de' Medici's first son, sickly François II, with his young bride, fifteen-year-old Mary Stuart, future Queen of Scots. Ostensibly the king came to Orléans to call a meeting of the Estates-Général. Actually, he meant to set a trap for two Huguenots: the king of Navarre, who outwitted him, and the Prince of Condé, the military leader. Before the Prince of Condé could be executed, François II died here in Groslot's home.

In front of the Hôtel de Ville, a statue of Joan of Arc is encircled with flowers. The sculptor, the Citizen King's daughter Princess Marie Louise d'Orléans,[63] made this bronze copy from her original marble statue, now in Versailles. Bullet holes are left from World War II.

In the Old Town on rue des Africains, behind the walls of a vinegar factory, is a deserted, dusty, half-timbered old house, which once belonged to Joan of Arc's widowed mother, who lived here eighteen years with her sons, Jean and Pierre.[64] Pierre was with Joan when the king sabotaged her attempt to take Paris,[65] and was captured with her at Compiègne. Her brothers were with their parents at the dauphin's coronation at Rheims, and suffered through their sister's four-month trial each day, when soldiers dragged her in chains from her cell. They also saw her burned. Their father died of a broken heart soon after.

The king's only acknowledgement of the family was a title and crest—no concern for their welfare. They existed on the charity of the Orléans city fathers, who donated this house. From here, year after year, they sent petitions to Rome for a review of the trial hearings. Two years before her death, Joan's mother learned that an inquiry set up by the good Borgia pope, Calixtus II, had reversed the verdict of heresy. The church where she worshiped, Église Saint Pierre le Puellier, is a short walk up the street.[66]

PARCS

The message of Orléans is *rejoice*—and Orléans does that—with flowers. The city, which has been beaten and battered for centuries, still celebrates the beauty of life and man's indomitable spirit with fantastic flower gardens, or parcs—five, in fact. In Parc Pasteur, *le petit train* is a gift from the school children in Wichita, Kansas; a token of friendship which began in 1944, when the 137th Infantry of Kansas liberated Orléans from the Nazis. In return, the people of Orléans sent a statue of Joan of Arc, a replica of the pensive Joan in front of the Hôtel de Ville. Wichita sent a smaller version of their Indian statue, "Keeper of the Plain." Like the original, it was made of rusted iron. When the statue arrived in Orléans, the people were chagrined to find it rusted! They removed the rust and treated the iron, lest it be thought they had neglected it. Today, the "Keeper of the Plain" Indian stands in all his glory on a floral island in the largest park in Orléans, Parc Floral, across the Loire near the University at La Source.[67] The Indian's top is steel blue, but his bottom is painted yellow—maybe to represent deerskin leggings?

22

Burgundy

Dijon: A Suburb and a "Resistance" Priest (who should have been a bartender) and an Owl That Brings Good Luck

DIJON

There she was, waiting for me at the train station; my wonderful friend, as if we had seen each other the day before. Actually we had met in Dallas a year ago, and now, on my tour through France, she welcomed me to her city—she and her beautiful mother. Their home in Talant, a suburb of Dijon, overlooks Lake Kir, named for Felix Kir, a priest and mayor of Dijon for twenty-two years (1946–1968). As mayor, to promote the sale of a local grape, aligote, he mixed the white wine with crême de cassis, a blackcurrant liqueur, and called it "kir." The famous priest-mayor was the first in France to call for resistance against the Nazis. From the pulpit of his parish church Felix Kir, the Curé de Bèze, on June 16, 1940 exhorted his parishioners to fight against evil. Two days later, Général de Gaulle broadcast from London his stirring call for resistance. The priest spent two months in a Gestapo cell for helping French prisoners escape.

The story of Talant and its old castle is interwoven with that of Dijon. In the thirteenth century, Eudes III, Duke of Burgundy,[1] built a castle-fortress in Talant with a sweeping view of the countryside. Later the castle was surrounded by walls and thirty-three towers. The duke built a town there and welcomed the wretched serfs trying to escape tyranny. He abolished taxes and military service and gave the people the right to govern themselves. In the fourteenth century, English king Edward III, the "Black Prince" who wore black armor, defeated French king John II at Poitiers. While the king was being held prisoner, his wife was stranded in the castle at Talant. Besides a ransom of $83 million, King Edward III received nearly half of the French king's territory. King John II died four years later and left the free duchy of Burgundy to his youngest son, fourteen-year-old Philip the Bold, who had fought at Poitiers with him. The future dukes of Burgundy became more powerful than the kings of France.

The castle at Talant remained intact throughout the centuries, until 1598. It might still be there if French king Henri IV, a former Huguenot, had not come to Dijon to stock up on wine. When Catholics in the castle[2] fired on him, the fort was ordered demolished.

The thirteenth-century Church of Saint Seine l'Abbaye is still there on the high bluff. It was built in the Old Market Town of Saint Seine over a sixth-century chapel, named for a holy man who founded the chapel near the source of the Seine River, eighteen miles from Dijon. The medieval church has flying buttresses and sculpture with a Burgundian flare—for instance, a typical Burgundian snail crawling in a sculptured vine. Inside, the church is filled with art treasures, such as lace-like carvings on a white marble altar and a delicate wrought iron altarscreen—as soothing to one's nerves as blowing soap bubbles in the sun.

From Talant, we drove into the medieval quarter of Dijon to visit the churches of Saint Bénigne (the Good) and the Church of Notre Dame. Saint Bénigne's Cathedral is built over the second-century tomb of the missionary-martyr[3] who brought Christianity to Burgundy. The present church (1001–1020) is built over a sixth-century Benedictine Abbey. The cathedral, dedicated to Our Lady of Good Hope, has fifty-six bells in the carillon, that ring out the buoyant spirit of the lovely city that was spared during two world wars.

The Flemish façade of the Church of Notre Dame is the only one of its kind in France. Three rows of gargoyles jut out, some at eye level, hoping to scare you. On a flying buttress of the cathedral, a stone owl, said to bring good luck, waits to be patted. In the left tower, a mechanical clock clangs out the time as the woodcutter Jacquemart smokes his pipe. The clock was carted from Flanders in 1382. Originally, there was only one figure, the Jacquemart, who represents the common people. In the seventeenth century, he was given a wife, and later, two children. Inside the church, on the right, the statue of Our Lady is the oldest wooden statue of the Virgin in

Burgundy

Church of St. Bénigne

France. She is the town's patron saint and has been worshiped here for nine centuries.

Nearby is the medieval palace of the dukes of Burgundy, where we climbed 350 steps to the top of a tower for a view of the city, with its colorful glazed tile rooftops in diamond-shaped patterns. We were up so high we looked down on the steep spires of Saint Bénigne's Cathedral.

Then it was lunchtime outdoors in place François Rude, named for the famous sculptor from Dijon. The artistically arranged luncheon plates knew how beautiful they were. Like a teenage girl dressed for a dance, mine seemed to say "Quick! Take my picture before I get messed up," which I did, as waiters either smiled or raised eyebrows. The veal, carrots, asparagus, and turnips could have been a Chardin painting. The chef's secret for the turnips was port, truffle juice, nutmeg, and chives. The salad was seasoned with walnut oil and sherry vinegar. When I asked the waiter the secret of Dijon mustard, he whispered, "sour wine."

The whole place François Rude calls for a camera. In front of a picturesque timber-framed house, a semi-nude male statue with his hands on his hips stands atop a fountain in a sculptured vat filled with sculptured grapes. He represents a Dijon winegrower crushing grapes with his bare feet. Although it is the work of French Jules Gérard, "the Bareuzar" looks more Italian than French. He seems lonely—as if he had recently arrived from Florence, and misses his friends in the Piazza Vecchio. Maybe the music and happy sounds from the gaily painted carousel will cheer him. He really needs a girl friend.

ALEXANDRE GUSTAV EIFFEL (1832–1923)
"Atsa My Boy"

Another friend in Dijon, Mme. Madeleine Laby, is a tour guide and author of two superb books about Burgundy. She showed me Gustav Eiffel's birthplace near the Port du Canal. The house is gone, and the port is now used for water sports and pleasure boats. A metal monument shaped like a pair of wings is dedicated to Eiffel and marks the former site of his parents' home.

His father fought under Bonaparte in three Italian campaigns. In 1824, he left the army and married a remarkable businesswoman who made a fortune. At the canal port of Dijon, she was the only one in charge of the warehouse for the Epinac coal mines. After eleven years of unloading ships, loading carts, building boats, and working from dawn until dusk, she sold the business and invested in a brewery.

Her brother, who owned mines that produced copper sulfate, named Eiffel his successor to manage one of the factories. Eiffel had been taking courses in mechanical and industrial engineering, but then he switched to chemistry—and failed all the courses. His sister's husband gave him a job in a blast furnace foundry where he studied metallurgy. Then he left for Napoléon III's Paris to become a railroad construction engineer—the beginning of his fantastic career.

His first assignment was to study the foundation in rivers. Next, he headed the research department. From there, he built bridges all over France. One was the Bordeaux bridge (1858–1860), with connections for two separate rail networks. In 1866 he started his own company, with a contract to build thirty-three locomotives in Egypt. His company built bridges and railroad stations throughout the world,[4] with offices in Saigon, Shanghai, and Lisbon. After the Franco-Prussian War, Eiffel worked with sculptor-architect Frédéric Bartholdi from Colmar, to design the infrastructure for the Statue of Liberty—a metal pier that could resist wind stress.

In 1889, out of 700 applicants, his company's design was chosen as a centerpiece for the Universal Exposition, celebrating the centennial of the

Burgundy

French Revolution. He proposed to build a tower made entirely of steel. Two of his engineers, Monsieur Nougruer and Maurice Koechlin, designed the tower. Their names are on the arch between the base and the first platform. Koechlin made 1,700 drawings for the skeleton alone. Another engineer, Pluot, made 3,629 drawings of 18,038 different parts. Names of the 199 permanent workers are also engraved on the site with their job descriptions: head barrow man, head carpenter, painting supervisor, masonry supervisor, and so on. Carpenters were the highest paid.

During a strike for higher wages as the tower grew, Eiffel gave a bonus to workers who continued to labor through long hours and all kinds of weather. Those still unsatisfied and not present the next day would be replaced. Instead of firing the ringleaders of the strike, Eiffel restricted

Eiffel Tower

them to putting up arches on the first level and forbid them to go above that level. The humiliation was as bad as being put in the front row in school with slower children. The ringleaders left when other workers laughed at them and called them "The Indispensables." The giant erector set was completed on time and under budget. On March 30, 1889, Monsieur Eiffel and a few dignitaries took a cable car to the third level, then climbed to the top to unfurl the French *tricolore*.

Gustav Eiffel's success story began when he failed chemistry and his uncle fired him because the Eiffels were Bonapartists. Uncle Mollerat believed all kings were rogues. The next chapter in the success story was the job offer by his brother-in-law, the metallurgist. And always behind the scenes was his pushy, ambitious mother. She even arranged his marriage to a girl with a generous dowry and "good disposition"—which meant she would raise children and not complain about an absentee husband. Even after the Exposition, when the tower should have been dismantled, Captain Ferrie, the father of military telegraphy, thought the tower would be an ideal base for experiments in adapting wireless telegraphy for the military. Eiffel agreed to have a radio and antennae placed on top, and by 1904, army posts 250 miles away could be contacted. Eiffel's experiments in meteorology and wind resistance led to research on airplane wings, propellers, and methods of releasing bombs. He died at eighty-eight, without revealing his secret for MENTAL STRESS management.

DUKES OF BURGUNDY
Names Don't Mean a Thing

From Eiffel's old neighborhood we drove to the Ducal Palace. In the Fine Arts Gallery (Musée Magnin), Mme. Laby knew every detail of every painting. My favorite was Delaroche's Frau Filippo Lippi on his knees, wooing (and winning) the beautiful nun, Lucrezia Butti, who ran away with him and became the model for his Madonnas. (Her sister and the three remaining nuns also came along.)[5]

The Ducal Palace was built by Philip the Bold,[6] the first Duke of Burgundy. Later he acquired, by marriage,[7] the cities of Bruges, Antwerp, and Brussels in Flanders. With two central governments, one for Flanders at Lille and one for Burgundy, he combined the accounting offices at Dijon and made it his capital. Both he and his grandson Philip the Good, who was born in Dijon, brought artists from Flanders and made Dijon a cultural center. They also started the pomp and ceremony usually associated

Burgundy

with Louis XIV. All four Valois dukes of Burgundy were brave, haughty, and had no qualms about raiding the French treasury. When they visited Dijon, trumpets announced their arrival and didn't cease all night long. Trumpets and bugles in the choirs were so loud, "You could not hear the thunder of God." Banquets served on gold and silver plates required twenty-five cooks and six huge fireplaces. Instead of a bachelor-party girl popping out of a cake—surprise! Twenty-eight musicians. The duke's huge stone banquet hall now houses the tombs of Philip the Bold and his son, John the Fearless.

Names don't mean a thing. The second Duke of Burgundy, John the Fearless, surrounded himself with bodyguards, and was so anxious to oust his cousin, King Charles VI, that he murdered the king's brother, Louis, duc d'Orléans. He told everyone it was for their own good. He even went to the funeral. The murder started a civil war, and Paris wasn't safe for twelve years. In the end, he was murdered by friends of the duc d'Orléans.[8] His tomb shows him lying next to his wife[9] on his back, with his head on a stone pillow, dressed in regal finery, his hands glued together piously praying. His tomb is an exact replica of his father's, Philip the Bold, which is also there. Angels with huge wings hover near their heads, with lions on guard at their feet. Surrounding the base of the tombs are forty mourning figures in flowing robes; the clergy in cowls, and laymen in hoods. The sculptured body language is wonderful. Some are desolate, some sedate, others just plain tired.

Outside in the courtyard, a lovely Renaissance staircase leads to an adjacent four-story tower, where Good King René of Anjou[10] was held prisoner twice by Philip the Good. The duke had extended his rule into the Netherlands and Luxembourg, but he also wanted Lorraine. He was not happy when René's title, "Duke of Lorraine," was confirmed.[11] Philip the Good was the one who had "at least thirty mistresses." The statue in front of the tower is by Flemish Klass Sluter, the sculptor who designed the dukes' tombs. We said goodbye to the dukes of Burgundy and bought a lot of Dijon's famous *pain d'epice*, gingerbread without ginger. A crusader brought the recipe back from Asia Minor.

BEAUNE
Balloons, Smallpox, and "The Wine of Your Life"

In Beaune, we met a couple from Maine who were celebrating the wife's graduation from college—after nine years and four children. The husband

Back to Europe with the BUSY BODY

admitted he was probably the number one Ugly American in Europe, but that morning in a traffic jam, he knew he had competition.

In the evening, another celebration was going on at an outdoor café near our hotel. A group of English people were celebrating a wedding anniversary, but the anniversary husband got tipsy and his wife left in a huff to sleep alone.

Craig, the business manager for Buddy Bombard's balloon flights, welcomed us in his informal office (strewn with peanut shucks) in the guardhouse of an old château. His life is never boring. One night at 11:00 o'clock a neighbor called to tell him Craig's dog had chewed off his cow's tail. Craig said his job was to worry about things like cows and washing machines working, while Buddy Bombard was concerned about balloons floating over just the right pond near someone's château.

The day we were to float through the air in Buddy Bombard's balloon, it was raining. At 6:00 A.M., we met the crew at Hôtel de la Poste. The smiling up-up people (excuse the metaphor) were as cheerful as if the sun were shining. We piled into a van and bounced around on country roads until we stopped in a field large enough to unfold the huge balloon. Despite the rain, it was a very colorful sight. The crew, in red raincoats, stood nearly shoulder deep in bright green grass. Some had picked yellow flowers to wear as boutonnieres. However, first there was a ritual. A farmer who had emerged from the tall grass was greeted with much *bonhomie* and jovial conversation. Then came a ceremony of uncorking a champagne bottle to toast the occasion—and the farmer's permission to use his land.

Now the famous balloon (decorated with enormous red tulips, bright orange-and-yellow daisies, purple irises, and butterflies), could be unpacked and spread out. Then followed energetic activity by five people, accompanied by a professional explanation of procedures and statistics, for example, winds under ten miles per hour are very, very safe, and the hot air heater is on only about twenty percent of the time. A man from UNESCO and I stayed dry in the van. He told me about the Montgolfier brothers' first experiment at Versailles six years before the French Revolution. Louis XVI, his court, and crowds of commoners watched as a sheep, a rooster, and a duck went for a ride in a wicker basket attached to the Montgolfiers' balloon. The ride lasted eighteen minutes, and the animals landed safely two miles away. A newspaper reported that the Montgolfier brothers' had given such a shock to the French that "It has restored vigor to the aged, imagination to the peasants, and constancy to our women."

Burgundy

After an hour of unfolding and untethering, a decision was reached. Perhaps it was too rainy to launch the balloon. Everyone still in high spirits, we folded up the balloon and piled back into the van with rainchecks to try again tomorrow. Unfortunately, my schedule didn't allow for tomorrow. When I returned home, it was just in time for the annual balloon festival in Albuquerque, New Mexico. Albuquerque doesn't have vineyards to float over, but it has balloons; huge and colorful, hundreds of them silently drifting, or absolutely motionless in the sky. We didn't see any châteaux, but after landing, we celebrated with French champagne.

HÔTEL DIEU (HOUSE OF GOD)
Red Curtains and a Pulitzer Prize

The main tourist attraction in Beaune is the charitable hospital, Hôtel Dieu, with its geometric, colored tile roof. The hospital was founded in the fifteenth century, fifty years before Columbus discovered America. Now a museum, the long rectangular ward is lined on each side with fourteen red-curtained built-in beds. At the far end of the room is an altar where patients could hear Mass. The red curtains fascinated me. When the hospital

Hôtel Dieu

was filled with smallpox patients, the red curtains were used as "red treatment" and nailed shut to keep out the light.

As early as the tenth century, the Japanese used this treatment, based on writings of Moslem physicians (980–1037). Moslem doctors wrapped patients in red blankets to "excite and assist nature in drawing pus to the surface of the skin where it would be excreted." Japanese babies wore little red caps, played with red toys, and ate red candy. Curtains and pictures in the sickroom were also red.

The Chinese, Indian, and Japanese all feared the goddess of smallpox. On the last night of the year, they wore masks to bed, hoping to trick the goddess into ignoring them. By the twelfth century, all Western countries knew that red objects had warming properties. Red treatment became popular throughout Europe. When England's Queen Elizabeth came down with smallpox and lay in a coma for four hours, doctors wrapped her in red cloth and laid her on a mattress in front of the fireplace. The smallpox scourge was halted in 1798, when Dr. Edward Jenner (in England) discovered vaccination. Napoléon even released English prisoners when Josephine mentioned Dr. Jenner's name. "Oh, we can refuse nothing to that name."

In Copenhagen, Dr. Niels Finsen (1860–1904) experimented with red light. In 1893, he devised a treatment for smallpox proving that rays from the sun have a stimulating effect on tissues, and especially on blood. In researching the effects of ultraviolet light, he chose red light. By filtering out the short-wave rays of natural and artificial light, his red light treatment of smallpox reduced the formation of pustules, diminished fever, and prevented scars. Two years later, his experiments demonstrated that the use of concentrated chemical light rays, free from heat waves, led to the successful treatment of other skin diseases.

Dr. Finsen was awarded the Nobel Prize in 1903 for dramatic results in curing the skin disease, *lupus vulsaris*. The Father of Photosynthesis was unable to accept the award personally. Anemic and exhausted, he suffered from Pict's disease; a thickening of connective tissue that required constant draining of fluid from his stomach. From his wheelchair, he acknowledged the award: "My disease is responsible for my research on the benefits of the sun and light and its effect on the blood."

The Hôtel Dieu was still used until World War II as a charitable hospital. Today, there are two modern buildings behind it. One is used as a hospital, the other as a home for the elderly—free. Money is raised by a fraternity (La

Burgundy

Confrérie des Chevaliers du Tastevins), that owns Château de Vougeot, where twice a year wine tastings are held. Wines that pass are given a special name and a special numbered label.

For centuries, the hospital has been given plots in choice vineyards. At an international auction each year, wines belonging to the hospital are auctioned off at exorbitant prices, especially Burgundies still young and in the case. Proceeds go to Hôtel Dieu.

BURGUNDY WINE
Paradise on the First Floor

Across the street from Hôtel Dieu, Marché Aux Vins is a wine-tasting center in the hall of an old Franciscan church, where you can help yourself to thirty-seven Burgundy wines (not advisable). Glasses are available at each display. Hold the glass by the foot to look sophisticated, and swirl the wine a little, then smell it. Before you drink, decide whether it is sweet, salty, acidic, bitter, smoky, woody, musky, spicy, floral, or fruity. My favorite descriptive adjectives are "blouzy" and "oaky on the nose." Try the "beautifully seductive" Vosny-Romanée. If you want to buy some, they will ship it overseas.

Beaune is the capital of the Burgundian wine industry.[12] Burgundian vineyards go back to Roman times; Charlemagne (742–814), and the crusaders. Ten miles south of Dijon[13] is the monastery of Cîteaux, founded by twenty monks in the twelfth century. They named it for the *cistels* (reeds) in the marshes, and called themselves "Cistercians."[14] Disillusioned by holy men who had become too worldly and drank too much wine, they started a reformed order. When a duke of Burgundy and other nobles went on a crusade, they donated their vineyard, Clos Vougeot, to the Cistercians. Saint Bernard and other austere monks, who approved of wine only as a "curative," now owned 124 acres of "medicine," the largest *clos* (or plot of land)[15] in Burgundy (God's sense of humor). Clos Vougeot was run by Cistercian monks until the French Revolution. Today it belongs to eighty wine growers called La Confrérie des Chevaliers du Tastevin, who use the château's former wine cellar as a banquet hall. Seventeen times a year, the public relations "knights" host parties for 500 guests.

Adjacent to Clos Vougeot is Romanée Conti, the most expensive and smallest *clos* (two acres). The red wine here, from pinot noir grapes and stony red soil, is considered the best in France. The monks who owned the vineyard sold it to equip themselves for a crusade, and the new owner sold it in 1760 to Prince of Conti. Mme. Pompadour wanted Louis XV to buy it, but the king gave it to his cousin. Red wine from nearby Chambertin was so impressive that one man,[16] remembering his favorite things, wrote, "I forgot the name of the place, I forgot the name of the girl, but the wine was Chambertin."

Clos Nuits-Saint Georges was so famous for its red wine, Louis XIV's doctor prescribed it when the king suffered from an ulcer on a "particularly unfortunate part of his anatomy—with the best possible results."

> Drink no longer water,
> But use a little wine for thy stomach's sake
> And thine often infirmities
> —1 TIMOTHY 5:23

The town of Nuits-Saint Georges, with its Roman ruins, is the dividing line between Côte de Nuits and Côte de Beaune. Nearby Corton-Charlemagne, donated to the Church by Charlemagne, produces a white "Grand Cru" (best growth). Originally Charlemagne planted red grapes, but as he grew older, the red wine stains on his white beard looked so funny, his wife suggested he plant vines for white wine. *Voila!* Corton-Charlemagne. Other famous wines from Côte de Beaune are Meursault and Pommard, each named for little villages, or *communes*. Meursault comes from Roman times, when soldiers on the march took a shortcut across a stream narrow enough to jump across. They named the place *muris saltus* or "leap of the mouse." The Celts renamed it Meursault. The vineyards around the ancient town are famous for white Premières Crus (next best growth), made from chardonnay grapes. Of all the Burgundian vineyards, the steep, sloping hills of Meursault are the most difficult to tend. Meursault is the second largest *clos* in Côte de Beaune. The red wines of Pommard are named after a Roman temple dedicated to Pomona, goddess of fruits and gardens.

Five minutes away is Montrachet, with five Grands Crus. According to experts, Puligny-Montrachet produces the best dry white wine in the world. Alexandre Dumas, author of *The Three Musketeers* and *The Count of Monte Cristo*, spent his last years writing a cookbook,[17] in which he declared that Montrachet should be drunk on bended knee with your hat off. Montrachet is the end of Côte de Beaune.

The next regions are Côte Chalonnaise on the Saône River and the Mâconnais. The Mâconnais produces both red and white wines; it was

Burgundy

originally planted by monks from the nearby Cluny monastery. The most famous vineyards are Saint Véran with its Pouilly Fuissé, a delicate chardonnay. South of the Mâconnais, the last region is Beaujolais, near Lyon, where wine is made from gamay grapes in granite soil. Moulin à Vent, named for a windmill that overlooks the vines, is best known outside France, but in France, Chiroubles is the favorite. The Chablis wine area is eighty miles northwest of Burgundy near Auxerre.

Wine-tasting caves are found in all the villages. In dark, cool cellars, rows of barrels and thousands of bottles are stacked along the walls, sleeping and aging until the wake-up call. During World War II, children collected spiders to spin cobwebs on hastily built walls, where the best wines were hidden from the Nazis. The joke in Burgundy is that heaven is on the first floor (cellar) instead of the second.

The best part of Beaune was our visit with Monsieur Claude Jaboulet, business manager for his family's vineyards and shipping firm in Côte de

Jaboulet-Vercherre

Beaune. Their twelfth-century château is the oldest and most handsome in Burgundy. It is in Pommard, the sleepy little wine village less than a mile from Beaune. The dramatic entrance is a sea of bright green vines, flowing acre after acre right up to the château door. Premiere red wine from their Clos de la Commaraine is one of the best known Pommard wines. In Côte de Beaune, where tiny parcels of land are divided among many proprietors, Jaboulet-Vercherre owns thirty acres and ships 750,000 cases of wine a year under a *negociant* (wine merchant) label. M. Jaboulet is very proud of the fact that, out of 3,000 bottles, there is only a breakage of fifty. He showed us the enormous stainless steel machines where grapes are crushed and separated from the skin and juice. The juice, skin, and seeds are then pumped into another large stainless steel machine to ferment for a couple of weeks. He explained the whole process, but it was those steel tanks in the cold, stone cavern that I remember—stark, impersonal, menacing monsters straight out of a sterile high-tech suspense story. The little medieval vine-covered chapel where wines are stored was more romantic. After lunch at the elegant Le Relais de Saulx restaurant, we talked about the twenty million hunters in France. When I asked our friendly, charming host how I might thank him, he told me to tell J. R. of *Dallas* fame (everyone's favorite bad guy) to stop mixing water with bourbon.

23

Provence

Grignan Castle
Marquise de Sévigné (1626–1696) and Her Daughter

GRIGNAN CASTLE

Grignan Castle, eighty miles southeast of Lyon, is the home of the daughter of the marquise de Sévigné, the famous letter writer. High on top of a rocky peak overlooking the plains, we found a parking place, and reached the castle's huge entrance hall just in time—before a sudden downpour. Others, not so lucky, straggled in like wet sheepdogs, not at all perturbed. Since English tours are Wednesday and Thursday at 11:00 A.M. and 2:30 P.M., we joined the Dutch tourists and trooped up the staircase to the first room; the music room, with green, round bottle windows. In the middle of a semicircle, two little blonde Dutch girls, ages two and four, sat on the floor cross-legged like Christmas card angels. In the count's room, with Greek decorations over the fireplace, the angels were still on the floor but bored playing with cords on roped-off areas. In the third room, they broke the monotony by twirling yellow tape draped across the chairs. In another room, the littlest angel's body felt like jumping up and down. Her father scooped her up, found a window bench to sit on, and parked both little girls, one on each knee.

Mme. de Sévigné's apartment included a sitting room and bedroom. The red draperies around her canopied bed reach the ceiling. On one wall hangs a portrait of her grandmother, Saint Jeanne de Chantal, from Dijon,

Grignan

who worked with Saint Francis de Sales to found the Visitation Order for young girls and widows. On another wall is a picture of Mme. de Sévigné's attractive daughter, Françoise.

From the two casement windows in Mme. de Sévigné's apartment you can see the whole county of Grignan, bordered in the distance by the Alps, Mt. Ventoux, and several smaller mountains. Before one of Mme. de Sévigné's visits, she wrote, "I am pleased to find my apartment already marked out. . . . Do not let anyone spoil my bed of red taffeta and clear those awful bugs from my room. The thought alone nearly kills me."

The final room on the tour is a long room with two fireplaces, a kettle drum, and a white iron bed on a raised platform. Our tall Dutch lady tour guide told us in English that the room was used for plays and musicals. The "entertainment" room, with a long, bare floor unencumbered by rugs or furniture, was the best part of the tour for the little blonde girls. Now they could wander all over the place.

Provence

By now the rain had stopped, and we could enjoy the view from the terrace. Winding our way down the cliff, along rose-covered walls carved into the rock we found the door to the Holy Savior Chapel, where Mme. de Sévigné was buried.[1] We also found a shop where artisans worked. The handcrafted shell-design earrings I bought were too beautiful to be true. (I knew I would lose one, and I did.) A statue below the castle depicts Mme. de Sévigné in a billowing dress, with a plumed pen in her hand. It would have been more realistic to show her in a nightgown, groping her way down a dark, cold hallway with a candle to help her seriously ill daughter. Although Mme. de Sévigné[2] lived in the seventeenth century, 300 years later, through her letters, we are exhausted reading about her journeys to Provence, and worry with her about her daughter's yearly pregnancies.

At eighteen, she had married twenty-one-year-old marquis Henri de Sévigné,[3] who brought her from Paris to live in Brittany at Château Les Rochers, his ancestral home;[4] a beautiful Gothic manor on a hill, surrounded by seventy acres of woods and farmland, where their two children were born; a daughter and, a year later, a son. After seven years, her husband, who slept with anyone available, was killed in a duel. Duels were very fashionable. One man whose date with destiny was in the rain came with his umbrella. He said he didn't mind getting killed, but he didn't want to get wet.

The marquis de Sévigné's beautiful, witty widow moved back to Paris, where she attended the court of Louis XIV, Molière's plays, and the most brilliant literary salons. She wrote down practically every thought in her head. When chocolate became a new fad at court, strange tales began to circulate. Mme. de Sévigné wrote, "The Marquise de Coetlogon took so much chocolate being pregnant last year, she brought to bed a little boy who was black as the devil." When a friend went to a spa in Vichy to be cured of a pain in her knee and came back with a toothache instead, Mme. de Sévigné noted, "I found her quite flat in the rear end."

Mostly she wrote to her daughter Françoise, who had married thirty-seven-year-old comte de Grignan, from one of the oldest families in Provence. Mme. de Sévigné had overheard at court that Louis XIV's lecherous eye had singled out her twenty-two-year-old daughter as his next mistress. As fast as possible, she arranged Françoise's wedding. Her cousin, comte de Coulanges, wrote, "The only thing that makes me fear for the prettiest maiden in France is that Grignan, not yet old, is already on his third wife; he goes through them like suits of clothes or at least carriages."

The Grignans had been living in Paris, but when the count was appointed Lt. Governor of Languedoc, they moved to his enormous castle[5] that required fifty servants to wait on the count's entourage. The castle is near Nyons, where the wind knocks you off your feet, and the icy mistral freezes your bones. Twice a week Mme. de Sévigné, a nervous wreck, wrote to her daughter, worrying about the count's debts, extravagance, and their sex life. After the birth of Françoise's second child in two years, she pleaded, "I implore you my darling, do not be over confident about sleeping in separate beds. The temptation is still there. Have someone else sleep in the room... I embrace the Count, but I love him better in his apartment than in yours."

In Paris, Versailles had recently been completed, with 1,000 windows. Louis XIV had jilted his first mistress, fathered five children by the second, and was now trying to conquer the Spanish Netherlands.[6] Mme. de Sévigné's son, twenty-year-old Charles, fought in all the king's horrible wars. He was with the flooded French army when the Dutch opened their dikes. "Everyone weeps for a son, brother, or husband. One would have to be very callous not to be affected at seeing all France depart."

In Brittany, the peasants tried to rebel against taxes that left them starving, and the king's troops poured into Rennes to punish them. "The hangings go on and on in Lower Brittany. Those poor fellows there. All they ask for is a drink and smoke before the rope goes around their necks. Poor homeless creatures wandering about weeping. No food, no bed..."

Mme. de Sévigné couldn't write to her son somewhere on a battlefield, but there was always Françoise: "Let me know how you were the sixth of this month. Your dresses are so well made... that figure of yours so prettily rounded in its natural state. Oh my God! Keep it that way...." When the count ordered a new coat, she was very upset: "That is a matter of seven or eight hundred francs. What happened to the beautiful one he had? In the name of God try to cut back somewhere on this terrible expense." But it was Grignan's gambling that really drove her crazy. "For a long time now your gambling has been ruinous to you. Fortune must be blind to treat you as she does."

Brittany was so cold in winter that she journeyed down the Rhône River to stay in Provence with them, but it wasn't any warmer there. She wrote, "Alas, my cousin, it is one hundred times colder here than it is in Paris. The wind lifts gravel from the terrace and hurls it all the way to the second floor with enough force to smash the windows."

Provence

It took five to six days to go from Paris to Lyons: "My equipage made it this far without any trouble. Then yesterday evening my horses were taken to be watered and one drowned. Now I have only five." Another time, returning to Les Rochers, she got as far as Orléans where she boarded a boat to Tours: "Hardly had we arrived there, then behold, there were twenty boatmen around us each boasting of the quality of persons he had carried before and the excellence of his boat." The boatman she chose was "a big well-made lad whose mustache and civil manner decided us." Good choice! During the voyage the boat ran aground several times, and she had to ride on the boatman's back to get ashore for the night.

Once, on the way from Paris to Les Rochers with her son, cousin, maids, and her daughter's ex-tutor, the road between Rennes and Vitré[7] (four miles from Les Rochers), was flooded, and they had to send for help: "Twelve strong fellows came. Some held us up, others lit our way with torches of flaming straw. All spoke Breton with accents so strong we thought we should die laughing. Thanks to the illumination, we arrived here, our horses exhausted, all our people soaking wet, and my carriage broken. . . ." Imagine being able to laugh, stuck in the mud in the dark and rain! On another trip back to Brittany, she left Orléans on the Loire River by boat but was stranded on a sandbar until midnight: "Found a miserable hovel of an inn but grateful for fresh straw on the floor to stretch out on without undressing. At break of day re-embarked despite wind and tide. All took an oar. . . ." She finally arrived at Nantes after twenty-four hours without food or sleep.

When she heard that her daughter was coming to visit, she implored, "Please my love, do not bring such a terrible amount of luggage. When I think of the thirty-two pieces you brought last time, I shudder."

During her daughter's last pregnancy (six in six years), Mme. de Sévigné journeyed down the treacherous Rhône River again to help. Although Françoise was near death, it was Mme. de Sévigné who died, at seventy—from stress and sleepless nights caring for her daughter. She wrote, "As for me, I am no longer good for anything. I have played my part, but we are lucky that it is God's will that orders life, like all things in this world." She never knew the count had contaminated his wife and children with syphilis.[8]

THE POET OF PROVENCE
Frédéric Mistral

Frédéric Mistral has nothing to do with the cold wind that bends cyprus trees and leaves olive trees twisted and gnarled... the wind that blows cars off the road between Arles and Les Saintes Maries de la Mer. Frédéric Mistral is the great poet of Provence. Since the time of Louis XIV, rulers had been enforcing the language of the north (French) throughout the country. In 1854, Mistral and six others who shared his dream vowed to restore the traditional language, wit, and humor of the people in his region. They called themselves "The Félibres," a word taken from a Catalan poem. The poem refers to Saint Anselm, a twelfth-century scholar, who "One day from his holy writing, rose to heaven where the Virgin told him her sorrows"—especially, the three days and three nights when her Son was in the temple disputing with the "Seven Félibres of the Law." When they read that, Mistral's friends shouted, "That's us! But who is going to establish the Law?" Twenty-five-year-old Mistral volunteered to draw up the laws that govern their Provençal language—a task that took twenty years.[9]

Sometimes the high-spirited Félibres met at Mistral's home in Maillane[10] near Saint Rémy, or on the heights of Châteauneuf des Papes, where they drank the famous wine. Throughout Provence, they collected stories—in Carpentras, Saint Baume, and Saint Maximin: "Where lizards gasp in the withered grass and cicadas sing madly in the dusty olive trees, bushes, and scrub oaks." From Grasse to Toulon, Marseille, Aix, Montpellier, and Narbonne, they recorded tales such as the girl from Monteux who went mad "bewildered like a bird in a storm"—or the mayor who ruled for fifty years, "cheerfully like a good shepherd who walks quietly in front of his flock playing the flute."

Mistral wrote: "We are the singers of the land. Warblers do not forget the warbling of their fathers. Nightingales do not forget what their fathers sang to them. So how could we forget the language of our mothers?" As he watched the farmhands follow the plow, singing as they went, "Glory Be to God," he began his 1904 Nobel Prize-winning epic poem, *Mirèio*[11] (or *Merèille* in French.) He saw Mirèio, his fifteen-year-old heroine, in the girls at Maillane who came to pick mulberry leaves for silkworms on his father's farm. He saw her in the wheatfields, the grapevines, olive trees, and among the haystacks. She was part of the workers on the farm who came and went from dusk till dawn. The poem begins,

Provence

> I sing the love of a Provençal maid
> How through the wheatfield of La Crau[12] she strayed
> Following the fate that drew her to the sea
> Unknown beyond remote La Crau was she
> And I tell the rustic tale of her . . .
> I'll build her up a throne out of my song
> And hail the queen in our despised tongue . . .

Mirèio is the tragic story of a wealthy farmer's daughter who loves a poor basket weaver's son, Vincent. Mistral's inspiration came from the shepherds and farmers of La Crau, from his dreamy, musical uncle, a born storyteller, and from a woodcutter who knew every secret of the Rhône. Mostly, Mistral was captivated by his cousin from a neighboring village, who could name every shepherd, farm, pasture, ranch, and Provençal expression—such as "the one who never lets anyone step on his corn," or "I was embarrassed as a basket with a hole in its bottom," or if a man was rich in property with buildings on it, it was said, "He owns seven acres of roofs."

He wrote about *Mirèio*, "I had decided to make love blossom between two beautiful Provençal children of different circumstances and let the ball of yarn run its course drifting before the wind at random in the unpredictable way of life."

Composer Charles Gounod came to Saint Rémy to write an opera about *Mirèio* and said: "When a beautiful Provençal girl with amorous dark eyes threw me a *Bonjour Monsieur* I was literally drunk with happiness. Musical ideas sprang to my mind like a flight of butterflies, and all I had to do was stretch out my hands to catch them." At a banquet the people of Saint Rémy had arranged, he played the score for *Mirèio* (or *Mireille*), which premiered in Paris in 1864. Mistral complimented him: "You came to discover Provence and you have succeeded."[13]

My friend and I came to discover Provence too, but we didn't compose music. We went swimming. In Saint Rémy, we stayed at the hotel where Gounod stayed.[14] The tile on the floor of our room looked like a big carpet with a border around it. The bad news was, we forgot to ask about the security code and got locked out. It was after midnight, and we seemed to be the only ones still awake in the dark little town. We sat in front of the locked door and prayed to every saint we had ever heard of. Then a heaven-sent man arrived who knew the secret code. The next day, our taxi driver tried to find Mistral's home in Maillane, and when we finally found it on a dusty corner hidden by overgrown bushes, it was closed for repair. In Arles, people acted as if they had never heard of Van Gogh. We climbed a mountain at Saint Baume to see where Mary Magdalene spent her last thirty years, and we got lost, but at the little fishing port of Les Saintes Maries de la Mer (that Van Gogh painted),[15] we sprawled in a chair and took off our shoes. We had finally discovered Provence.

We had come from Arles on a bus through the marshy Rhône delta, flooded with rice fields, past tall grass, black bulls, and beehive-looking adobe dwellings with thatched roofs like those in Africa. Silhouetted against the sky were pink flamingos and beautiful white horses with flowing manes.

THE HOLY MARYS OF THE SEA
Les Saintes Maries de la Mer

The Holy Marys were Jesus' aunts, the Virgin's sister Mary Jacobe, and Mary Solome, mother of the apostles James and John.[16] According to tradition, after the Crucifixion, when Christians were tortured and killed, the two Marys were at Jaffa, the port for Jerusalem, with Mary Magdalene, Martha, Lazarus, and several other disciples.[17] Instead of killing them, they were thrown into a boat without sails, oars, rudder, or food, to perish at the mercy of the waves. Miraculously, they crossed the Mediterranean and landed near Marseille at today's Les Saintes Maries de la Mer. Accompanying them was the gypsy, Sarah.

THE GYPSIES' PATRON SAINT
Sarah

In the tradition of Belgium gypsies, while Sarah of the gypsies was living on the banks of the Rhône with her tribe she had a vision, that the saints who had been present at the death of Jesus would come, and that she must help them. One day she saw their boat on the rough sea. Throwing her dress on the waves, she used it as a raft to float toward the saints and help them reach land. They baptized her, then went their different ways to preach the gospel—Lazarus to Marseille, his friend Saint Maximin to Aix, Saint Trophimus to Arles, and Saint Martha to Tarasçon. Mary Magdalene lived for thirty years in a grotto high in the mountains of Saint Baume. (A Celtic name for "holy cave.") Only the two Marys, already old, remained onshore, where people came to hear about the new faith. When they died, native fishermen built a little chapel over their graves.

A gypsy child kisses the cheek of the statue of Saint Sarah

Between the ninth and twelfth century, when Saracens raided the coast, the present fortified Romanesque church was built over the shrine and dedicated to the Virgin, Notre Dame de la Mer. So many miracles happened in the fifteenth century that King René of Provence ordered an investigation. Excavations revealed the remains of the two Marys in a double sarcophagus. In 1448, the Church instituted a commemoration of their landing. The official appearance of Sarah took place a little later.[18]

In the fifteenth and sixteenth centuries, it was customary to give pilgrims and holy people safe-conduct passes when they wandered dressed as penitents. The gypsies dressed themselves as pilgrims and claimed they were condemned to roam for forty years because of a curse imposed by their ancestors in Egypt, who had refused to receive the Holy Family when they fled from Herod. The king of Hungary gave them a safe-conduct letter because Pope Clement V had decreed they were to make a pilgrimage to

Rome. While on their pilgrimage, the relics of the Holy Marys were found at the shrine by the sea in the Camargue,[19] a vast delta of the Rhône River. The gypsies mingled with other pilgrims who came to the church and adopted Sarah as their patron saint. Her Feast Day is celebrated on May 24. The solemn celebration begins with an all-night vigil; Rosary, Benediction, Stations of the Cross, and Mass. The following day the sacred relics of the two Marys, locked in a chapel high above the altar, are slowly lowered through an opening on a rope decorated with flowers. The relics are reverently returned, and Sarah's statue, draped in several elaborate robes, is taken from her blazing, candle-lit chapel below the main altar and carried out of the church on a platform, on the shoulders of four devout gypsies.

The Holy Marys performed a miracle for us, too. We found the last space on the sea wall to sit and watch as *Gardians*[20] on white horses escorted Sarah through the crowded streets to the beach and into the sea where the miraculous boat once landed. A priest blessed the water in thanksgiving for the saints' safe voyage, then Sarah was returned to her ninth-century chapel.

Actually there is no proof of Sarah's existence. However, as Curé Father Heckenroth says: "If the idea of a Saint Sarah helps the gypsies to pray, so much the better." One time in 1967 the national chaplain of the gypsies[21] came from Paris to desanctify Sarah, and the gypsies threw him into the sea. The archbishop of Aix had to rush to his rescue when the gypsies stood on the beach with knives in their hands.

If there were gypsies in colorful costumes and jangly, gold jewelry, we didn't see them. These are the real gypsies, who live in poverty—for whom life is a struggle to exist—as reflected in the faces of the worn, haggard, undernourished women. Pope John Paul II celebrated his sixty-eighth birthday with the exiles—"Refugees always on the move, wayfarers without repose . . . here (referring to the Church) at last you will find a station, a campground where you are welcome."

But more than Sarah, we remembered Mistral's *Mirèio*, "Child of the merry sun whose dimpled face bloomed into laughter. . . ." When the teenagers, Mirèio and Vincent, were forbidden by her parents to meet, and Vincent was wounded by a rival suitor, Mirèio fled to the church of the Les Saintes Maries de la Mer. Vincent had told her "If ever any harm betide you, go quickly to the holy saints who cure all ills."

"Under the pouring fire of the June sky like lightning doth Mirèio fly . . . to the church of the Les Saintes Maries de la Mer over the salt encrusted waste, on through the tall marsh grasses, on reeds and rushes haunted by the gnat she speeds. Exhausted and suffering from sunstroke she sank to her knees on the cold flags of the chapel floor . . . Poor little one . . ." Before she died, in the presence of her stricken parents and distraught lover, she whispered to Vincent: "Dearest I would you saw my heart this minute as in a glass, all the comfort in it. Comfort and peace like a full fountain welling through all my happy spirit."

The poem ends with a prayer to the saints, "So when the penitents heart-broken sue for pardon at your door, flood their souls with peace unspoken, white flowers of our briny moor."

THE FRENCH NATURALIST
Jean Henri Fabre (1823–1915)

If I were a beetle,
I would wake up in the morning sun
I would drink for my breakfast
A single drop of dew.

While Mistral and his merry Félibres roamed the countryside, a few miles from Mistral's home Jean Henri Fabre, seven years older, was on his hands and knees in the blazing Vaucluse sun with a magnifying glass, spying on insects. To visit the home of the famous naturalist at Sérignan,[22] we stayed in Orange (fifty miles from the Mediterranean) at a perfect hotel, Lou Cigaloun;[23] owned by a young couple with two beautiful little preschool boys who kept peeking around corners. A fifteen-minute taxi ride down a narrow dirt road, bordered by feathery brown reeds, brought us to Fabre's small, two-story house, now a museum. It's hidden behind a wall, surrounded by a green, tangled jungle of plants and bushes. Director of Harmas de J.H. Fabre, Pierre Téocchi and his wife greeted us, then left us alone to hero-worship.

Born of illiterate peasants, as a child Fabre was lucky to find a bunch of grapes to eat. To exist, he sold lemons in the market square, and worked on the railroad; but God had blessed him with natural talents, a brilliant mind, and, above all, curiosity. Although his schooling ended in the fifth grade, he read and devoured knowledge, winning scholarships in chemistry, physics, algebra, and geometry. At nineteen, he was appointed teacher of a primary school in nearby Carpentras under dreadful conditions—in a damp, dark cellar—for $140 a year. But his students loved him.

Back to Europe with the BUSY BODY

After seven years, he had an opportunity to teach physics in Corsica[24] at a big pay raise, $360 a year. Four years later he came down with malaria and returned to France, where he took the best job offer—at Lycée d'Avignon ($3200 a year). He was also appointed drawing master and director of the Réquien Museum of Natural History in Avignon.[25]

When the French minister of education[26] visited, he was so impressed by Fabre that he recommended him for the Legion of Honor in Science and Literature. Fabre left Avignon long enough to receive the medal in Paris, presented by Emperor Napoléon III, then hurried back to his classroom.[27] After teaching for seventeen years at the same salary, he was fired.

His famous free evening lectures, open to girls as well as boys, included botany. For teaching about the pollenization of flowers and plants, the clergy and jealous colleagues accused him of heresy and scandal. They claimed he was corrupting the girls' innocence. He lost his position at the museum and was evicted with his sixty-year-old father, five children, and a sick wife.

But God does provide. The famous English economist-philosopher, John Stuart Mill, who had come to Avignon to study botany and worked with Fabre at the museum, gave Fabre money to rent a little house near Orange. It was at the edge of fields, connected to the main road by an avenue of plane trees filled with birds and cicadae. But how to feed his family? The only thing he possessed was his strange collection of insects. He traded his professor's long frock coat for a peasant's blouse, and for nine years wrote school manuals for chemistry, mechanics, mushrooms, volcanoes, butterflies, bees, and more. He also wrote the first of many volumes of his famous *Souvenirs Entomologiques* (*Memoirs of Insects*). Louis Pasteur came to consult with him about the silkworm disease,[28] and was appalled at Fabre's poverty. When the landlord cut down the plane trees and destroyed his precious bugs, he moved to Sérignan, a few miles down the road, and named his new home "Harmas,"[29] an old Provençal word meaning "plot of uncultivated land." He earned enough money to repay his friend, John Stuart Mill, but the Franco-Prussian war ended his income. "Today the weathercock has turned. My books no longer sell in the grip of that terrible problem of daily bread."

Fabre lived at Harmas for thirty years in obscurity and terrible poverty. God knows how he fed his family. He lost a son he adored,[30] and his wife, a schoolteacher he had met at Carpentras, died after having seven children. Fabre remarried two years later and had three more children. All the while he continued to observe his little insects and write about them, one volume every three years; in all, nine more volumes of his famous *Souvenirs Entomologiques*.

He wrote about insects as if they were real people with personalities. He calls the glowworm a gad-about, a trot-about. "The male is correctly garbed in wing cases, like the beetle that he is, and the female, to guide the lover, lights a beacon like a spark fallen from the moon," or the dung beetle, "forgetful of himself, heedless of the intoxicating delights of Spring, although it would be so good to see something of the country, to feast with his brothers, or pester the neighbors, but no, he collects food to nourish his children."

Fabre has been called the "Homer of the Insect World," but he writes like Balzac, with detailed descriptions of clothes and interior decorating, such as "the great Peacock moth[31] is clad in maroon velvet with a necktie of white fur. The Kamasutra [beetle] appears in the balcony of her boudoir. . . . She awaits the visit of the spouse, the gentle Bomyx, who for the ceremony, has donned his feathery plumes and his mantle of black velvet. If he is late, she gets impatient and goes off to find him."

For thirty years, Fabre observed and wrote about insects. Everyone helped; the village schoolmaster, a blind carpenter, farmers, gardeners, truffle hunters, even the butcher. His son Émile sent a nest of wasps from Marseille, a daughter sent research documents, and his youngest son, Paul-Henri, gathered handfuls of dead moles and repulsive caterpillars as if he were picking strawberries. The town children helped too. One little boy brought him a moth he had been looking for for thirty years. A young shepherd, on the lookout for pill-rolling beetles, found a scarab beetle (like our ladybug), the largest of the dung beetles. Fabre was as excited as if he had found the sacred scarab representing the sun, that the Egyptians worshipped as a symbol of immortality.[32]

His whole family accompanied him on field trips. They saw red ants ransack neighboring black ant hills to steal the children and use them as servants. They stared bug-eyed (pardon the expression) at the praying mantis,[33] "with a dainty muzzle that seems made for billing and cooing. . . . Those arms folded in prayer are cut-throat weapons. They slay whatever passes within range. . . ." With his children, he watched a wasp scoop up mud to build her nest, "like a skilled housekeeper with her clothing carefully tucked up so it won't get dirty."

Fabre's patient observation revealed the puzzlement of little round disk-like holes on plants, like the ones in my canna leaves, that look as if someone had used a hole puncher or a machine gun. The bees did it; the leaf cutters. They use the little disks they cut out to seal a series of cells that hold eggs and store up food for the larvae. Fabre counted forty-two disks or lids needed for each cell. The bees know by instinct exactly what size is needed.

He also solved the mystery of the white, slimy stuff on stems of grass and weeds that look as if someone had spit on them. Under his microscope, he discovered that the foam is the home of soft-bodied little insects, immature frog-hoppers. Inside the foam, they grow and molt until they emerge as winged adults. The frog-hopper, a bubble blower, gives off secretions from tiny glands in the abdomen that stiffen the foam. By lantern light, he watched spiders weave a web which "becomes a fairy rose window." The most exciting experiment was the day he borrowed the town cannons and set them off to see if the noisy cicadae would stop their raucous screeching. When the roar of the cannons didn't faze them, he concluded they were deaf.

For thirty years his books sold very slowly. Literary critics disapproved of introducing literature into science, and scientists frowned on their brilliance and charm. Fabre chuckled: "They fear lest a page that is read without fatigue should not be the truth."

He used the big table on the first floor of his Harmas as a laboratory. It was covered with specimens of his constant companions, the insects. Around and around the table he paced, smoking his pipe. The whole family watched a wasp paralyze its prey by stinging it in its nerve center to keep it alive and at its most nutritious for her young to eat. They saw a wasp capture a bee to feed her larvae, but before carrying the bee to her offspring, she squeezed out the honey. Instinctively she knew the honey would poison them. They observed caterpillars (the ones that chew up pine trees) parade around the top of a bowl in procession. They saw them spin a fine thread of silk, to which each caterpillar clings and follows, while they add a thread of their own making a shiny white ribbon. "The caterpillars are more sheep-like than sheep. Where the first one goes, the others follow, unable to turn aside from their charmed circle day after day even though they face starvation."

He put a female Peacock moth that had just emerged from a cocoon into a wire mesh cage with strong smelling naphthalene, to disguise any odor, then left the windows open. That night, the house was invaded by

Provence

A Fabre watercolor

hordes of giant male Peacock moths that had flown miles through the dark. "Peacock moths in darkness over hills and valleys, with heavy wings spotted with hieroglyphics, find their sleeping beauties drawn by unknown odors." Fabre proved that instinct is born in these little creatures. He saw low-IQ insects with fixed habits using extremely complex behavior patterns. "An ant is knowing and wise but doesn't know enough to take a vacation."[34]

When Frédéric Mistral came to buy some watercolors for the museum he had established in Arles,[35] he was shocked to see eighty-five-year-old Fabre practically destitute. He was also astounded at the 700 awesome, meticulous paintings of plants, flowers, and fungi. Fabre wrote, "I had to let them go with bitterness like the tearing off of a piece of my skin."

Back to Europe with the BUSY BODY

Mistral informed the General Council of the province of Vaucluse of Fabre's predicament and arranged a festival to honor him. Public relations people went to work, and two years later, on his eighty-seventh birthday, a carriage arrived to take him to Sérignan where, at a banquet, he was given a gold plaque engraved with his portrait. The Choral Society marched down the main street, and famous writers, scientists, and French Academy officials sent messages. Forty years after he had received the Legion of Honor, people finally discovered his books. His Harmas swarmed with visitors, including the president of France, Reymond Poincaré. Five years before Fabre died, at ninety-two, the French government granted him a pension. "A peach offered to me when I am beginning to have no teeth to eat it." He joked about his life's work: "To appoint oneself . . . an inspector of spider webs . . . means joining a not-over-crowded profession." When asked if he believed in God, Fabre replied, "I see Him everywhere." He also told his brother "Above all, don't ever be discouraged. Time is nothing provided the will is never distracted."

As we toured Fabre's Harmas, we saw photographs, awards, diplomas, and astonishing, delicate, watercolors. Among the congratulatory letters is one from Edmond Rostand,[36] author of *Cyrano de Bergerac*. He told Fabre his books were a delight during his long convalescence from tuberculosis and depression after the Franco-Prussian war. He said one of his sons was so enthusiastic about Fabre's stories that he had decided to be an entomologist. Two letters are from Charles Darwin. Fascinated by Fabre's observations, he wanted to cooperate in experiments with the homing instinct of bees. Fabre began to study English to reply, but Darwin died (1882). Fabre could not accept Darwin's theories of evolution. "Facts disincline me to accept his theories."

Upstairs at the Harmas, Fabre's study is lined with cabinets displaying various collections, including broken Roman pottery and Roman coins he found while digging. A reference book, written in minute, spidery handwriting with a goose-quill pen, is on a tiny worktable he used for fifteen years. He bought it when he married at twenty-one. The satchel he carried that held his magnifying lens, glass bottles, trowel, and tweezers is there, too. The black marble clock was a present from the girls in his class at Avignon. If he had not been fired for teaching the girls, he never would have written his beautiful books.

24

The Grand Duchy of Luxembourg

ON A HOT, SUNSHINY DAY in Luxembourg City I set off all by myself to visit the American Cemetery, where General Patton[1] and 5,076 other Americans killed during the Battle of the Bulge are buried. I found the bus stop in the Old Town, climbed aboard for a short two-mile ride, and asked to be let off at the suburb of Hamm, where people step out of ancient stone houses onto a narrow, cobbled street. The bus driver left me on the highway at Hamm and pointed toward the horizon. For fifteen minutes, I walked among scrubby weeds and thirsty buttercups beside whizzing cars. Around a curve, the road ended in a circle. Noisy grinding, banging bulldozers, forklifts, and sand trucks halted the hike. Later, I learned they were making road improvements for the fiftieth anniversary of the Battle of the Bulge. Oops—wrong year. Back to the bus.

    I had come by train in the morning from Frankfurt. Waiting in the aisle for the train to stop, I asked the man ahead of me with a briefcase if he were going to Luxembourg on business. He smiled dreamily and said, "No, for pleasure." I wondered what his pleasure looked like. In the railroad station, a conveyor belt quietly moved suitcases up the steps, as a grown man flew by on a skateboard.

    My hotel was the Grand Cravat, where United Press correspondent Walter Cronkite stayed during World War II. One of his dispatches said: "Here was the fur-lined foxhole of all times. Ben Wright, as Ninth Air Force Public Relations Officer, had just ensconced his forces at the Cravat Hotel when the Battle of the Bulge[2] began. While the Third Army press corps camped out in a miserably cold school room . . . over in Esch, those of us lucky enough to affix ourselves with Ben's ministrations, lived in luxury in hot baths and flowing champagne. . . . The night the Germans managed to drop a few mortar shells into Luxembourg City almost ended that idyll."

Opposite the Grand Cravat Hotel, la place de la Constitution overlooks a crater-like hole in the ground. The spectacular ravine separates the Old Town and New Town with flights of steps, winding streets, and viaducts over the Petrusse and Alzette Rivers. The picturesque Old Town evolved around a tenth-century castle. In 963, Count Sigfrid, from the House of Ardennes, bought 150 acres from the monks in Trier, where Luxembourg City is today. On a cliff above the Alzette River, Count Sigfrid rebuilt a Roman fortress protected by three miles of walls and seven towers.[3] The castle was handed down to the Count of Vianden, whose most famous descendant was John the Blind. As Count of Luxembourg and king of Bohemia, the blind knight-errant galloped through Europe, charging into battles with his horse hitched between two of his knights' bridles. His son, Charles IV, when elected Holy Roman Emperor (1355), made Luxembourg a duchy that included today's Belgium and the Netherlands. In medieval times, Belgium and the Netherlands were a mass of disconnected countries, duchies, and feudal districts; some in France, some in Germany. Over the centuries, various rulers sliced away at the Luxembourg pie.

CATHEDRAL OF OUR LADY OF LUXEMBOURG

In the cathedral down the street behind the hotel, a workman on a scaffold was repairing a stained glass window. In the crypt under the ancient Jesuit church, the Grand Ducal family is buried in a vault, with two bronze lions guarding the entrance. But it is John the Blind, flamboyant as usual, who steals the show. An effigy shows him laid atop an empty tomb, looking like Christ taken down from the cross. Five large-scale mourners standing behind the cenotaph express their sorrow in varied poses; one woman is brushing away her tears.

The cathedral was originally the chapel of a Jesuit college and then a parish church. In 1870 it became a cathedral dedicated to Our Lady of the

Immaculate Conception. In the center, a miraculous statue of Our Lady, "Consoler of the Afflicted," is dressed in a Spanish medieval costume. In one hand she holds a scepter; in the other, the Infant Jesus with a globe in His hand. Both wear jeweled crowns.

The origin of the statue is unknown, but in 1624 it was carried in procession outside the city walls. So many pilgrims came to beg the Virgin's intercession that a special chapel was built, then enlarged. In 1666, Our Lady, "Consoler of the Afflicted," was made patroness of the city and the duchy of Luxembourg. The statue remained outside the city walls until the French Revolution, when it was returned to the Jesuit church in town.

For three centuries, Luxembourgers have prayed, "Father of pity and God of all consolation, You wished that Mary the mother of Your Divine Son be also our Mother. In Your bounty You gave her to us to guard and protect us, to be our comfort and consolation through Jesus Christ Our Lord" *(Notre Seigneur)*.

Through the centuries, she has been their "Consoler of the Afflicted"—most recently during World War II, when thousands were prisoners in Germany, and families lived like animals in icy cellars. Today, Luxembourg is one of the wealthiest countries in the world; but a new generation with cradle-to-grave benefits ignores Our Lady. It is she who needs consoling. Maybe the Grand Duke Henri (2000) will make a difference by stirring their Christian consciences. In his inaugural speech he acknowledged: "We have received a great deal." Then he asked, "Do we still notice people less fortunate . . . ? Are we not too selfish?"

VIANDEN
Exiled Victor Hugo, a Famous Fortress, and Mary Poppins

A new friend, Romain, brought me to Vianden, twenty miles north of Luxembourg City, where a ninth-century castle overlooks the ancient town sprawled below. On a pretty arched bridge over the Our River flowing through town, Rodin's statue of Victor Hugo commemorates nineteenth-century France's leading poet, novelist, playwright, artist, and hypocrite, who preached morality but didn't practice it. When the composer Berlioz visited Hugo's home in Paris he said, "The salon was full of monstrous old women ugly enough to make a dog bark." Even at seventy-five, he was a licentious sex addict. Once, when the police caught him in bed with another man's wife, Alexandre Dumas said, "He should take lessons on how to pull on his trousers faster." Whatever—Rodin has captured in stone the intellectual giant. Rodin's Hugo appears to be either dozing or lost in concentration, but it is the power of his mind Rodin has captured.

Victor Hugo, author of *Notre Dame de Paris* (*The Hunchback of Notre Dame*)[4] and *Les Misérables,* championed the oppressed and lived through two revolutions, as well as Louis Napoléon's *coup d'état,* the Franco-Prussian War, and the Communard's Civil War. During bloody revolutions, he printed anti-government pamphlets, manned barricades, and harangued crowds to put down their firearms and work peacefully for "social justice." Disillusioned with Louis Napoléon's government, he formed a Resistance Committee, and barely escaped with his life. Thanks to his long-suffering mistress, Juliet Drouet, who copied practically every word he wrote, he left his family behind and escaped to Brussels. Juliet, a beautiful actress who gave up her career for him, coached and disguised him as a typesetter with smudges on his face, stooped shoulders, and greying hair. He shuffled into the Paris railway station, Gare du Nord, carrying a small bundle containing a sausage sandwich reeking of garlic. When he reached for his passport with dirty fingernails and greasy hands, the conductor glanced at it and hurried away. Juliet followed two days later, with suitcases filled with manuscripts. In Brussels, he was ordered to leave. They didn't condone unfaithfulness in marriage. (Finally, at seventy-six, before his wife died, he swore on the Bible and on a copy of *Les Misérables* to be faithful to his mistress, Juliet.)

He and Juliet fled from Brussels to the Isle of Jersey, then to the Isle of Guernsey, where his family joined them. Juliet was practically his childrens' second mother. In Guernsey, Hugo delighted in shocking neighbors and tourists by taking cold showers in the nude, outdoors on his second-story deck. When Louis Napoléon, now emperor, granted amnesty to exiles, Victor Hugo pompously declared, "When liberty returns, I shall return." He returned to Paris after the emperor's downfall in 1871, to bury his son Charles, who had died suddenly in Guernsey of apoplexy. The funeral procession arrived in the midst of the bloody Commune uprising. Although Hugo's sympathies were with the wretched poor, he advised them to take office by legitimate means. When their rage turned to madness, he fled to Brussels again (at seventy) and loudly proclaimed that any Communard would be safe under his roof. A disgusted mob attacked his home, ready to lynch him. When, again, he was expelled, he found refuge in Vianden where he bought two homes, one for his family, another for himself and Juliet. His house next to the bridge, now a museum, contains letters, furniture, and reproductions of his Vianden sketches.

To visit the famous fortress in Vianden, we parked under a tree halfway up Mount Saint Nicholas, and climbed the rest of the way to the castle of the counts of Vianden.[5] Families with toddlers laughed and chatted as they pushed babies in strollers over bumpy cobblestones straight up the mountain.

The first thing you see at the top is a gargantuan empty room with Byzantine trefoil windows open to the elements. Below the Byzantine Hall, on the ground floor, a huge vaulted hall once held 500 men. The hall, with palm tree pillars and gothic arches, is divided into two rooms: the Captain's Hall and the armory, with exhibits of ancient weapons and suits of armor. One of life's great mysteries is how men could fight or even move, encased in fifty to seventy pounds of steel. I laughed, remembering "the old man" in Robert Ruark's book *The Old Man's Boy Grows Older,* as he tells "the boy" about a knight-errant: "When he come fourteen he graduated into an esquire. . . . He was supposed to be able to fork a horse on the gallop wearing a full suit of boiler plate and jump streams and scale walls and such strenuous things. . . . They used to lose a lot of esquires that way because if a guy tried to jump a deep stream and didn't make it, he plumb sank. And when a wall scaler missed his foothold, all you heard was clank."

In the Count's Hall, a chapel with high, slender pillars opens down to a lower Romanesque chapel, where servants and townspeople heard Mass. Above the ground floor is an enormous Knights' Hall, with its thirteenth-century gothic door and magnificent Gobelin tapestries. My favorites were *Ulysses, Joan of Arc,* and the Habsburg Emperor, *Maximilian of Austria.*

Eight tapestries show Ulysses returning to Ithaca after the fall of Troy. The victorious Greeks, returning home, encountered wild adventures, and a scene here portrays Ulysses and two companions with the beautiful sorceress, Circe, who turned men into swine. Another tapestry shows Joan of Arc and her soldiers at Fort des Tourelles on the Loire, in the battle that ended the siege of Orléans. My special favorite is Maximilian I (who inherited the Low Countries and Luxembourg) on horseback in a hunting scene, a popular theme. Anything pertaining to multitalented Maximilian would have been fine with me.

There should have been a great view from the Knights' Hall, but it was raining. Waiting for the shower to stop, we sat on the ledge of a big bay window and had a picnic with my ever-ready peanut butter crackers and water. When the rain slowed to a drizzle we left, and again saw good-natured couples under umbrellas, with plastic-draped babies in buggies.

Lunch at the renowned Heintz Hotel was a delicious experience. The hotel-restaurant, originally a fifteenth-century convent, was built by the Trinitarian Order, founded during the Crusades to rescue prisoners from the Saracens. The Trinitarians planted grape vines in the area, but the wine was so bad, it was said that three men were required to drink; one to pour it down his mouth, another to make him swallow, and a third to stop him from running away.

Our wine at lunch was perfect—crisp, white Mosel, to accompany the melt-in-your-mouth trout and a hot plum wrapped in bacon. A thin slice of melon, with a sliver of prosciutto hoisted on a toothpick for a sail, resembled a *bateau*. For dessert, we enjoyed *sabayon* sauce over raspberries and whipped custard. No wonder royalty, prime ministers, and famous authors have dined here for centuries.

Life, however, is not always raspberries and cream. During World War II, after the Grand Duchy had been liberated from the Nazis, on December 14, 1944, at 11:00 P.M., most of the GIs quartered in the Heintz Hotel were asleep. At a dining room table, while several soldiers were patching a boat, they talked about a German they had picked up who kept telling them the Germans would come that night. He begged them to flee and take him with them. The next day, Vianden was bombed and captured by the 5th German Parachute Division.

We couldn't leave Vianden without a ride in the chair lift over the lovely town. The rain was nearly over, but gliding through the air, under Romain's black umbrella, visions of Mary Poppins popped into my friend's head.

THE BATTLE OF THE BULGE
Diekirch

A few miles from Vianden, the Battle of the Bulge Museum in Diekirch honors the memory of General George Patton, Jr., and Americans who lived through hell and died to defend a crossroad. Dioramas and photographs in the War Museum prove one picture is worth a thousand words, such as bridge builders in the Engineer Corps, wading knee-deep in icy water to lay foundations for bridges.

The Grand Duchy was invaded by the Germans on May 10, 1940. They occupied the country for four years until it was liberated by the 5th U.S.

The Grand Duchy of Luxembourg

Armored Division and the First Army.[6] While Americans controlled the Grand Duchy, the Germans dug in at the Siegfried Line. On December 16, 1944, Hitler launched a desperate drive through the Ardennes to reach the port of Antwerp.

General Patton, stationed in Nancy, ordered his 10th Armored Division to the Ardennes, where unprepared Americans were outnumbered six to one. In a chapel at his new headquarters[7] in Luxembourg City, he prayed in his inimitable fashion: "Sir, this is Patton talking. The last fourteen days have been straight hell. Rain, snow, more rain, more snow—and I'm beginning to wonder what's going on in Your headquarters. Whose side are You on, anyway? . . . Up until now You have given us Your unreserved cooperation. But now You've changed horses in midstream. You seem to have given von Rundstedt every break in the book and frankly, he's been beating the hell out of us.

"But now Sir, I can't help but feel that I have offended You in some way. That suddenly You have lost all sympathy with our cause. That You are throwing in with von Rundstedt and his paper-hanging god. You know without me telling You that our situation is desperate . . . I don't like to complain unreasonably, but my soldiers from the Meuse to Echternach are suffering the tortures of the damned. Today I visited several hospitals, all full of frostbite cases, and the wounded are dying in the fields because they cannot be brought back for medical care. But this isn't the worst of the situation. Lack of visibility, continued rains, have completely grounded my air force. . . . Not only is this a deplorable situation, but, worse yet, my reconnaissance planes haven't been in the air for fourteen days, and I haven't the faintest idea of what's going on behind the German lines. Damn it, Sir, I can't fight a shadow. Without Your cooperation from a weather standpoint I am deprived of an accurate disposition of the German armies and how in hell can I be intelligent in my attack? . . . You have just got to make up Your mind whose side You're on. . . . Sir, I have never been an unreasonable man. I am not going to ask you for the impossible. I do not even insist upon a miracle, for all I request is four days of clear weather.

"Give me four clear days so that my planes can fly, so that my fighter-bombers can bomb and strafe, so that my reconnaissance may pick out targets for my magnificent artillery. Give me four days of sunshine to dry this blasted mud, so that my tanks may roll, so that ammunition and rations may be taken to my hungry, ill-equipped infantry. I need these four

Back to Europe with the BUSY BODY

days to send von Rundstedt and his godless army to their Valhalla. I am sick of this unnecessary butchery of American youth, and in exchange for four days of fighting weather, I will deliver You enough krauts to keep Your bookkeepers months behind in their work. Amen."[8]

He told Chaplain O'Neil to publish a prayer for good weather. "See if we can't get God to work on our side." The Chaplain's prayer was passed out to men in a driving snow storm: "Almighty and merciful God, we humbly beseech Thee of Thy great goodness to restrain these immoderate rains with which we have had to contend. Grant us fair weather for battle." The next day Patton looked out the window to see swarms of planes in the air. "Hot dog! I guess I'll have to have another 100,000 of those prayers printed. The Lord is on our side, and we've got to keep Him informed of what we need."

Ettelbruck

Memorials honoring heroes of the Battle of the Bulge are everywhere in the Grand Duchy. The town of Ettelbruck (known as Patton Town), celebrates "Remembrance Day" each year in gratitude to General Patton[9] and his Third Army, who liberated them on Christmas Day, 1944.

Clervaux

Clervaux in Luxembourg, a lovely castle town twenty miles east of Bastogne, Belgium, is behind the main crossing of the Our River. On December 17, 1944, 200 German tanks roared into the town, designated as a rest area for American GIs. From every hotel, non-combat servicemen (clerks, cooks, or electricians), were hastily summoned to defend the castle. Today, the happy resort city with its restored castle and red-roofed Benedictine abbey has been rebuilt, and Edward Steichen's[10] 273 photographs of people from sixty-eight countries, "The Family of Man," was on exhibit in the Castle Museum. The title is perfect for the collection, depicting the universality of man, especially here in Steichen's native country, where the hotel wake-up call is in three languages: French, English, and German.

Wiltz

Americans of the 28th Infantry were stationed here in 1944 on December 6, the day Saint Nicholas traditionally brings presents to children. To make sure Saint Nicholas had something to give them, the soldiers collected their rationed chocolate, cookies, and candy. Nine days later, Wiltz[11] was overrun by Nazi troops.

The Grand Duchy of Luxembourg

While Patton's tanks skidded north on solid ice, a wiry little sixty-three-year-old priest, Prosper Collins, promised Our Lady of Fatima he would build a shrine to her and the Sacred Heart of Jesus if they were saved. The people were to say a novena consisting of the "Credo," the "Our Father," a prayer for repentance, a song to Saint Sebastian (the town's patron saint), and the song, "I Am a Christian and I'll Stay a Christian."

On the ninth day of the novena, as the priest was singing High Mass in the bombed-out church in Lower Wiltz, the shivering little congregation heard the clanking of hobnailed boots on the cobblestones. The Germans were leaving. On the last day of the novena, the town was free.

Today, the beautiful town of Wiltz, left in shambles, has been rebuilt, with an outdoor theater behind the château. The shrine, as promised, stands on a hill overlooking the town.

Eschweiler

The little town of Eschweiler has a population of 200. In 1944, a twenty-four-year-old American soldier, George Mergenthaler, arrived there with the First Army's 28th Division, which had battled its way across France from Normandy. When they reached Luxembourg, the Grand Duchy had already been liberated.

The Princeton graduate was quartered for five weeks with the parish priest, Father Antoine Bodson, who spoke English. George spoke French, German, and English. On December 16, the American GIs' vacation from war became a nightmare when the Germans returned. George Mergenthaler attended Mass in the small white parish church,[12] said goodbye to Father Bodson, and left to take his post on the road to Bastogne, Belgium, where German tanks were moving up. Months later, a crude grave marker was found with a GI's helmet hung on it. The priest identified the body as that of his friend by the beautiful vest under his uniform, which his parents had sent for Christmas. Today, George Mergenthaler is buried in the parish cemetery. The place in the woods where his body was found is marked with a gray stone slab and a simple headstone. To this day, the people of Eschweiler bring fresh flowers to the American they loved as a son.

Echternach

Echternach, fourteen miles from Luxembourg City, is a quaint medieval town with pretty yellow houses and mansard roofs in the middle of a gloomy forest. Each year, on the Tuesday after Pentecost, thousands of pil-

Back to Europe with the BUSY BODY

grims come to dance around the tomb of Saint Willibrord,[13] who brought Christianity here in the seventh century. Miracles and cures are attributed to the saint, whose marble tomb is in a crypt in the ancient clifftop Benedictine monastery he founded.

Saint Willibrord, patron saint of the Netherlands, was born in Northumbria, educated near York, and ordained in Ireland. He established an abbey first in Utrecht, then at Echternach. Today, the abbey is a school.

A single company of American riflemen held Echternach during the Battle of the Bulge. The town on the Sauer River was completely destroyed during weeks of battle. It has been restored, thanks mainly to one man, Robert Schaffner, who, after being sent from one concentration camp to another, when peace came made his way back to Luxembourg to search for his wife and two-year-old daughter. The miraculous happy ending occurred in Echternach where his wife and baby had returned, after hiding in the Black Forest a year and a half.

LUXEMBOURG CITY
At Night

Before leaving the Grand Duchy of Luxembourg, a wonderful girl I met at a bus stop in Luxembourg City gave me a night tour of the floodlit city, which included: the American Embassy (22 boulevard E. Servai); the Grand Rue; place d'Arm, a pretty square ringed with lime trees and a bandstand in the center; Marché aux Poissons, the most ancient square, where Roman roads intersected; and the oldest café, called "Under the Pillars." Opposite Hôtel de Ville is the Grand Ducal Palace, and in place Guillaume, atop a fountain-monument commemorating Michael Rodange's epic poem, *Renert*, sits Reynard the Fox, with his pointy little ears alert as always.

My pretty guide said that Pont Adolphe, a beautiful bridge day or night, is named for Grand Duke Adolphe, who founded the Luxembourg dynasty (1890). Two enormous complexes tower above the town house; the European Banking Center and the secretariat of the European Parliament. Other European Union buildings are the European Court of Justice, the European Investment Bank, and the European Board of Auditors.

In Clairefontaine Square, a statue honors Grand Duchess Charlotte[14] (1896–1985), who became a symbol of Resistance during World War II. Along a winding hill, we looked down on the eerie ruins of Luxembourg's ancient fortress, with its three remaining towers crowned with ornamental acorns.

The magical evening ended at Café des Artistes, a hole-in-the-wall, where a fantastic piano player knew every song anyone could think of—where young people gathered 'round the piano and sang in four languages: "He's Got The Whole World in His Hand," "Michael Row the Boat Ashore," "My Bonnie Lies Over the Ocean," and so on. With music, we celebrated the theme of Steichen's photographic exhibit, "The Family of Man." In churches throughout Europe sermons stress Hope and Faith. In quiet Luxembourg City, soft lights glow in the dark.

THE LUXEMBOURG STORY
Sex, Love, and Power

Belgium, Holland, and the dukes of Burgundy are part of the Luxembourg story. The first duke, Philip the Bold, inherited five provinces from the Count of Flanders, who died fifteen years after Philip married his daughter. From then on, Burgundian dukes added more and more land. The second duke, Philip the Good (who really wasn't), seized the duchy of Luxembourg in 1430 by threatening to kill the husband of the heiress, Jacqueline.[15] The last Duke of Burgundy, Charles the Bold (or Rash), tried to create a kingdom between France and Germany, but was killed by the Swiss during a battle near Nancy in 1476. When his daughter, Marie, married Maximilian of Austria, Luxembourg came under the Austrian Habsburgs. Their son, Philip the Fair (who wasn't fair), inherited the Netherlands from his mother. Born and raised in Ghent, eighteen-year-old Philip I married Juana (Joanna), daughter and heiress of Ferdinand and Isabella of Spain.[16] After the wedding in Antwerp, she wrote a letter home, horrified at the Dutch people, "They swill gallons of something called beer and fall dead drunk into the canals." Juana, a brilliant linguist and musician, was also exceptionally eloquent. "She could sway her worst enemy." Tragically, the twenty-five-year-old princess was not prepared for marriage. She had never even held hands with a boy. She thought sex meant love. Others, including her husband, coveted the Spanish crown—and she had to go. After six children and forty-seven years of solitary confinement and torture (mental and physical), she was driven insane. She died on Good Friday of 1555, the year her son, Emperor Charles V, abdicated and left all those Spanish descendants named Philip.

Back to Europe with the BUSY BODY

Philip II of Spain and William the Silent of The Netherlands

"Tho all should fail us, we shall at least have earned the honor of having done what no other nation did before us."
—WILLIAM THE SILENT

Philip II's father was Emperor Charles V, "who had more in the back of his head than in his face." Philip's mother, Isabelle of Portugal, died in 1515 when he was twelve, and although Philip rarely saw his father (busy fighting French king Francis I, German Protestants, the Turks, and Barbary pirates), the Emperor found time to write letters recommending piety, patience, and modesty. "Never allow heresies to enter your realms." Mostly, he warned of power-seeking nobles. Unlike his father who ruled on horseback, Philip II governed his empire from a desk. He was not the soldier type; besides, he got diarrhea when he was nervous.

By the time his father abdicated, Philip had been married twice. His first wife, Marie of Portugal, died four days after the birth of their son, Don Carlos. His second wife, Mary Tudor, ten years older, was queen of England. Poor homely Mary! He didn't care a thing about her, but he thought the marriage would make him king of England and, eventually, Ireland. After their wedding at Winchester Cathedral, Philip stayed in England fourteen months.[17] Two years later, he stopped by on his way to Flanders. Mary Tudor died the following year at forty-two of syphilis, inherited from her father, King Henry VIII, thus ending Philip's hopes of becoming king of England.

Philip's contemporary, William, Prince of Orange-Nassau (1533–1584), became famous as William the Silent, for his ability to keep his usually talkative mouth shut; a survival technique he learned in a family of sixteen brothers and sisters. At eleven, when he inherited the principality of Orange in southern France and estates in the Netherlands from his cousin,[18] he became the wealthiest noble in Europe.

Emperor Charles V summoned the outgoing, happy little boy to be brought up at the royal palace in Brussels and educated by Flemish noblemen. Court life for the independent boy took a little getting used to—especially the nuisance of being dressed by servants. In Germany, where his father was Count Nassau-Dillenburg, William had been raised among country people. In 1551, at eighteen, the prince married Anne of Buren,[19] a bride the same age. Two children later, Anne wrote that she knew her husband no better after six years than on the first day they met.

The Grand Duchy of Luxembourg

William of Orange was in Flanders with the army when he was recalled to Brussels. Emperor Charles V, worn-out at fifty-five, was abdicating—leaving the Netherlands, land of his birth, for Spain. His humorless, twenty-eight-year-old son, Spanish Philip II, had been trained to succeed him, but it was twenty-two-year-old William, Prince of Orange, on whose arm the gouty emperor leaned as he hobbled down the Great Hall of the palace in Brussels, where the Palais Royal is today. Trailing behind came Philip and Margaret of Austria,[20] who had ruled as Charles' regent of the Netherlands for twenty-five years. William of Orange, a gregarious charmer, was not Philip's favorite person, but he was valuable as a public relations man with the wealthy Dutch merchants.

The same year that William's twenty-five-year-old wife, Anne of Buren, died (1559), forty-two-year-old Spanish king Philip II married the thirteen-year-old daughter of Catherine de' Medici and French king Henry II.[21] She was supposed to have married the king's son, Don Carlos, but Philip wanted her for himself. France had sued for peace in their long war with Spain, and the marriage was part of the negotiations. William of Orange went to Paris for the signing of the treaty and the proxy wedding, where the little bride cried all through the ceremony.[22] Her father had recently been killed in a jousting tournament. While stag hunting in the Chantilly forest, her father, the king, had confided to William his plan to help Spain crush Protestant heretics in the Netherlands. William was speechless! He had been raised a Lutheran. For seven years, he remained silent about his plans.

William tried to persuade King Philip to cooperate with the people of Netherlands, whose constitutional rights date back to a 1356 charter. William was as successful as the American colonists were with King George III. Bigoted, despotic Philip believed he was divinely appointed to rid the Church and State of dissenters. Any opposition was treason. His solution, like the Red Queen's in *Alice in Wonderland*, was "Off with their heads."

When Emperor Charles V died, leaving an empire that included Mexico and Peru, Philip returned to Spain after four frustrating years in the Netherlands. Before he left, he had appointed his father's illegitimate daughter, Margaret of Parma,[23] regent. He also demanded that the Estates-General (the highest authority) advance him credit for the next nine years. Grudgingly they did, but leaders of seventeen provinces presented him with a protest. They demanded withdrawal of Spanish troops, an end to religious persecution, and respect for their representative government. One

Back to Europe with the BUSY BODY

of Philip's advisers called the 200 aristocratic petitioners 'beggars,' and as the revolution grew, its backers defiantly adopted the name. Philip knew the Prince of Orange was influential with delegates of the Estates-General, and when William tried to reason with him, the angry king interrupted: "Without help from higher quarters [meaning William], the Estates never would have given trouble." William knew the Netherlands without foreign allies could never defeat Spanish troops. He also knew that only militant Calvinists would fight. He joined the Calvinists, resigned as *Stadholder* (governor), packed up his family, and headed for Germany to raise money and recruit troops. Two thousand nobles and burghers signed a document (1568) demanding an end to Philip's Inquisition and edicts dictating religion.

He had been gone three years when Regent Margaret sent for him. A starving mob led by Calvinist nobles was heading for Antwerp, and he was the only one able to restore order—which he did, urging the people to tolerate each other and live as Christians. As soon as he left Antwerp for Brussels, the mob sacked the cathedral, churches, chapels, and monasteries.[24] As rioting spread, William left for his principality of Nassau in Germany.

Merciless Spanish king Philip II sent the sixty-year-old Duke of Alba and 60,000 Italian troops,[25] with orders to stamp out all resistance. Alba stepped up his atrocities, which Peter Breugel painted in *The Massacre of the Innocents;* a gray winter landscape with Dutch peasants clutching murdered babies. Regent Margaret of Parma resigned.

While William was in Cologne gathering an army, the princes of Holland and Zeeland (where William was *Stadholder*), revolted and declared their independence. Alba accused the Prince of Orange of treason, seized William's fourteen-year-old son, and sent him to Spain a prisoner. Two Catholic nobles, Egmont[26] and Hoorn, loyal to both Emperor Charles V and King Philip, were executed in Brussels for petitioning the king to alleviate the suffering and stop the horrible Inquisition.

During the bitter winter of 1572–1573, as William's messengers skated across frozen canals, his mercenaries suffered one defeat after another by Alba's professionals. William the Silent, Prince of Orange, one of the wealthiest, most respected noblemen in Europe, lost battles, his fortune, and his reputation. Only when Alba imposed a ten percent tax affecting their wallets did apathy turn to action. When Zierickzee was blockaded and the people left to starve, William wrote his brother: "We will not be down-hearted, but will hope that when all the world abandons us, the Lord

The Grand Duchy of Luxembourg

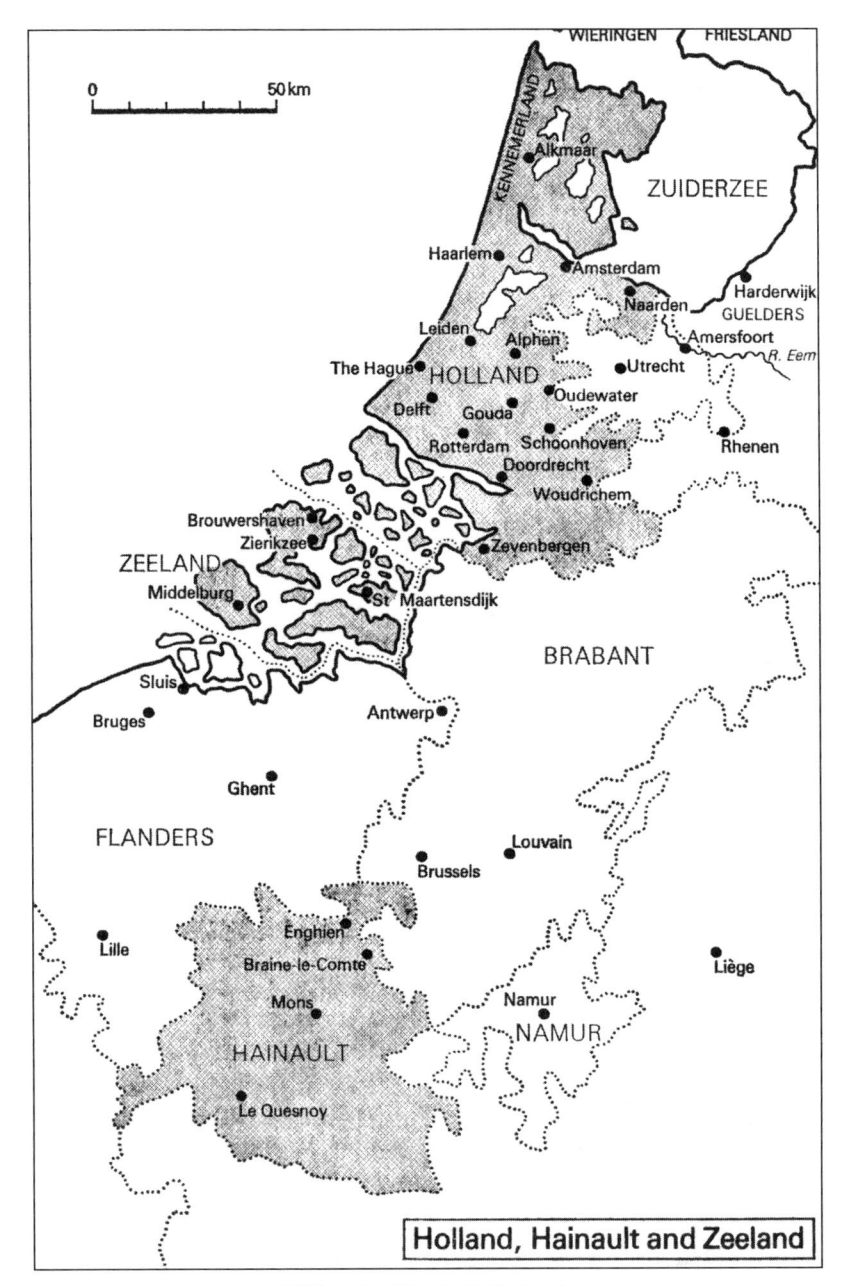

William the Silent's Netherlands

Back to Europe with the BUSY BODY

God will stretch His hand over us."

In Dillenburg, Germany, William wrote his famous "Justification," signed by ten provinces. It opened with a quotation from Psalm 37:32: "The wicked watcheth the righteous and seeketh to slay him." The document justifying the revolt vindicated himself as a rebel and turned the accusation toward King Philip. The main idea was that, as a shepherd, the Spanish king had maltreated and forsaken his flock, and forfeited his right to rule the Dutch.

The gauntlet was thrown and the stage set for tragedy. Characters were established, the conflict made clear, and the plot was building toward a climax—with William the Silent in the role of mediator.

William's next biggest problem was his mentally unstable second wife, Anna of Saxony, who had just given birth to a puny little boy, Maurice. Her tantrums and drunken behavior shocked the whole Rhineland. In Dillenburg, pregnant again, the sixteen-year-old girl escaped from William's family estate and fled to Cologne, where her baby girl was born. She sent the infant to William's parents to raise, and took a lover, Jan Rubens. The guilty pair were arrested, and Rubens promptly confessed, while hysterical Anna insisted they should both be killed. Luckily, William the Silent was not the vengeful type. Rubens, thanks to his wife, was released on honorable detention after two years in prison. Reunited with his wife, six years later a son was born—the genius artist, Peter Paul Rubens. Meanwhile in King Philip's Spain, Cervantes was writing about his "Knight with the Woeful Countenance," and El Greco was painting masterpieces. Thirty miles northwest of Madrid, Philip II was building the remote palace-monastery, El Escorial,[27]—so enormous (one hundred miles of passageways) that it is classified as a city.

Philip's son Don Carlos, who despised the Inquisition, had hoped to be sent to the Netherlands as governor. When the Spanish king learned his son sympathized with the dissenters, he arranged his murder. In the royal palace in Madrid, the king, in full armor, with his companions, appeared in his son's room at night while he slept. On being awakened, the twenty-three-year-old youth asked "Have you come to kill me, Father?" He was seized, imprisoned, and died five months later of poison. Verdi's opera *Don Carlos* commemorates him as another victim sacrificed in the name of power and fanaticism. The king's young wife, Elizabeth of Valois, also

The Grand Duchy of Luxembourg

twenty-three, died four months later. Within two months, Philip II married a fourth wife, Anna of Austria, his twenty-one-year-old niece, half his age.

In 1573, the Duke of Alba and his son were recalled from the Netherlands and replaced (after six years) by elderly Don Louis de Requesnes, son of King Philip's old tutor—who went under protest. "I can find one thousand reasons for not accepting." Calvinists, protesting another Spanish governor, sacked 4,000 churches in Flanders alone.

When Leiden was blockaded, William the Silent convinced the Estates-General of Holland that the only way to save the city was by cutting the dikes, as they had at Alkmaar.[28] It was a gamble but the only way. Water had to flow twenty-two miles from Rotterdam.[29] With a strong wind and high tide, it would be possible, although thousands would be homeless and their land ruined by the gray, saltwater. The Estates voted yes—a small price to pay for freedom.

While relief preparations were under way William nearly died of malaria, but a dietitian from Alkmaar prescribed a special diet and a tonic made of beer, wine, and sugar. William recovered, like the old mule with sore feet who lay down and refused to budge. One shot of whiskey and he was on his feet, frisky as a colt.

From his headquarters in Rotterdam, William sent word to Leiden that help was on the way. Leiden had been under attack for four months. Despite famine and plague, Burgomaster van der Werff defied every demand for surrender. He shocked a hungry mob into silence by daring them to eat his flesh: "But surrender, never!" To Spanish taunts, he replied: "Ye call us dog eaters. It is true. So long as ye hear a dog bark or a cat meow within the city, ye may know that the city holds out."

Leiden was rescued by the "Sea Beggars," who fought Spain on the sea. Fierce, illiterate peasants manned 200 barges to save their countrymen. To float the vessels, dikes holding back the North Sea were cut in sixteen places. At Zoeterwande, one terrified enemy left a note saying, "Farewell little forts who are abandoned on account of the waters, not on account of the force of the enemy."

Five miles from Leiden, the water receded and the wind died, leaving the barges stranded. When it blew again, it came from the wrong direction. Miraculously, a steady wind from the northwest coincided with a high tide, and the sea poured through the holes in the dike. At midnight, boats loaded with herring and white bread sailed on giant waves. On Sunday, October 3, 1574, rescuers reached the city wharves, where survivors, weak from hunger, could barely stand.

William, whose court was in Delft, was praying in the confiscated convent of Saint Agatha with his household and townspeople when a sentry handed him a note with news of the miracle. William passed the note to the preacher who read it aloud. God had answered their prayers and, as usual, never said, "I told you so." William left immediately for Leiden, where he established the University of Leiden to honor their obstinate defiance against the enemy.

William, now forty-two, had married thirty-year-old Charlotte de Bourbon. As a baby, she had been bundled off to a convent to save dowry money. She escaped to Heidelburg in her late twenties, where she met William. The chemistry was right, and three years later, they married. Both were exiles and poor (William's lands had been confiscated), but both shared the same dream of freedom.

After the terrible "Spanish Fury" (1576), when starving Spanish troops descended on Antwerp, burning a third of the city and slaughtering more than 6,000 citizens, seventeen provinces (Catholics and Calvinists) signed "The Pacification of Ghent," calling for withdrawal of Spanish and German troops, self-government, religious tolerance, and the return of William's son, who, at fourteen, had been seized by the Duke of Alba and kept prisoner in Spain for twenty-six years.[30]

When Governor Requesnes died of typhoid fever, King Philip sent his brilliant half-brother, Don Juan of Austria,[31] to rule. The twenty-six-year-old hero, Don Juan, admiral of the Spanish Navy, had recently (1571) defeated the Ottoman Turks in the Battle of Lepanto in the Gulf of Corinth, where 15,000 Christian slaves were freed, and where Cervantes, author of *Don Quixote*, lost his arm.

Handsome, fearless Don Juan arrived in Luxembourg from Vienna, disguised as his friend's Moorish slave. When he reached the Luxembourg fortress, he washed his face. There was one problem. The Dutch refused to let him enter the United Netherlands until he agreed to the terms of the "Pacification" treaty. Romantic Don Juan's passion in life was to rescue a maiden in distress, Mary Queen of Scots, and he would need a Flemish port. He agreed to everything. He even loaned the bankrupt Estates-General money to pay their German mercenaries. Then he galloped from his Luxembourg headquarters into Brussels to rule a United Netherlands.

The Grand Duchy of Luxembourg

The United Netherlands didn't stay united. The predominantly Catholic South had agreed to a Calvinist leader, William the Silent, to oust the Spanish, but there remained the memory of slaughter, desecrated churches, and confiscated church property. When Calvinists continued to destroy churches, William, whose goal was a permanently united Netherlands, told the Estates-General: "You are acting as a wounded man who tears off bandages like a madman and instead of submitting to treatment, plunges a dagger into his own heart." Tolerant Don Juan had arrived in Brussels in the midst of mayhem. King Philip, apprehensive about sending him to the turbulent Netherlands, (he regularly disobeyed), also sent the thirty-three-year-old Duke of Parma, with 2,000 fresh troops. His mother was Philip's half-sister, Margaret of Parma, who had ruled as regent for him. Her son, the well-liked duke, had grown up in the Netherlands. After he had won over five southern provinces for the Spanish king, five northern provinces united with Holland and Zeeland.

The northern provinces elected William the Silent *Stadholder* and declared their independence from Don Juan. Two years after Don Juan's gung-ho entrance into the Netherlands' inferno, he died in Namur at thirty-one of typhoid fever. The Duke of Parma took over as governor and called William a traitor. He told the people King Philip would have given them peace if it were not for one man, William of Orange.

King Philip proclaimed the Prince of Orange an outlaw and made it a crime to obey him. For the prince's assassination, the king offered 25,000 gold crowns. William's reply, endorsed by the Estates-General of the United Netherlands, stated the reasons for their revolt and opposition to the Spanish king. It also proclaimed William's commitment to the Netherlands. The document, printed in four languages, was shipped throughout Western Europe.

The Apology, or Repudiation stated:

> A Prince is constituted by God to be ruler of a people, to defend them from aggression and violence as the shepherd his sheep; and whereas God did not create the people slaves to their prince to obey his commands . . . but rather the prince, for the sake of the subjects, to love and support them as a father his children or a shepherd his flock . . . and when he does not behave thus, but . . . oppresses them, seeking opportunities to infringe their ancient customs, exacting from them slavish compliance, then he is no longer a prince but a tyrant,

and they may not only disallow his authority but legally proceed to the choice of another prince for their defense.

With the repudiation of King Philip as ruler, tensions that had been mounting for nine years erupted like a gusher in an oilfield. With his family, William the Silent escaped to Middleburg in the north. His only hope was Francis, Duke of Anjou, Catherine de' Medici's youngest son, who could provide money and troops. No one wanted the unscrupulous Anjou with his silly minions, but William insisted that only by making him "Protector" could they legally change their allegiance from Philip. Reluctantly, thirteen of the seventeen provinces voted for the French duke.

Meanwhile, with permission to kill, a Portuguese merchant boasted to the Duke of Parma that he had hired a clerk to murder the Prince of Orange. The twenty-year-old clerk, Juan Juaréguy, had never done this sort of thing. He had never even held a pistol. He decided to use twice as much gunpowder as he had been told.

At the palace in Antwerp, as William led his dinner guests across a crowded room to examine a new tapestry, the assassin pushed through the sightseers and fired. The pistol, with the extra gunpowder, exploded, blowing his hand to pieces. William's hair and ruff caught fire, and the bullet flew through his neck, under his right ear, through the roof of his mouth and out under his left jaw. To stop the bleeding, friends took turns plugging the hole with their thumbs. Twice, after the wound was apparently sealed, it broke open. After hours of hemorrhaging they cauterized it. A small pellet of lead was stuck in the hole and held there by various thumbs for seventeen days. Five weeks later, miraculously, the Prince of Orange was able to leave his bed.

His wife, Charlotte, the ex-nun, never left his side. After visiting Our Lady's Cathedral in Antwerp for eleven consecutive days to thank God for her husband's life, she died—exhausted by her five-week vigil and six pregnancies in seven years.

William, "Chief disturber of the whole state of Christendom," continued his efforts to save the southern provinces, but his new French troops were not cooperating. The Duke of Parma captured city after city[32] for Philip II. As the Calvinist minority in the provinces of Brabant and Flanders continued to attack the Catholic majority, Catholics turned more and more to the Spanish duke of Parma—and still William argued for Anjou, the French duke.

The Grand Duchy of Luxembourg

After William finally won over the Estates-General, Anjou attacked Antwerp in a *coup d' état* to rule the Netherlands himself. Appalled at the betrayal, William for the first time lost his celebrated cool and called him a lot of censored names. Anjou, on the other hand, could not believe Catholics in Antwerp did not welcome him. Instead, they had stretched chains across the streets and fired on him from rooftops. Once more, William the Silent was summoned. The first time it was against the "Spanish Fury." Now it was the "French Fury."

Even after the betrayal, William insisted it was necessary to keep Anjou under control rather than have him join the Duke of Parma; but no way could William regain the peoples' confidence. He sent Anjou to Dunkirk in Flanders, where the duke was so bored that he returned to France. The officer left in charge surrendered to Parma, who blockaded the port of Antwerp. William's popularity poll, either high or low, now plunged off the chart.

After his wife's death William had married Louise de Coligny, daughter of the French Huguenot, Admiral de Coligny. Both her husband and father had been killed during the Saint Bartholomew Massacre in Paris, when 2,000 Huguenots were murdered—leaving her a widow and orphan at eighteen. Louise de Coligny made a wonderful mother for William's children, but the Dutch didn't care what kind of mother she was. The Prince of Orange was still promoting the hated French duke of Anjou, and now he had taken a French wife. Again, William was forced to leave Antwerp and head for safety in the United Provinces, north of the province of Brabant. With his court and family he settled in Delft, in the former convent of Saint Agatha. Today, The Prinsenhof, (home of the prince) is a museum.

Despite the reward for his head, William the fatalist, now fifty-two, left his life in God's hands. He still received petitioners, with an open door to everyone. One petitioner determined to collect Philip's reward money was Balthasar Gérard, a secretary with the Duke of Parma's staff, headquartered in the Luxembourg fortress. Carrying a handful of forged passes, he told the Prince of Orange he was a Calvinist and wanted to serve him. He hoped the prince might use the passes behind enemy lines. William said thanks, but no thanks. Maybe the Duke of Anjou could use them, and he sent Gérard off with a courier to find Anjou. That was not in Gérard's plan. Besides, he still didn't have a weapon. When he reached the French border, he learned that Anjou had died—another typhoid victim. Volunteering to carry the report back to the Prince of Orange, he showed up in William's

Back to Europe with the BUSY BODY

bedroom, where everyone hung out. He looked so bedraggled, William remembered him and asked why he hadn't gone to France. Gérard told him he needed money. His shoes were worn out.

William gave him twelve crowns, but Gérard still didn't leave. He said the roads were dangerous, and he might be attacked. With the money the Prince of Orange had given him, he bought two pistols; one with two bullets, the other with three.

As the family entered the dining hall, Gérard shoved forward and asked for a passport for his journey. William promised he would get it, then escorted his wife into dinner. Outside, Gérard looked around for an escape, then joined the crowd of petitioners and waited, the pistols hidden beneath his coat. When William and his family left the dining hall, Gérard shot the prince with both pistols. Five bullets ripped through William's lungs and stomach. He fell at the foot of the staircase and was dead before the doctor arrived. The drama was over—and the assassin butchered.

Compassionate William the Silent, the first ecumenical ruler, was raised a Lutheran, became a convert to Catholicism, then a Calvinist by necessity. He is buried in the New Church in Delft, where an elaborate black-and-white marble baroque tomb marks his grave. A bronze statue shows him seated in armor, with his famous white pug dog at his feet. The inscription reads: "To the everlasting memory of William of Nassau, Father of the Fatherlands."

Epilogue

After Philip had disposed of William the Silent, he sent 12,000 troops to the Netherlands and re-established his authority. He died at the El Escorial in Spain at seventy-one, in a tiny bed overlooking the chapel, after months of agony, leaving Spain bankrupt. The Dutch fight for independence continued as Philip's daughter, pious Isabella, and her husband, Archduke Albert,[33] ruled the Spanish Netherlands, and William the Silent's seventeen-year-old son, Maurice (by rebellious Anna),[34] recaptured cities taken by the Spanish. William's youngest son, Frederick-Henry (by his last wife), was another *Stadholder*. He ruled the United Provinces during a twelve-year truce (1609–1621) negotiated by Rubens, court painter for the Spanish Netherlands.

Five years after the truce ended, in 1626, Peter Minuit, governor of New Netherland (owned by the Dutch West India Company), bought Manhattan Island from the Indians for $24 worth of trinkets. Thirty-eight years

The Grand Duchy of Luxembourg

later, in 1664, the English[35] bribed wealthy Dutch landowners to surrender their colony, New Amsterdam—today's New York.[36]

In 1648, Spanish king Philip IV recognized the independence of the United Provinces, despite the United Provinces' condition that the port of Antwerp on Spanish-held River Scheldt be closed. Antwerp became a ghost town, while Amsterdam became Europe's busiest seaport.

Peace ended abruptly. French cardinal Richelieu continued Europe's Thirty-Year War against the Habsburgs, leaving the path to Austria across the Low Countries a wasteland. Young Louis XIV's state minister, Cardinal Mazarin, concluded a peace[37] which gave Luxembourg and part of Flanders to France. When greedy Louis XIV became king he coveted the wealthy Netherlands, and sent troops first to the Dutch Republic. As his soldiers advanced over the ice almost to Amsterdam (1672), a sudden thaw sent them wading home. Six years later, in a second attempt, French troops poured into the United Provinces but were chased back by crashing waves, when William the Silent's great-grandson, William Henry,[38] flooded the canals. The Dutch war with Louis XIV lasted nearly forty years.[39]

William Henry (William III) had married Mary, Protestant daughter of the English king's brother[40]—a Catholic. To prevent a Catholic from gaining the throne, in 1688 seven English Protestants offered William Henry the English crown. During his "William and Mary" reign in England, he arranged an alliance with the Holy Roman Emperor to drive the French from the Netherlands. Troops under John Churchill, the Duke of Marlborough, defeated the invaders at Blenheim, Bavaria. Victory for the "Grand Alliance" transferred the Spanish Netherlands and Luxembourg to Austria. From then on, countries jumped in and out of bed with whoever made the best offer.

In Spain, Philip IV's son, pathetic, crippled King Charles II, the last descendent of Emperor Charles V, was dying. Louis XIV and the archbishop of Toledo forced him to leave his empire to the French king's grandson, Philip V. Other countries objected, and the result was a thirteen-year war over the "Spanish Succession." A 1713 treaty among England, Holland, and France ended the argument.[41] At the price of thousands of lives, Louis XIV bought a crown. King Louis XIV finally died, succeeded by Louis XV. During the War of Austrian Succession (1744–1748) and the Seven Years War (1754–1763), European troops of all nations ravaged the Low Countries.

In America, Paul Revere hopped on his horse to alert the colonists that the "redcoats" were coming.[42] After the Americans miraculously defeated the British Goliath, the United Provinces of the Netherlands[43] was the second nation (after France) to recognize the new United States of America. Three Dutch banks gave John Adams loans, and John Paul Jones ("I have just begun to fight") was given a hero's welcome. Freedom in the United Provinces[44] bewildered a class-conscious Englishman, who wrote home saying there was no way of knowing a servant from the mistress of the house.

During the French Revolution both the United Provinces and Austrian Netherlands had welcomed revolutionary troops, with their promise of liberty, equality, and fraternity, only to discover that liberty could not be won with foreign aid. They were forced to quarter 25,000 French soldiers, take orders from the Directoire in Paris, and fight in France's war with England. When England blockaded the Dutch coast, both North and South suffered.

Napoléon united the Netherlands into a nation (1806) and made his brother, Louis, king. Louis had been bossed around by Napoléon all his life—even told to marry Empress Josephine's daughter, Hortense. He ruled three years as king of Holland before Napoléon fired him for being too lenient. Napoléon sent 1,500 Dutch boys to Russia. A few hundred straggled home.

After Napoléon's defeat at Waterloo, twelve miles south of Brussels, the Congress of Vienna made tactless Protestant William I[45] king of Holland, which included the Catholic Netherlands in the South, the United Provinces in the North, and Luxembourg. It was a miserable marriage. Riots broke out in July, 1830, and three months later, Catholic Netherlands declared themselves an independent state of Belgium. The following year, a conference of the major powers divided the Grand Duchy in two. The largest part (today's Belgium, the size of Maryland) was granted independence and neutrality, with money-minded German prince Leopold of Saxe-Coburg as the first king of Belgium. The smaller portion, under Dutch king William I, stayed in the Germanic Confederation, with the Luxembourg fortress held by Prussians. The Grand Duchy of Luxembourg was now less than half its original size. Holland's King William I was not happy with his small piece of the pie, although he was given the title "Grand Duke of the Grand Duchy of Luxembourg."

During the 1848 revolutions in Europe, Belgium, under Leopold II, was the only country without violence—protestors were jailed and starved. In 1866, the Confederation of German States was dissolved. Luxembourg City

The Grand Duchy of Luxembourg

was no longer a federal fortress, although Prussian soldiers still manned the fort. Germany, France, and Belgium, three "Cinderella" step-sisters, fought over the Luxembourg fortress until it was decided the only solution was to tear it down and declare the Grand Duchy of Luxembourg independent and neutral (1867).

In 1867, the year the United States bought Alaska, the kingdom of Holland passed to the female line. The Grand Duchy of Luxembourg went to the House of Nassau. During World War I, only Holland escaped German occupation. Belgium and Luxembourg, despite their neutrality, were invaded. Luxembourg had been courted by, married to, and dumped by Germany. After World War I, defiled and helpless, the country returned to the arms of its deceitful "protector," who promised diamonds and pearls. But naïve innocence and trust were gone. They knew they were being used and would suffer again. In 1940, their protector turned on them. Today, Holland, Belgium, and the Grand Duchy of Luxembourg are centers of arbitration.

In Luxembourg City, the poet Rodange's wily fox, *Renert*, atop Rodange's monument, could be a tribute to the people of the Low Countries. Constantly involved in a battle of wits with powerful enemies, Reynard the Fox is a survivor—like the people of the Low Countries. The Luxembourg story ends in Delft, where William the Silent was murdered. We went there via Brussels, Antwerp, Ghent, Scheveningen (Skáy-ven-in-gen), and The Hague.

25

Belgium

Brussels:
An Opera, Comic Books, and a Puppet Show

BRUSSELS

Brussels—the Common Market Headquarters, where we never saw a brussels sprout. It rained in Brussels and my pocket-size umbrella[1] flew apart. Bought a new one with a Betty Boop design. We stayed at the only nineteenth-century hotel in Brussels, Hôtel Metropole, on de Brouchere Square. It's where movies are made and international conventions held, for example, in 1911, a physics convention was attended by Mme. Curie and Albert Einstein. Inaugurated in 1895, guests have included Richard Strauss and Sarah Bernhardt, and more recently, Placido Domingo, and many movie celebrities. Gerard Depardieu filmed *Les Anges Gardiens* here. Could he possibly have slept in my bed? Oh well—wishful thinking. The sumptuous hotel, with its warm, elegant beauty, soothes the mind and soul, but it is the friendly staff that makes it unique.

If you take a city tour, a guide rounds up his flock, stands them in one corner of the enormous Grand Place, and points in the air with his black umbrella. Necks swivel, but no one is quite sure what is where. Then he herds you onto a bus for a canned talk.

Just off the Grand Place is the Théâtre Royal de la Monnaie, where the Mint used to be and where the 1830 riots began—right in the middle of Auber's opera.[2] When the crowd outside heard the applause after the aria

Belgium

"For the love of our country, give us daring and confidence," they hoisted the flag of the duchy of Brabant and set torches to the homes of Dutch government officials. Nearby is the Stock Market (the Bourse), and the Church of Saint Nicholas, where the history of Brussels is depicted in a manger scene. The miniature pie carriers are copied from Breughel's *Wedding Scene*.

The Comic Strip Museum in Brussels was a must—to see Tintin, the comic book little boy with a funny blond hairdo, and his dog, Snowy. Their adventures, which take them to exotic places throughout the world, have been translated into English. Another priority was Toone's Puppet Show in an old inn.[3] Can you imagine a puppet version of *The Three Musketeers?*

Toone and his marionettes

The dueling was hysterical. The quiet audience, mostly in their twenties, sat on wooden benches in a small, packed theater, but no one laughed. Toone's puppet theater continues a tradition started when Spain ruled the Netherlands. Spanish authorities, incensed by ridicule and insults from the stage, closed the theaters. However, by using puppets, the people continued to revile their oppressors.

The Brussels cathedral, usually known as Saint Gudule's, is named for an eleventh-century pious lady who faithfully prayed at a little chapel dedicated to Saint Michael. It was on the site of today's cathedral. The Devil, who disapproves of prayers, amused himself by blowing out her candle as she walked across the marsh. Saint Gudule was buried in the little chapel, and after the church burned, it was rebuilt and dedicated to both Saint Michael and Saint Gudule. Calvinists and French Revolutionaries destroyed it, and Napoléon I gave the first donation toward its restoration.

Another church is Notre Dame du Sablon (Sand). In 1304, the Crossbowmen built a chapel here on a sandy patch in the marsh. Forty-four years later, in Antwerp, another holy lady, who prayed regularly before a neglected, tiny black statue of the Madonna, had a vision of the Virgin. She was told to bring the statue to Brussels and place it in the recently built chapel of the Crossbowmen. Their devotion to the Blessed Mother was so great that they built a larger church which, after 100 years, developed into the present one, above place du Grand Sablon—far from the crowds near the Grand Place. Across the street, near the Egmont Palace in the Petit Sablon Gardens, we sprawled on the grass and had a picnic by a lovely fountain. Enjoying the picnic with us were statues of counts Egmont and Hoorne, victims of King Philip II of Spain.

That night we ate at a restaurant off Grand Place, where eight girls and one lone male at a window table waved us in from the street. From the enthusiastic welcome, you would have thought we were old friends. We chose a table in a corner, away from the laughing, singing, and possibly slightly inebriated welcome committee.

ANTWERP
Site of the First Attempt to Murder William the Silent

Antwerp, an international port fifty-six miles from the sea, was off-and-on rain, but not cold. Central Station, with its stained glass ceiling and wrought iron metalwork, is worth a long look, as well as the shop windows in the Jewish area, filled with gold and diamond jewelry. Antwerp is the world center for cut diamonds. We used the underground train to whiz back and forth to our hotel near the Royal Opera House.[4] At the hotel, there was only one language problem; we thought the desk clerk was talking about a parakeet. When we said, "Parakeet?" She laughed. "No. Spare keys."

We tracked down Rubens' paintings all over town. In Saint Paul's Dominican Church, there are two paintings: *The Scourging at the Pillar* and *Adoration of the Shepherds*. One of the chapels in the Dominican Church is dedicated to the Battle of Lepanto in 1571, when dashing Don Juan of Austria defeated the Ottoman Turks. The fleet sailed under the protection of Our Lady of the Rosary, and all the chaplains were Dominican friars.

Rubens' statue is in front of the Cathedral of the Holy Virgin.[5] His *Descent from the Cross* in the cathedral impressed the painter Delacroix so much that he climbed a ladder to see it better. The enormous fifteenth-century Church of Saint James (Sint Jacobskerk), with enormous white marble statues, contains two other Rubens paintings. While we were there, a man preparing to make a pilgrimage to Saint James' tomb in Compostella, Spain, was being given a special blessing. Rubens, who painted while Shakespeare wrote plays, is buried in Saint James Church, behind the altar, with his family. His home at 9–11 Wapper,[6] an open pedestrian area with fountains and benches, had a big note on the door, apologizing for not being open due to repairs. We compensated with fresh fruit at the nearby Saturday market.

GHENT
Picture Perfect

If Brussels' Grand Place seems lacy and feminine, Ghent is macho-masculine. Now I know where Rembrandt found his black-clad serious merchants. Severe, step-gabled Guild Halls, lined up stolidly on *Korn Markt*, present a unified front in battle formation against rulers attempting to deprive the people of their ancient privileges.[7] At the end of the thirteenth century Ghent was the capital of Flanders and the main cloth-weaving city in Europe. It was larger than Paris, but English competition and an eighty-year religious war changed all that.

In the Town Hall, or *Stadhuis*, the first Duke of Burgundy, Philip the Bold, married the Count of Flanders' daughter and inherited her lands. Burgundian Philip the Good spent his youth here, and Juana of Spain gave birth to future Emperor Charles V. In Ghent William the Silent's "Pacification of Ghent" was proclaimed, by a League protesting Spanish tyranny.

Ghent

Here, too, Calvinists and Catholics took time out from their terrible war to sign a twelve-year treaty;[8] peace for the first time in forty years. Also in Ghent, Marie, daughter of the last Duke of Burgundy, Charles the Rash, was forced to sign The Great Privilege, which gave back to the people the charter protecting their rights.[9] From America, John Quincy Adams and Henry Clay came to sign The Treaty of Ghent, ending the War of 1812 with the British. The infant American fleet had defeated England's great naval power on Lake Champlain in the Baltimore harbor. The treaty was signed in 1815, the year Napoléon was exiled to Elba and General Andrew Jackson won the Battle of New Orleans.

In the rain at the train station, a taxi driver suggested we stay at Hotel Eden, a lovely 'European' hotel; warm, softly lighted, and filled with elegant antiques. The next day, still in the rain, we toured the city built on one hundred islands.[10] In the Gothic Cathedral of Saint Bavon,[11] to the right of the entrance, is Jan and Hubert van Eyck's famous painting, *Mystic Lamb of God Who Redeemed the World from Sin.* Adored by angels, the Lamb stands on an altar, blood flowing from its side into a chalice. In the center is Christ Triumphant.

After a wet walk in the rain through the picturesque city, with its many bridges and canals, the sun shyly peaked through the clouds, and we ate

Belgium

outdoors. The restaurant overlooked Graslei quay, lined with medieval guildhouses mirrored in the water. We ordered everything the waiter suggested: asparagus and *waterzooie* (chicken in vegetable juice served in cream sauce; hare with onions and prunes); *spekulatius* (spicy biscuits); and *pain armanndes* (almond bread). When we tried to adjust the table umbrella, tons of water dumped on us. When we asked the waiter to please take our picture, we made the mistake of saying "Cheese." The waiter said, "Oui, oui, *fromage,*" and went off to get some cheese.

26

The Hague

Scheveningen, with Its "Cure" House

KURHAUS

Although Scheveningen, a famous beach resort on the North Sea, is part of The Hague, it is an independent town one mile northwest of the Hague. We spent most of our time on the beach and at the Kurhaus, an internationally renowned hotel with the personality of a heavy-set dowager, as indomitable as the sea at her back. *Kurhaus* means cure house. Originally, it was a wooden bathing house, built when Jane Austin's society world (1818) flocked to the ocean to bathe and breathe salt air. Two bathing carriages trundled ladies from the bathhouse and deposited them modestly into the water. The old wooden bath house was replaced by a brick municipal bathing house with 120 rooms, a concert hall, and a gambling casino. Concerts that originated in the bath hall have made Scheveningen an international music center, with celebrities such as Leonard Bernstein and violinist Mischa Elman. When the late Mischa Elman (1891–1967) was seventy he told a reporter: "When I made my debut as a twelve-year-old in Berlin, people said, 'Isn't he wonderful for his age?' Now they are saying the same thing."

As you enter the hotel at the top of a Grand Staircase, glorious space welcomes you with wide-open arms. However, cozy cocktail tables, thick rugs, and discreet lighting in different areas create quiet intimacy. The

The Hague

gambling casino on the elegant mezzanine has a different ambience. The long line of people filing in were there to gamble—period. From the patio at sunset, we watched an awesome ball of fire slip into the North Sea—a subtle reminder that the spectacular sunset was not manmade. Long after midnight a constant flow of men, women, children, and dogs promenaded along the brightly lighted beach.

MADURODAM, THE MINIATURE CITY
Bring Binoculars

The next day, a ten-minute tram ride brought us to Madurodam,[1] the largest miniature city in the world. One hundred twenty-one models of famous sites in the Netherlands are built to scale at $1/15$ their actual size. Looking down on the Lilliputian city for the first time, with its tiny trees and joyous flowers, suddenly it's Christmas—with a feeling of holiday cheer and goodwill toward everyone. While church music floats from tiny churches, a miniature barrel-organ captivates a carnival crowd. The little city bustles with activity; trains run, windsails glide, ships move through canals, a ferris wheel turns, and windmills work. Busy people scurry around, going somewhere or doing something.

In a tiny square outside the miniature Alkmaar Cheese Museum,[2] the famous Alkmaar cheese carriers, in traditional white suits and straw hats with colored ribbons dangling from the brim, carry heavy loads of big round cheese on litters to delivery trucks. Working in pairs, the cheese carriers jog along at a funny gait to prevent the cheese from spilling.

The historic Esso oil refinery[3] in Rotterdam is represented by a little fire boat, with water jets dousing a fire on an oil tanker. Beautiful architecture enhances the charm of the fairy tale city: the Railway Station in Groningien, the Peace Palace at The Hague (donated by American Andrew Carnegie),[4] a thirteenth-century castle at Murden with turreted towers and drawbridge, and the fourteenth-century bell tower in Utrecht.

Other buildings are the Anne Frank house in Amsterdam, Queen Beatrix's residence, and the administrative center, the *Binnehof* (Innercourt) at The Hague, where a gilded Cinderella-like coach, drawn by eight pairs of horses, is followed by horse-drawn carriages headed for the Knights Hall.

Also in the miniature village is The Frans Hals Museum in Harlem, with its enclosed garden that once housed the Old Men's Almhouse, where Hals painted his famous portraits of old men. The Tree Nurseries in Boskeep are reproduced to scale with 1,730 acres of tiny trees. In the spring 20,000 miniature tulips bloom. All proceeds from Madurodam go to charity. The Canadian Pine Forest was donated in memory of thousands of Canadians who died during World War II, detonating mines in the icy North Sea.

REMBRANDT AND VERMEER
Rembrandt at the Mauritshuis Art Museum

Another short tram ride brought us to The Hague (where international treaties are signed) and the famous Mauritshuis Art Museum[5] we had seen on a small scale at Madurodam. Instead of a golden chariot opposite the Knights' Hall, there is an ice-cream stand in the Inner Court. Another added attraction was a mini-skirted model with pop-out breasts, posing on a low stone wall ornamented with a wrought-iron fence. People gathered 'round as she twisted into come-hither positions and smiled seductively for the camera. Leaving the burlesque show, we entered the museum and a world of beauty.

The Mauritshuis Museum, a seventeenth-century mansion, belonged to Johan Mauritis, great-nephew of William the Silent's youngest son. Today, his bedroom is used to exhibit Rembrandt's paintings. Early in his career, Rembrandt painted the dramatic black and white *Anatomy Lesson of Dr. Nicholas Tulp,* the doctor who prescribed fifty cups of tea a day for his patients. He is lecturing to seven men during a post mortem examination. His knife is pointed toward a sheet-covered corpse, but it is not the corpse we notice; it is Dr. Tulp and the remarkable faces of the observers above their white ruffs. The positioning of the men and their ruffs at different angles forms a composition a stage director would appreciate.

Rembrandt (1606–1669) was raised by a deeply religious mother. Biblical characters were as familiar to him as his own family, and he painted them with empathy, such as *The Prodigal Son* and *The Jewish Wife.* His most famous painting is in the Rijks Museum in Amsterdam. People still call it *The Night Watch* (1642),[6] although when it was cleaned in 1946,[7] it turned out to be a daytime scene. For twenty years Rembrandt had it all—worldly success, a happy marriage, and material possessions. His last twenty years brought personal tragedy,[8] bankruptcy, and humiliation. He withdrew from society and created hundreds of etchings, landscapes, and masterpieces. One of his self-portraits is in the Mauritshuis, as well as *Adam and Eve in Paradise,* which he painted with Jan Brueghel. His last painting, *Simeon with the Christ Child in the Temple,* is there, too. At the

The Hague

end of his life, his hand crippled with arthritis, Rembrandt thought of old Simeon who, at the end of his life, was privileged to see the Holy Family in the Temple, where they had come to offer a sacrifice according to Jewish law.

Jan Vermeer at the Mauritshuis Art Museum

If you have only a short time to visit the Mauritshuis, look for Rembrandt's contemporary, Jan Vermeer's *View of Delft* and *Girl with a Pearl Earring*. In *View of Delft*, he painted the city before a rainstorm, from across the wide Rotterdam Canal. *View of Delft* is mostly a view of a gloriously lighted sky with church steeples, turrets, gables, and chimneys piercing the flat horizon. Light reflected from the sky shimmers in the water with shadows from buildings, bridges, and boats.

Vermeer's *Girl with a Pearl Earring*

Girl with a Pearl Earring, probably one of Vermeer's daughters, responds on cue: "Turn toward me," and she does. She looks directly at you—lips slightly parted. She is young, innocent, vulnerable, trusting—the greatest attraction at the Mauritshuis. Her blue Dutch headkerchief is silhouetted against a yellow background and mysterious dark wall. A dot of paint becomes a luminous pearl earring. When very few knew of Vermeer, van Gogh said in amazement: "This strange painter's palette consists of blue, lemon-yellow, pearl grey, black, and white."

Vermeer's reverence for the Blessed Mother is revealed by an idealized respect for women. His wife Catharina and his daughters were the center of his life. When the economy collapsed, he moved with his family into his mother-in-law's home several blocks away, where he painted simple domestic scenes. He used the corner of one room, lighted from the north. By changing furniture, draperies, and wall hangings, he painted different scenarios: the maid pouring milk into a bowl, Catharina writing or reading a letter, or baking bread. By his magical use of light, you can almost see the texture of the bread.

One of his last works, *Allegory of Faith,* is now worth millions. A darkened room with heavy draperies drawn across the window is lighted by candles and torches. His model, probably Catharina, is dressed in white, looking toward heaven with her hand on her heart. Beside her on a table are a crucifix and Bible. In the background, a huge painting depicts the Virgin looking up at her crucified Son. The Virgin's foot, representing Virtue, is planted triumphantly on a globe (the world). A serpent, Evil, is crushed under a cornerstone and an apple in the foreground represents Original Sin. A glass sphere hanging from the ceiling reflects everything in the room. While Louis XIV's armies devastated the country, Vermeer's corner was an oasis of quiet serenity.

When Vermeer died, impoverished, at forty-three, his paintings were confiscated to pay debts—even his wife's favorite, *An Artist in His Studio.* Three hundred years later, Hitler paid $700,000 for it. Allies found it hidden in a salt mine near Salzburg; now it is safe in the History of Art Museum in Vienna.

Vermeer lived during the end of the Golden Age of Dutch painting; a time that blossomed full-blown like a brilliant Dutch tulip. The soothing effect of a Vermeer painting calms harassed mothers, cures anxiety, and saves executives a session with their psychiatrist.

27

Delft
Never on Sunday

WILLIAM THE SILENT'S home in Delft is twenty minutes from The Hague. From the train station, on a beautiful warm day, we inquired our way along a canal to the uncrowded Market Square, to buy wooden shoes and eat a Belgian pancake the size of a frisbee. The new (fourteenth-century) Dutch Reformed Church, where William the Silent, Prince of Orange, is buried, occupies the east side of the square. About twenty grey-haired couples in their Sunday best had disappeared into the enormous Gothic church, where descendants of the House of Orange are buried behind William the Silent's marble tomb. Bad news; the church is open to tourists only on weekdays. Never on Sunday. We wandered behind the church, where Delft pottery shops were open, and took pictures of a little arched bridge over the canal.

At the tourist office on the square near the New Church, we bought loud-colored, tulip-decorated neckties for quiet, conservative friends. A busy but patient salesgirl taught us to say "hollow" (hello), "dankuvel" (thank you), and "Whodunduck?" (How do you do?). She also told us a lot of funny translations. The only one I remember *is*, "We'll cross that bridge when we get there." They say: "Who lives then, will worry about it then." *Wie dan Leeft, wie dan Zorgt.*

Back to Europe with the BUSY BODY

She pointed directly across the square to the site where Jan Vermeer once lived. Today, the house has a green awning. The original building, a combination home and tavern, belonged to Vermeer's father. Jan Vermeer worked with his father in the tavern and sold art as a sideline. When he married, he lived there with his wife and eleven children.[1]

THE FATHER OF INTERNATIONAL LAW
Hugo Grotius (1583–1645) and a Heavy Trunk

The Market Square in Delft is dominated by a huge statue of Hugo Grotius,[2] Father of International Law—called by some the greatest intellectual genius since Aristotle. Born a year before William the Silent was murdered (1584), Grotius lived through the horrible Thirty Years' War, and like William the Silent, deplored intolerance and cruelty.

After graduating from the University of Leiden at fifteen with a law degree, he spent a year in France as a diplomat. At The Hague, he represented the Dutch East India Company and was made attorney general by William the Silent's son, Maurice—who later became his enemy. Calvinist Maurice, as intolerant and fanatical as Catholic Philip II of Spain, was determined to rid the Netherlands of Spanish troops by force. He was more than annoyed with the twelve-year truce of 1609 and with those responsible for negotiating it. (In the same year, Henry Hudson discovered the Hudson River.)

Grotius, already famous for his attempt to prevent war, disagreed with a professor at the University of Leiden who believed that God chose to save only a few "elect." Grotius and others, contrary to the belief of Prince Maurice, believed in God's goodness and justice for all men. Militant Calvinists, however, persecuted their fellow Protestants as unmercifully as the Spanish king persecuted Protestants. Grotius was arrested, sentenced to life imprisonment, and sent to a ninth-century fortress, where he was allowed two rooms for his wife and seven children. Fortunately, he was permitted unlimited books, which his wife (accompanied by soldiers) obtained from a shop in town. After two years, she arranged Grotius' escape in a four-foot trunk supposedly filled with books. Instead, it contained Grotius in his underwear and silk stockings. Panting soldiers carried the heavy chest three miles to a book merchant's shop. Disguised as a mason in work clothes, with plaster smeared on his hands, Grotius escaped to Paris, where King Louis XIII gave him asylum. In France, he wrote his famous *Law of War and Peace*,[3] based on truth and justice in international law, rather than Machiavellian deceit.

Delft

Louis XIII made him French ambassador to Sweden, where he became counselor to young Queen Christiana. On his way to Rostock, after three days aboard ship in a violent storm, and a sixty-mile ride in an open wagon, Grotius died—soon after his arrival, at the age of sixty-five.

Ironically, he is buried in the New Church in Delft with the dukes of Orange, including his enemy, Maurice, who made him an outcast. He wrote his own rueful epitaph, "This is Hugo Grotius, captive and exile of the Dutch but envoy of the great Kingdom of Sweden."[4]

Four hundred years later, arguments about the justification of war continue, and negotiations are as frustrating as ever. According to some wit, even Moses had to compromise. Supposedly, when he came down from the mountain with the Ten Commandments, he said: "Well, we reasoned together. I got Him down to ten, but adultery is still in."

WILLIAM THE SILENT'S PRINSENHOF
Sex on the Menu

We left Market Square to find William the Silent's Prinsenhof, or "Prince's Court," opposite the eleventh-century Old Church where Vermeer is buried. It's called the "leaning church." To prevent more leaning, the church was closed for repairs.

The three-story Prinsenhof is in Old Delft, across the canal on a shady street. The building was purchased by devout ladies of the Third Order of Saint Francis. Enlarged and dedicated to Saint Agatha,[5] 108 nuns were living there when the Calvinists confiscated it (1568). The States of Holland made the building available to William the Silent, and when his last son, benevolent Frederick Henry,[6] was born there, the building was officially given to the prince.

We entered the Prinsenhof through an arched wooden gate on the left of the stone building and found ourselves in a small, shady courtyard, where the only open door led into a restaurant. That was a shock—what next? After we had adjusted to the idea of a restaurant in our hero's home (on second thought, maybe the old stone cave-like ambiance could be romantic), but then another shock—worse. Pictures on the menu featured near-nudes instead of food! Sex on the menu in Saint Agatha's convent! At one end of the restaurant, formerly the nuns' Assembly Room, a tiny duck-your-head door is carved from rock and leads into the Historical Hall—not open yet. Waiting for opening time, we walked through the garden for a better view of the 600–year-old large building that once housed

William the Silent's court. A dozen tourists had gathered outside the locked door, and at two o'clock, a dour, key-jangling woman opened the door as brusquely as if she were herding cows through a gate. At the end of an entrance hall, once part of the old chapel, she led us toward the Historical Hall, formerly the refectory, where today souvenirs and tickets to the museum are sold. I headed straight for the bottom step of a staircase, where three bullet holes are covered with plastic. After the assassin's attack on William the Silent, he was carried into the dining hall opposite the staircase and laid on a hastily cleared table. Today the comparatively small, oblong table, covered by an elegant tapestry, is placed dramatically alone in the large, empty room.

28

Kraków

A Poet, an Engineer, and a Piano Player

ON THIS TRIP, with two friends, we brought a wheelchair in which to pile "things." At the train station we bought Polish money. One zloty equals two French francs. We piled our luggage into the wheelchair and pushed it up and down steps and over curbs to the Francuski Hotel, a few blocks away, inside the remains of a medieval wall. The wall was plastered solid with brightly-colored paintings. After making ourselves at home in the beautiful turn-of-the-century eclectic hotel, we began our city tour in the huge medieval Market Place (Rynek Glówny), surrounded by outdoor cafés. The famous landmarks are the Cloth Hall, the Town Hall Tower, the Barbican (fortress), and Florian Gate, named for a Roman officer martyr, one of their patron saints. The monument in the center of the square is dedicated to Michiewitz, the national poet.[1]

Saint Mary's Church with its two uneven towers dominates the square. From the higher tower, in the thirteenth century, a nineteen-year-old sentry-trumpeter stayed at his post playing a hymn to Our Lady, while savage Tartans invaded and burned the city. His song ended when an arrow pierced his throat. In his memory, every hour a trumpeter blows five long, sad notes that end abruptly. Most people use the fanfare to check their watches for the correct time.

Back to Europe with the BUSY BODY

Medieval wall used as art gallery

Saint Mary's glory is the triptych wooden altarpiece with 200 carved figures. The facial expressions are wonderful! One lady has that dubious "I don't think so" look. Kraków has thirty-nine churches and twenty-five convents. We didn't visit them all, but it seemed that way.

On top of Wawel Hill (Vavel Hill), the Italian Renaissance castle was the home of Polish kings. Elizabeth Sforza, the Italian wife of one of the Augustus kings,[2] brought architects and artists with her. One collection of Belgian tapestries, (a set of 136) is the largest in Europe. The exciting story of the collection should be called "The Case of the Missing Tapestries." On September 3, 1939, Nazi tanks invaded Poland. Two days later, to save the tapestries, they were floated down the Vistual River on a coal barge that took them to Romania, out to the Black Sea along the Mediterranean coast to Cornwall, then to London, Nova Scotia, and Ottawa, where they were stolen. Twenty-two years later, in 1961, the tapestries arrived just as mysteriously, back in Poland.

The most fun we had in the castle was in the six rooms filled with Persian rugs and Turkish tents, that conjure up visions of Omar Khayyam's *Rubaiyat* and sensuous, silk-clad, dancing girls in *Tales of the Arabian Nights*. In the Throne Room or "Heads' Room," 194 Italian Renaissance wooden faces peer down from the ceiling. Five hundred years ago, when that same Augustus (with the wife from Milan) was about to sentence a woman accused of stealing a belt from the market place, a voice from one of

Kraków

the heads called out: "King Augustus, pass a just sentence." The terrified king pardoned her, but quickly ordered a sculptor to carve a wooden band over the mouth that talked. And there it is—the mouth still gagged.

The Cathedral, where kings and queens were crowned and buried, is also on Wawel Hill. Outside the door, a pretty, dark-haired girl asked if we would like a tour in English. We certainly would. In perfect and audible English she explained the history of the awesome beauty. As she guided us through crowds she condensed her encyclopedic knowledge with expert timing. Outstanding is the marble and silver sarcophagus of Saint Stanislaus,[3] an archbishop murdered in 1079 by a king who didn't like church rules. Another magnificent sarcophagus is Queen Jadwika's. Against her will, she was married in 1386 to the Grand Duke of Lithuania, who was crowned king of Poland under the title of Wladislaus II. Jadwika sacrificed her true lover to unite Lithuania and Poland under one king. The duke's conversion to Catholicism accomplished what Teutonic Knights had attempted by tyranny and bloodshed for 200 years.

In the ornate "Chapel of the Two Sigismunds," both kings recline in niches, one above the other, in the same nonchalant position—each propped up on an elbow with one leg crossed over the other. Sigismund the Old (on top) looks as if his neck is killing him. Our pretty guide told us that the crypts of four Polish heroes are under the cathedral: Kosciuszka, an engineer; Michiewicz, a poet; and Paderewski, a concert pianist. Also buried there is King John III Sobieski who, with his Polish army in 1683, rescued Vienna from the Turks after a two-month siege. To celebrate the victory, Vienna bakers invented croissants in the shape of the Moslems' small crescent moon.

THADDEUS KOSCIUSZKA (1746–1817)
Unlucky in Love but Lucky for Americans

After a disastrous love affair, when his girlfriend's father had him beaten up, thirty-year-old Thaddeus Kosciuszka, tall, blond, and handsome, left Poland and arrived in Philadelphia, in 1776, to help the American colonists in their fight for freedom. His own country had recently been divided among Russia, Prussia, and Austria.[4] In Poland his friends called him "Thad," but in America, General Washington called him "Kosci" (Kosciuszka was too much even for George Washington). Since Thad had studied engineering and architecture under the famous French engineer Peyronnet, the Continental Congress assigned him to build fortifications

Back to Europe with the BUSY BODY

along the Delaware River. Thanks to his plans, Washington crossed the Delaware, December 8, 1776, safely, with the enemy only six miles behind. On Christmas Eve Washington crossed the Delaware again—in a blinding snowstorm—to reach the Pennsylvania side, where he captured supplies and 1,000 British mercenaries.

Next, Thad was ordered to find and fortify a site to stop General Burgoyne, marching from Canada along the Hudson River. Kosciuszka chose Bemis Heights, ten miles from Saratoga in upstate New York. The site, on top of two hills, overlooked woods and the river. The Battle of Saratoga marked the turning point for the colonists in their struggle against Britain. Despite the victory, led by brilliant Benedict Arnold (wounded during the assault),[5] Washington's troops at Valley Forge were freezing to death and starving. Saratoga, to the north, was even colder, with four-foot snowdrifts.

Kosci's next assignment was to choose and fortify a site on the Hudson River, the most important area to be defended. Kosciuszka chose West Point, where he met General Washington for the first time. When the British retreated, Kosci was the toast of the Hudson River Valley, and Washington named him chief engineer of the Southern Army. After five years as an engineer, he was given command of an advance post. A few days later, Cornwall surrendered at Yorktown. In appreciation of Kosciuszka's genius, Washington presented him with a sword, two pistols, a cameo ring, and membership in the Honorary Society of Cincinnati.[6]

Back in Poland (1784), Thad, now thirty-eight, fell in love a second time. But like his first love, the romance ended the same way, with the girl's furious father forbidding Thad to ever see his daughter again. Thad's nobility wasn't high enough on the nobility scale, and, besides, Thad was dangerous. He wanted to free the peasants. Most nobles wanted them to remain serfs.

When Thad was asked to lead a Polish revolt against Russia, Prussia reneged on a treaty to help the Poles, and Polish king Sigismund I, despite his promise to back the uprising, gave in to Empress Catherine of Russia. Prussian troops took Kraków and Warsaw, then Austrian troops joined Russia and Prussia, and the revolt collapsed. Thad, unconscious with a saber wound in his head and three bayonet gashes in his back, was taken to Saint Petersburg, where he lay in a tiny cell for two months. When his wounds didn't heal, the empress had him transferred to the Orlov Palace in Saint Petersburg. Two years later, in 1796, he was still there when she died. Her son, Tsar Paul I, freed Thad and gave him money to visit America—far away. When Thad asked pardon for 12,000 Polish prisoners, the tsar granted his request, on the condition that he never return to his native land, which had been wiped off the map (1794).

In America he was welcomed as a hero. Dr. Benjamin Rush, signer of the Declaration of Independence and surgeon general of the Continental Army, treated his wounds and partial paralysis, and by the time he left America, he walked with only a slight limp.

American–French diplomatic relations had gone from a high to a deep-freeze low. The penniless new nation had not helped France in her war with England. Vice President Jefferson suggested that Thad visit Paris merely as a friend of France. In Paris, Thad successfully persuaded the Directoire (now in power after the Revolution) to release American seamen seized illegally, and to accept an American ambassador.

After Napoléon's fiasco in Russia, semi-liberal Tsar Alexander I rode into Paris as conqueror, and paid public tribute to Kosciuzka. He also declared a pro-Polish policy, but at the Congress of Vienna two years later, Prussia and Austria said "No way." For the third time, Poland was parceled off to Russia, Prussia, and Austria. General Thaddeus Kosciuszka, who had spent his life fighting for freedom for the colonists in America and for his Polish people, lived his last two years with Polish friends in Switzerland.[7]

COUNT CASIMIR PULASKI (1747–1779)
A Brilliant Cavalryman Comes to Help

A year after Kosciuszka landed in Philadelphia (1776), another Polish freedom fighter, Count Casimir Pulaski, arrived at Marblehead Bay, Massachusetts. Today, 176 counties, cities, and towns are named for him.[8]

His father, Count Joseph Pulaski, a lawyer and wealthy landowner, whose estate overlooked the Vistual River, led the resistance of Polish Patriots against Russian invasion. The once-powerful Polish army, after years of peace and disarmament, was too weak to stop the invaders. The count's three sons trained the recruits. Overpowered by thousands of troops sent by Empress Catherine of Russia, Joseph Pulaski died in a Turkish prison, his sixteen-year-old son died in Siberia, and his eldest son, Francis, was found hacked to death on a battlefield.

The empress offered a huge reward for twenty-year-old Casimir, especially after his incredible defense of Czestochawa, the Polish national shrine. Furious, she demanded, "How can one man hold off our armies?"

When Austria and Prussia joined Russia to partition Poland, Casimir

Back to Europe with the BUSY BODY

fled: first to Turkey, then to Marseille, France, where he was thrown into debtors' prison. Thanks to friends who sent money, he was eventually freed (1775). At the harbour in Marseille, he watched sailors loading Beaumarchais' ships with weapons and supplies for the American colonists fighting for their freedom. Since he could no longer help his countrymen, he decided to help the Americans. A friend in Paris introduced him to seventy-year-old Benjamin Franklin, the American ambassador, who gave him a letter of introduction to the colonists' Commander-in-Chief, George Washington.

Casimir, now thirty, hero of Polish patriots, left for America from Nantes. Here again, sailors stored desperately-needed supplies aboard ship for the American colonists. A month later, the *Reprisal* arrived at Marblehead Bay Massachusetts. An American general who spoke French welcomed him, gave him a horse and a map, and pointed that-a-way to Philadelphia. Somehow, without knowing a word of English, he reached Washington's headquarters a few miles south of Philadelphia, where twenty-two-year-old marquis de Lafayette met him. (Pulaski brought him a letter from his wife.)

Most of Pulaski's American experience was plain frustration. Washington appointed the fierce thirty-year-old freedom fighter as his aide, but Casimir wanted to use his expertise in cavalry and guerilla tactics, to win battles as he had in Poland. The colonists used horses only as messengers. Finally, during a disastrous retreat at the Battle of Brandywine, his brilliant tactics saved so many lives, he was promoted to brigadier general.

At the Battle of Chestnut Hill, off the Jersey shore, although Pulaski couldn't shout commands in English, his men charged behind their ferocious-looking leader (wild black hair and huge mustache) as he led them in a surprise attack toward the enemy, brandishing his sword high in the air, shouting Polish war-hoops. When the astonished British troops fled, Pulaski's ragged soldiers were even more astonished at their victory.

Five months later, after no orders, he resigned his commission. At least during the horrible winter at Valley Forge he had received permission to bring the horses to Trenton, so they wouldn't freeze to death.

After his resignation, General Washington, at Casimir's suggestion, put him in charge of a corps of cavalry and infantrymen to act only under Washington's orders. Congress gave him $50,000, 68 horses, and 200 infantrymen. At headquarters in Baltimore, Maryland, he set up a rigorous training program, and transformed inexperienced, undisciplined men into fighting cavalry troops, proud of themselves and their accomplishments. Glamorous uniforms helped, too; gold buttons glistened in the sun, and sky-blue cloaks, tossed over their shoulders with panache, showed off the different colors of their divisions. One proud soldier wrote home: "I feel like a General myself in this fancy outfit"—and still no action.

Finally, orders came to proceed to Charleston, where his 300 troops defeated 3,600 British redcoats at a high price—swamp fever. Shaking with chills and fever, they waited weeks for a promised French fleet to arrive to help liberate Savannah. In September of 1779, they spotted the 22 ships, with 5,000 men under the command of Admiral Charles d'Estaing. Then the ships disappeared! Pulaski and his men galloped out of camp to find them. Along the way, he captured so many British, he had more prisoners than men. He found the fleet off the sandy dunes three miles from the colonists' headquarters, at Greenwich on the Wellington River. Despite the kissing and hugging welcome, d'Estaing, without telling the Americans, had sent word to the British in Savannah to surrender. They said, "Give us twenty-four hours." He agreed, and the British proceeded to use the time to build up barricades.

French ships bombarded Savannah, and the French infantry moved in—in torrential rain. Drastic action was needed, and Pulaski was named commander of both the French and American cavalry. As they discussed strategy, a traitor eavesdropped and reported the entire plan of attack. Pulaski's cavalry raced to help, but in the battle, Admiral d'Estaing was wounded, and thirty-two-year-old Casimir Pulaski died of gangrene from cannonball wounds in his thigh and chest.

Casimir Pulaski's tomb is not in the Kraków Cathedral. He died clutching a medal of Our Lady of Czestochowa, and was buried at sea off the coast of Georgia.

ADAM MICKIEWICZ (1789–1855)
The Voice of Poland

I call him Poland's "somehow" poet. He was born in Lithuania, which at that time was ruled by Russia. His father, a police court lawyer, died when Adam was fourteen, leaving a widow and five children practically penniless. Somehow, Adam went to the University at Vilna, where he joined a secret youth society and wrote about freedom. He and other students were arrested and sentenced for a year and a half in a Russian jail.

After a five-year exile he somehow obtained a passport from Tsar Alexander I, and permission to leave Russia (1824). Now, the poor twenty-six-year-old somehow got himself to Germany and Italy, where he became friends with James Fenimore Cooper and Samuel Morse, painter and inventor of the telegraph. After the 1830 Revolution in Paris and Brussels, he arrived in Paris, where he worked with seventy-year-old Lafayette and others to form a Franco-Polish Committee to free his fellow countrymen left without a country. Somehow, he found time to write a masterpiece, *Pan Tadeuxz*, a nostalgic poem about wealthy Poles before Napoléon.

Wherever there was an uprising against tyrants, he was on the scene. When the 1848 Revolution exploded throughout Europe, Mickiewicz returned to Italy to organize a Slavic Legion to free Italians from Austrian rule. During the Crimean War, he went to Turkey to organize Polish troops to fight Russian aggression. He died of cholera in Constantinople, but his poetry and literature continued to give hope and encouragement to persecuted people. Polish shipyard workers, striking for bread and freedom from Communism in 1980–1981, defiantly sang their national anthem: "Poland has not perished while we still live." Their leader, Lech Walesa, had professional actors read to them Mickiewicz's *The Polish Nation* and *The Polish Pilgrimage*. Each worker wore a cross with a picture of Our Lady of Czestochowa. Attached was Mickiewicz's translation of Byron's poem, "The Giaour": "The battle of freedom once begun, bequeathed by father, passes to the son. A hundred times crushed by the foes' might, still it will be won." Somehow, after once being obliterated, Poland somehow survives.

IGNACE PADEREWSKI (1860–1941)
A Concert Pianist with a Mission — and a Spider

Paderewski was three when Poland was divided between Russia, Prussia, and Austria. During the 1863 revolt, his father, an estate manager for a wealthy family, was literally carted off to prison by Russian Cossacks for his dangerous thoughts, but was released after a year. When Paderewski's mother died, soon after his birth, relatives raised him. His always-optimistic father recognized the little boy's musical genius and arranged for the best possible training. At the University of Warsaw, twenty-year-old Paderewski married and had a son, but his young wife died in childbirth. Paderewski, and now his son, were cared for by friends and relatives.

After studying in Berlin, Vienna, and Strasbourg, Paderewski got his big break when an actress (his piano teacher's wife), invited him to play onstage between her dramatic recitations. At twenty-seven, he was giving concerts throughout Europe. Tall and handsome, his distinguishing feature was a mop of bushy, bronze-colored hair. In Berlin, when a cab driver asked him where he wanted to go, a stranger yelled: "To a barber shop."

At thirty-seven, he married Helena Gorska, a widow. She and her husband, Paderewski's friend, had cared for his son until the boy died of polio at twenty. Wives of brilliant men require a special talent to continually bolster their husband's faith in themselves. After each concert Helena was there to congratulate him; she'd find him weak and drenched with perspiration. Never would she allow a word of criticism about her husband: "Criticism is not friendship and loyalty. Besides, no one knows him better than he knows himself."

Wealthy and famous, they bought an estate in Switzerland,[9] where Paderewski composed music for six of Mickiewicz's patriotic poems. As he practiced, he noticed that every time he played notes up the scale, a spider climbed upward. When he played down the scale, the spider came down. Anyone want to check that out?

When he toured America in 1915, under the sponsorship of the Steinway Piano people, he bought a ranch in California[10] and campaigned for Woodrow Wilson as president. During his concerts, he appealed to Americans, especially the nine million Americans of Polish descent, to help his destitute countrymen.

At the beginning of World War I tsarist Russia was overthrown, and the part of Poland held by Russia was freed (for a short time) before Russian Communists took control. After the Armistice Paderewski returned to his ravaged homeland. He was elected prime minister and a delegate to the Versailles Peace Conference, where Poland was declared a free nation. Jubilant, Paderewski returned to Poland—to find arrogant landowners once again in power. The superb statesman and diplomat resigned rather than deal with political intrigue and petty spitefulness.

His fortune, given to Polish charities, was gone. To regroup, in 1926, he returned to the concert halls and to more fame. In America (at age seventy), he visited President Hoover, whom he had met twenty-five years before, when Hoover was an engineering student at Stanford University. Hoover arranged food and supplies for starving Poland and other war-ravaged European countries. Then came another war. On January 23, 1940, Paderewski addressed the National Assembly in Paris, pleading for his people after Hitler decimated Poland. That summer France also fell to the Nazis. In America, Paderewski talked with President Roosevelt and addressed Congress, again appealing to Polish-Americans for help. On Christmas, 1940, on a radio talk-show, he thanked God for permitting him to come to the land of the free. He died the next year at eighty-one.

SISTER FAUSTINA (1905–1938)
and American Money

Besides the castle and cathedral on Wawel Hill, another place we visited was the chapel where Christ appeared in 1931 to a twenty-six-year-old nun in a convent outside Kraków. We had no idea where it was but our taxi driver, Hendryk[11] (the joy of our visit to Kraków), brought us there. During the twenty-minute ride to Ladiewniki, Hendryk, who speaks many languages, entertained us. Hendryk is big. He could have hugged all three of us at once. Happy one minute, melancholy the next, his voice changed from one dramatic nuance to another: "I laugh so I won't cry." He helped us with our Polish vocabulary: goodbye, *Do widzenia*; thank you, *dziekuje*; please, *groze*; excuse me, *przepraszam*; yes, *tak*; no, *nie*.

We arrived at the convent chapel of The Sisters of Mercy in time for Mass. To the left of the altar is the painting of Christ as He described it to Sister Faustina and asked to have it made, depicting a God of infinite mercy.

Sister Faustina Kowalska, poor and uneducated, lived during terrible World War I and brutal German and Russian occupations. When Christ appeared to her in 1931 and 1933, He told her she must tell mankind to draw close to His merciful heart and He would fill all with peace. She was to bring the devotion of His mercy to the world. When the Blessed Mother appeared on August 15, 1936, she said: "When hearts are sincere, His mercy will always prevail over His justice. You must proclaim His mercy and prepare the world for His Second Coming."

Sister Faustina predicted that, for twenty years, nothing would become of the devotion, but suddenly it would be a new splendor for the Church, a spark of light. She died at thirty-three of tuberculosis, in 1938. Six months after becoming Pope John Paul II, Karol Wojtyla, former archbishop of Kraków, took the first step toward her sainthood by declaring her "Blessed." On April 30, 2000, credited with two miracles,[12] both in the United States (Boston and Baltimore), she was canonized a saint.

Today, the devotion of God's mercy is being revived for the first time since the fourteenth century, when Christ appeared to Saint Catherine of

Siena, and said: "The sin that is never forgiven is the scorning of my mercy." Maybe now people will notice the motto on American money: "In God We Trust."

THE WIELICZKA SALT MINES
Seeing Is Believing

Someone had told us we must see the salt mines. We inquired at the hotel and the desk clerk arranged reservations for transportation and a two-hour tour in English. The salt mines, seven miles south of Kraków, are really a museum, listed by UNESCO as a World Heritage Monument, along with the Taj Mahal and The Leaning Tower of Pisa. For more than 700 years, salt has been mined here.

At the entrance to the mine we joined ten other tourists. Our guide, another twenty-ish, pretty, dark-haired girl, was accompanied by a seventy-ish man wearing a miner's hat with a little lantern on top. He is a descendant of generations of miners. They led us down a spiral wooden staircase (378 steps) to the first of fourteen chambers, one more incredible than the other. The first one has a statue carved from salt of Nicholas Copernicus, the astronomer who toured the mines in 1493 while attending the University of Kraków. He wears a medieval scholar's robe and holds a globe high above his head.

Another room is dedicated to Saint Anthony of Padua, who finds things for you. The miners prayed he would find the spot where they should dig for salt. Life-size Saint Anthony, carved in salt, holds the Baby Jesus. In another chamber, three salt-carved figures represent miners who crawled to the top of the caves with a torch suspended on a long pole to detonate pockets of gas from a safe distance. They wore hooded cloaks to protect themselves from burns in case of an explosion. In the next room, eight little gnomes are hard at work with pickaxes, wedges, and clubs. In one chamber, an enormous wooden crucifix hangs above a salt-carved altar. A statue of Our Lady of Victory is dedicated to miners who fought Swedish troops during the Thirty Years' War. Our pretty guide explained that the drudgery of underground life and hard physical labor required a lifting of minds and hearts to God and the saints in heaven. The statues inspired their imagination and provided expression for their artistic and engineering talents. Throughout the tour, our guide often deferred to the retired miner who accompanied her, then translated his contribution.

The path, well-lighted and non-claustrophobic, led to a large balcony, where we looked down into an enormous room honoring saints, kings, and thirteenth-century Polish queen Kinga from Hungary. According to legend, she wanted to bring a special gift to her subjects to make them happy, and miraculously found the salt mines in Poland. She led a saintly life and was beatified in 1690. Five colossal crystal chandeliers, electrically lighted, sparkle and glisten like those in Versailles's Hall of Mirrors to except these are carved from salt. Mass is celebrated here on July 24, December 4, and December 24.

From the balcony to the room below, we descended a salt staircase with an elegantly carved balustrade. Constantly, we had to remind ourselves that everything is carved from salt: the regal figure of Saint Kinga, the altar that took four years to complete, and a tableau from the New Testament decorating the walls. The artists' perspective skill is incredible, especially *The Last Supper*. A statue of Pope John Paul II is also here, but when he visited Kraków on June 13, 1999, he wasn't well enough to see it.

In one room along the way a band was playing "The Beer Barrel Polka." The feet of the uninhibited Americans (us) automatically began to dance. The musicians, in black uniforms, beckoned us to have our picture taken with them. They seated us in a front row and put their red-plumed hats on our heads. The picture is very funny. The black hat on my head is so big, all you can see is a nose and mouth under enormous red feathers.

The last cavernous room has a post office, gift shop, and café with tables and benches. It is so enormous that during winter it is used for soccer and basketball games. We stayed there about ten minutes, breathing the cool, salt air before being whisked to the top of the mine in an original miners' lift.

CZESTOCHOWA
A Tour Guide Out of Uniform

We couldn't leave Poland without visiting the town of Czestochowa, to see a painting of Poland's patron saint. The original painting, destroyed in a fire, was a Byzantine icon representing the Mother of God, Theotoko.[13] A Hungarian prince brought it to the Paulist monastery here in the fifteenth century.

Czestochowa is a two-hour train ride from Kraków. When we arrived, we wondered: "Now what?" A little bald-headed seventy-ish man in a black sweater smiled at us and asked in English if he could help. "We came to visit

Kraków

Our Lady of Czestochowa." His beautiful smile absolutely beamed: "Just follow me." We climbed aboard a crowded trolley car for a few blocks, got off, crossed the street, and boarded another one for a few more blocks, then hopped out in front of a beautiful enormous park. As we walked up a hill, our escort told us he was a priest at the monastery and had been visiting his family in Kraków. Ahead of us, at the top of a hill called Jasna Gora (Mount of Light), we saw a church steeple and a sprawled-out monastery, in a park-like setting that holds thousands of pilgrims. At the monastery, two guards greeted our little priest with big grins. Before saying goodbye, the gentle priest, who had survived fifty years of sadistic Nazi and Communist rule,[14] directed us to the chapel of Our Lady.

As we entered, Mass had just begun. We found seats on a wooden bench in the small Baroque church and sang along with the Polish people—not happy, joyful songs; more like repetitive, pleading petitions. We didn't understand a word. Priests distributed communion among men, women, and children, who knelt on the hard marble floor. After Mass, we took a closer look at the elaborately framed painting above the altar. The dark-faced Madonna holding her Infant Son looks straight at you. Large jeweled crowns on the Mother and Son create sparkling halos of light above their dark faces. Two slashes on the Madonna's face are left from a forty-day siege in 1655 by Swedish troops. The national shrine at Czestochowa is a world-famous pilgrimage place, symbolizing liberty and patriotism for the Polish people. During the successful shipyard strike at Gdansk against the Communists in 1980 and 1981, the leader, Lech Walesa, and the workers wore a picture of Our Lady of Czestochowa, queen of Poland, around their necks.

To think we had to leave Kraków and the beautiful hotel with the elegant mahogany staircase—not to mention our last breakfast. By now we knew enough to sit near the buffet table to shorten our many trips for omelets made to order, weiner-schnitzel, cereal, sauerkraut, fruit, cheese, ham, breads, juice, and more and more. Thank heavens the chef, in his tall hat, stood at the opposite end of the room.

After breakfast we shopped at the beautiful medieval Cloth Hall, which is lined with booths on each side of a central arcade. We bought amber jewelry, sheepskin rugs, and cozy rabbitskin-lined slippers. The enormous marketplace was filled with people, pigeons, and merchants selling their wares. We bought some roses to put on the Virgin's altar at nearby Saint

Back to Europe with the BUSY BODY

Mary's and had our picture taken with the little man selling them. Musicians and dancers in native costumes performed on a platform, and from below, we had a good look at their fancy rope shoes.

The only language problem was the word "music." We made reservations at a restaurant that advertised "music" and hurried to be on time to sit near the big baby grand piano. But no one ever came to play it! It just sat there laughing at us, part of the decor. Who knows? Maybe the word for music is "piano." Other nights, we ate at different cafés on the main square and watched vacationers being driven in horsedrawn carriages *(droshkies)*, or zooming around in do-it-yourself vehicles—all this activity while being serenaded by musicians and singers. The best musicians were an old man making music with a saw, accompanied by a young girl violinist at a street corner. But a policeman gave them a ticket. What we didn't like were the older, costumed musicians walking around passing a hat. We left money for those who didn't ask for it.

Our visit to Kraków ended at a small restaurant in the Jewish quarter, where Russian folksingers livened up the quiet, staid atmosphere. Out in the street, however, Jewish girls joined hands in a circle to sing and dance. Saturday was their celebration day. The next morning, inside the small Balice Airport, people with luggage, jam-packed together, waited patiently.

On our British Airways flight to London and home, an article in a Kraków magazine quoted the mayor of Kraków during an interview. In reference to a proposed new center in a historic site near the railway station, Mayor Gótas stated: "I tend to be cautious and skeptical. . . but I think reserve may cushion possible failures that are part and parcel of one's life. Not all our hopes need to come true." I'm glad he said that. Now I feel better.

29

Greece
Paris to Athens

RUE DE LA HUCHETTE in Paris, lined with Greek restaurants and bursting with vitality, happy music, and delicious aromas, was our home for awhile in Paris. We couldn't end our trip without visiting Greece, where the motto is: *Ysou Ke Harasou,* "Be Happy!"

In 4000 B.C. the Greek name for Adam was *Enkidu.* He comes into the world totally innocent and is introduced to a prostitute. "Eat bread, Enkidu [it's] the custom of the land. Enkidu ate bread until he was full; he drank beer, seven goblets. His mind reeled, he became giddy, his heart pounded. His face became flushed. A barber dressed the hair of his body. He anointed himself with oil and became a human being."

If anyone can put life into perspective, it is the Greeks. Six thousand years ago a Greek poet in Egypt wrote: "My wife is thanking God for all he has given her. My mother is prostrate beside the sacred river. There is not, methinks, much hope of dinner."

ATHENS
You Gotta Have a God — Maybe Twenty

The Athens airport, the Olympic Terminal, resembles a big-city post office. No problem about getting lost and no problem with carry-on luggage. Step outside, cross the street, stand in line for a taxi, and try to guess the relationship between people. Greek men are a real challenge. Their blasé behavior toward the women they were meeting was so different from that of enthusiastic Americans, I decided most of them were meeting their mothers-in-law.

Although the late March sky was overcast, the moist air was balmy. On this trip, my constant (and sometimes not-so-constant) traveling companion was a tall, handsome male who could pass for a Greek or a Hollywood movie producer. Our taxi driver, affable, English-speaking George, drove us to an upscale hotel fifteen minutes from the airport, near a race track and the port of Piraeus. No complaints, except for constant commuting into town. Hadrian's Arch and the columns of Zeus' Temple became old friends waiting for us to drive by one more time. The biggest surprise at the hotel was a blonde saleslady from Fort Worth, Texas, in the gift shop. A Texas accent in a Greek gift shop? What was she doing there? There had to be a man involved.

CAPE SOUNION

Since we had missed the city bus tour from the hotel, we took the only afternoon tour available—to Cape Sounion, a beautiful half-hour drive along the Saronic Gulf to the Aegean Sea. Up, down, and around curves, we passed barren cliffs that plunged to the depths of blue-green water.

At Cape Sounion white Doric columns, silhouetted against the sky, stand atop an acropolis surrounded by the Aegean. Only the columns remain of a fifth-century temple dedicated to Poseidon, Greek god of the sea.

Temperamental Poseidon, brother of the number-one god, Zeus, lived in a golden palace in the depths of the Mediterranean Sea, where he held court, rode in his seashell chariot, and carried a trident. He always sided with the Greeks, but one never knew when he might become angry. His son Aeolus, ruler of the wind, was just as predictable. Thousands of years ago, Greek sailors offered a last sacrifice to Poseidon in the temple before leaving the safety of the Saronic Gulf for the dangers of the open archipelago. The gods were always a first priority with the Greeks, and when their prayers were answered, they erected beautiful monuments in thanksgiving. Today, they worship their Christian God with the same fervor. The warmth and courtesy of the Greek people reflect the joy of their religion.

Our bus driver deposited his twenty or so passengers at the foot of the hill, where we started an easy climb. We stood at the top surrounded by sea and sky. The wind was blowing and a slight rain stirred visions of fierce storms, small boats, and ancient mariners rounding the cape. Sunset at dusk or blue skies over sparkling water would have been more colorful, but whatever the setting, the haunting simplicity of the majestic, stone-topped columns speaks of eternity and our place in it.

THE ACROPOLIS AND DIONYSUS' THEATER
Or, "Come, Josephine, in My Flying Machine"

The second overcast day in Athens, our taxi driver brought us to the world-renowned Acropolis and Parthenon. The climb to the top is comparatively easy. One scenic view overlooks the remains of the theater of Dionysus, where 3,000 people once brought pillows to sit on—where drama as we know it developed from the worship of the god Dionysus. Dionysus, one of lusty Zeus' many sons, was the Greek god of the vine, springtime, and fertility. The Greeks believed he once lived on earth and traveled from coun-

The Theatre of Dionysus

try to country, teaching men to grow grapes and to make wine. He rode through the sky in a chariot drawn by lions and leopards, attended by dancing girls and satyrs.

In the sixth century Pisistratus, the good tyrant with the funny name, proclaimed a religious festival in Dionysus' honor to celebrate the end of winter. Originally, the raucous festivities included processions, dances, singing, and contests for new poems and songs. Leaders of different processions exchanged jokes and repartee with other leaders, and eventually the good-natured banter became written comedy; *komos* (revel), and *ode* (song).

Tragedy evolved from the minstrels' songs, rhapsodizing the gods, and Homer's heroes. Their songs, or epic poems—*rhapsodes*—came from *rhaptein* (to stitch together). This new entertainment, "tragedy," was named after goatskins the chorus wore (*tragos-goat*). In Greek mythology, goat-like satyrs provided lute music for Dionysus. As part of the devotion, a bull was sacrificed on one side of the orchestra, in a *skene* (tent). Poetry became plays, and the tent or *skene* became a building used for costumes and props. The façade of the *skene* formed the scenery. The area in front of the *skene* became the *proskenion,* or proscenium, with two or three doors for entrances to a house or palace. Later, appropriate costumes for the chorus replaced goatskins. Dialogues and choruses evolved into plays after the dramatist, Thesbis, chose one actor to play the main character in his poem.

Looking down on the ancient amphitheater, we imagined elaborately-robed actors clumping around on stage in high platform soles, attempting to appear larger-than-life. Enormous masks with huge eye openings represented the characters portrayed. Megaphones were concealed in the mouth openings, and reed pipes and flutes provided music. They had a thunder machine, and their god machine flew characters up to Mount Olympus; Herakles, for one, the Greeks' greatest hero. He wasn't too brainy, and he certainly couldn't control his emotions, but he possessed a virtue Greeks admired most, courage—and confidence that no matter who was against him, he could not be defeated. What made Herakles truly great was his sincere repentance for his wrongdoing and his willingness to repent.

Herakles:
A Dastardly Deed and the Wrath of Gods

Herakles was one of Zeus' many bastard sons. Zeus, the number one god, was married to jealous Hera, who hated this child by another woman.

Greece

When she sent serpents to kill him in his cradle, the infant strangled the snakes with his strong, chubby hands. As a boy, his studies included music. While Herakles sat on a stool with the lyre on his knees, his teacher, Linus, stood over him, keeping time. Music was not Herakles' thing. He hit so many discords that Linus thought he was doing it deliberately. How dare he humiliate a god! When Linus punched Herakles in the jaw, Herakles bashed him over the head with the lyre. Linus cracked his head on the stone floor and that was the end of the music lessons—and Linus.

When Herakles chose a life of virtue over vice, Hera was furious. She made him go berserk and kill his wife and children. To atone for his crime, his cousin gave him twelve impossible tasks to perform—but with Athena's help, he accomplished them.

As winner of a wrestling contest, Herakles won a beautiful wife who owned a vial of poisonous blood, a gift from an evil centaur, who guaranteed it would keep her husband faithful. Unaware that it was poisonous, she soaked a new tunic in the magic blood and sent it to Herakles. When the poison took effect, he threw himself on a funeral pyre to die; Zeus, however, came to the rescue, and whisked him away to Mount Olympus in the convenient god machine.

Many performances at Dionysus' theater were taken from Homer's *Iliad*,[1] tales of the Trojan War. Ares, god of war, and soft-hearted Aphrodite, the love goddess, were aiding the Trojans against the Greeks. Outraged, Hera found her husband, Zeus, and demanded: "Aren't you furious with Ares for these violent deeds? Do you mind if I smite him and chase him from battle in sorry plight?" Zeus shrugged. "Go get him. Set upon him Athena [protectress of Athenians] who is wont to bring sore pain against him." Athena donned her armor and, with Hera, sped across the sky in a chariot, while Hera "smote the horse with a stinging lash." When she found the Greek hero Diomedes,[2] she helped steer his chariot straight into Ares, the war god. "They wounded him sore. Ares bellowed as loud as when 10,000 warriors cry out in battle." He fled from the field, and flew back to Mount Olympus in the god machine.

According to Homer's *Iliad*, the Trojan War began when Paris, son of Hecuba and King Priam of Troy, was selected to judge a beauty contest among three goddesses. They all tried to bribe him, but Aphrodite's offer was the best. She promised him the most beautiful woman in the world—Helen, wife of King Menelaus of Sparta. When Paris abducted her, her husband appealed to his brother, Agamemnon, king of Mycenae, to avenge

Back to Europe with the BUSY BODY

the dastardly deed. Homer's story of King Agamemnon and his wife, Clytemnestra, was dramatized by the playwrights Aeschylus[3] and Sophocles, and performed in Dionysus' theater.

Aeschylus' *Agamemnon*:
The Face That Launched a Thousand Ships

Agamemnon is a tragedy of warfare, political and domestic. Of the many conflicts it presents, the main one is right against right—each person insisting on his right—and the kind of conflict that brings tragedy into divorce courts.

Performed during the time of art patron Pericles (495–429 B.C.), *Agamemnon* is part of a trilogy. Agamemnon, king of Mycenae, was all set to sail the Greek fleet to Troy to punish Paris and the Trojans for harboring Helen, his brother's wife. However, there was no wind, and the *triremes* (oars) couldn't budge the warships. The Oracle declared that Artemis, the Huntress, was keeping the ships from sailing until Agamemnon's eldest daughter, Iphigenia, was offered as a sacrifice—so they sacrificed her! Her father called to his men: "Lift her with strength of hand . . . as you might lift a goat for sacrifice. . . ." After she was burned on the altar the wind blew, sails billowed, and the fleet headed for Troy.

During Agamemnon's absence his wife, Clytemnestra, takes her husband's cousin as a lover.[4] She sends her son, Orestes, away but keeps her daughter Electra. Ten years later, when Agamemnon returns with Cassandra, the Trojan king's daughter, as his "war prize," Clytemnestra and her lover kill them both. Poor Agamemnon. He only tried to help his brother. But there's more—his son, Orestes, returns to kill his mother and her lover.

Although the Oracle had told him to "slay those who slew," his conscience bothers him about killing his mother, and he wanders around pursued by his tormentors, the Furies. During his wanderings, he learns that no crime is beyond atonement—even he could be made clean. When he begs Athena for forgiveness she accepts his pleas, and tells him that those who desire to be purified cannot be refused. Five hundred years later, Saint Paul told the Athenians about One who died on a cross who did just that. (*Acts* 17)

Sophocles (496–406 B.C.)

Sophocles, a younger contemporary of Aeschylus, also used myths, but unlike Aeschylus, who blamed the gods, Sophocles thought that man's

Greece

downfall or fate was determined by some character flaw or overwhelming force outside himself, over which he has no control. In *Oedipus Rex* a former king of Thebes brings on his ruin with serious "flaws"—pride and arrogance—very displeasing to the gods. He discovers his bride is actually his mother. She commits suicide, and Oedipus blinds himself, doomed to wander through Greece with his faithful daughter, Antigone. Sophocles was the first to deal in personality traits and interpersonal relationships.

Euripides (480–406 B.C.): Talk About Rejection!

Euripides wrote ninety-two plays and never won a prize. Outside Athens, however, he was the favorite playwright. With Aeschylus and Sophocles, Euripides lived through the Persian and Peloponnesian wars. Each playwright saw the rise and fall of Athens. Euripides portrayed the unjust suffering of women and innocent victims of war, especially in *The Trojan Women*. In *Medea*, performed in the amphitheater, the chorus intones: "The voice of time will change . . . womankind will be honored." Compassion for women? Judges for the play contests thought he was mad. Since Euripides had no answer to man's inhumanity to man, he solved dilemmas by whisking his characters off to Mount Olympus in the god machine.

Medea ("How Dare You Leave Me!")

Nineteenth-century English playwright William Congreve said it better. "Hell hath no fury like a woman scorned." The king of Thessaly wanted to retire, but since his son Jason was too young to rule, he made Jason's half-brother, Pelias, regent. The Oracle, however, warned Pelias to "Fear a man wearing only one sandal."

Jason grew up in a distant village, and, years later, returned to his father's palace[5] on the Aegean coast, to claim his throne. However, on the way, he had lost a sandal and came limping into town with one shoe on and one shoe off. The next thing Jason knew, he was being hurried out of town by Pelias to find a ram's fleece made of gold, hidden in a sacred grove in Colchis (today's Russia). The king's daughter, Medea, with her magic powers, helped Jason subdue the dragon guarding the Golden Fleece. Mission accomplished, Jason sailed back to Thessaly with the Golden Fleece—and Medea. Eventually Jason became king of Thessaly (after Medea poisoned Pelias), but, unfortunately, he failed to be faithful. To punish him, Medea killed her rival, the princess of Corinth, by sending her a poisoned wedding-robe. She also killed the princess' father, the king of Corinth. To further punish her unfaithful husband, she killed their two young sons. When Jason discovers her crimes, he searches for her, but she disappears into the heavens in the well-oiled god machine.

The gods could not condone her behavior, and neither could Euripides. However, in the fifth century B.C. Euripides blamed a society where women's rights were ignored and children were punished for their parents' sins—a society in which marriage vows were meaningless. "Gone is the respect for oaths. Nowhere in all . . . Hellas is honor any more to be found."

Audiences at Dionysus' theater knew all the stories by heart, but they came to see what each new playwright would do with the script. Comic playwright Aristophanes once sent a character up in the god machine to ask the gods for peace. No one was home but mischievous Hermes, the messenger, who informed him that the gods were tired of humans and had all gone on vacation.

Aristophanes (445?–385 B.C.)

Aristophanes' *Clouds* won third place in the Great Dionysian Festival. The play ridiculed new theories of education being taught by philosophers (represented by Socrates). The title suggests fuzzy, shifting, cloud-gathering thinking. When Socrates saw the play, twenty-four years after it was written, he laughed and stood up, so the crowd could see how closely the actor's mask resembled his face. He said, "When they break a jest upon me in the theater, I feel as if I were at a big party of good friends."

Clouds (The Thinkery School)

Pheidippides, a playboy son who spends his time and money betting on chariot races, has run his father into debt, and creditors are threatening to sue. According to the distracted father, it is all his wife's fault. He is a good ol' country boy and his wife is a social climber. She has spoiled the boy, who must have inherited her genes.

The father wants his son to attend school where he can learn something. He should go to "The Thinkery" School. When the son says "No way. I'll lose my tan," his father decides to go himself. A chorus of Clouds enters, and tells him that the Clouds are the only true gods, not Zeus. Strepsiades, the father, says he doesn't want to become a philosopher—only to learn eloquence and sophistry, so he can win in law court over his creditors. He wants to appear without conscience or fear.

> Bold, hasty, and wise, a concocter of lies,
> A rattler to speak,
> A regular claw of the tables of law
> A Shuffler complete, well worn in deceit.
> A supple, unprincipled, troublesome cheat;
> A hand dog accurst, a bore with the worst,
> In the tricks of the jury-courts thoroughly versed.

When Strepsiades flunks out, the Clouds tell him to send his son to the school. When told that the son refuses, they ask: "Is he your master then?" Strepsiades' reply is something like "No damn it, but he's bigger than I am. I'll go get him, and if he won't come, I'll turn the ingrate out of the house."

Pheidippides finally agrees, but says, "You'll be sorry." The father is ecstatic. He knows they teach two kinds of logic: Right Logic Law and Wrong Logic Law. He tells Socrates to make sure the boy learns how to out-talk Right Law, the old-fashioned method. Right Logic says, "I shall speak of the time when there was no trace of indecency . . . when justice was held in veneration. Evil you will avoid like plague . . . you will have regard for those who brought you up and spend your days in the gym glowing with strength and health."

Wrong Logic pleads that the new learning will give youth the ability to contradict the old laws, and to argue oneself out of any difficulties a life of sensual pleasures may lead to. "You love, seduce, you can't help that, hold nothing base to be. Why if you're in adultery caught, your place will still be ample. You've done no wrong you'll say."

The Chorus tries to warn Strepsiades against Wrong Logic, but the father is too excited. In court, his son will win over the creditors. He tells him: "You have ruined me. Now save me."

The last day of the month (the Old and New Day) arrives when debts must be paid. His son, Pheidippides, instructed in Wrong Logic, argues there can be no such day as "Old" or "New." On this technicality, Strepsiades refuses to pay his creditors, on the grounds that he has made a mistake about the gender of a word. The old man is in his glory. He won! But his son has learned all the Wrong Logic. Instead of saving his father, he beats him up, and informs him that he can prove he was right to beat him:

Back to Europe with the BUSY BODY

"I can also prove it is right to beat my mother." The heartbroken father realizes he has corrupted his son. He admits he was a fool for having abandoned fair dealing and reverence for Zeus, to follow sophistic logic and scientific atheism: "You have insulted all the blessed gods in heaven." Then he burns the Thinkery School.

No matter how serious the subject (presented in a hilarious manner), Aristophanes always leaves his audience with hope. In *Clouds* he advises, "Trust in the old ways and the old gods and this sort of thing won't happen to you."

Peace (A Rescue and Dirty Deeds)

In *Peace,* produced two years later, Pericles, the Greek ruler, has died, and the Peloponnesian states have been at war for ten years. Trygaeus, a vintner, flies to heaven in the god machine to beg Zeus for peace. When he knocks at the door Hermes greets them. He had been left behind "to guard the pots and pans and jugs and like o' that." Hermes tells the vintner that the gods have all gone to the topmost cell of Heaven's hive, because they were disgusted watching the Greeks fight each other. Peace was deep in a dungeon—a prisoner of war.

The male Chorus gets so excited at the prospect of rescuing Peace that they begin a frenzied dance that gets wilder and wilder. The vintner finally calms them down, and bribes Hermes to help them rescue Peace. While the Chorus loosens stones with pickaxes at the dungeon entrance and lowers a rope to haul up the goddess' statue, the vintner and Hermes drink a toast to Peace: "May a Greek man never have to go to war again . . . but live at home in peace beside his girl with naught to do but love and poke . . . the fire!" After Peace is rescued, Hermes gives the vintner the goddess, Floria, to take back to his farm: "Marry her and raise a crop of healthy, handsome . . . grapes."

Because of the religious origin of Aristophanes' comedies, he and other comic playwrights were allowed what was known as *sacred release,* a polite phrase for permission to be obscene. It was considered good medicine for people to occasionally let it all out—all their inhibitions and anxieties. It was perfectly acceptable to ridicule the gods, drink too much, and get down in the gutter with sex, sex, sex. They called it *catharsis,* or purging one's emotions. Sacred release was supposed to drive away evil spirits. Obviously, it didn't work. Evil spirits and demons are still rampant.

Greece

THE ACROPOLIS AND THE MUSEUM
Or, I'm Still Here

As we continued past Dionysus' theater, to the top of the Acropolis, the sun slid out from behind the clouds. It is not enough to simply climb the Acropolis in Athens. Flags should be planted, commemorating the early Greeks who worshipped here and who established the first attempt at democracy. Fifth-century B.C. temples, too beautiful to be called ruins, were built during the Age of Pericles, under the supervision of the sculptor Phidias.

Crowning the Acropolis, the Parthenon temple honored Athena the maiden (*parthenos*), goddess of war and peace, for whom the city is named. In Greek mythology, Zeus decreed that the city should be awarded to the god or goddess who could create the most useful gift. Poseidon, the sea god, conjured up a horse, but Athena, the wise virgin, won the contest with an olive tree that provided food, wood, shade, and oil for lamps and cooking. Athena's gigantic statue could be seen for miles by sailors rounding Cape Sounion. John Ruskin called her "Queen of the Air." If she were still around, she would be choking in the polluted air. The Greeks, who prided themselves on physical fitness, knew their athletes must have strong lungs, achieved by exercise and fresh air. They knew the importance of oxygen. Victory usually came to those who had the best breath control, not necessarily to the strongest. Today, Athenians can barely see each other in their smoke-filled offices.

Near the Parthenon are the remains of a temple that once had nine gates, the Propylaea. Gunpowder stored there during Turkish rule was struck by lightning in 1656: Twenty-four columns have survived, some better than others.

The "Porch of the Maidens," near the Parthenon, is part of the Erechtheon, a shrine dedicated to Poseidon's son Erechtheus. (Under Turkish rule, it was a harem.) Six gracefully-gowned ladies, the *caryatids*, have been holding the porch roof on their heads for more than 2,000 years.

Inside the Acropolis Museum

Most of the statues are thankful they still have noses, but there they are—statues influenced over thousands of years by the Babylonians, Assyrians, and Egyptians. The museum is inside a huge cave in the rock. In one room, Herakles is killing the many-headed monster, Hydra, that he fought during his Odyssey. (Each time one head was cut off, two more grew in its place.)

Back to Europe with the BUSY BODY

The Porch of the Maidens

Greece

In another room, a lamb is slung over a shepherd's shoulders. Three rooms are devoted to the sweet-faced Koraie, smiling maidens with a born-to-obey look. Whatever they did, they must have enjoyed it. Two thousand years later, they are still smiling.

The early Koraie, in long, straight skirts, stand stiff and straight as a pharaoh. A century later they were given a new look, as if a designer, with a mouthful of pins and a bolt of cloth, had swathed them in voluptuous drapes, padded their breasts, and named them "Classicism."

In the largest room, comfortably seated on a marble slab, Apollo, the sun god, and Poseidon, god of the sea, are deep in conversation. Seated with them is demure, lovely Artemis, goddess of the moon and guardian of purity among youths. The graceful fourth-century B.C. frieze shows a mastery of anatomy, and illustrates the Greeks' belief that a man's body, as well as his soul, has a glory.

A statue of Athena in her battle helmet, leaning on a lance, was practically ignored. The main attraction was sensuously draped Nike, goddess of victory, bending over to unfasten a sandal strap. So many sculptors used that pose, sandals seem to have been a problem. Either the straps kept breaking, or they had to stop and dump out sand and pebbles. Today Nike, the sexy goddess of victory, is associated with sensible shoes.

A sculpture by Phidias, *The Panathenaean Procession,* represents the city's greatest holiday, held every four years, when various tribes of Attica came to Athens to honor Athena. The sculpture shows crowds surging through the city gates, parading along the Panathenean Way through the Agora (marketplace) and up the Acropolis, to offer sacrifices to the gods before the contests. They came in chariots, on foot, and on horseback. The sculpted high-spirited horses—galloping, rearing, and charging—have inspired artists for centuries.

THE AGORA (MARKETPLACE) THROUGH THE CENTURIES

In the Acropolis Museum we had met a doctor from Ireland and a pretty, twenty-three-year-old girl from Connecticut who taught math in Cairo. A visit to the Agora was a must for her, since her aunt had participated in an archaeological dig when the American School of Classical Studies excavated the Agora in the 1950s.

From the foot of the Acropolis, we followed her along a path overlooking the once-crowded, noisy Agora. We had a balcony view, where we could envision the ancient Athenians.

Back to Europe with the BUSY BODY

Solon and a Waltz by Strauss

Johann Strauss II wrote waltzes for every occasion and for any convention that came to town. He composed "Solon's Spruche" for a ball given to honor law students at the University of Vienna. The waltz is a tribute to Solon, the ancient Greek legislator.

The good tyrant, Solon (638–559 B.C.), started the Panathenean Festival, and replaced the tyrant Draco's code and its harsh punishments (usually death), with his own more lenient code. He was the first to write down the laws posted in the Agora on wooden tablets, and, later, on stone columns. He set up a Council of four hundred to guide the city and check on the judges. Any citizen could be elected to the Council, with the right to vote in the assembly. To prevent land barons from buying up little farms, he limited the amount of land a man could own. He freed farmers who had been made slaves and declared that every father should teach his son a trade. His motto was "Nothing in Excess."

When Solon built a new shopping district, the Stoa, with shaded colonnades around the marketplace, it became the meeting-place for people throughout the Mediterranean. They exercised there, discussed politics and Egyptian philosophy, read poetry, or just hung out in the barbershop exchanging jokes (like the one about the absent-minded professor who wondered what he looked like when he was asleep, so he sat in front of a mirror with his eyes shut). One man in the Agora greeted an old friend with "I thought you were dead." The friend replied: "Well you can see I'm not." The first one said: "I don't know what to believe, you're such a liar."

Pisistratus the Builder

When Solon's cousin, Pisistratus (the good tyrant who added play contests to the Dionysus Festival), seized power, he continued Solon's democratic reforms, built white stone temples to replace the old wooden ones, built a new Parthenon, and started a temple for Dionysus. He also decreed that every four years the Panathenean Festival should include international games and contests. Citizens of every Greek city flocked to Athens—except the Spartans, who believed that soldiers who tried to out-do each other became rivals instead of a team.

Cleisthenes (506 B.C.):
Inventor of Ostracism

The next good tyrant who strolled in the Agora, Cleisthenes invented democracy—with a few flaws. Most of the Athenians were slaves. Jury duty was paid entertainment for as many as 500 jurors who hadn't the foggiest notion of what the law should be. Only native-born Athenian citizens could vote for all city officials, including army generals.

To protect the new democracy, Cleisthenes invented "ostracism." Citizens wrote the name of the man they wanted expelled from office on a piece of clay, then put their ballots into jars placed in the Agora. The man receiving the most votes was exiled for ten years. That solved the overcrowded jail problem. The democratic experiment[6] was a success, but Athens was a man's city. Women had no more rights than slaves. They stayed home, weaving and spinning; those who waited too long for marriage were called spinsters.

THE PERSIAN WARS
The Battle of Marathon

When Persian king Darius sent messengers to the Athenians demanding surrender and tribute, the Athenians threw them into a pit. Darius had already conquered Egypt and Phoenicia; now he was ready to tackle Greece. During a first attempt, his fleet of *triremes* sailed too near the rocky coast, and a storm smashed them against the shore. Two years later, the Persians successfully crossed the channel and landed at Marathon. Terrified Athenians sent their champion Olympic runner, Pheidippides, to Sparta for help. He ran two days and two nights, swimming rivers and climbing mountains. The Spartans said they couldn't come until the moon was full. Pheidippides, who had run 300 miles nonstop to Sparta and back to Marathon, then buckled himself into a heavy bronze shield to fight. Alone, against impossible odds, the Athenians defeated the Persians. After the victory, Pheidippides ran twenty-six miles to Athens to bring the good news. On the outskirts of the city, he managed to gasp "Rejoice. We conquer," then collapsed and died. To honor him, the Marathon race was made an Olympic event when the games were revived, in 1896.

After the Battle of Marathon a young politician, Themistocles, warned the Athenians that the Persians would return. He persuaded them to repair

Back to Europe with the BUSY BODY

the port of Piraeus and build dozens of *triremes*. With their powerful new trading fleet, Athens grew rich.

Leonadis (Lion's Son): Brave as a Lion

The Persians waited ten years for the next assault. King Darius had died, but his son, Xerxes, had vowed to avenge the defeat at Marathon. At the Hellespont, a strip of land north of Troy, forty-six nations joined the Persian fleet, bringing soldiers dressed in the battle gear of their homelands; foxskin caps, bronze helmets, leopard skins, lion skins, others in high boots and colored cloaks. When their boats were lashed together for the huge army to cross the water, all Asia sailed against the Greeks. At Thermopylae the Spartan commander, Leonidas, had blocked off a narrow pass between the mountains and the sea, the one place the small Greek army could hope to hold off Xerxes' hordes. Twice the Persians were turned back, but Xerxes found a Judas, a betrayer who showed him a way through the mountains. By nightfall, heroic Leonadis and his Greek soldiers were dead. Xerxes ordered his swarms to move on to Attica, the region around Athens.

Themistocles to the Rescue

When news arrived of the disaster at Thermopylae, the whole city prayed to Athena, begging her to ask Zeus for some promise of hope. The answer was given by the Oracle at Delphi, who prophesized: "The wooden wall shall not fall but will help you. . . ." Themistocles, who had warned them about the Persians, realized that the wooden wall meant a barricade of ships. He urged the Athenians to flee to the island of Salamis, a few miles east, where the fleet would protect them. When Xerxes arrived in Athens and found the city deserted, in childish revenge he burned and destroyed the homes and places of worship on the Acropolis.

At Salamis, Themistocles tricked Xerxes into believing that he would switch to the Persians' side. The ruse worked. Persian ships were trapped in the narrow waters of Salamis, and sunk before they had a chance to fight. On shore, Xerxes shouted and cursed. He had lost more than 200 ships. The rest fled for the Hellespont, Xerxes with them. On land, thirty miles from Athens, the Persian army was also defeated.[7]

Athenians rebuilt their burned city. Themistocles, responsible for the victory, built four miles of walls connecting the city with the port of Piraeus. He also organized a league of city-states, to help the Athenian navy

Greece

protect Greek cities and islands. In exchange for protection they contributed money and ships. Since the money was kept on the island of Delos, they named it the Delian League, but Themistocles, who organized it, was exiled. The new favorite, big, jolly, Cinon, was also ostracized.

THE PELOPONNESIAN WARS
and Pericles

That left Pericles as the leading citizen. Besides being a nobleman, a general, and a scholar, he was also the grand-nephew of Cleisthenes, who started Athenian democracy. Under Pericles, Athens rose from its ruins.[8] The Delian League treasury was transferred to Athens, where Athenians helped themselves to "protection" money, to rebuild their temples. The small city-states watched, as Athens became the cultural center of the Hellenic world[9]—and the most powerful. Greed comes with power, and under the guise of protection Athens gobbled up smaller cities and islands. (No democracy for the victims.) Jealous Sparta also began collecting cities. The Peloponnesian War started when Spartan troops invaded Attica, burning homes and crops.

Pericles herded Athenians behind Themistocles' walls, where refugees were penned up in appalling filth for months. Pestilence and plague killed one out of three, including Pericles, his two sons, and his sister. All this occured during the Golden Age of Pericles.

When Pericles died Athenians floundered around, electing one leader after another. Aesop wrote a fable about frogs who were grieved because they had no king. They sent ambassadors to Zeus requesting a ruler. Knowing frogs are stupid, Zeus threw a log down into a pond. When the frogs noticed that it didn't move, they grew to despise the lifeless ruler. They requested another sovereign. This time, Zeus sent an eel into the pond. Easy-going and good-natured, he made a poor king. The frogs still were not satisfied. Exasperated, Zeus finally sent a stork who, each day, ate up a frog or two. Soon there were none left to croak and complain.

A Chess Game and More Aesop's Fables

Seven years later, during the second Peloponnesian War, Pericles' nephew, Alcibiades, massacred every man on the island of Melos, then sailed off to conquer Syracuse in Sicily, the largest city in the Greek world. When messengers arrived to arrest him he defected to Sparta, and spilled the Athenians' secret plans.

Back to Europe with the BUSY BODY

The Persians aided both Sicily and Sparta against Athens with money. After two years, the Athenian fleet was defeated in the harbor at Syracuse, and Sparta, with Persian gold, built their own navy.

The third Peloponnesian War lasted eight years. Sparta's fleet destroyed the Athenians' and blockaded the harbor of Piraeus, starving the people into surrender. Spartan general Lysander and his Thirty Tyrants began an eight-month reign of terror. For nine years, Sparta ruled Athens under Critias, a traitor, until democracy was restored by an uprising.

Meanwhile Persia played a game of divide-and-conquer.[10] They switched support to their old enemy, Athens, and helped to rebuild the harbor at Piraeus. Now Sparta and Athens were both beholden to Persia, the enemy their Greek ancestors had defeated at Salamis. The once-proud rivals, Sparta and Athens, became vassals.

Sparta called the first disarmament conference in history (371 B.C.), but the conference collapsed when delegates from Thebes stalked out. The Persian king chuckled and moved another pawn on his chessboard.[11] This time he would back Thebes. With Persian aid, Thebes, forty-four miles north of Athens, defeated Sparta and became the most powerful city-state in Greece. King Philip of Macedon smiled, knowing that only an outside force could unite the Greeks. "If a house be divided against itself, it cannot stand." (Mark 3:25) Aesop, in his *Bundle of Sticks,* wrote about four sons who quarreled constantly. Their father asked each to break a bundle of sticks. None could. But each could break an individual stick. The moral was if they stuck together as friends, they could be as strong as a bundle of sticks.

Socrates (469?–399 B.C.): A Different Drummer

Another ancient in the Agora was short, stocky, Socrates, the philosopher, in bare feet and rumpled toga; the man who changed the course of human thought. After the Peloponnesian Wars people were torn with moral confusion. Socrates made them think for themselves, by asking questions such as, "What is the best way to wealth?" Answer: "Cutting down on your wants." To teach, he used maxims: "To found your life on one hope is like mooring a ship with only one anchor." Once he stood in the same spot all night, pondering a problem. He drove his neglected wife[12] crazy.

Athens under Spartan rule was no place for a philosopher. The Spartans' cruelly disciplined lives did not include discussions. Their bare-

Greece

necessity philosophy, requiring minimum speech, was called "laconic"—for Laconia, the land around Sparta. Once, an ambassador, after a lengthy address, ended by asking what he should report back to his people. The Spartans replied: "Tell them we found it as hard to listen as you did to stop talking."

Socrates' enemies arrested him for heresy and for corrupting the minds of youths. The chief instigator, a leather merchant, was the father of a student whom Socrates had advised to study philosophy, instead of working in his father's tannery business. A notice for Socrates' arrest was posted in the Agora near the prison where he spent his last ten days. He could have escaped (his friends had bribed the guards), but he chose to die for his beliefs. With friends at his side, he talked of the soul's immortality, then carried out his death sentence by drinking poison. Like the early Christians, he died defending his beliefs.

Plato (427?–347? B.C.):
Platonic Love

Short, pug-nosed Socrates was a sharp contrast to his twenty-eight-year-old student, handsome, aristocratic Plato. As Socrates' friend, he, too, was under suspicion, and forced to flee. He went to Syracuse, where he tried to teach the monarch to rule according to Socrates' ideas. The king nearly killed him; instead, he sold him into slavery. Fortunately for Plato, he was sold to a man who appreciated his ideas. The man freed him and allowed him to return to Athens. Plato, now forty, founded a school, "The Academy," near the Agora, where he taught and recorded Socrates' ideas of an ideal state, based on "platonic" love and the four Greek virtues: courage, temperance, wisdom, and justice.

Aristotle (384–322 B.C.):
The Doctor's Son

Plato's student, Aristotle, was descended from a line of physicians to the kings of Macedonia. He idolized Plato, although they disagreed about communism and equal rights for women. Aristotle believed that what everyone owns, nobody cares about, and that people are inclined to evade a duty which they expect someone else to do.

Aristotle traveled, married a princess, and became tutor to King Philip of Macedonia's wild thirteen-year-old son, Alexander. When Philip was murdered, Alexander, not yet twenty, set off to finish his father's dream of world conquest. Before he left he gave Aristotle four million dollars for scientific research, and ordered animals and plants from conquered countries to be sent back for study.

Aristotle founded a school, The Lyceum, near the Agora, and hired nearly one thousand assistants. He started the first scientific research, recorded in hundreds of reference books that were used for nearly 2,000 years. Aristotle laid the foundation for all sciences and philosophies. One day, as he waded through paperwork, a non-stop talker droned on and on and finally paused for breath. He said "I hope I'm not boring you." Aristotle replied: "Not at all. I'm not listening."

King Philip of Macedon and Demosthenes

Aristotle and the famous orator, Demosthenes, master of lung power, lived and died at exactly the same time (384–322 B.C.). While Aristotle was tutoring future Alexander the Great, Alexander's father, King Philip, was conquering the Hellenes.

Fifty years after the Peloponnesian Wars, Sparta ruled Athens. Sparta was then ousted by the Thebans, and Athens' democracy disappeared. They wanted security more than freedom. All the Greek city-states were fighting each other—exactly what King Philip of Macedon had been waiting for. During three years in Thebes as a hostage, Philip had studied the Theban king's battle tactics, paying special attention to rivalries among the Greeks. When freed, he turned his Macedonian peasants into a well-trained army, seized the Thracian gold mines, and built a navy—then conquered a Greek port town on the Aegean.

The only one concerned about all this was Demosthenes in Athens, who insisted that Philip of Macedon, not the Persians, was the most dangerous threat. In a series of famous speeches against Philip, called The Philippics, Demosthenes begged Athenians to beware of Philip of Macedon. He reminded them that they were the last hope of Greece.

Philip's first target toward world conquest was Greece. To win collaborators, he hired speechwriters and public relations men. One declared that King Philip was really a Greek at heart. He was a fine speaker, beautiful to look at, and a good companion over a cup of wine. Demosthenes climbed to the speaker's platform, interrupting the campaigner. He argued that anyone could become a good speaker. "Good looks become a woman, and the claim that Philip soaks up wine could be matched by any sponge."

Week after week, Demosthenes spoke against Philip and his Greek col-

Greece

laborators. While Athenians were making up their minds, Philip copied a Persian technique. He acquired support by secretly funneling money to pro-Macedonian parties in Greek cities. His policy paid off. When he supported Thebes in a quarrel with their neighbor, as payback, the Thebes admitted him into their inner councils—like Aesop's camel, who, at first, merely stuck his nose into a tent, but was soon inside.

Philip's victories and maneuverings finally alarmed the Athenians. When Philip appeared in Greece with his army, he said he came as a friend. He spoke of his love for Greece and his dream to lead them against the Persians—luring them on, like fish. When he sent messengers to ask the city-states whether they wanted him to come as a friend or as an enemy, Sparta replied: "Neither." Athenians finally took Demosthenes' advice. They persuaded Thebes to join them in battle,[13] but King Philip of Macedon defeated them and became master of Greece.

Remnants of all this history—vases, sculptures, laws of Solon, and much more—are found in the museum of the restored Stoa in the Agora, including a chunk of stone from the ancient library that says "No book shall be removed for we have taken an oath. Open from the first hour to the sixth."

Journey's End

Back home, where life had gone on as usual without me, I went to an outdoor performance of *King Lear*, Shakespeare's version of Sophocles' *Oedipus Rex*, whose king of Thebes refused to believe Apollo, the god of Truth. When Truth is revealed, as Apollo had foretold, the king, in despair, blinds himself.

In the performance of *King Lear* that I attended, during the storm scene when the old king goes raving mad, a real storm blew in with lightning, crashing thunder, and torrential rain. As everyone ran for cover, the loudspeaker informed us we would get a rain check.

Notes

1. LONDON'S "THE SAVOY"

1. King Henry III (1207–1272) was eldest son of King John (son of Eleanor of Aquitaine and Henry II). His wife was the daughter of the Count of Provence.

2. French king John, born in Ghent, Belgium, was captured at Battle of Poitiers and held prisoner at the Castle of Savoy. He had such a good time, he didn't want to leave.

3. Sir Arthur Sullivan, son of a bandmaster, wrote *Onward Christian Soldiers* and *The Lost Chord*. Sir William Gilbert, son of a surgeon, was a playwright who wrote the lyrics to *Onward Christian Soldiers*.

4. The Savoy Theater is adjacent to the Savoy Hotel and the Savoy Theater Box Office. Tel: 01.836.8888. Convenient to Covent Gardens and Trafalgar Square.

5. In each room, beside the bed, a small silver buzzer with three buttons summons a maid, valet, or room service.

6. 1899 and 1901. His son was in London studying English.

7. The backer for the Ritz Hotel in Paris. He invented the cordial, Grand Marnier.

8. It was said that when Escoffier wrote about food, even the words gave off an aroma.

9. Try a "Royal Love" cocktail: ⅓ Mandarin Napoléon, ⅓ apricot nectar, ⅙ Crème de Cassis, ⅙ orange juice.

10. Words by Andy Razas. Music by Benny Goodman.

2. NOTRE DAME

1. State-owned since 1905. All authority under Public Works Department under minister of The Cathedral, 62 rue Antoine.

2. Masses 10:00 A.M., 11:30 A.M., 5:30 P.M.

3. John of Brienne. The crown of thorns had been in the Church of Saint Sinai. In 1060, they were taken to Constantinople.

4. English Henry V and his French bride, Catherine, are the ones in Shakespeare's *Henry V*'s funny courtship scene trying to communicate in each other's foreign language.

5. And heir to the throne of France.

Notes

6. *Te Deum*, the abbreviated title from the opening words of the hymn *Te Deum Laudamus* (We Praise Thee, Lord).

7. Anne of Austria bought the mansion of a former abbey and established a Benedictine convent. On the birth of her son, Louis XIV, she built the beautiful church, Val de Grace, in thanksgiving for her prayers being answered. In the 1850s the buildings were used as a graduate school specializing in military medicine. Since 1992 the convent has been called "Mucée du Service de Sante des Armees au Val de Grace."

8. Architect and painter Alexandre Marie Lenoir rescued the broken smashed statues and artwork. He cataloged them and declared them state property. The original heads are now in the Cluny Musée.

9. Originally they were the bodyguards of Turkish slaves.

10. Red, signifying immortality, was Napoléon's favorite color. From Egypt he brought back (in his boots) seeds of field poppies for dye.

11. Pope Pius VII.

12. See *The Coronation of Napoléon* by artist Jacques-Louis David (1748–1825) in the Louvre.

13. On the day that an abandoned infant was found at Notre Dame, the Introit of the Mass began, "Quasi modo genti enfantes . . ." meaning "as newborn babies . . ." The child was named Quasimodo, and Victor Hugo used the name for his character in *Hunchback of Notre Dame*.

14. They tore the blue and white from the flag of the Republic.

15. Commune—the revolutionary committee that governed Paris from March 18 until May 28, 1871 (from "commune," meaning division).

16. ". . . The stained glass windows in bloom, stone foliage always budding, loaded with birds in the thickets of Saxon capitals . . ."

17. After the treaty with Prussia, (when France lost Alsace and Lorraine).

18. At Hôtel Maurice, the German headquarters.

19. Today, a memorial plaque marks Leclerc's headquarters at Gare Montparnasse. Five years before, he had liberated French territory around Lake Chad in Central Africa from Petain's collaborators.

20. Communists and Gaullists were vying for control of Paris. The Insurrection began August 23. August 24, three tanks from General Leclerc's Second Armored Division rolled into Paris and headed for the Hôtel de Ville in the midst of violent fighting. The following day the whole division (6,000 men, 2,000 tanks) entered Paris. At 4:30 P.M., August 25, Général de Gaulle arrived in an open car to a hero's welcome at the Hôtel de Ville. That night, lights went on all over Paris for the first time in five years (September 3, 1939). War correspondent Ernie Pyle's dispatch read, "Describing Paris in words today is like trying to paint a desert sunset in black and white." To impress the Communists that de Gaulle was backed by full Allied power, August 28 the U.S. 28th Infantry Division, with jeeps, cannons, and hundreds of planes overhead, rolled through Paris and out on their way to one more battle.

21. A Carmelite priest, d'Argenlieu was drafted into the French navy during World War II. Captured at Cherbourg, he escaped and reached safety at a Carmelite

Notes

monastery in England. He joined the 10,000 French evacuated from Dunkirk, and answered de Gaulee's call for Resistance volunteers. In 1939 he went to Africa with Leclerc and others to regain French Africa from Petain's collaborators. D'Argenlieu commanded French naval forces during the Normandy Invasion. After receiving the highest awards from England and France, he resumed his life as a Carmelite.

22. Mary's reply when Elizabeth greeted her with "Blessed art thou amongst women..."

23. After Mass each man went his separate way. Waiting in a car driven by a very tall man, whose hat and uniform were covered with ribbons and medals, was Thèrése de Hautecloque, Général Leclerc's widow.

3. THE LOUVRE

1. After Rachel toured the United States, a member of her troupe, returning to Paris aboard ship, wrote, "They mix rice with cream and gooseberries, currants with peppers. My palate was completely baffled by strange, unnatural marriages." He was also amazed at politicians who thought their portraits would captivate the electors.

2. Catherine de' Medici built the Tuileries Palace, connected to the Louvre by a mile-long passageway. Louis XIII, as a little boy, raced up and down the long hall in a miniature coach pulled by two dogs.

3. The handsomest man at court. She sailed from Leghorn, Italy, and landed at Toulon, then Marseille, Avignon, and Lyons.

4. Queen Marie de' Medici had six children in ten years.

5. He was crowned at Rheims, at age thirteen.

6. At Saint André in Bordeaux.

7. Maréchal of France with title marquis d'Ancre.

8. The duc de Luynes carried it out.

9. He turned son against mother and mother against son.

10. Known as "The Day of Dupes."

11. He established despotism and left an empty treasury—an inheritance compounded by the next three kings until the Revolution.

12. Saint Vincent de Paul organized his charities to help *"les miserables,"* victims of wars under Richelieu and Louis XIV. When Louis XIV revoked the Edict of Nantes, thousands of Huguenots died as galley slaves.

13. Henriette-Marie.

14. King Louis XIII later publicly apologized and had her remains returned to France.

4. CAFÉ PROCOPE AND MIRABEAU (1749–1791)

1. Molière's theater, "Illustre Théâtre," after 1689 known as "Théâtre de Comédie Française."

2. The new calendar months eliminating Sundays and Holy Days were named for the weather: Brumaire (November fog), Frimaire (sleet), and so on.

Notes

3. Mme. Tussaud made death masks of Marat and Charlotte Corday. Marat, who advocated a Napoléon-type dictatorship, was stabbed to death by twenty-five-year-old Corday as he soaked in a shoe-shaped bathtub to relieve a painful skin disease. After her execution, her Bible in Caën was found opened to Judith 13, where Judith slays Holophernes.

4. "The only man in the Revolution whose genius could direct men and impel an Assembly" (Mme. Roland).

5. Daughter of Louis XVI's financial minister, Jacques Necker.

6. Comte de Honoré Gabriel Riqueti Mirabeau.

7. "Oh Ça Ira"—Actor and opera singer, Lainez. "All Will Go Well" (1789). During the Revolution its meaning changed to "It will go on."

8. At La Salle des Menus Plaîsirs.

9. Held at La Salle des Menus Plaîsirs, 22 avenue de Paris; the royal theater's storage warehouse held 2,000 spectators—near Versailles palace. When Jefferson arrived in Paris, John Adam's wife Abigail warned him, "To be out of fashion is more criminal than to be seen in a state of nature, to which Parisians are not averse."

10. Duc de Liancourt, aged archbishop of Vienne, president of the National Assembly.

11. Headed by thirty-two-year-old Lafayette, commander-in-chief of the National Guard.

12. President of the Third Estate (1789); he was guillotined by Robespierre.

13. Influenced by the English Bill of Rights, the Constitution of the new United States and the American Bill of Rights written by George Mason, friend and neighbor of George Washington. Thomas Paine wrote his "Rights of Man" during ten months in a French prison. (Sentenced by Robespierre.)

14. Jefferson wrote, "The king goes for nothing. He hunts half the day, is drunk the other and signs whatever he is bid."

15. In Tuileries' old riding school, La Salle de Manège.

16. Talleyrand's home in Paris was at rue St. Florentin and rue de Rivoli; today it is the U.S. Embassy. The fate of Napoléon I was decided there by the Allies.

17. When Desmoulin and Danton called for moderation during the Terror, Robespierre ordered them guillotined—also, Desmoulin's twenty-three-year-old wife.

5. SAINT SULPICE CHURCH

1. Saint Sulpice is located between rue de Vaugirard and rue de Tournon on the site of a twelfth-century church. The church is named for a sixth-century bishop of Bourges.

2. *Fountain des Quartre Points Cardinaux.*

3. The four priest were Bosset, Fénelon, Massillon, and Flechier.

4. Fénelon was tutor to Louis XIV's son, the dauphin. At one time he was also in favor with Mme. de Maintenon, the king's secret wife.

5. The shells were given to King Francis I by the Venetians. Louis XV gave them to the church in 1745.

Notes

6. The duel took place between King Louis XIII's guardsmen and Cardinal Richelieu's guardsmen.

7. The street takes its name (Duckling Street) from the low roof at #18. The former seminary is at #9.

8. Confessor to Louis XIII's Queen Anne of Austria. He dedicated his life to charity for *les misérables* during Richelieu's wars and founded the Sisters of Charity and Daughters of Charity, who worked with the destitute and galley slaves.

9. Olier (1608–1641) was a friend of Saint Vincent de Paul. Both had the same goals: missionary work and education of the clergy, most of whom could neither read nor write. Father Olier founded thirty-four parish schools and several libraries, and he held retreats for engaged couples. He also began construction of the present church.

10. Today the seminary is at Fory la Moulineaux outside Paris.

11. Sulpicians were sent to French Canada. In America they traveled down the Ohio River valley to Detroit, west to Saint Louis, and down the Mississippi to New Orleans.

12. During the Revolution, eighty-year-old Pope Pius VI was taken prisoner (1798) and dragged all over Italy—Sienna, Certosa, Parma, Piacenza, Turin, Grenoble, and Valence, France, where he died six weeks later, on August 29, 1799.

13. Pope Pius VI.

14. Emmitsburg. Her teaching methods are still used in public schools.

15. In a coup d'état November 9, 1799, Napoléon replaced the Directoire with a Consulate.

16. A Concordat signed by the next Pope, Pius VII, in July 1801, reestablished the Church in France, but it was Napoléon who waved the baton as he orchestrated the proceedings. For instance, he made his brother, Jerome, divorce his wife and crowned himself emperor (1806). Three years later, he united the Papal States with France and took Pope Pius VII prisoner.

17. 1810.

18. Pius VII was taken prisoner in 1809 and brought to Savona, Italy, near Genoa. In 1812 he refused to recognize bishops appointed by Napoléon. He was brought to Fontainebleau while Napoléon was in Russia and in 1813 declared invalid all official acts of bishops appointed by Napoléon. On May 24, 1814, he returned to Rome.

19. Father Francis Libermann (1802–1852) was the founder of Congregation of the Holy Heart of Mary and the second founder of the Holy Ghost Fathers or Sulpicians.

6. GARNIER'S OPERA HOUSE

1. In reparation and atonement to the Sacred Heart of Jesus, the basilica of Sacré Coeur was built atop Montmartre.

2. The first opera house was located on rue Peletier.

3. The bomb was thrown by an Italian, Orsini, who wanted to establish a republic in Italy and France. He also talked Eugénie into a war in Italy. The emperor acquiesced and sent troops in exchange for Nice and Savoy.

Notes

4. Construction of the new opera house began in 1861 but was halted by the Franco-Prussian War.

5. The original is in the Louvre.

7. OPÉRA COMIQUE AND BIZET'S *CARMEN*

1. The setting she describes is from the dream scene of *Les Bardes* or *Ossian* by LeSeur (1760–1837). Ossian was a third-century Irish warrior poet.

2. At age nineteen he sight-read for Liszt's concert at La Madeleine. At age nine he played and knew all of Mozart's sonatas. At age twenty-four he wrote *The Pearl Fishers*.

3. Théâtre de l'Odéon. Louis XVI bought the gardens of Hôtel de Conde for the new home of the Comédie-Française.

4. Author of *Around the World in Eighty Days, Twenty Thousand Leagues Under the Sea,* etc.

5. Bizet was the only man Saint Saëns admired.

8. NAPOLÉON III (1808–1873)

1. *Matter of Pride*—title of a book by the author's dear friend, Emily Crofford (1981, Carol Rhoda Books)

2. The empress officiated at the opening of the Suez Canal in Egypt 1865. For the occasion, Verdi wrote *Rigoletta* for her. At the performance in Cairo, all the jewels worn on stage were genuine. Her husband, the emperor, was in Paris suffering a gallstone attack. Ferdinand de Lesseps, in charge, was the cousin of Eugénie's mother.

3. Empress Eugénie bought Hortense's home overlooking Lake Constance. Today it is a museum. The drawing room is a replica of that at Malmaison.

4. Eugénie also bought Malmaison, now a museum.

5. The Duke of Reichstadt died in 1832.

6. 1837.

7. One man was shot and one man was drowned.

8. Manuscripts and books by the cartload were sent from all Europe.

9. His passport was denied in 1846. He was imprisoned in Concièrgerie and tried in Luxembourg on September 28.

10. December 21, 1852, was the official date of entry.

11. Mountains were reforested and land between the Atlantic and Gironde was cultivated. He improved conditions for delinquents and victims of child abuse. Women were educated for professions. Postal service and telegraph positions were opened to women. He started adult education classes and vocational training. He was known as Napoléon the Well-Meaning until the end of the Empire.

12. In wine, oxidation can occur any time after the grapes have been crushed. Now winemakers take great pains to avoid exposing wine to excessive amounts of air.

Notes

13. Five hundred lives were lost and nearly 3,000 men were imprisoned or sent to Algeria.

14. "His heart was as far from fraud as heaven from earth."—William Shakespeare, *Two Gentlemen from Verona*.

15. The marriage took place January 29, 1853.

16. At first in alliance with Sardinia, he sent troops to free Piedmont and half of Italy from Austrian rule, but to protect the pope from freedom fighters he made a deal to give the provinces back to Austria. In exchange, France received the province of Piedmont, which included the cities of Nice and Annecy.

17. When Russia, under the pretext of a religious issue (shrines in the Holy Land), attempted to partition Turkey for control of the Mediterranean, Louis Napoléon sent troops to the Crimea to help Austria and England, who wanted free access to trade routes on the Black Sea.

18. According to de Toucqueville, she said, "If Mexico were not so distant and if my son not a mere baby, I myself would place him at the head of the French armies so I could write with his sword one of the most shining pages in the history of this country."

19. Mexico was in debt to France (Juárez had stopped payment on the debt he owed to England, France, and Spain). In order to expand the empire and retrieve the debt, Eugénie arranged to have Maximilian of Austria put on the throne in Mexico. Unable to maintain French troops, the emperor withdrew support. Maximilian was shot by a firing squad in 1867.

20. The throne was offered to a German Hohenzoller prince distantly related to Prussian king William I. The offer was refused. France demanded that the German king guarantee that his relative would never accept the Spanish throne. A telegram from France was reworded by Otto von Bismark, inciting France to declare war.

21. They left from Saint Cloud Railroad Station.

22. Wilhelmshöhe.

9. CHOPIN (1810–1849)

1. After Napoléon's defeat, Poland was at the mercy of Russia. An 1830 revolt was crushed, as well as uprisings in 1846 and 1849.

2. Balzac said, "She is more of a man than she wants to be."

3. Chopin lived at 5 rue Tronchet, Sand at 16 rue Pigalle.

4. After four nights in a stagecoach, he arrived in Perpignan looking "as fresh as a rose and as pink as a beet root."

5. Specifically, he composed Opus 4 in D Minor, Funeral March in E Minor, Sonata in B-flat Minor, and Opus in D-flat.

6. Alexandre Dumas, when asked for a donation for the burial of a bill collector (bailiff), gave them forty francs and said, "Here, bury two." His son had a large house with a small garden. Dumas told him, "You should open the drawing room to air out the garden."

Notes

7. "She shows us a Chopin in a most ignoble detail," asserted Delacroix. "She has outrageously mistreated my friend, Chopin," said Henrik Heine.

8. Rev. Aleksander Jelowicki. Solonge was at his bedside.

9. The organist also played Chopin's Sonata in B-flat Minor. Jane Stirling sent everything from place Vendôme to Chopin's family in Poland.

10. Edgar Allan Poe died the same year. Balzac died the following year. Famous English writers were Carlyle, Thackeray, Dickens, Scott, and Emily Brontë, author of *Wuthering Heights*.

10. THE PALAIS ROYAL

1. This cannon was triggered by sun coming through a magnifying glass. It broke down 1914. So today a man from a gunsmith's shop on rue de Richelieu sets off a loud boom from the tiny cannon, which has been there since 1786.

2. This started as a hut where coffee was sold, called Café de Chartres, Égalité's youthful title. During the time of the Citizen King, the name changed to Grand Véfour. Ashtrays are in the shape of George Sand's hands.

3. Colette's apartment was #9 rue de Beaujolais.

4. Anne was the daughter of Philip III of Spain, from the Spanish branch of the Habsburgs of Austria.

5. This was a prelude to the Revolution. It started with nobles in Parliament trying to limit royal authority and excessive taxes. Instead, the monarchy was strengthened under Louis XIV, who famously declared, "I am the State."

6. His first wife (for nine years) was Henriette Marie, widow of Charles I, the English king beheaded by Parliament.

7. The king's first mistress, Louise de Vallière, who bore three children by him, was dismissed, and after five years' recuperation she joined the Carmelite Order of nuns. When her replacement, Mme. de Montespan, was discarded, she visited Louise at the convent on rue St. Jacques, hoping to be consoled.

8. Général Foy.

9. When they learned their mother had been exiled to Spain, they left America to join her but were detained in Havana eighteen months. Permission to enter Spain was denied, but they found refuge in England.

10. The director of the Théâtre du Vaudeville donated military costumes.

11. Dumas pawned his medals, his most precious possessions, to buy a burial plot for penniless actress Marie Dorval, once the toast of Paris. His son wrote, "My father is a great child I had when I was quite young."

12. Louis Philippe commissioned fifteen paintings of the Indians for the Louvre.

11. IN MEMORY OF MOLIÈRE (1622–1673)

1. Béjart was also the business manager for the company. When she died (February 17, 1662) she had to renounce her profession to have a Christian burial. Molière died exactly one year later: same day, same month.

Notes

2. An actor in 1650 was considered "infamous."

3. Prince de Conti adopted the troupe as his own. Later it was under patronage of "Monsieur," Louis XIV's brother.

4.. Armande was the most celebrated member of the company.

5. *Le Bourgeoise Gentilhomme* staged at Chambord Château on the Loire.

6. The modern version was accepted in 1669.

7. Molière lived next to the Hôtel de Grou de Beaufort. Intersection rue de la Planchete and Grand Rue; he had been separated from his wife for four years.

8. The archbishop of Paris refused burial in consecrated ground. Louis XIV ordered a Christian burial, but the archbishop compromised. Molière was buried at night, somewhere in the cemetery of Saint Eustache, with no ceremony.

12. PLACE DE LA BASTILLE AND BEAUMARCHAIS (1732–1799)

1. "The ultimate recognition of the U.S. is definitely the work of Beaumarchais," noted Alexander Hamilton. Thomas Jefferson, John Jay, and former American minister to France John Bigelow (1870) agreed.

2. Count Paris-Duveney, who died owing Beaumarchais 15,000 francs. When Beaumarchais submitted a claim, Duveney's heir accused him of fraud and forgery.

3. Duc de Chaulnes.

4. Judge Advocate Göezman.

5. In Act I, Don Bazile advises Dr. Bartholo that slander will be a most effective way of driving Count Almaviva from Seville.

6. His company was named Rodrique Hortalez et Cie.

7. These were located at 66 rue Raynouard in the suburb of Passy.

8. When Mozart set *Le Mariage* to music (1786), German emperor Joseph II refused his approval, saying there were too many notes. When the opera was finally approved, Mozart gave the role of Figaro to Irish tenor Michael Kelly, who Italianized his name to Signor O'Chelli. His contract included lodging, fuel, and four wax candles per day.

9. The future King Charles X.

10. Chérubin in *Le Mariage* was Beaumarchais as a precocious teenager, chasing girls and associating with undesirable companions. His father made arrangements with a neighbor to take the boy in. When the prodigal son repented, Monsieur Caron drew up a peace treaty laying down conditions for his son's return: Rise at 6:00. In winter, 7:00. Abandon entirely your wretched music and, above all, the company of young people. No more supping in town. No excuses for lateness on errands. One quarter of profits to be handed over. Not only did Beaumarchais sign the agreement, he kept all the conditions "with the help of the Lord."

11. The name Odéon is from a Greek word meaning "small theater."

12. Danton.

13. In Lucek.

Notes

13. PASSY: MAISON DE BALZAC AND HONORÉ BALZAC (1799–1850)

1. He named his characters after shop signs.
2. The street was named for Italian astronomer who directed the Royal Observatory in Paris 1625–1712. Balzac lived there nine years.
3. Two of his characters in *Père Goriot*, Rastignac and Vautrin, lived at today's place St. Jacques between Val de Grâce and the Pantheon.
4. *Les Jardies* was located at 14 rue de Basse Ville d'Avray near Versailles, where he tried to grow pineapples.
5. Contessa Visconti, who settled his debts for years.
6. "He who owns land has a war on his hands" became the theme of Les Paysans.
7. Paris critics couldn't forgive his attacks on corruption of the press in *Lost Illusions*.
8. Monsieur de Brugnol.
9. These were *Lost Illusions, Lucien Chardon, Eugénie Grandet, Cousin Pons,* and *Cousine Bette*.
10. Lirette Borel from Neuchatel, Switzerland, was governess for Mme. Hanska's daughter and later entered Convent of the Visitation.
11. A former Swiss Calvinist, she converted to Catholicism to enter the convent.
12. In Russia.
13. His pain was caused by tension, fatigue, and caffeine poisoning. Gangrene had set in after he banged his leg on a chair.

14. RUEIL MALMAISON: CHÂTEAU MALMAISON

1. He dismissed the Assembly of 500 and made himself first consul; founded the Bank of France; made a treaty with the pope; united church and state in France (this lasted until 1905); codified laws (Napoleonic code); created state system for schools; created the University of France to supervise education (the New York State Board of Regents was modeled after Napoléon's centralized system); built roads and bridges; established the Legion of Honor; and abolished serfdom and other feudal practices.
2. The Louisiana Purchase (1803) was arranged by President Thomas Jefferson. (Louisiana was named for Louis XIV. New Orleans was named for Regent Louis Philippe.)

15. NORMANDY

1. These words are taken from a U.S. Navy hymn written by English clergyman Rev. William Whiting (1860). It begins, "Eternal Father strong to save/Whose arm doth bind the restless wave/Who bids the mighty ocean deep/Its own appointed limits keep..."
2. A Corsair is a patriot who pillaged ships for his king.
3. Nine miles of sand surround Mont Saint Michel.

Notes

4. The angel who is the protector of God's people . . . "until finally Michael, one of the chief princes came to help me" . . . Daniel 10–13 . . . "Michael and his angels battled with the dragon, . . . that great dragon was cast down . . . he who is called the devil and Satan." Apocalypse 12–7.

5. This was Tiphaine Raquenel from Dinan, Brittany, wife of Bertrand du Guesclin, who was marshal of France under King Charles V and a Breton hero who drove out the English 1373. Mont Saint Michel was the safest place he could think of for Tiphaine.

6. Becket clashed with Henry regarding the issue of clergy being tried under civil law rather than church law.

7. Henry II falsely accused her of poisoning his mistress, Rosamond.

8. Philippe II was also called "Augustus" since he was born in August.

9. Queen Adele of Champagne.

10. Pentecost is the feast celebrated by Jews on the fiftieth day after Passover. *Pentekoste* is Greek for "after the Passover." Christians celebrate the feast day as the day the Holy Spirit descended upon the Apostles. From the white garments worn by candidates for baptism held on this day, the feast day is also known as white or Whitsunday.

16. AQUITAINE

1. They were influenced by the love poetry of Andalusia and Arabia, where Arab poets had been worshiping their ladies for at least 200 years.

2. Only the eldest son inherited land.

3. By Lawrence Dernier, Joe Galdo, and Raphael Digil.

4. River Isle joins Dordogne River. Together they flow to meet the Garonne estuary. Libourne is the center of the Saint Émilion, Pomerol, and Fronsac wine district.

5. Aquitaine is divided into five departments: Gironde (Bordeau and Saint Émilion), Dordogne (Bergerac-Les Eyzies, Périgueux, and Sarlat), Landes, Lot et Garonne, and Pyrenees Atlantiques (Bayonne, Biarritz, and Pau).

6. The lion represents military valor and protector of liberty.

7. In 1988, the people of Cognac, France contributed to a large plaque with Mr. Munson's portrait in bronze, displayed at the Training Centre of the Munson Memorial Vineyard in Denison, Texas. The same year Texas vintners dedicated a memorial to French scientist Pierre Viala and his family in Cognac, France. Most of the T. V. Munson collection in France is near Montpellier at Vallal.

8. The seventy-nine acres were recently sold to Gerard Perse.

9. Jean Capdemourlin.

10. Panel called Commission de la Belle consists of five tasters per wine.

11. A Grand Cru must have earned its status for at least ten years before it can apply for promotion to Premier Grand Cru Classé.

Notes

12. The white wines from Bordeaux come from two main areas, The Graves (gravelly) and the Sauterne area.

13. The Jurade no longer has civil power.

14. On his sixty-eighth birthday, Pope John Paul II celebrated an evening Mass in the rain at their campground twenty-five miles outside Rome. Law forbade them more than twenty-four hours within the city of Rome.

15. Robert from Arbissel near Rennes, Brittany.

16. This was her headquarters for years as she traveled (e.g., a trip to Spain to arrange a wedding between her Spanish granddaughter and the son of her enemy, French king Philip II).

17. King Philip II was the son of Eleanor of Aquitaine's first husband, King Louis VII, and his third wife.

17. BRITTANY

1. 1528.

2. The Spider King's daughter, Anne of Beaujeau, arranged the marriage of her brother to Anne of Brittany.

3. He had his marriage to Claude of France, daughter of King Louis XI, annulled.

4. Mazarin, who was made a Roman Catholic Cardinal, was never even ordained a priest.

5. From the château, walk toward the cathedral. It's the terraced house on the left corner behind the walls.

6. Marie Louise and Pauline dui Guigny.

7. Simon Dentz.

8. The others were Charles de Mesnard, a faithful sixty-two-year-old equerry, Achille Guibourg, and Sylite Kersabiec, sister of the lady who accompanied her into Nantes.

9. Coe du Cayla.

10. She prayed to Saint Spiridion, a holy bishop of Crete, Saint Janarius, Saint Roch, and Saint Clement.

11. They lived near the lake of Brunn.

12. He wrote nearly 100 books.

13. Edgar Allan Poe's "The Gold Bug" was Verne's favorite. Verne dedicated *The Narrative of Arthur Gordon Pym* to Poe.

14. At this time Verne wrote *The Clipper in the Clouds, The Flight to France, Gilbraltar, Two Years' Holiday, North Against South,* and a play, *Mathias Sandorf.*

15. Later that year, pretty twenty-two-year-old Nelly Bly (the pen name for journalist Elizabeth Chochrane from Pennsylvania) visited the Vernes on her journey around the world. She and Jules Verne, author of *Around the World in Eighty Days,* toasted each other: "Good Luck, Nelly Bly." She made it in seventy-two days, six hours, and eleven minutes.

Notes

16. The seven-year-old was his daughter's son, Benjamin Franklin Bache, and the older boy, William Temple, was the son of Franklin's illegitimate son.

17. Le Modèrn Hôtel.

18. At this time Shakespeare's plays were published, Rembrandt was painting in Leiden, and Velasquez was painting in Spain. Bernini, the architect and sculptor, was in Rome, and the Dutch were organizing their colony of New Netherlands.

19. In 1961, the park was designated a national cemetery dedicated to those of all faiths killed during World War II.

20. Among others, these included Cezanne, Degas, Pissarro, and Toulouse-Lautrec.

21. He depended on anyone who would give him canvases, paints, brushes, and tobacco.

22. These included *Vision After the Sermon, Yellow Christ, Breton Shepherdess, Woman Herding Cows on Beach at Le Pouldu, Four Breton Women Chatting Over a Wall,* etc.

23. Maxime du Camp.

18. AUVERGNE

1. Our Lady of France is dedicated to the Virgin's Assumption into heaven. The Statue was made in 1860 from melted-down Russian cannons captured at Battle of Sevastopol during the Crimean War. It is painted red to match the rooftops below.

2. This was on the eve of the Council of Ephesis, which proclaimed Mary the Divine Mother. In the eleventh century the city was called Le Puy Sainte Marie.

3. The lyrics of the chant are "Hail Holy Queen, Mother of Mercy, our life, our sweetness and our hope. To thee do we cry, poor banished children of Eve. To thee do we send up our sighs, mourning and weeping in this valley of tears. Turn then, most gracious advocate, thine eyes of mercy toward us. And after this our exile, show unto us the blessed fruit of thy womb, Jesus. O clement, O loving, O sweet Virgin Mary, pray for us, O Holy Mother of God, that we may be made worthy of the promises of Christ."

4. From Monteil.

5. Raymond of Aiguilhe, who accompanied the bishop, wrote about the crusade.

6. The statue was burned during the French Revolution: the present one is a duplicate.

7. This was left from the fourth-century Roman occupation of the town.

8. At the foot of Saint Michel d'Aiguilhe, a chapel is dedicated to Saint Gabriel, the Annunciation angel. The chapel opens onto a terrace garden.

9. According to Webster's Dictionary, a hero is a man of extraordinary courage who performs great deeds.

10. 1945: Cofounder of the U.N. 1949–1950: president of U.N. General Assembly. 1952–53: Ambassador to U.S. from Philippines. 1955–62: Ambassador to U.S.

Notes

11. He died while fighting the English at Battle of Minden, 1759, near Hanover, Germany, where the British demolished the entire French cavalry.
12. It was confiscated during the Revolution. Lafayette's wife was imprisoned there.
13. Famous for their motto "All for one, one for all."
14. Today it is Hôtel Saint James et Albany.
15. Jefferson wrote from Nîmes, "Louis XVI long in the habit of drowning his cares in wine. His religion borders on bigotry. He is too much governed by his queen."
16. His ship, *Hermione,* is being reconstructed at Rochefort, and is scheduled to make a memorial maiden voyage of good will to the U.S. in 2007.
17. It sailed from the Spanish port, Los Pasayes.
18. "We the people of the United States in order to form a more perfect Union, establish justice, insure domestic tranquility [I love that one], provide for the common defense, promote the general welfare and secure the blessings of liberty to ourselves and our posterity, do ordain and establish this constitution for the United States of America."
19. George Washington (president of the 1787 Constitutional Convention), ". . . If to please the people, we offer what we ourselves disapprove, how can we afterward defend our word? Let us raise a standard to which the wise and honest can repair. The event is in the hands of God." Washington was childless. Alex de Toqueville described him as tall, of hard countenance yet with a very young look. With an easy soldier-like air and gesture, he speaks with a very determined style and accent. He was first president of the United States 1789–1797.
20. At Valley Forge, Washington gave him command of a division of Virginians.
21. December 23, 1777.
22. Thomas Paine, *The Crisis.*
23. On Freeman's farm and Bemis Heights near Saratoga, Oct. 1777.
24. Members of Continental Congress met at Raleigh's Tavern.
25. For a reward offered by King George III.
26. He was under house arrest for one week.
27. Young Lafayette recaptured Virginia from Cornwallis. Even "Papa" Rochambeau, a French general before Lafayette was born, declared the boy "has conducted himself perfectly." Rochambeau's statue is in King's Park, Newport, Rhode Island. The Vernon House was Rochambeau's headquarters in Newport.
28. On the York River, sixty miles from Richmond. Near where Lafayette first landed.
29. "And there was a General Washington, Upon a strapping stallion. A-giving orders to his men, I guess there was a million. Yankee Doodle, keep it up, Yankee Doodle, Dandy. Put a feather in his cap, and called it Macaroni. . . ." (Elegant gentlemen's clubs in England were called Macaroni clubs).
30. General Rochambeau stayed with his troops at Williamsburg, Virginia, for one year, to meet a possible English counterattack. He left in 1782.

Notes

31. She was named for his favorite state—the home of Washington and Jefferson.
32. July 1, 1784.
33. With eighty-three different banners.
34. French revolutionaries adopted the Phrygian or "freeman's" cap. Natives of Phrygia (in today's central Turkey) were captured by Romans, and when given their freedom, they wore a red cap. Represented in Greek art, the soft red cap with a forward curl was called a Phrygian cap.
35. At the urging of Marie Antoinette.
36. It was composed by Rouget de Lisle, stationed in Strasbourg.
37. They were imprisoned in the tower of the Temple, the remains of a fortress built by the Knights Templar.
38. He was captured in the Belgian town of Rochefort, August 19, 1792.
39. Morris was a financier from New York City. Gouverneur Morris replaced Jefferson as minister to France.
40. The fifth U.S. president, he was remembered for the Monroe Doctrine, written by John Quincy Adams. In 1803, Jefferson sent him to France to buy Louisiana from Napoléon.
41. James Monroe replaced Morris as minister.
42. Lafayette had smuggled a letter to England. It was written with a quill dipped in a mixture of soot and sour wine on the blank pages of a book. It was publicized in Europe, describing prison conditions.
43. It was deliberate harsh treatment. Austrian emperor Joseph II, brother of Marie Antoinette, blamed Lafayette for his sister's death.
44. Comtesse de Tessé. She wrote about Lafayette, "He had the simple-minded faith and calm fearlessness of those old navigators in the sixteenth century who set out to explore the world in ill-equipped ships with mutinous crews."
45. He had overthrown the Directoire and made himself consul.
46. Napoléon ordered Fouché, the police chief, "Let the newspapers constantly attack England. They must serve my government."
47. The estate had belonged to Adrienne's seventh-century ancestor, a lady-in-waiting to Ann of Austria, wife of King Louis XIII.
48. He endured a 40-day torture, strapped into an experimental contraption.
49. 1807. She was buried in the cemetery of Picpus, on the grounds of the Augustinian monastery, where victims of the guillotine are buried. The guillotine, originally located across from Louvre, was moved to the place de la Concorde, then to the place de la Bastille, and finally to the place de la Nation. Lafayette and his wife bought part of the grounds surrounding the monastery. The chapel, convent, and several small buildings on the property have been renovated.
50. Louis XVIII had to be wheeled around in an armchair.
51. Especially Benjamin Constant.
52. Lafayette's secretary was Auguste Levasseur. His valet was named Bastien.

Notes

53. President James Monroe was seventy-four; Jefferson was eighty-one. He was entertained by Daniel Webster, Henry Clay, Andrew Jackson, John Adams, and others.

54. He stayed four days in Alexandria, Virginia, at Gadsby's Hotel, now a museum.

55. September 6, 1825.

56. On May 20, 1834.

57. They were forbidden to carry arms.

58. Which Lafayette had designed.

59. Today it is the Polish church, it is located off rue St. Honoré between rue de Castiglioni and rue Royale.

60. The Convent of the Sacred Heart was confiscated in the name of the Republic during the Terror, and the guillotined heads and bodies (including Adrienne's family) were dumped into shallow pits dug in the convent's garden. Wanting to be buried near her family, she bought a plot, and the couple were eventually buried there. An American flag is displayed over Lafayette's grave.

61. John Quincy Adams, at sixteen, had accompanied his father, John Adams, representative to France (1783).

62. Other French nobles who fought with the colonists founded The Society of Cincinnatus, named for a fifth-century B.C. Roman patriot.

19. BERRY

1. It is named for the wealthiest man in France during the sixteenth century.

2. A diplomatic genius who invented the Cold War. Spun a web of foreign policy with propaganda and economic pressure throughout Europe.

3. Four dozen or more buttons were on a woman's dress, half as many on a man's doublet.

4. England held land in both Scotland and France.

5. According to legend, after Clovis won a big battle in a field of iris, he chose the iris as a symbol for his banner. Louis VII made the flower the symbol of France. His followers called it "fleur-de-Louis," and the name evolved into *fleur-de-lys*.

6. Aubigny sur Nère's population is 5,700, a town of ancient houses in jumbled streets with big squares. The Town Hall is the old Stuart château.

7. Louis XII granted free naturalization to all Scots, to be treated as French subjects.

8. Chambord.

9. Scottish king James V allied himself with France against Henry VIII.

10. He dissolved three Parliaments and ruled eleven years without them.

11. His most famous mistress was the actress Nell Gwyn.

12. She relied on "tears, beauty and hard-headed business sense." She was given exorbitant sums for herself and her son Charles Lennox, first Duke of Richmond. Some of the money came from a new law requiring wine merchants to purchase a

Notes

license. Year after year, King Louis XIV issued royal decrees postponing her execution.

13. Children will love the goat farm with piped-in music that makes goats produce more milk.

14. 31 place de la Hall. Tel: 48.54.00.81.

15. Crottin de Chavignol—goat cheese.

16. After the French Revolution, when the plates were scattered among neighbors, the marquis of Maupas retrieved them by trading two white plates for each collector plate. The men on the tour were more interested in a collection of horns—deer, elk, and ibex.

17. A music box (1830), a toy room with dolls, a child's spinning wheel, and a Punch and Judy Theater.

18. Eldest daughter of the king of Naples.

19. He was murdered outside the opera and was carried to the director's office, where he lay dying as the unsuspecting audience roared with laugher. The program was a one-act opera, *La Rossignol* (The Nightingale), and two ballets, *Le Carnival de Venis* (The Carnival of Venice), and *Les Noces de Gamache* (The Wedding of Gamache). He died 6:30 A.M. February 13, 1820.

20. When King Louis XVIII died, his brother Charles X (her father-in-law) became king. During the July 1830 Revolution, he fled to Scotland, and Louis Philippe, the Citizen King, was put on the throne. The duchess claimed that since King Louis XVIII had no heir, her son was next in line.

21. Le Windsor.

22. Alain Fournier's *Le Grand Meaulnes* (The Wanderer).

23. The cathedral was built between the thirteenth and sixteenth centuries. Climb 406 steps to the top of the north tower.

24. He hired Flemish artist Pol de Limbourg and his brother to create *Trés Riches Heures du Duc de Berry* (in the Musée Condé, Chantilly, France), the most exquisite "illuminated" or lighted manuscript known. The intricately designed prayer book is inlaid in gold, almost like bright jewels. His *Book of Hours*, also by the two Limbourg brothers, is in The Cloisters Museum in New York City.

25. Each guild had a fraternity club that cared for the sick, aged, and needy. Baptisms, marriages, and funeral Masses were held in the different trade chapels.

26. Born near Annecy.

27. He borrowed money from the cook.

28. Mehun sur Yèvre

29. He was the diplomat responsible for negotiating trade with the sultan. He settled a Vatican dispute and negotiated a treaty between the Knights of Rhodes and the Arabs.

30. Treaty of Aaras, peace between French king Charles VII and Philippe the Good of Burgundy, who had been England's ally.

Notes

31. Agnes Sorel is buried in Collegiate Church in Loche. A graceful sculpture over her tomb shows her reclining on her side.

32. He bought up twenty estates of nobles ruined during the Hundred Years' War. Jacques Coeur was eight years older than the dauphin.

33. His son Ravant, a lawyer in Avignon, played an important role in the rescue and accompanied his father to Rome.

34. Pope Nicholas V was a good Spanish Borgia pope (except for the nepotism). Pope Eugene IV (1431–1447) had chosen Jacques Coeur for negotiations. As a result, the Hospitallers occupied Rhodes for nearly a century. Tolerant Arabs had respected Christian shrines. Pope Eugene ordered the Crusaders to end their war with the Egyptians.

35. In 1453 Turks captured Constantinople. It was the end of the Eastern Roman Empire (Byzantium). 1453 also marked the end of the Hundred Years' War.

36. Jacques Coeur lived there only four years before he was arrested.

37. "Watch, therefore, for you do not know at what hour your Lord is to come." (Matthew 24:42)—(All the sculpture had a double meaning).

38. (1462–1515) Cousin of Charles XIII. He continued the union of France and Brittany by discarding his first wife to marry Anne of Brittany.

39. He was the cup-bearer to King Louis XI, the Spider King.

40. The Fatimids were a Moslem dynasty that ruled over northern Africa and parts of Egypt, A.D. 907 and 1171.

41. The same time as Charles Martel defeated the Moslems at Poitiers (1095).

42. It was the First Crusade, led by Godwin of Bouillon, duke of Lower Lorraine. He came with two brothers. Godwin's sword and spurs are preserved in the sacristy of the Church of the Holy Sepulchre in Jerusalem. His 12th-century castle in today's Belgium is a tourist attraction.

43. Peter the Hermit (he wore a hermit's cape) was an itinerant monk who preached from his donkey. His crusader army that left from Bourges included women and children who walked across Europe.

44. His older brother was pious Godfrey of Bouillon.

45. Troyes is ninety miles southeast of Paris.

46. In 1185, the Knights Templar were established in London.

47. Louis VII left from Metz; his court was in Bourges.

48. She departed with a dozen other high-born ladies. Eleanor was duchess of Aquitaine and countess of Poitou. Her territories extended from the Auvergne to the sea, and from the Loire to the Pyrenees. Her father's castles were in Bordeaux, Tours, and Poitier.

49. Raymond wanted to strike the Saracens at Edessa before they could build up defenses against Antioch. Louis wanted to march directly to Jerusalem. Eleanor committed her Aquitaine knights to her uncle Raymond.

50. Their three daughters were to remain in France to be married off politically.

Notes

51. A four-year truce was broken by a crusader who ambushed a Moslem caravan.

52. Unity between the Latin Empire and Byzantine Empire ended 431 A.D. The Byzantine Empire included Syria and Egypt.

53. Philip Augustus was King Philip II, son of French king Louis VII and his third wife, Adele of Champagne. (Eleanor of Aquitaine was King Louis VII's first wife.) He doubled the size of his French domain.

54. The term *crusade* comes from "taking the cross," after the example of Christ.

55. The bride's name was Burengaria—from Navarre.

56. He was shipwrecked. In disguise, he made his way through enemy territory. He was recognized, and handed over to Emperor Frederick I, and jailed.

57. They rejected all the sacraments and denied that Christ had been truly human.

58. Frederick II, ruler of Germany (1212-1250), was in Sicily. His court was a meeting place of Arabic, Greek, and northern scholars. A menagerie of falcons traveled with him. He wrote and illustrated a book, *The Art of Hunting and Falconry*, in which he proved his statements by experiments.

59. Saint Louis died at the same time that Marco Polo went to China.

60. Charles de Bigny.

61. Trying to assert flimsy claims in Italy, Louis XII spent years fighting gory battles against Pope Julius II. His queen hated the wars and went off to Brittany, where she ruled in her separate court.

62. Since 1954, the history of Ainay le Vieil has been portrayed in a *son et lumier* (sound and light). Summer programs include a series of concerts and plays.

63. He was now also minister of France (1664).

64. When he tired of his first mistress, Louise de la Valliere, she joined the strict Carmelite order. Her *Reflections of the Mercy of God* is still in print.

65. The marquis de Seignelay; Colbert had six sons and four daughters.

66. Charles Perrault's brother, Claude, a physician, scientist, and architect, designed the east front of the Louvre.

67. Her real name was Aurore Dudevant.

68. Hugo wrote *Les Miserables* in 1841, at the same time that Edgar Allan Poe wrote the first mystery story, *Murder in the Rue Morgue*.

69. Lady Mary Montague, wife of an English ambassador, wrote about George Sand: "On the whole 'tis the most miserable stuff—declaring all she thinks to all the people she sees without reflecting that in this mortal state of imperfection, fig leaves are as necessary for our minds as our bodies. It is as indecent to show all we think as to show all we have."

70. No wonder the short, dumpy lady loved him. In *Poor Richard's Almanac* he wrote, "A ship under sail and a big-bellied woman are the handsomest things that can be seen in common."

Notes

71. He was poet, novelist, art and theatrical critic, travel writer, literary critic, and journalist.

72. Sand sent her daughter, Solonge, to live with the girl's gloomy father in Gascony.

73. *Marionettes and Guignols,* by Ernest Maindron.

74. Maurice married the granddaughter of sculptor Houdon, and left a collection of 200 puppets.

75. He finished Opus 60, Barcarolle, and Opus 61, Polonaise Fantasy, two of his greatest. His last composition at Nohant was Opus 65, Sonata in G Minor.

20. TOURAINE

1. Chenin blanc grape. Look for labels of Marc Brédif or Gaston Huet.

2. The remains of the monastery, Marmoutier, are on the opposite side of the river 1½ miles from town. Part of the cloister survives in a convent in rue Descartes; It is now occupied by Sisters of the Sacred Heart. 2:00 P.M. tour includes cave cells where early hermits dwelt. Saint Martin prayed here, as well as the third-century Saint Gatianus, first missionary to Gaul. (No fee for the tour. Be sure to give the nuns some money.)

3. The present nineteenth-century monolithic church is part of the ancient basilica.

4. Before presenting the grill, Louis XI checked out Saint Martin's genealogy. He learned that Martin was a kinsman of a Roman senator, and Flavius, king of Hungary.

5. Ussé is high on a hill above three terraces. A steep path leads to lovely chapel and another path leads uphill to the château. An Orange grove is near the entrance. The Royal bed chamber was built for Louis XIV, who never came. The only king who did was Hailé Sélassie of Ethiopia, who popped in for a lunch and a nap.

6. Balzac visited the Margonne family here between 1829 and 1837. He modeled Mme. Grandet in *Eugénie Grandet* after Mme. Margonne. The parish priest in *Le Curé de Tours* was inspired by the canon of Église Saint Denis in Saché.

7. The stagecoach from Paris to Tours took twenty-three hours. He walked two hours to Saché.

8. His homey low-ceilinged room, always reserved for him, is on the first floor. A small desk faces a window and soothing scenery. Balzac wrote *Louis Lambert* and *Lyle dans la Vallée* here.

9. In longhand, he rewrote a manuscript sixteen or seventeen times. He condensed 2,000 words to 200.

10. Named for World War I American president Woodrow Wilson.

21. LORRAINE

1. He later moved to 4 rue Auxonne. He stayed eight months at Nancy.

2. On August 11, 1944. Leclerc's Free French Forces had fought all the way from Africa.

Notes

3. Fuel for the tanks was diverted to the First Army.

4. The Resistance in Nancy and Strasbourg was organized by Marie-Madeleine Fourcade, the only woman to head a major Resistance network. She ordered Resistance data on German positions and strengths for General Patton, when his Third Army would arrive to liberate Alsace-Lorraine.

5. On the last day of fighting, September 14, twenty-four French Resistance Fighters were killed in Nancy.

6. The same territory where the famous World War I New York City 69th (Rainbow) Division fought in muddy trenches. When relieved by another New York City outfit, as they silently passed each other at night near enemy artillery, the new division quietly hummed under their breath, "Give my regards to Broadway, Remember me to Herald Square."

7. Museum of the School of Nancy.

8. One of the rooms was bought by the Musée des Arts Decoratifs in Paris. It includes vases by Gallé, jewelry by René Lalique, panels carved like trees, etc.

9. His father was a mirror manufacturer. Gallé added table glassware to the business.

10. *As You Like It*, William Shakespeare.

11. His studies included the formation of crystals.

12. His studies also included the contents of sailors' logs brought together in a study of the sea by American Matthew Maury (1806–1873) and the valuable observations in oceanography during expeditions of Capt. James Cook, as well as the scientific expeditions of Sir John Robs (north) and Sir James Robs (south) during their polar explorations around the world in 1872 and 1876.

13. 1870.

14. He was born in what is now the Bishop's Palace.

15. Tours was to Louis XI what Prague was to Mozart. He was loved there.

16. At the Basilica of Saint Martin of Tours.

17. After Spider defeated the British at Dieppe, his father gave a huge celebration in his honor. Before the battle he prayed for victory at Church of Saint Jacques. He promised the Blessed Virgin he would enlarge and glorify her Church near Orléans. During the battle . . . a sudden change—and victory.

18. The main cities in the Dauphiné; Montélimar, Valence, Briançon.

19. Spider made a pilgrimage to La Saint Baume, a cave atop a mountain where Mary Magdalene spent her last thirty years.

20. "Alas what a pity when the Head of State gives such a bad example to his people."

21. Charlotte of Savoy's father, the Duke of Savoy was "gate-keeper" to Italy. Married in Chambéry in the castle chapel.

22. He was given a castle at Genappe outside Brussels, a pension, and preferential treatment.

Notes

23. When he learned his father had died, he jumped on a horse belonging to his uncle's wife and galloped to Paris without even saying "au revoir."

24. Marie of Burgundy, who married Maximilian of Austria.

25. Anne, who inherited her father's skill as a diplomat. She married Pierre de Beaujeu, brother and heir to Duke of Bourbon. In tenth century, the Bourbons were the greatest barons in France. Before he died, Spider made Beaujeu marshal of France. Anne of Beaujeu and her husband were in complete charge of the twelve-year-old dauphin.

26. He studied international finance, medicine, law, and history and became fluent in Italian.

27. The towns along the Somme River had been temporarily ceded to the first Duke of Burgundy. Charles VII had sold them to Philip the Good.

28. Also Duke François II of Britany, Jean II of Arragon, etc.

29. Secretaries, agents, commanders, and spies.

30. Spain, Portugal, Italy, England, and Scotland.

31. Duke of Bourbon.

32. The funeral was at Saint Donatian in Bruges. He was buried in Dijon, capital of the duchy of Burgundy.

33. His brother, duc de Berry and the Duke of Brittany, Francois II (both allies of Rash), quarreled over the spoils in Normandy. The Normans seized Spider's brother and imprisoned him in Rouen. Spider rescued him and assigned him to Roussillon—far away. His brother changed his allegiance from Rash to Spider. Spider also made a truce with Rash's ally, Duke François II of Brittany—then went to thank the Virgin at Noyon in a church founded by Charlemagne.

34. The towns were Saint Quentin and Amiens.

35. He wanted Liège in order to expand into Germany.

36. King Louis exempted the town from taxes and decreed that the women could walk in front of the men during their annual saints' day procession. They could wear jewelry and any dress they chose. Louis also provided a wedding for Jeanne and her fiancé, as well as a dowry. He gave donations to Notre Dame de Cléry, Our Lady of France at Le Puy en Velay, and Saint Martin of Tours.

37. From Holland, Flanders, Germany and Austria.

38. The Angelus

> The Angel of the Lord declared unto Mary
> And she conceived of the Holy Spirit. Hail, Mary!
> Behold the hand maiden of the Lord
> Be it done unto me according to Your Word. Hail, Mary!
> And the Word was made flesh.
> And dwelt among us. Hail, Mary!
> Pray for us Oh Holy Mother of God
> That we may be made worthy of the promises of Christ
> Let us pray

Notes

Lord pour forth we beseech thee the grace unto our hearts that we to whom the incarnation of Christ Thy Son was made known by the message of the angel, may be brought by His passion and cross to the glory of His resurrection through the same Christ our Lord, Amen.

39. June 22, 1476, at Lake Morat.

40. Spider said he was suffering from heart tremors, migraine headaches, and hemorrhoids due to the fact that he hadn't had sexual intercourse lately.

41. After the Battle of Nancy, death vanquished Spider's old enemies: his brother, Charles of France (formerly duc de Berry), Rash's daughter and heir, Marie of Burgundy, and when René II of Lorraine and his nephew, Count of Maine (last of the Anjou family) conveniently died without heirs, Spider got Marseilles, Provence, Maine, and Loire valley all the way to the border of Brittany. Spider went to thank Our Lady of Cléry eight miles from Orléans. At his death (1483), he left France a unified and envied nation.

42. France had three rulers: 1. A kingdom under Henri VI of England, ruled by a regent; 2. Kingdom of Bourges, under dauphin; and 3. Duchy of Bourgogne, under Philippe the Good (Duke of Burgundy).

43. Saint Michael, one of three archangels. Daniel 10:3, Jude 5:9.

44. Saint Catherine was the patron saint of Joan's older sister, who had died. Saint Catherine from Alexandria (310), martyred by Emperor Maxentius (see Tours Chapter).

45. Her fifteenth-century statue is in the nearby National Basilica, as is the baptismal font where Joan was christened.

46. Jean de Metz and Bertrand de Poulengy.

47. Wife of King Charles VI. During one of the king's bouts of insanity she signed a treaty with the English and Burgundians, disinheriting the dauphin. Their daughter was given in marriage to English king Henry V, enabling their son to inherit the French throne.

48. Charles Martel was said to have left his sword in a ruined chapel. The chapel was rebuilt by a blind, paralyzed knight who was miraculously cured. Saint Catherine became patroness of French soldiers captured by the English and Burgundians. Those who escaped left chains and ropes as votive offerings.

49. It is still there on Grand Carroi.

50. His mother was a nymphomaniac and had implied she didn't know who his father was.

51. Joan's mother, Isobelle Romée, met him on a pilgrimage to Our Lady in Le Puy en Velay, and persuaded him to accompany her daughter.

52. She told him she knew he had prayed at the castle in Loche and that, if he was not the true son of Charles VI, he might be allowed to seek refuge in Scotland or Spain. He still hesitated and demanded proof of her virginity.

53. Sword that Charles Martel had used to defeat the infidels at the Battle of Tours in 732.

Notes

54. One was Mark Twain's favorite character; blustering, bragging Paladin.
55. They went to confession—at the church of Saint Sauveur.
56. It was presented by the archbishop of Rheims. The banner with the royal gold *fleur-de-lys* and the words Jesus-Maria (dictated by her Voices), shows a seated Baby Jesus holding a globe in one hand and the other raised in a blessing. Angels kneeling on either side offer more lilies. The reverse side shows a scene of the Annunciation and the crown of France.
57. Although he was the illegitimate son of Louis, duc d'Orléans, the label was honorable since his father was a noble. Joan called him her "Gentle Bastard." After Joan's death, he later drove the English from Paris.
58. The English had fortified the Church of Saint Loup, but, so far, the city had not been cut off completely.
59. The cathedral was built at the end of the fourth century by the first bishop of Orléans, who dedicated it to the Holy Cross, which had been discovered by Constantine's mother at Golgatha earlier that year.
60. The letters were tied to an arrow which a bowman shot across the broken bridge.
61. It was Pont Royal. During World War I, it was renamed Pont George V when England and France were allies. English king George V gave up his German titles and changed the name of the English Royal House to "Windsor" (formerly Saxe-Coburg Gotha).
62. The tourist train starts here.
63. Married to Leopold I of Belgium.
64. Her eldest son, Jacques, died during Joan's trial.
65. Held by the English. She prayed at the small Saint Denis de la Chapelle in Paris 18e (#16 rue de la Chapelle). When she attacked the fort, defended by a moat, she was wounded in the thigh and given first aid in the square at #4.
66. To see the house, inquire at office of vinegar factory, 2 Cloitre Saint-Pierre.
67. The source of the Loiret, a small river that flows into the Loire.

22. BURGUNDY

1. The dukes of Burgundy date back to 1032, when French king Robert II gave the duchy of Burgundy to his son, who became King Henry I.
2. The Catholic Guise family had captured the fortress castle.
3. In the lower level, his crypt is in a chapel copied from The Holy Sepulchre in Jerusalem.
4. Eiffel envisioned a "Panama Canal." He later designed and built ten locks.
5. Lippi and Lucrezia had a daughter and a son who resembled his homely father.
6. His father, King John II, gave it to him for bravery during the Battle of Poitiers (1363).
7. He married Margaret of Flanders.
8. They were called Armagnacs for their leader, Count Bernard d'Armagnac.

Notes

9. Margaret of Bavaria.

10. King René was also Duke of Bar, which is now in the Ukraine. The tower is called "Tour de Bar."

11. Basle, 1434.

12. The Côte d'Or region is divided between Côte de Nuits near Dijon and Côte de Beaune farther south. (*Côte* means slopes.) Although both sections produce red and white wines, the northern section, Côte de Nuits, is renowned for reds and the southern part, Côte de Beaune, for its dry whites, from chardonnay grapes. Each winegrower has his own winery which is passed on from generation to generation.

13. Region of Côte de Nuits. Nuits is from the Celtic words "un win" that means stream in a valley.

14. Fifty monks still pray and work there.

15. *Clos* originally meant land closed in by a wall. Now it means a small plot of land.

16. The famous English author, Hillaire Belloc, born at Saint Cloud, France.

17. *Grand Dictionarie de Cuisine,* Simon and Schuster, 1958.

23. PROVENCE

1. She was buried in a crypt below the castle in the Collegiate Church of the Holy Savior. In 1793 during the Revolution, a mob broke open the caskets and dumped the bones into a common grave.

2. Maria de Rabutin-Chantal. Her father, Baron de Chantal, was the son of Saint Jeanne Chantal, widow who "provided" for her seven children and founded the Order of nuns called the Visitation Order. Saint Vincent de Paul and Saint Francis de Sales encouraged women to visit and help the poor and sick, instead of just praying for them.

3. Count Françoise Adhemar de Monteil Grignan. Aix, Marseille, Arles, Nîmes, and Toulouse were all under his jurisdiction.

4. Today the château, a half mile from Vitré, is privately owned, but a small chapel and a few rooms are open to the public. An eighteen-hole golf course on the estate is free and open to the public, as well as jogging paths through the woods.

5. The castle housed the Provençal Parliament.

6. Louis XIV ordered Grignan to seize the fort at Orange which belonged to his enemy, Dutch William of Orange.

7. Vitré—one of best preserved towns in Brittany.

8. They had half-moon erosion of their teeth; today it is proof of syphilis. They had to give up the castle and move to Marseille. Françoise died of smallpox. The count remarried and died at age eighty-three.

9. He wrote *Tresor dóu Félibrige,* a vast dictionary of Provençal grammar, words, and proverbs.

10. Maillane—a town near the farm—was named for the month of May, Mary's month. Mistral was born September 8, 1830, on the Feast of Our Lady—her birthday.

Notes

11. Mirèio was a name used by his mother and grandmother to tease or as a word of endearment.

12. *Crau*—a vast arid plain of stone and pebbles.

13. Parisians couldn't relate to the problems of lower-class peasants. After ten performances, Gounod cut it from five to three acts and let Mirèio live with the prospect of marrying Vincent.

14. Hôtel Ville Vert.

15. *Bateaux a Saintes Maries* (Fishing Boats on the Beach at Les Saintes Maries de la Mer) (1888). He wrote to his brother, "The little green and red and blue boats are so pretty in shape and color that they made one think of flowers."

16. Both Marys were with Mary Magdalene at Christ's empty tomb.

17. These included Cleon, Eutropuis, Marcellus, Zachaeus, Joseph of Arimathea, Maximum, and Sidonuis, whose sight Jesus restored.

18. A monk in the twelfth century wrote, "In a bronze chest was afterwards found the various human remains which were believed to be those of Sarah, a follower of the Holy Marys."

19. The region is thought to be named for Caius Marius, a Roman general who was defeated near Saint Rémy.

20. Caretakers of horses and bulls. The breed of horse, the Camargue, often called "the horse of the sea," has existed in this region since prehistoric times. Small herds run wild in the marshland, and today the breed is strictly protected. Like our cowboys, the Gardians train the rugged horses to manage the bull herd as well as to provide visitors the opportunity to explore the region by horseback.

21. During the Holocaust, when thousands of gypsies were sent to Nazi gas chambers, Father Fleury in France founded the National Gypsy Chaplaincy.

22. Ile de la Barthelasse, Avignon.

23. Lou Cigaloun, 4 rue Caristie 84100 Orange. Tel: 90.34.89.76, Fax: 90.34.10.07.

24. At Ajaccio (ah YAH cho), birthplace of Napoléon.

25. The museum was named for a retired botanist. 67 rue Joseph Vernet. Tel: 90.82.43.5.

26. Victor Duruy.

27. He taught himself Latin, Greek, geometry, and algebra. He received his diploma in physics and chemistry from Montpellier, a diploma in biology from the University of Toulouse, and a degree in biology from Faculty of Science in Paris.

28. Napoléon III's government assigned Pasteur the task. Pasteur, who knew nothing about silkworms, said it was like going to a fire without knowing where it was and without a fire engine or hose.

29. Harmas, acquired in 1922, is administered by the Entomological Laboratory of the National Museum. Closed Tuesday. Tel: 90.70.00.04.

30. His son, Jules, to whom he dedicated the first volume of his *Souvenirs Entomologicques:* "It was for your sake that I began this volume . . . I shall continue in the bitterness of my mourning . . ."

Notes

31. The Peacock moth is the largest in Europe.

32. The sacred beetle was carved in precious stones and buried with Egyptian mummies.

33. The praying mantis came to the U.S. from southern France via Rochester, N.Y., in packing material around nursery stock.

34. Quote by Clarence Day.

35. After Mistral received the Nobel Prize in Literature for *Mireille* (1904), he established the Arlaten Muséum, dedicated to Provence.

36. In Rostand's poem, "Blue Morning," all nature recites the Lord's Prayer in Latin: the sky, earth, plants, animals, and insects.

24. THE GRAND DUCHY OF LUXEMBOURG

1. There has been no official report of an accident that paralyzed and led to the death of the four-star general and American hero. There is nothing in the Army Military Center about the accident. There was no official investigation. The driver responsible for the accident was never interrogated. Nothing is known about the driver to this day.

2. Germans swarmed into the "bulge" that they had made in the American line.

3. The fortress had sixteen miles of tunnels.

4. When *Notre Dame de Paris (The Hunchback of Notre Dame)* was published in 1831, Hugo moved to #6 place des Vögues in Paris, now The Victor Hugo Museum.

5. Under the reign of King William I, the castle was sold piece by piece. Restored in 1890, it was given to the State.

6. Defenders of Luxembourg territory were men of the 4th and 28th U.S. Infantry Division and the 9th U.S. Armored Division.

7. It is now a retirement home called Pescatore Foundation.

8. "Battleground—Luxembourg Remembers—44 the Bulge by Luxembourg National Tourist Office Publishers."

9. There is a nine-foot statue of General Patton in battle uniform scanning the horizon with binoculars.

10. Steichen was born in Berchem in southern Luxembourg.

11. Colonel Daniel Strickler, in command of Wiltz, became a straggler like thousands of other GIs. With two others, he struggled through snow and freezing rain for fifteen miles, without food or sleep for six nights. Miraculously, the famished, exhausted men reached their Division Headquarters across the Belgian border in Vaux lez Rosieres, Queen of the Rosary.

12. The parish church of Saint Mauritius has been rebuilt. Behind the altar, in a large bright mural, Christ sits in the middle of a throng surrounded by baskets of bread and fishes—a biblical picnic. Standing beside Christ is George Mergenthaler, dressed in a long brown robe over his uniform—happily at home with the apostles and saints.

Notes

13. The strange eighth-century zig-zag dance begins at 9:00 A.M. and lasts a half-hour. Each group of pilgrims is accompanied by its own brass band.

14. Both her husband, Prince Felix, and her son, Grand Duke Jean, served with the Allies during World War II.

15. Philip's cousin, beautiful, talented Jacqueline, was the only daughter of William VI of Holland. When he died, in 1417, cities of Hainut, Holland and Zeeland promised to support her claim to succession. Instead, she was betrayed by everyone. She was the most fascinating person in the history of Holland, except for William the Silent—of course.

16. How Philip became king of Spain is a diabolical tale: a bride betrayed and imprisoned, first by her husband, Philip I, then by her father, and later by her son.

17. He didn't speak English. Mary taught him to say "goodnight" to the court ladies.

18. In 1522, Emperor Charles V gave his friend, Prince Philbert, the province of Orange in France and possessions in the Netherlands. He was succeeded by his nephew, son of the Count of Nassau, who gave the title and land to his young cousin, William of Dillenburg (William the Silent).

19. An heiress of the Egmont family—giving him more estates in Holland.

20. She was the daughter of Marie of Burgundy and Maximilion of Austria.

21. Elizabeth of Valois.

22. Her father, King Henri II, died from wounds in a jousting match during the festivities.

23. Daughter of Emperor Charles V and Jeanne van der Gheymst, daughter of a weaver. Her education was supervised by Margaret of Austria and Mary of Hungary.

24. Priceless treasures were destroyed. Fathers brought children carrying hammers into churches to find an "idol" to destroy.

25. The king's troops under Alba were a brilliantly uniformed army accompanied by elegantly attired wives. Mercenaries were accompanied by their wives and "camp followers"—a polite term for you-know-what.

26. Beethoven dedicated his famous *Egmont* overture to him.

27. Spanish royalty are buried there. Philip's wife, Mary Tudor, queen of England, is buried in Westminster Abbey.

28. In Alkmaar, freedom was so precious, people sacrificed homes and land by cutting the dikes. The North Sea, five miles away, rushed in, drowning cattle and crops.

29. They opened the sluices of the Ysel and Neuse river above Rotterdam.

30. Released at age forty-six, a broken man.

31. Emperor Charles V's illegitimate son.

32. Conquered Ghent, Brussels, Antwerp, etc.

33. Son of liberal Maximilian II, king of Bohemia and Hungary.

34. William's second wife.

35. Under the reign of English Restoration king Charles II.

Notes

36. The colony was named for the king's brother, James, Duke of York. Before the betrayal, a defense wall had been built from today's Wall Street across Manhattan.

37. Peace of the Pyrénées.

38. Nassau Hall at Princeton University is named for him. His portrait is there.

39. Louis XIV took Strasbourg, then invaded Spanish Flanders and took Luxembourg in 1684.

40. King Charles I, beheaded by Cromwell's government.

41. The treaty gave today's Belgium and Luxembourg to Austria.

42. A man from Boston, who was tired of hearing a Texan bragging about the Alamo, asked the Texan if he had heard of Paul Revere. The Texan drawled, "Isn't that the man who had to call for help?"

43. The perseverance of William the Silent and the American colonists recalls a story about the devil, whose favorite tool is "discouragement": "If I can get that wedge, discouragement, under a man, it opens the way for all my other tools."

44. Holland, Zeeland, Friesland, Gelderland, Utrecht.

45. Son of William V of Orange. He was Queen Victoria's uncle.

25. BELGIUM

1. The umbrella was invented in 1740 by British merchant and philanthropist Jonas Hanway. Everyone laughed at him and paraded after him with sieves balanced on broom handles.

2. *La Muette de Portici,* based on 1647 Revolution in Naples.

3. 6 Petite rue des Bouchers. Operated since 1835 by the same family of puppeteers.

4. The Meir is the main street connecting the Old Town with the area around Central Station.

5. In 1566, it was pillaged by Calvinists; it was pillaged ten years later by Alva's starving Spanish soldiers.

6. In medieval times a canal that ran under a bridge brought clean water to the breweries. The brewers built a large wooden fork with a long beam, a "wapper," on the bridge to raise the barrels of water.

7. Granted in the twelfth century by the first Count of Flanders.

8. November 8, 1576.

9. Ignored by successive rulers.

10. Ghent is connected to the North Sea via the Adegern Canal.

11. Saint Bavon was a seventh-century wealthy landowner who gave up everything to live in poverty and prayer.

26. THE HAGUE

1. It was named for George Maduro, a lieutenant in the Dutch Tank Regiment who died in the Dachau concentration camp. His parents donated the initial money.

Notes

2. This staged event is held each Friday morning from 10:00 A.M. 'til noon. Since the seventeenth century, cheese has been sold by auction to wholesale dealers. The "weight" house was once a spiritual house of rest for poor travelers.

3. Esso is the trade name for Standard Oil of New Jersey. Today it is called Exxon, but many foreign affiliates have kept the name Esso.

4. Son of a Pennsylvania mill worker. Carnegie donated $350 million for the public good, including the Carnegie Endowment for International Peace.

5. The museum was named for Johan Mauritis van Nassau-Siegn, governor-general of Dutch West India Co. (1604–1679).

6. French Louis XIII died the next year, 1643, leaving a five-year-old son, future Louis XIV.

7. The actual title is *The Shooting Company of Captain Frans Banneng Gocq*.

8. Rembrandt's wife died the year he finished his famous *Night Watch*. His son by a second wife was the only survivor of several children.

27. DELFT

1. Three boys and eight girls. Four died early.

2. Hugo de Groat (Grotius) was born on Easter 1583, a year after William the Silent was murdered.

3. *Law of War and Peace* (1625) was considered the first definitive text of international law. While not condemning all war, it maintains that only certain causes justify it.

4. In 1621 he renounced his Dutch allegiance. He pledged his allegiance to the queen of Sweden.

5. Third-century martyr from Catonia, Sicily.

6. He was born in 1583, six months after his father's assassination. His mother was Louise de Caligry.

28. KRAKÓW

1. The monument in Matejko Market Square was donated by Paderewski to commemorate a 1410 Polish victory at Grunwaldt over the Teutonic Knights.

2. Sigismund Augustus II (1592–1572).

3. Beheaded in the Church on the Rock, on the bank of Vistula River.

4. Catherine II of Russia, Frederick of Prussia, and Maria Theresa of Austria.

5. Over Washington's protests, Congress had promoted five brigadier generals of junior rank over Arnold.

6. Named for a fifth-century B.C. Roman consul, Cincinnatus, who left his farm twice to defend Rome. Mission accomplished, he returned home.

7. Canton of Solothurnn in Northwest Switzerland.

8. Also a monument on Cockspur Island, Georgia, and a marble bust in the capitol Rotunda in Washington, D.C.

9. Near town of Morges in the canton of the Vaud.

10. Paso Robles.

11. Henryk Migocki. Tel: (+48) 0 601, 448 545.

12. Miraculous healings of Maureen Digan, 1992, and Father Pytel, 1999.

13. The title, which means "bringing forth God," was given to the Virgin Mary by The Third Ecumenical Council at Ephesus.

14. In 1940 the Russians massacred 4,321 Polish officers in the Katyn Forest between Minsk and Moscow, near Smolenski.

29. GREECE

1. Greek word for Troy. Homer, the first European poet, lived 800 B.C. According to legend, he was blind.

2. One of Homer's bravest heroes in Trojan War.

3. Aeschylus (525–456 B.C.), "the father of tragedy," wrote the first ghost scene when the ghost of Persian emperor Darius appeared, warning his people of their doom. Aeschylus used two members of the chorus to portray separate characters. He won the Greek play contest thirteen times, but was prouder of his role as a soldier in the Battle of Marathon.

4. Aegisthus.

5. In Iolcus.

6. While Greeks were experimenting with democracy and sacrificing animals on altars, the Prophet Ezekiel in Babylonia reminded the protesting, exiled Jews that God was the only reason for their existence. He pleaded with them to keep their faith.

7. At Plataea.

8. Pericles had arranged a truce with Sparta. The result was fourteen years of peace.

9. The culture, ideals, and lifestyle of classical Greece, especially that of Athens during the Age of Pericles, spread throughout the Mediterranean near Europe into Asia after Alexander the Great's conquests.

10. To incite Hellenic rivalry.

11. The Persians invented chess.

12. Zantippe.

13. At Chaeronea in Boeotia.

Places of Interest

1. LONDON

The Savoy Group (Tel. 1-800-223-6800) includes: Claridge's, The Berkeley, The Connaught, Forest Mére Spa Health Resort, The Savoy in London, and the sixteenth-century Lygon Arms in the Cotswolds Village, Broadway. In Paris, The Lancaster.

The Tabard Inn	Southwark, South London, where Chaucer's *Canterbury Tales* pilgrims gathered.
Mermaid Tavern	London's Bread Street, where Sir Walter Raleigh, and playwrights Ben Jonson, Beaumont, Fletcher, and probably William Shakespeare met.
The Cheshire Cheese	Fleet Street, where William Butler Yeats read poetry. Also a favorite haunt for Boswell, Oliver Goldsmith, and Samuel Johnson.

Restaurants

Savoy Grill	Savoy Hotel River Restaurant
Wiltons	55 Jermyn Street (near Saint James Palace) Tel. 01.629.99.55

Limousine Service

From Heathrow Airport	Tel. 01.759.1305

3. THE LOUVRE

The Louvre	Metro Louvre
Luxembourg Palace	Residence of Marie de' Medici after death of her husband King Henri IV. Mansion named for original owner, duc François de Luxembourg. Today, residence of president of the Senate. Includes cloister and chapel of a convent founded by the queen. Metro Odéon.
Notre Dame des Victories	Dedicated by Louis XIII. Famous for annual pilgrimages to the Virgin since 1836. Place des Petits Pères. 4 Metro rue Montmartre.

Places of Interest

Val de Grace Church (Valley of Grace)	A church on the site of a Benedictine Convent commissioned by Queen Anne of Austria, mother of Louis XIV, in gratitude for his birth (1645). During the French Revolution, the church and convent were saved by a decree from the National Convention, making Val de Grace a military hospital. Today, a university for research and advanced studies of military medicine. 284 rue St. Jacques. Metro Port Royal.
Church of Saint Denys du Saint Sacrement	Delacroix's Deposition: (Ask to have Pieta lighted.) Rue de Turenne in the Marais. Metro Saint Paul.
Delacroix's Studio	Where Delacroix painted portraits of Chopin and George Sand. He had a piano there for Chopin to play when he visited. The piano is now in the Louvre. 17 rue Visconti. Metro Odéon.
Museum	Delacroix's home and studio, built 1857. A staircase joins the apartment to the studio overlooking a little garden. 6 rue de Furstemberg. Metro Saint Germaine des Pré.

4. CAFÉ PROCOPE AND MIRABEAU (1749–1791)

Café Procope	13 rue de l'Ancienne Comédie
Mirabeau's home	46 rue de la Chaussée d'Antin
Saint Eustache Church	Mirabeau's funeral
Pantheon	Mirabeau buried there.
Nationale Musée du Château at Versailles	David's painting, *Oath of the Tennis Court*.
Musée Carnavalet	Marat's shoe-shaped bathtub, Forum des Halls. Metro Saint Paul.
Saint Nicholas des Champs	Lafayette's church where Louis Braille (1809–1852) played the organ. République Metro.
Assembly Hall	La Salle des Menus Plaîsirs, 22 ave. de Paris, Versaille.

5. SAINT SULPICE CHURCH

Saint Sulpice Church	Rue St. Sulpice
Seminary	Formerly #9 rue St. Sulpice. Today Faubourg Moulimaux.
Motherhouse	30 rue Lhomond
Eugène Delacroix Museum	#6 rue de Fürstemberg

Places of Interest

6. GARNIER'S OPERA HOUSE

Opera Library and Museum — Rue Scribe, on the site of the private entrance for Emperor Napoléon III. The courtyard and projecting wing were designed for season ticket holders (subscribers). The library contains 80,000 books. The Museum displays costumes and reduced-scale model sets used since 1669 (reign of Louis XVI), as well as genuine jewels worn on stage designed by the greatest artists of the times. Exhibits of sets and costumes for operas by Gounod, Berlioz, Meyerbeer, Verdi, Mozart, Rimsky-Korsakov, Gluck, Puccini, and Strauss among others.

7. OPÉRA COMIQUE AND BIZET'S *CARMEN*
George Bizet 1838–1875

Born: 6 rue de la Tour d'Auvergne, Bougival, near Paris.

Baptized: l'Église Notre Dame de Lorette, Paris. Metro Notre Dame de Lorette.

Residence: 22 rue de Douae, place Pigalle in Montmartre near the Moulin Rouge. At that time only gardens, grass, and trees. Gounod, Degas, and Doré lived nearby.

Funeral: l'Église de la Trinité off rue Taitbout. Metro Châteaudun

Monument: Père Lachaise Cemetery. Metro Père Lachaise.

Paris Theaters

Odéon — *The Pearl Fishers* produced there 1863, and *The Fair Maid of Perth* 1867. Metro Odéon.

Opéra Comique or Salle Favart — Rue Marivaux off rue des Italiens. Built by duc de Choiseul on his land for the comic opera company Les Italiens, which later changed to operettas and light operas by Offenbach and Johann Strauss. Metro Opéra.

8. NAPOLÉON III (1808–1873)

Born: 8 rue Lafitte, Paris

Buried: Saint Michael's Memorial Church in Farnborough, Hampshire, England. The church is an exact replica of Église Saint Augustin in Paris, which he built. Boulevard Haussman. Metro Saint Augustin.

Parks — Parc de Buttes—Chaumont
Parc de Monceau
Bois de Boulogne
Bois de Vincennes

Places of Interest

9. FRÉDÉRIC CHOPIN (1810–1849)

Statue: Luxembourg Gardens. Metro de l'Austerlitz.
Funeral: Church of the Madeleine. Metro Madeleine.
Buried: Père Lachaise Cemetery. Metro Gambetta.

Paris Residences	5 rue Tronchest. Metro Madeleine.
	Square d'Orléans (intersection of rue Taitbout and rue Notre Dame de Lorette) Apartment #9. Metro Saint Georges.
	74 rue Quentin Bauchart (between #10 and #16 near Saint Pierre de Chaillot.) At the time, it was outside Paris, where the air was cleaner. Today, nearby, is Place États Unis (United States) and the American Cathedral in Paris. Metro Georges V.
	#12 place Vendôme Residence at time of death Metro Tuilleries
Musée de La Vie Romantique	16 rue Chaptal. Metro Saint Georges.
Nohant	George Sand's estate in the province of Berry. 166 miles south of Paris near Châteauroux.

11. IN MEMORY OF MOLIÈRE (1622–1673)

Statue: Rue de Richelieu opposite his home.

Baptized: Church of Saint Eustache (named for a Roman general; a convert to Christianity). Les Halles Beaubourg between rue Rambuteau and rue Montmartre. Metro Halles.

Married: Church of Saint Germain Auxerrois, opposite the Louvre. Metro Palais Royal.

Home: 40 rue de Richelieu. Metro Palais Royal.

Tomb: Père Lachaise Cemetery. Metro Père Lachaise.

Theater	Palais Royal. Metro Palais Royal.
Comédie-Francaise	Theatre that evolved from Molière's first theater. Opposite Palais Royal. Metro Palais Royal.

12. PLACE DE LA BASTILLE AND BEAUMARCHAIS (1732–1799)

Beaumarchais

Statue: Rue St. Antoine. Metro Saint Paul.
Married: Saint Paul–Saint Louis. Metro Saint Paul.
Prison: 107 rue de Faubourg St. Denise. On site of former leper hospital founded by Saint Vincent de Paul. Today, a hospital again (1935), Maison Saint Lazare.
Tomb: Père Lachaise Cemetery. Metro Père Lachaise.

Places of Interest

Homes	Born, rue St. Denise. Street famous for jewelers and clock makers. Lived with parents and five musical sisters who adored him. Metro Les Halles.
	26 rue de Conde where he wrote *The Barber of Seville*. Lived with his widowed father and two unmarried sisters. When convicted of fraud, his furniture was taken and house confiscated. After retrieving the honor of Marie Antoinette, he bought the house back. Metro Odéon.
	47 rue Vieille du Temple and rue des Rosiers in the Marais. Home was also headquarters for his export-import company. Wrote *The Marriage of Figaro* there. Today it is Hôtel Amelot de Bisseuil. Once was Hôtel des Ambassadeurs de Hollande used by Dutch Ambassadors' chaplain. Metro Saint Paul.
	Restaurants
Bastille Area	Brasserie Bofinger 3–7 rue de la Bastille rue de Lappe
	7 La Tchaika (Russian)
	9 La Balajo (Afternoon tea dances except Monday).
	17 Tapas Noctunes (Spanish)
	43 El Barrio (Spanish)
	41 La Galoche d'Aurillac (Auvergne) rue de la Roquette
	13 Le Baltzar Brasserie rue St. Savin
	12 La Petite Fabrique (chocolates)

13. PASSY: MAISON DE BALZAC AND HONORÉ BALZAC (1799–1850)

Statue: By Rodin. Carrefour Vavin blvd. Raspail and blvd. Montparnasse. Metro Montparnasse Bienvenue.

Home: Maison de Balzac (1840–1847), 47 rue Raynouard in Passy. Metro Trocadero.

Funeral: Saint Philippe du Roule. Place Chassaigne Goy. Metro rue de Courcelles and Myron T. Herrick.

Buried: Père Lachaise Cemetery (near tombs of Beaumarchais and Rabelais).

His Publisher	30 place St. André des Arts. Metro Odéon.
Printing Shop	17 rue de Visconti parallel to rue des Beaux Arts. In his late twenties (1826), he lived in an apartment above the shop and lugged water from the fountain at blvd. St. Michel. Metro Odéon.

Places of Interest

14. RUEIL MALMAISON: CHÂTEAU MALMAISON

Tourist Office	Parc de l' Amitié, 160, ave. Paul Doumer, 92500
Josephine's Home	60 rue de la Victoire, Paris, where she and Napoléon lived as newlyweds
Malmaison	From Gare d'Austerlitz take Metro Express (RER) line A to Saint Germain en Lay. Then #158 bus to Rueil Malmaison. Tel. (1) 47.49.20.07
Restaurant	Pavilion Josephine, 19 ave. Bonaparte. Tel. 17.51.01.62
l'Église Saint Pierre	Tombs of Empress Josephine and Queen Saint Paul Hortense

15. NORMANDY
MONT SAINT MICHEL

Tourist Office	Tel. 1.900.420.2003
Saint Malo	28 miles
Dinan	47 miles
Caen	80 miles
Hôtel du Mouton Blanc	Tel. 99.60.14.08
Hôtel La Mère Poulard	Where tourists peer through the window to watch chefs whip up frothy omelets to a syncopated rhythm of their whisks—a Breton version of Vachel Lindsay's "beat, beat, beat of the tom-tom." (run by the government). Tel. 03.91.11.01
Mass Schedule	12:15 P.M. daily. Sunday 9:30 A.M. and 11:00 A.M.
Suggestions	To avoid crowds, don't go on a weekend. Order omelet and salt-marsh-fed lamb. Visit Saint Aubert's Chapel. Also visit Gabriel Tower to see sunset and tide.

16. AQUITAINE
SAINT ÉMILION (THE FAMOUS WINE TOWN)

Hospices de la Madeleine	Underground Museum of Pottery, History and Art. 21 rue André Loiseau. Tel. 05.57.55.51.65, Fax 05.57.51.61
Train of the Great Vineyards	www.visitesaint-emilion.com. Tel. 05.57.51.13.76, Fax 05.57.01.99
Le Doyenne Place des Crémeaux	

Places of Interest

Hotels

Hostellerie de Plaisance	Place du Clocher. Tel. 05.57.55.07.55 or 05.57.74.41.11
Auberge de la Commanderie	Rue des Cordeliers. Tel. 05.57.24.70.19. Stone archway a few steps away; it remains one of the oldest buildings—former residence of Garrison officers.
Logis des Ramparts	Rue Guadet. Tel. 57.24.70.43
Hôtel Château Grand Barrail	Two miles west of Saint Émilion. Tel. 33.57.55.37.00

Restaurants

Auberge de Gros Figeac	Next to Hôtel Château Grand Barrail. Lunch and dinner in a château. Owner, Vincent Querre. Tel. 33.57.55.37.00
Le Clos du Roy	12 rue de la Petite Fontaine. Tel. and Fax 05.57.74.41.55
L'Huitrie	Près rue de la Grand Fountaine
Le Medieval	Place de la Porte Bouqueyre. Tel. 05.57.24.62.94
La Babanne	Place du Marché.
Logis de Cadéne	Place Marché au Blois
Michel Poupin	Rue Guadet

Suggestions	Buy: 1. Replicas of ancient pottery and artwork at Museum of Pottery, 21 rue André Louiseau. 2. Chocolate at Rémy Ertle Patissier, rue Grand Fontaine. 3. Almond macaroons at Brocante Antiques. 4. Wine at Maison du Vin—around corner from Place Mayrat, Syndicate d'Initiative.

17. BRITTANY

Jules Verne (1828–1905)

Married: Église Saint Eugène, Amiens
Buried: Cemetery of La Madeleine, Amiens
Monument: Blvd. Longueville, Amiens. Paid for by public subscription from all over the world.

Homes	6 rue Charles–Dubois, Amiens 44 blvd. Longueville, Amiens

Restaurant

Eat	Pont Levis Restaurant. Nantes.
Höedic	Take a boat trip on the Morbihan Gulf from Auray.

Places of Interest

Vocabulary

ville close	walled city
pou or *ple*	parish (Ploudaniel means Parish of Saint Daniel)
loc	place (Loc Maria = Mary's place)
traon or *trou*	valley (e.g., *tro* melin = Valley of the Mill)
lit clos	enclosed bed

18. AUVERGNE

Office de Tourisme	Place du Breuil 43000 Le Puy en Velay. Tel. 71.09.41
Le Petite Train	Opposite Tourist Office 16 blvd. Marechal Fayolle.
Musée Crozatier and Jardin Henri Vinay	Tel. 71.09.38.90. A paradise for geologists. Most beautiful lace collection in France. Look for cross of boatmen, which they display on prow of their barges; Jesus' body pierced by lance surrounded by objects recalling His Passion, e.g., ladder and discarded purse of Judas. On top of the cross is a cock, symbol of Peter's denial, but also the herald of dawn—the Resurrection. Pamphlets on display include *How to Participate in the Prevention of Juvenile Delinquency*. (Picture of boy on ladder painting a house.) Information on mediation and counseling.
Cathedral	On the porch, funny carvings on capitals represent the seven deadly sins; for example, Gluttony: a cake, Avarice: a purse with the strings drawn, and so on.

Special Events

Classical Music Festival	August 1–10
Feast of the Annunciation	March 25
King of the Bird Festival	Fête de L'Oiseau September 13–17

Hotels

Hôtel Christel	15 blvd. Aclair. Tel. 71.02.24.44
Hôtel Bristol	7 ave. Foch. Tel. 71.09.13.38
Hôtel Ibis	1 ave. d'Aiguilhe. Tel. 71.02.22.22
Hôtel Licorn	25 ave. Charles Dupuy (near train). Tel. 71.02.46.22
Hôtel Régina	34 blvd. Maréchal Fayolle. Tel. 71.09.14.71

Restaurants

Restaurant Sarda (cave)	12 rue Chenebouterie

Places of Interest

Bateau Ivre	5 rue Portail
Crêperie Pomme d'Api	17 rue Vibert
Michel Datessen	5 rue Portail d'Avignon
Licorn Hôtel	Order coffee and get free dessert. 25 ave. Charles Dupuy
Lapierre	6 rue des Capucins
Outdoor Cafes	Bring paper napkins to cover drinks at sidewalk cafés (bees). Also bring folding cup for unexpected, welcome, drinking fountains. Bring home green lentils and raspberry liqueur.

CHAVANIAC

American Memorial. Owned by American Lafayette Memorial Trust c/o Friends of Lafayette. Lafayette College, Easton, Pa. To help maintain Lafayette's birthplace in France send contributions to: Château Natal du Général de la Fayette, Chavaniac-Lafayette, 443230 Paulhaguet. Tel. (16-17) 77.50.32

PARIS

Picpus Cemetery	35 rue de Picpus opposite a Renault garage. Metro Picpus, Bel-Air. Sisters of Sacred Heart Retreat House (closed during August). 1,306 victims of French Revolution buried here. 1,298 names recorded. In smaller enclosure, victims of 1870 Commune, including sixteen Carmelite nuns. Most famous member of Sacred Heart Order is Belgian Father Damien, who cared for leprosy victims. Plaques in cemetery in memory of arrival of General Pershing and the American Army, July, 1917, donated by Daughters of the American Revolution, Benjamin Franklin Chapter. Lafayette's burial site.
Lafayette's Statue	Place du Carrousel, in Paris. Gift from 5 million American students, who raised $50,000. U.S. Congress matched the sum.

19. BERRY

Contact	Directeur Générale, Comtesse Marie-France de Peyronnet, 1 rue Madame, 75006 Paris, France. Tel. 1-45.44.19.77

GIEN

Restaurant

Hôtel du Rivage	On the banks of the Loire. 1 quai de Nice. Christian Gaillard, Proprietor. 45500 Gien. Tel. 38.67.20.53

Places of Interest

Office de Tourisme	11 rue Anne de Beaujeu. Tel. 38.67.25.28
La Musée de la Chasse	In the château of Gien
Gien's faience (earthenware) factory with its museum and shop	Tel. 38.67.00.05
Musée Alain–Fournier	Between Gien and Bourges.

Le Verrerie Château

Good overnight stop southwest of Gien, halfway between Paris and Bourges. Seven elegant guest rooms with private bath and breakfast in bed. Individually decorated rooms. Tennis, bicycle and horseback riding. 17 miles south of Aubigny sur Nère. 18700 Aubigny sur Nère. Tel. 48.58.31.01. Open March 1 to December 1 from 10 A.M. to noon and 2 P.M. to 7 P.M.

Maison d'Hélène	Housed in a seventeenth-century farm on the estate. Specializing in family recipes. Cottage with a huge fireplace. Nearby town of Aubigny sur Nère, town of the Stuarts. Tel. 48.58.06.91. Open February 15 to December 31 except Tuesday.

SANCERRE

Restaurant de la Tour	31 place de la Hall. Tel. 48.54.00.81
Syndicate d' Initiative	Maire de Sancerre 18300 de Sancerre. Tel. 48.54.00.26
Hôtel Panoramic	Rampart des Augustins. Tel. 48.5.22.44
Hôtel de France	Rue St. Martin. Tel. 48.54.00.52

Castle Maupas

Castle tour	Open Palm Sunday to November. Tel. 48.46.41.71

BOURGES

Office de Tourisme	21 rue Victor Hugo B. P. 145 F-18003 Bourges Cedex. Tel. 48.24.75.33
Hôtel d'Angleterre	1 place des Quatre Piliers Town Center. Tel. 48.24.68.51
Hôtel Restaurant Le Windsor	Tournedos, au crotin de chavignol, rognons de veau a la berrichonne. For dessert, charlotte aux péches. 3 rue Jacques Coeur. Tel. 48.24.68.51

BOURGES OLD TOWN

Rue Mirebeau	Shopping. Near La Place Gardaine.
Rue Ed Branly	l'Hôtel des Echevisn
Rue Pelvoysin	Hôtel Pelvoysin (note slanted windows).

Places of Interest

Rue des Aremes	Berry Museum
Rue des Trois Maillets	Where church money was stored in the "Tithe Barn."
Place Gordaine	Sidewalk cafés and Hôtel Lallemont, the Museum of Decorative Arts. Two levels with two courtyards.
Rue Roubonnoux	Sidewalk luncheon at Bar Remparts, north of cathedral. One of the most picturesque streets in Bourges. Remains of third-century Roman walls.
House of Three Flutes	Corner rue Rourbonnoux and rue Joyeuse
Place de la Nation	Site of Roman amphitheater.
1 rue d'Auron	Home of Jacques Coeur's father-in-law.

Chateau de Meillant

18200 Meillant. Follow the sign "Promenade en Miniature" in the former wine cellar. Walk through the Middle Ages, Renaissance, eighteenth, nineteenth, and twentieth centuries. From a tiny medieval village to the twentieth century symbolized by Art Deco style. Hours: 9–11:30 2–6:30. Tel. 48.63.30.58 or 48.63.32.05

Commanderies in France

Berry	Stay at La Commanderie; seven beautiful rooms. Breakfast; special arrangements for dinner. For reservations contact: Countess B. de Jouffroy Gonsans. 18200 Farges-Allichamps. Tel. 48.61.04.19
Saint Émilion	Auberge de la Commanderie rue des Cordeliers 33330 Saint Émilion. Tel. 56.24.70.19
Geux	31 miles N.E. of Aix en Provence on mountain top. Largest existing Templar castle in Europe.
La Rochelle	Off rue du Palais, a covered arch leads to the courtyard of former site of The Knights Templar Commanderie. An enormous Maltese Cross is emblazoned on the pavement and the tomb of their commander is under a restaurant on the square.
South of Dôle	Temple restaurant in a stone cellar. Arched roof supported with massive pillars from Templar period. On river Doubs is hamlet of Molay, District of Jacques de Molay, last grand master of the Knights Templar. Burned at the stake in Paris, 1314.
Near Roquefort	Medieval Templar town of La Couvertoirade between Avignon and Aix. The Commanderie is in a perfectly preserved medieval town. A red wine, La Bargemone, is labeled with the sign of the Templars' cross.

Places of Interest

Paris	Place de la Republique, site of the Temple in Paris, headquarters of the Order in Europe, near the Church of Saint Nicholas des Champs, where Louis Braille played the organ. The Temple Tower, built by Philip IV as a prison after the Templars' arrest, was on the site of today's Carreau de Temple, an open-air clothes and costume market (9:00 A.M. 'til noon, except Monday).
Troyes	34 miles N.W. of Paris is a farm in Barbonne Fayel, the first donation to the Templars in France. Still called La Commanderie.
Dôle	S.E. of Paris is Le Temple Restaurant. Located in a stone cellar, with arched roof and massive pillars from the Templar period.

Commanderies in England

London	Chancery Lane in Westminster. The former Temple, The Knights Templar banking center. Today it is the lawyers' chapel hidden between two Inns of Court, built over the site of the original temple.
Essex	Cressing and Witham Manors
Oxford	Crowley Manor

Castle Ainay Le Vieil

Open to visitors all week. February–November 30th. 10 A.M.–noon and 2:00 P.M.–7:00 P.M. Closed Tuesday during February, March, and November.

Pageant	"The Castle by Candlelight." 1,000 torch flares, period costumes. Also performances of *Gilles de Rais (Bluebeard)*. More than 100 performers.
Gardens	Open from May 15th–Sept 30th. Tours July and August, 10:00 A.M.–7:00 P.M. Tel. 48.63.50.67 or 48.63.50.03
Noirlac	Beautiful Cistercian Abbey founded by Saint Bernard 1150 near Ainay le Vieil. For visits and concerts contact: Friends of The Abbey of Noirlac Hôtel du Departement 18014 Bourges Cedex. Tel. 33.48.70.71.72

NOHANT

Château Nohant	Home of George Sand. 2 hours on train from Gare de l'Austerlitz in Paris to Bourges. 43 miles from Bourges to Nohant; 45 minutes by bus from Bourges.

Places of Interest

Musée George Sand	In Chatre, a small town 3 miles from Nohant. Located in a tower formerly a prison.
Musée de la Vie Romantique	In Paris: small museum in a shaded courtyard. Souvenirs of George Sand and her Paris friends. 16 rue Chaptal. Tel. 48.74.95.38

20. TOURAINE

TOURS

Tourist Office	Place du Mal Leclerc. Tel. 47.05.58.08
Tours to Ussé and Saché	Depart 1:15 P.M. place de la Gare. Platform 20.

ORLÉANS

Office of Tourisme	Place Albert. Tel. 38.53.05.95. Inquire about underground parking, Jacques Coeur Tour of châteaux and Jeanne d'Arc Festival May 7 & 8.
Cathedral Saint Croix	Tourist train leaves from here. 45-minute tour.
Maison de Jeanne d'Arc	Home of Jacques Boucher: place du Général de Gaulle.
Museum of Beaux Arts	Rue Paul Belmondo
Museum of Natural Science	2 rue Marcel Proust
Church of Saint Aignan	Remains of Saint Aignan, second bishop of Orléans are here. In 451, Attila and his Huns threatened the city. Although an old man, the bishop went to Nîmes to appeal to Roman general there. When Attila came to the gates of Orléans, the old bishop mounted the ramparts in full regalia and spat in the pagan chief's direction. Instantly a terrible storm turned day into night. Attila was so astonished, he retreated before the Roman legions arrived.

Restaurants

Saint Pierre Hôtel and Restaurant	Rue de St. Catherine and blvd. de Verdun. Eat outdoors and note wonderful old facades. Les Antiquaires 2–4 Lin. Tel. 38.53.52.35
Serrurerie J. Lawreau	Rue de Borgogne
La Cremaillere	34 rue Notre Dame de Recouvrance. Tel. 87.49.17

Hotels

Sofitel Orléans	44–46 quai Barentin. Swimming pool. Walking distance to center of town. Tel. 62.17.39
Terminus	40 rue de la Republique opposite railroad station.

Places of Interest

Saint Martin	52 blvd. A. Marlin. Near Cathedral. Close to restaurants. Tel. 64.47.47

Parks and Gardens

Parc Floral	La Source of Loriet—100,000 roses and dahlias.
Parc Pasteur	Le petit train de Wichita, rue Egéne Gignat
Jardin des Plantes	Ave. du Jardin des Plantes.
Jardin d'Eveche	Adjacent to the Cathedral.
Ile Charlemagne	Rue de Courtenay with lake. Center of town.
La Source	University located here. Make reservations for sightseeing boat for cruise on Loiret at Hotel–Restaurant Madgascar.

Nearby

Beaugency	Château Dunois. Today a museum. Each room decorated in different period. 11 miles from Orléans. Great view. Tel. 38.66.12.58
Cléry Saint André	Dunois Chapel, where Joan's brilliant commander, the "Gentle Bastard," is buried in chapel he built for Our Lady, whose ancient statue was found here. Devout King Louis XIII, the Spider King (Dauphin's son) prayed at Dunois' tomb (his cousin). For tour, apply at Rectory 10–12 and 2–7.
Olivet, a suburb along the Loiret (little Loire)	King Louis VII, first husband of Eleanor of Aquitaine, returned from Second Crusade with priests from Mount Zion in Jerusalem and gave them land, which they named from the Mount of Olives.
Saint Benôit (Benedict)	Eleventh-century monastery near Fleury. Once a celebrated center of learning. Look for sign "La Basilique." In 703, monks stole relics of Saint Benedict from monastery of Monte Cassino in Italy, ruined by Lombards a century before. His bones and those of his sister, Saint Scholastica, brought here. Italians, in uproar, appealed to pope who said okay to keep bones, but "send us back a few." Saint Scholastica's bones given to monks of Le Mans, who had provided safe escort to Italy. Gregorian Chant: Vespers: 6:15 P.M. Mass: Sunday 11:00 A.M.; weekdays–noon. For tour, inquire at book shop.
Fierbois	Chapel of Saint Catherine where Joan worshipped before meeting dauphin in Chinon.

Places of Interest

21. LORRAINE

Office de Tourisme	14 place Stanislas. Tel. 03.83.35.22.41, Fax 03.83.35.90.10
The Grand Rue	Where dukes of Lorraine made their entry into Nancy.
Porte de la Craffe	Two fourteenth-century gates in medieval wall and Porte Nicolas.
Lorraine Historical Museum	Church of Cordeliers, former monastery and remains of Ducal Palace which houses Georges de la Tour's *Woman and the Flea*.
Church of Saint Epvre	Place Stanislas
Museum of Fine Arts	Houses painting of *Battle of Nancy* by Eugène Delacroix.
Hôtel de Ville	(Town Hall) rue P. Fournier.
Opera	Théâtre de Nancy, 1 rue St. Catherine.
Parc de la Pépinière	Behind Amphitrite Fountain 1 rue St. Catherine.
Aquarium rue Catherine	Near place Stanislas.
The Cathedral	6 rue des Chanoiness (money changers).
Musée de l'Ecole de Nancy	36 rue du Sergent Blandan. Closed Tuesday.
Our Lady of Refuge	(Notre Dame de Bonsecours). Originally a chapel built during reign of René II to commemorate his victory over Charles the Bold.
Aviation Museum	Largest civil aviation museum in Europe; Plateau de Malzeville.

Restaurants

Capucín Gourmand	31 rue Gambetta

Hotels

Thiers	Place Thiers
Excelsior	Place de la Gare
Angle Terre	Place de la Gare

Outside NANCY

City of Toul	Daum Works in rue des Cristalleries.
Town of Baccarat	Baccarat Crystal.
Luneville	Medieval town. Château of former dukes of Lorraine.

Places of Interest

Town of Saint Nicholas de Port	Basilica of Saint Rémy, 1477. Duke René II prayed there before Battle of Nancy. Built basilica in thanks for victory.
Notre Dame de Cléry	Future King Louis XI, as dauphin, prayed for victory in Dieppe, promised to enlarge and glorify her church in Cléry. After victory, kept his promise.
Dijon, France	Famous tombs of two dukes of Burgundy, John the Fearless and Philip the Good. Tower where Philip the Good imprisoned "good king René." Palace of dukes of Burgundy where gargantuan banquets were held.
Bruges, Belgium	Church of Notre Dame—Tomb of Charles the Rash, Duke of Burgundy. Saint Donation— Funeral for Philip the Good.

22. BURGUNDY

Office de Tourisme	Rue de l'Hôtel Dieu
Bombard Society	6727 Curran St., McLean, VA 22101
Notre Dame Basilica	Fifteenth-century Belgium tapestries of "Life of the Virgin."
Musée du Vin	Former residence of dukes of Burgundy, rue Paradis.
Hôtel de Ville	In former cloister of Ursuline Convent.

Hotels

Modern Hôtel Bourgogne	Ave. Général de Gaulle. Tel. (80) 22.22.00
Hostellerie de Bretonniére	43 Faubourg, Bretonniére
Hôtel de la Poste	1 blvd. Clémenceau. Tel. (80) 22.08.11
Le Cep Hôtel	27 rue Maufaux. Tel. (80) 22.35.48

Restaurants

Le Relais de Saulx	16 rue Louis Very. Tel. (80) 22.01.35
Auberge Saint Vincent	Place de la Halle (opposite l'Hôtel Dieu). Tel. (80) 22.42.34
Jacques Laine	10 blvd. Fuch. Tel. (80) 24.76.10
de la Poste Hôtel	Restaurant, 1 blvd. Clémenceau. Tel. (80) 22.08.11

23. PROVENCE
BRITTANY

Office de Tourisme de Vitré	Place St. Yvres 365 Vitré Tel. (99) 75.04.46, Fax (99) 74.0201
Château Les Rochers	In Brittany near Rennes and Vitré. Two hours from Montparnasse Station in Paris via TGV.

Places of Interest

PARIS

Church of Saint Gervaise and Proteus	Married there. Rue Françoise Miron near Hôtel de Ville.
Hôtel Carnavalet	22 rue de Sévigné. Mme. de Sévigné's last home in Paris, now Museum of the History of Paris. Tel. (01) 42.72.21.13

PROVENCE

Office de Tourisme	5 ave. van Gogh BP16, 13732 Les Saintes de la Mer, France Maries. Tel. (04) 90.97.82.55, Fax (80) 90.97.71.15
Château Grignan	Mme. de Sévigné's daughter's home near Montélimar or Nyons.
Comité Départmental de Tourisme de la Drôme	31 ave. du President Herriot 2600 Valance. Tel. (75) 82.19.26, Fax (75) 56.01.65
Folco de Baroncelli Museum	Les Saintes Maries de la Mer. Founded by the poet Marquis de Baroncelli (one of the Félibres) to preserve the traditional costumes and language of the Camargue.
Boisset's Cafe	Where gypsies dance and sing after Sarah is returned to her shrine.
La Petit Train	The Gardiane Cross at the Pont du Maur.
The Tzigane (Gypsy) Museum	Tel. 90.87.82.85
Statue of Mirèio (Mireille)	Les Saintes Maries de la Mer.
Wax Museum	Includes wax replica of van Gogh's *Les Barques aux Saintes Maries*.

24. THE GRAND DUCHY OF LUXEMBOURG

Office of Tourisme	Luxembourg National Tourist Office B. P. 1001 L-1010 Luxembourg. E-mail: info@ont.lu. www.ont.lu. Tel. (352) 42.82.82-1, Fax (352) 42.82.82.38
Grand Cravat Hôtel	29 blvd. Roosevelt. Tel. (352) 22.19.75
Hôtel Hilton	12 rue Jean Engling, Dommeldange. Tel. 4.37.81

Eat at Patisserie Namur and Lea Linster's Letzbeurger Kaschthaus.
Minitrain leaves from place d'Armes.

ARDENNES

Hotel–restaurant Leweck in Lipperscheid
Hôtel Vieux Moulin d' Asselborn

Places of Interest

CLERVAUX

Castle and Benedictine Abbey of Saint Maur and Saint Maurice

DEIKIRCH

Museum of the Battle of the Bulge

ESCH SUR SURE

Hôtel Beausite Mondorf–Les Bains
Luxembourg's Spa
Moselle River Cruise
SS Princesse Marie-Astrid

VIANDEN

Syndicate d'Initiative	37 rue de la Gare, L-9420 Vianden (Luxembourg). Tel. 84257
Heintz Hôtel–Restaurant	Hostellerie des Trinitaires, 55 Grand rue. Tel. 83.155
Folklore Museum	96–98 Grand rue
Doll Museum	96 Grand rue (500 dolls)

Huge hydroelectric underground power plant, the most powerful pumping station in Europe—a spectacular engineering feat.

Thirteenth-century Trinitarian Church and Cloister

Thirteenth-century Church of Saint Nicholas

Thirteenth-century Church of Saint Rochus. A yearly pilgrimage to a tiny 1848 chapel (with a miraculous statue of "Our Lady") takes place at the end of August.

WILTZ

Seventeenth-century Château of Wiltz, Eisenhower Square, and site of International Open-Air Theater and Music Festival in July.

25. BELGIUM

BRUSSELS

Belgian Tourist Office	Place de Brouchre. Tel. 02.18.05.20 780 Third Ave., #1501, N.Y. Tel. 212.758.8.130. www.visit-belgium.com
Grand Place	26, 27 Le Pigeon. Victor Hugo lived here 1852.
King's House (Maison du Rois)	Breughel's Wedding Procession here. Also 450 costumes and uniforms of Manneken Pis.
Manneken Pis	Rue l'Etude and rue du Chêne
Place Royale	Site of destroyed Castle of Coudenberg where Emperor Charles V abdicated.

Places of Interest

Comic Strip Art	20 rue des Sables. Tel. 219.19.80.20
Hôtel de Ville	Grand Place—Bombed by Louis XIV 1695 for thirty-six hours. Thousands of homes and buildings destroyed. Hôtel de Ville with statue of Saint Michael remained untouched.
Musée Breughel	132 rue Haute in Marolles district
Église Saint Jean Baptiste	Place du Beguinage au Beguinage
Bastogne	American Cemetery 2 miles N.W. of village Henri Chapelle where 7,989 American were killed holding the Bastogne Crossroads during the Battle of the Bulge.
English Book Shop	W.H. Smith 71 ba A. Max. Tel. 219.27.08
Belgian Tourist	111 blvd. Anspach (32.2).Tel. 513.74.84

Reservations

Bruxelles Accueil	6 rue de Tabora. Tel. 511.27.15; 511.81.78 (Times of religious services, etc.)
La Boutique de Tintin	13 rue de la Colline. Tel. 514.51.52 or 514.45.50
La Cheval Blanc	Rue St. Guidon Collectors' Place (posters, boxes . . .) 10:30 A.M. to 3:00 P.M. and 4:30 A.M. to 8:00 P.M. Tel. 521.33.31

Others

La Truite d'Argent	23 quai au Bois a Bruler. Tel. 219.95.46
Roue d'Or	Rue Chapeliers (beautiful interior)
Le Nostalgia	49–51 rue de la Fourche. Tel. 513.32.91
Le Grand Mayeur	Place du Grand Sablon. Tel. 512.80.91 (gypsy orchestra restaurant with Slavic specialities)
Ultieme Hallucinatie	Rue Royale, art noveau. Tel. 217.06.14
Au Vieux Spijigen Duivel	Chaussée d'Alsemberg. Tel. 344.34.55 (one of the oldest taverns)
La Capannina (Italian)	12 Petite rue au Beurre. Tel. 512.05.45 or 502.67.67

Shopping

Galeries Royales	Place de Louise
Saint Herbert (Tintin Shop)	Streenstraat 3; rue de Namur

Hotels

Metropole	31 place de Brouchre 84. Tel. 217.23.00 or 218.02.02
La Legende	35 rue du Lombard 35. Tel. 512.82.90 or 512.34.93

Places of Interest

A La Grande Cloche	Place Rouppe 10–12 (Marolles area). Tel. 512.61.40
Hôtel Sabine	Rue de Nord 78 (near place Madou). Tel. 218.26.37
Hôtel Noga	Rue de Beguinage 38 (Saint Catherine area). Tel. 218.67.63
Hôtel Metropole	Place de Brouchre 31. Tel. 217.64.50
Hôtel Amigo	1–3 rue de l'Amigo 1–3. Tel. 547.47.47 or 513.52.77
Hôtel Le Dixseptieme	25 rue de la Madeleine. Tel. 502.57.44 or 502.64.24
Hôtel Arlequin	Rue des Bouchers. Tel. 514.16.15
Ibis Saint Catherine Hôtel	Rue du Marche aux Herbes 100. Tel. 514.40.40
Hôtel Albert Premier	20 place Rogier. Tel. (02) 217.21.25
Clubhouse Hôtel	Rue Blanche. Tel. 537.92.10
Astoria	103 rue Royale. Tel. 217.62.90 or 217.11.50
The Mozart	15A rue de Marché aux Fromages. Tel. 502.66.61
Hôtel Welcome	Rue de Peuplier. Tel. 219.95.46 (Brussels' smallest hotel)

Restaurants

De Marina	Rue des Chartreux 36. Tel. 502.06.36
Le Perroquet	Rue Watteeu ave. (ave. Louise area). Tel. 512.99.22
Le Fine Fleur	Rue de la Longue Haie 51 (ave. Louise). Tel. 647.68.03
La Quincaillerie	Rue de Page (ave. Louise area). Tel. 538.25.53
Aux Armes de Bruxelles	Rue des Bouchers (near Grand Place). Tel. 511.55.98
Aux Armes de 't Kelderke	Cellar below #14 (near Grand Place). Tel. 513.73.44
Aux Armes Bonsoir Clara	Rue Dansaert 18 (near Grand Place). Tel. 502.09.90
Café Metropole	Place de Brouchers (near Grand Place). Tel. 219.23.84
In't Spinnekipke	Place du Jardin aux Fleurs (Saint Catherine area). Tel. 511.86.95
La Villette	Rue de Vieux Marche aux Grains 3 (Marolles area). Tel. 512.75.50
Comme Chez Soi	Place Rouppe 23 (Marolles area). Tel. 512.29.21
Around the Grand Place	Aux Armes de Bruxelles
Taverne du Passage	30 gal. de la Reine.Tel. 512.37.31. Scheitema (fish)
L'Ogenbilk (bistro)	1 gal. des Princes. Tel. 511.61.51
La Roue d'Or (bistro)	26 rue des Chapeliers. Tel. 514.25.54
t'Kelderke (basement)	6 Grand Place. Tel. 513.73.44

Places of Interest

ANTWERP

Tourist Office	Pelikaan Stratt. Tel. 03.32.01.03
Plantin Moretus Museum	25 Vrijdagmarkt Home of famous printer-publisher, Plantin. He printed prayer books for the Church and under William of Orange, he was the publisher for the states-general and City of Antwerp. Rubens worked as an illustrator for Plantin. Several Rubens works here.
Boat Excursions	1 ½ hrs. Steenplein. Tel. 231.31.00
Mayer van den Bergh	Lange Gasthui'straat 19

Museums

The Steen	The name means "castle moat." Ninth-century castle now houses National Maritime Museum. In an open-air section of the museum, a plaque honors the 1st Canadian Army, which, with British and Polish units, liberated the Scheldt estuary in 1944 by detonating mines under the icy sea to reopen the port of Antwerp.
Stadhuis (City Hall)	on Grote Markt
Royal Museum of Fine Arts	Leopold de Wallplaats 1–9
Diamond Museum	Lange Herentalsesstraat 31–33
Cathedral of Our Lady	Near Grote Markt
Saint Jacobskerk	Lange Nieuw Straat (Begun 1491)

Hotels

de Witte Lelie Keizerstraat	16–18 (Old City Centre). Fax 234.00.19
Antigone Hotel	Jordaenkaai 11–12 (Central Station area). Tel. 231.66.77
Hotel Postiljon	Blauwmoezelstraat 6 (Old City Centre).Tel. 231.7.75
Hotel Eden	Lange Herentalsestraat 25–27 (Central Station area). Fax 233.12.28
Hotel Prinse	Keizerstraat 63. Fax 225.11.48
Hotel Rubens	Oude Beurs 29, (near Grote Markt). Fax 225.19.40
Astrid Park Plaza	Koningin Astridplein 7. Fax 203.1251
Hotel Industrie	Emiel Banningstraat 52 ('t Zuid area). Fax 258.86.88
Pension Cammerpoorte	Steenhouwersvest. Fax 226.28.43

Restaurants

De Matelole	Haarstraat. Tel. 231.32.07
Sir Anthony Van Dyck	Oude Koornmarkt 16. Tel. 231.61.70

Places of Interest

T Fornuis	Reyndersstraat 24. Tel. 233.62.70
Eetjioske de Stoemppot	Vlasmarkt 12. Tel. 231.36.86
Het Nieuwe Palinghuis	St. Jansvliet 14. Tel. 231.50.53
Pottenbrug	Minderbroedersrui 38. Tel. 231.51.47
De Gouden Ecu	St. Michielsstraat. Tel. 232.71.25

GHENT

Tourist Office	Borluutstraat 9. Tel. 09.25.36.41
Stadhuis (Town Hall)	64 Koningin Maria Hendrik Aplein opposite Sint Pieters Station.
Cathedral of Saint Bavon	Fifteenth and sixteenth century. Crypt dates from 941.
Les Beguinages	Thirteenth-century convent surrounded by walls and moats. Many small houses, eighteen convents, and a church. Occupied by 700 Beguines; women devoted to good works. Famous for lace-making.
Audeburcy	Twelfth-century castle, built by the first counts of Flanders.
Former Hotel D' Haene Steenhuyse	Refuge of French king Louis XVIII during Napoléon's "Hundred Days." In Vedlstraat.
Former Hotel Schamp	John Quincy Adams and Henry Clay stayed here. Signed Treaty of Ghent ending War of 1812 with England.
The Belfry	Excellent view and audiovisual of The Ghent Experience. Thirteenth-century Botermarkt (great view).
Flower Show	April
Music Festival	Last two weeks of August.
Bijloke Museum	In thirteenth-century abbey (Flemish furniture and paintings).
Fine Arts Museum	Nicolaas de Liemaeckereplein
Museum Voor Schrene	Karel de Kerchovelaan
Kunsten School Museum	In north wing of former Abbey of Saint Peter (near Citadel Park). Audiovisual of Ghent history. Also history of the computer.
Ruined Abbey	1369: Wedding of Philip the Bold of Burgundy to Benedictine Margaret of Flanders, daughter of Count Louis de Male.
Gravensteen	Twelfth-century count's castle Saint Veerleplein.
Canal Cruises	Depart from Grceslei and Korenlei (45 minutes).
Ghent to Burges Canal	Cloth industry ruined by English competition.

Places of Interest

Hotels

Hotel Sofitel	Hoogpoort 63. Tel. 09.233.33.31
Novotel E.	Goudenlieu Plein. Tel. 09.12.42.230
Jorishof E.	2 Botermarket Restaurant and pool (near Cathedral). Tel. 091.24.24.24
Hotel Flandria	Barrestraat 77. Tel. 223.06.26, Fax 259.00.77
Hotel Adoma	St. Denijslaan 19. Tel. 222.65.50, Fax 245.09.37
St. Jorishof	Botermarkt 2. Tel. 224.24.24, Fax 224.26.40
Hotel Gravenstein	Jan Breydelstraat 35. Tel. 09.225.11.50

Restaurants

Eethui's Avalon 1	Geldmunt 32. Tel. 224.37.24
Togo	Vrouwebroersstaat 21. Tel. 223.65.51
Keizerhof	Vrjdagmarkt 47. Tel. 223.44.46
Het Waterhuisaan	Overlooking Groenten Markt.
De Bierkant	Outdoor Terrace.
Brasserie Moka	Koestraat 46. Tel. 09.225.00.54
Hotsy Totsy	Penitentenstraat 24. Tel. 09.234.07.08
Het Nieuwe	St. Jansvliet. Tel. 231.74.45
Pottenbrug	Minderbroedersrui 38. Tel. 231.51.47

26. THE HAGUE

SCHEVENINGEN

Kurhaus Hotel	Tel. 317.04.16.26.30, Fax 3170.416.26.40
Sea Life Centre	Strandweg 13. Walk through a transparent tunnel to see hundreds of tiny shrimp, starfish, crabs, sting rays, sea eels, and sharks.
Fishing Village	92 Neptunusstraat. Traditional dress and life of fishing people. A video of the historic fishing seaside resort.

THE HAGUE

The Hall of Knights	Inner Court in the Binnenhof, a medieval banquet hall where the Dutch Parliament meets.
American Embassy	102 Lange Voorhout.
Old Court, Palace	The States of Holland rented it (1591) for William the Silent's widow and her children. Later it was given to her and her son, Frederick Henry.
Carnegieplein	A gift from the American philanthropist, Andrew Carnegie. Furnished by countries from all over the world.

Places of Interest

27. DELFT

DELFT

Tourist Office	Market 85 Guided Tours. Fax 001.31.15.15.86.95
Old Church	Founded 1240 Helige Gesestkerhof
New Church	On the main square (1383–1510)

Hotels

3 Star Leeuwenbrug	Koor Market 16.26.11 EE Delft. Fax 31.15.159759
Hotel Devlaming	Vlamingstraat 52,26,11 KZ Delft. Fax 31.15.122006

28. KRAKÓW

Cultural Information Center	Ul. S.W. Janaz. www.Karnet.Karków2000.pl
Polish National Tourist Office	272 Madison Ave., #1711, N.Y. Tel. 212.338.9412, Fax 212.338.9283
Rynek Glowny	On the east corner of the square is the Jagiellonian University, founded in 1364. Statue of astrologer Copernicus, who studied here. The second-floor museum contains instruments used by Copernicus and the German Dr. Faustus, who inspired plays by Christopher Marlowe and Goethe, as well as music by Berlioz, Gounod, Liszt, and Schumann. #45—Kosciuszka lived here as a young officer, #6 was his headquarters in 1794. #16 is the famous restaurant Boris Godunov.
Saint André	To the right of garden, Pope John Paul II lived at #9 and later at #21.
Monument	2½ miles N.W. of Kraków is a monument to Kosciuszka, on top of a pile of dirt from battlefields where he fought. Take Tram 1, 2, or 6 from Place Dominikainski to Salwator; walk up.
View	Take cable car to terrace café on Gubalowka. Also, an eleventh-century Benedictine Abbey at Tyniec overlooks Vistula River.
Opera and Operettas	12 Bracka St. 31-005 Kraków. Tel. 422.62.10.421.28.13, in Kraków. Fax 422.57.26 or 422.08.79 www.opera.kraków
Church Services	English S.W. Idzi Church, Grodzka St. near Wawel, Sun. 10:30 A.M.
German S.W. Barbary Church	Sat. & Sun. Holidays 5:00 P.M., 8 Maly Rynek
French S.W. Jana Church	7 SW Jana St., 1st Sunday of month confession available before Mass.

Places of Interest

Dominican Basilica	Eighty Seminarian monks preparing for priesthood sing Gregorian chant every evening at 7:00 P.M.
Sister Faustina Convent In Ladiewniki	Tel. 012.266.58.59, Fax 012.266.23.68
Wieliczke Salt Mine	Tel. 0048(12) 278.73.02.278.73.66, Fax 278.73.33
Czestochowa,	70 miles N.W. of Kraków. Tel. 0048.34.365.38.88, Fax 0048.34.365.43.43
Stay at Orbis Patria	Tel. 034.24.53.59, Fax 034.24.63.32
U Moniaka (Jazz Club)	Florianska St. Thurs., Fri. & Sat. at 9:30 P.M.
Auschwitz Concentration Camp	½ hour from Kraków. 1.5 million people were exterminated there by the Nazis—Jews, Catholics, and Gypsies.

Hotels

Francuski	13 Pijarski St., 31.015 Kraków. Tel. 48(12)422.51.22, Fax 012.422.52.70. Email: francuski@orbis.pl
Grand Hotel	Art Nouveau decor. Tel. 421.72.55, Fax 421.83.60
The Royal Hotel	Below Wawel Castle. Tel. 421.49.79, Fax 421.58.57
Pod Roza	Near Main Square. Tel. 422.12.44, Fax 421.75.13 Email: podroza@hotelcom.pl
Wanda Hotel	Folklore music in garden 15 Armii Krajowej Av. Thurs. & Fri. 7:00 P.M. Tel. 637.16.77
Dionisos	Live music 4 Dominikanski Square. Tel. 0501.424.316

Restaurants

Krewi Roza	at Rezydent Hotel .Tel. 429.61.87
U Ziyade in castle at Prizegorzaly	8 minutes from city center. View of Vistula River. Tel. 429.71.05
Cyrano de Bergerac	Candlelit courtyard. Tel. 421.72.88
Slaw Kowska 26	Tel. 012.429.54.20
Hawelka in Spiski Palace	Main Market Square. Tel. 422.06.31
Na Wawelu Wawel Castle	Lunch. Tel. 411.65.98
Chlopskie Jadlo	Tel. 421.85.20
Pod Aniolami	Medieval Cellar. Tel. 421.39.99

Cafés

Graffiti Film Café	ul S.W. Gertrudy
Jama Michalike Literary Café	Established in 1895. Ul Florianska 45

Places of Interest

29. GREECE

NAUPLION

Old World Venetian seaport atmosphere. Visit Peloponnese Folklore Museum. Stay at Venia Palace Hotel overlooking Gulf of Argos. To visit town, take elevator through rock. From Nauplion visit Corinth, Mycenae and Epidaurus, first capital of modern Greece.

CORINTH

On Isthmus of Corinth, a canal connects two gulfs. Ornate "Corinthian" column invented by architect from Corinth. Saint Paul with Timothy and Silas, on second voyage 50–53 A.D., lived and preached here a year and a half.

MYCENAE

Center of power between 1600 and 1100 B.C. Royal family residence and burial place. Famous Lion Gate. Stone above portal weighs 120 tons. Beehive tombs of King Agamemnon and wife, Clytaemnestra. Ruins excavated by Heinrich Schliemann, 1876. Proved Homer's tales were fact.

EPIDAURUS

One-day trip north of Athens. A fourth-century Lourdes near the village of Palaia. A king of Thessaly, Askelepios, was such a successful healer, he was worshiped as a god. Shrines were dedicated to him, and since the Oracle said he had been born in Epidaurus, the sanctuary there became famous. In the museum, seventy inscriptions on stone slabs testify to seventy miracles. Also displayed are replicas of the anatomy cured and surgical instruments used by the priests. World-famous summer festival of Greek tragedies and comedies performed in the restored 2,300-year-old amphitheater. Festival Box Office Athens. Tel. 1.322.1459

DELPHI

Wild gorge to Gulf of Corinth. Beautiful setting. Famed temple of Oracle. Stay at Vouzas Hotel, hanging off a cliff.

NORTHERN GREECE

MACEDONIA

Thessalonika, capital of Macedonia. Alexander the Great was born in nearby Pella, where Saint Paul preached. International Trade Fair most important industrial event. Held in September.

Fly to Rhodes	$195.00 round trip. Visit Knights Hospitallers' medieval city.

Bibliography

1. LONDON

Aresty, Elizabeth B. *The Exquisite Table: A History of French Cuisine.* Indianapolis, NY: Bobbs-Merill, 1980.

Ayre, Leslie. *The Gilbert and Sullivan Companion.* New York: Dodd, Mead, 1972.

Bailey, Leslie. *Gilbert and Sullivan and Their World.* New York: Penguin, 1979.

Cellier, Francois. *Gilbert and Sullivan and Their Operas with Recollections and Anecdotes of D'Oyly Carte and Other Famous Savoyards.* Boston: Little, Brown, 1914.

Gourmet Magazine Gourmet Cook Book. New York: Gourmet Magazine of Good Living, 1957.

Montagne, Prosper. *Larousse Gastronomique.* New York: Crown, 1961.

2. NOTRE DAME

Anderson, Robert Gordon. *Biography of a Cathedral.* New York: Longmans, Green, 1945.

Collins, Larry, and Lapierre, Dominique. *Is Paris Burning?* New York: Simon and Schuster, 1965.

Gimpel, Jean. *Cathedral Builders.* Grove Press, 1983.

Huddleston, Sisley. *France, the Tragic Years.* New York: Devin-Adair, 1955.

Hugo, Victor. *Hunchback of Notre Dame.* New York: Dodd, Mead, 1947.

McNaspy, C. J. *Guide to Christian Europe.* S. J. Loyola University Press, 1963.

Temko, Allan. *Nôtre Dame of Paris.* New York: Time, 1952.

Schoenbrun, David. *Soldiers of the Night.* New York: E. P. Dutton, 1980.

Winston, Richard, and Clara Winston. *Nôtre Dame de Paris.* Newsweek Book Division, 1971.

3. THE LOUVRE

Baudelaire, Charles. *Art in Paris 1845–1862.* Phaidon Publishers, 1965.

Corley, Thomas A. *Napoléon III: Democratic Despot.* London: Barrie Rockcliff, 1961.

D'Auvergne, Edmund. *Napoléon III.* Eveleigh Nash Gray and Son, 1929.

Bibliography

Delacroix, Eugène. *Delacroix's Watercolors of Morocco.* Paris: Fernaud Hazan, 1951.
Laugh, John. *Introduction to Seventeenth Century France.* London: Longmans, Green, 1954.
Mahoney, Irene. *Royal Cousin: Life of Henry IV of France.* New York: Doubleday, 1970.
Marvick, Elizabeth Werth. *Louis XIII.* New Haven, CN: Yale University Press, 1986.
Prideaux, Tom. *World of Delacroix* 1798–1863. New York: Time-Life Books, 1966.
Roche, Alphonse V. *Alphonse Daudet.* Boston: Twayne (G. K. Hall).
Saward, Susan. *Golden Age of Marie de Medici.* Ann Arbor: MI: University of Michigan Press, 1982.
Shennan, J. H. *Philippe, Duke of Orléans.* London: Thames and Hudson, 1979.
Smith, W. H. *Napoléon III.* New York: St. Martin's Press, 1972.
Spector, Jack J. *Death of Sardanapalus.* New York: Viking Press, 1974.
Stewart Jean. *Eugène Delacroix.* New York: Abrams, 1971.
Tapie, Victor L. *France in the Age of Louis XIII and Richelieu.* New York: Macmillan, 1974.
Yvonne, Deslandies. *Delacroix: A Pictorial Biography.* New York: Viking, 1963.

4. CAFÉ PROCOPE AND MIRABEAU (1749–1791)

Bernier, Oliver. *Lafayette: Hero of Two Worlds.* New York: Dalton, 1983.
Bernier, Olivier. *Words of Fire, Deeds of Blood.* New York: Little, Brown, 1989.
Colette. *Collected Stories of Colette.* New York: Farrar Straus Giroux, 1983.
Cronin, Vincent. *The Romantic Way.* Boston: Houghton Mifflin, 1966.
Davidson, Mickie. *Louis Braille: The Boy Who Invented Books for the Blind.* Hasting House, 1972.
Grun, Bernard. *Timetables of History.* New York: Simon and Schuster, 1975.
Kimball, Marie. *Jefferson: The Scene of Europe.* New York: Cowan-McCann, 1950.
Martin, Sylvia I. *Mme Tussaud.* New York: Harper and Brothers, 1957.
Michelet, Jules. *History of the French Revolution.* Chicago: University of Chicago Press, 1967.
Randall, Willard Sterne. *Thomas Jefferson.* New York: Henry Holt, 1993.
Schama, Simon. *Citizens New York.* New York: Alfred A. Knopf, 1989.
Severy, Merle. *National Geographic.* Vol. 176, no.1, 1989.
Vallentin, Antonina. *Mirabeau.* Clifton, NJ: Augustus M. Kelley, 1973.

5. SAINT SULPICE CHURCH

Dictionary of the Bible Vol. II. New York: Saint Sulpice Biblical Library Educational Book Guild, 1956.
Kaufman, Christopher J. *Priests of Saint Sulpice in the United States.* Baltimore, MD: Provincial House, 1989.

Bibliography

Kauffman, Christopher J. *Tradition and Transformation in Catholic Culture.* New York: Macmillan, 1988.

Kennedy, Richard. *International Dictionary of Religion.* New York: Crossroad, 1984.

Koren, Henry J. S. C. Sp. *The Spiritans History of the Congregation of the Holy Ghost.* Pittsburgh: Duquesne University Spiritan Series l Maurice Serullaz, 1958.

Leflon, Jean. *Eugène de Mazenod, Vol. I (1782–1814).* New York: Fordham University Press, 1961.

Leland, Jamison. *Light for the Gentiles.* Philadelphia: Westminister Press, 1961.

Pollart, Claude. *Spiritual Writings of Father Claude Francis Pollart.* Pittsburgh: Duquesne Studies Spiritan Series 3, 1959.

Prideaux, Tom. *World of Delacroix 1798–1863.* New York: Time-Life Books, 1966.

6. GARNIER'S OPERA HOUSE

Aillalud, Charlotte. Marc Chagall. *Architectural Digest,* August 1984.

Ewen, David. *Encyclopedia of the Opera.* New York: Hill and Wang, 1959.

Gischford, Anthony. *Grand Opera: The Story of the World's Leading Opera Houses and Personalities.* New York: Viking, 1972.

Life of Rossini-Stendhal. New York: Criterion, 1957.

Machlis, Joseph. *Romanticism in 19th Century Music.* New York: Music Treasures of the World, 1954.

Makarius, Michel. *Chagall.* New York: Portland House, 1988.

7. OPÉRA COMIQUE AND BIZET'S *CARMEN*

Curtiss, Mina. *Bizet and His World.* New York: Alfred A. Knopf, 1958.

Dean, Winton. *Bizet.* London: J. M. Dent, 1948.

Geras, Adele. *The Random House Book of Opera Stories.* New York: Random House, 1997.

Harding, James. *Saint-Saëns and His Circle.* London: Chapman-Hall, 1965.

Lyon, Sylvia. *Life and Times of Prosper Mérimée.* New York: Dial Press, 1948.

Musical History of Opera in France, Vol. B.

New Groves Dictionary of Opera in France, Vol. 2.

New Groves Encyclopedia of Music, Vol. 2.

Rait, A. W. *Prosper Mérimée.* New York: Charles Scribner's Sons, 1979.

8. NAPOLÉON III (1808–1873)

Barschak, Erna. *Innocent Empress.* New York: E. P. Dutton, 1943.

Corley, Thomas Anthony. *Democratic Despot Napoléon III.* London: Barrie and Rockcliff, 1961.

Kallmyer, Nina Athanassoglou. *Delacroix Prints, Politics and Satire.* Yale University Press, 1991.

Eric Plaut. *Grand Opera.* Chicago: Ivan R. Dee, 1993.

Bibliography

D'Auvergne, Edmund. *Napoléon III.* London: Eveleigh Nash and Grayson, 1929.

Kurtz, Harold. *Empress Eugénie.* Boston: Houghton Mifflin, 1964.

Maclis, Joseph. *Music Treasures of the World.* New York, 1954.

Pinkey, David H. *Haussmann and Louis Napoléon and Rebuilding Paris.* Princeton, NY: Princeton University Press, 1958.

Richardson, Joanna. *La Vie Parisienne (1852–1870).* New York: Viking Press, 1971.

Saalman, Howard. *Haussman, Paris Transformed.* New York: George Braziller, 1971.

Smith, W. H. *Second Empire: Napoléon III and His Parisien Prefect.* New York: St. Martin's Press, 1972.

Stendhal, Henri Beyle. *Life of Rossini.* New York: Criterion Books, 1957.

Thompson, J. M. *Louis Napoléon III and The Second Empire.* New York: W. W. Norton and Co., 1967.

9. FRÉDÉRIC CHOPIN (1810–1849)

Delacroix, Eugène. *Eugène Delacroix: Selected Letters.* New York: St. Martin's Press, 1964.

Delacroix, Eugène. New York: Abrams, 1971.

Gavoty, Bernard. *Frédéric Chopin.* New York: Charles Scribner's Sons, 1974.

Grebanier, Frances. *Life of the Heart: George Sand and Her Times.* New York: Harper and Brothers, 1978.

Grunfield, Frédéric. Chopin Without Tears. *Horizon Magazine,* vol 2, 1969.

Jacobson, Robert. *Chopin: His Life and Times.* New York: Funk and Wagnalls, 1849.

Jordan, Ruth. *Nocturne: A Life of Chopin.* New York: Taplinger, 1978.

Kallmyer, Nina Athanassoglou. *Delacroix Prints, Politics and Satire.* New Haven, CT: Yale University Press, 1991.

Marek, George R., and Maria Gordon-Smith. *Chopin.* New York: Harper Row, 1978.

Prideaux, Tom. *The World of Delacroix.* New York: Time-Life Books, 1972.

Sand, George. *The Intimate Journal of George Sand.* London: Haskell House, 1973.

10. THE PALAIS ROYAL

Baldick, Robert. *Goncourt Journal.* New York: Oxford University Press, 1978.

Baronesse de Stoeckl, Agnes. *King of the French: Portrait of Louis Philippe.* New York: Putnam, 1958.

Bernier, Olivier. *Louis the Beloved: Life of Louis XV.* New York: Doubleday, 1976.

Billy, André. *Goncourt Brothers.* New York: Horizon Press, 1960.

Deschamps, Fanny. *Louis XV: The King's Garden.* New York: Harmony Books, 1984.

Gounod. *Autobiographical Reminiscences.* London: Da Capo Press, 1970.

Grebanier, Frances. *Life of the Heart: George Sand and Her Times.* New York: Harper and Brothers, 1945.

Harcourt, Lewis. *Scandalous Regent.* New York: W. H. Brace and World, 1961.

Bibliography

Harding, James. *Gounod*. New York: Stein and Day. 1973.

Kleinman, Ruth. *Anne of Austria, Queen of France*. Columbus, OH: Ohio State University Press, 1985.

Kroll, Maria. *A Woman's Life in the Court of the Sun King: Letters of Liselott 1652–1722*. New York: McCall, 1971.

Laugh, John. *Introduction to Seventeenth Century France*. London: Longmans, Green, 1954.

Lewis and Galantiers. *Goncourt Journalists*. Garden City, NJ: Doubleday, 1958.

Louis Philippe, King of France. *Diary of My Travels in America*. New York: Delacorte Press, 1977.

Lyon, Sylvia. *Life and Times of Prosper Mériméé*. New York: Dial Press, 1948.

Marx, Karl. *Class Struggles in France 1848–1850*. New York: International, 1976.

Maurois, André. *Alexandre Dumas*. New York: Alfred A. Knopf, 1955.

Mitford, Nancy. *Madame de Pompadour*. New York: E. P. Dutton, 1984.

Rait, A. W. *Prosper Mérimée*. New York: Charles Scribner's Sons, 1979.

Roche, V. *Alphonse Daudet*. Boston: Twayne (G. K. Hall), 1976.

Sand, George. *Intimate Journal of George Sand*. London: Haskell House, 1976.

Saward, Susan. *Golden Age of Marie de' Medici*. Ann Arbor, MI: University of Michigan Press, 1982.

Shernan, J. H. *Philippe Duke of Orléans*. London: Thames and Hudson, 1979.

Tapie, Victor L. *France in the Age of Louis XIII and Richelieu*. New York: Macmillan, 1974.

Voltaire. *Age of Louis XIV*. New York: Dutton (Everyman's Library), 1961.

11. IN MEMORY OF MOLIÈRE (1622–1673)

Fernandez, Ramon. *Molière: The Man Seen Through the Plays*. New York: Hill and Wang, 1958.

French, Samuel. *Le Malade Imaginaire*. New York, 1959.

———. *Tartuffe (The Imposter)*. New York, 1950.

Howarth, W. D. *Molière, Stage and Study*. Oxford, UK: Clarendon Press.

Laugh, John. *Introduction to Seventeenth Century France*. London: Longman, Green, 1954.

Molière. *Comedies*, vol. I. New York: E. P. Dutton, 1929.

———. *Le Bourgeois Gentilhomme*. New York: Harcourt Brace, 1947.

———. *Le Misanthrope* and *Le Tartuffe*. New York: Harcourt Brace, 1965.

———. *Le Tartuffe*. New York: Harcourt Brace, 1963.

———. *School for Husbands (École de Maris)*. New York: Harcourt Brace, 1994.

———. *Tartuffe and Other Plays*. New American Library, 1967.

———. *The Learned Ladies (Les Femmes Savantes)*. New York: Harcourt Brace Jovanovich, 1978.

Bibliography

Palmer, John L. *Molière*. New York: Brewer and Warren, 1930.

12. PLACE DE LA BASTILLE AND BEAUMARCHAIS (1732–1799)

Beuve, Saint. *Portraits of the Eighteenth Century,* Vol. II. New York: Ungar, 1964.

Cox, Cynthia. *The Real Figaro*. New York: Howard McCann, 1962.

Deschamps, Fanny. *The King's Garden*. New York: Harmony Books, 1982.

Frischauer, Paul. *Beaumarchais and the War of American Independence*. Boston: R. G. Badger, 1918.

Kite, Elizabeth. *Beaumarchais the Adventurer*. New York: Viking Press, 1935.

Krehbiel, Henry. *Book of Operas*. New York: Garden City Publishing, 1916.

Lemaitre, George. *Beaumarchais*. New York: Alfred A. Knopf, 1949.

Sunglowsky, Joseph. *Beaumarchais*. New York: Twayne Publishers, 1974.

13. PASSY: MAISON DE BALZAC AND HONORÉ BALZAC (1799–1850)

Balzac, Honoré. *Bachelors House*. New York: Juniper Press, 1956.

———. *Cousin Bette*. New York: Random House, 1958.

———. *Droll Stories Collected from the Abbeys of Touraine*. New York: Bell, 1985.

———. *Père Goriot*. New York: Airmont, 1965.

———. *The Chousans*. Middlesex, UK: Penguin Classics, 1972.

Benjamin, René. *Balzac*. New York: Alfred A. Knopf, 1927.

Cronin, Vincent. *The Romantic Way*. Boston: Houghton Mifflin, 1966.

Gerson, Noel V. *Life and Times of Honoré Balzac*. New York: Doubleday, 1972.

Pritchett, V. S. *Balzac*. New York: Alfred A. Knopf, 1973.

Walker, Howell. *National Geographic,* July 1972.

Zweig, Stefan. *Balzac*. New York: Viking Press, 1946.

14. RUEIL MALMAISON: CHÂTEAU MALMAISON

Castelot, André. *Josephine*. New York: Harper and Row, 1967.

Cole, Hubert. *Josephine*. New York: Viking Press, 1963.

Epton, Nina. *Josephine: The Empress and Her Children*. New York: W. W. Norton, 1975.

Mosiker, Frances. *Napoléon and Josephine: A Biography of a Marriage*. New York: Simon and Schuster, 1964.

Pitman, Jon L. Napoléon. *National Geographic,* vol. 161, no. 2, 1982.

Southerland, Christine. *Marie Walewska*. New York: Viking Press, 1979.

15. NORMANDY

Adams, Henry. *Mont Saint Michel and Chartres*. New York: Houghton Mifflin, 1905.

Aubert, Marcel. *Mont Saint Michel*. Grenoble, France: B. Arthaud, 1938.

Butler, Isabel (trans.). *Song of Roland*. New York: Houghton Mifflin, 1904.

Bibliography

Kleinman, Ruth. *Anne of Austria, Queen of France.* Ohio Univ Press, 1985.

Morel, Pierre. *Visitors' Guide.* Grenoble, France: B. Arthaud, 1938.

Peck, Ira. *Patton.* New York: Scholastic Book Services, 1970.

Pernoud, Regine. *Eleanor of Aquitaine.* New York: Coward McCann, 1967.

Roberts, Mesta. *Companion Guide to Normandy.* Englewood Cliffs, NJ: Prentice Hall, 1983.

Seward, Desmond. *Eleanor of Aquitaine: The Mother Queen.* New York: Dorset, 1978.

Slocombe, George. *William the Conqueror.* New York: G. P. Putnam's Sons, 1959.

16. AQUITAINE

The Book of France. Secaucus, NJ: Chartwell Books, 1980.

Cole, Robert. *A Traveller's History of France.* New York: Interlink Books, 1995.

Collis, Louise. *Memoirs of a Medieval Woman: Life and Times of Margery Kemp.* New York: Harper Colophon, 1983.

de Troyes, Chrétien. *Story of the Grail.* Chapel Hill, NC: University of North Carolina Press, 1952.

Early English Text Society. 1866.

High School Subjects Self Taught. Garden City, New York: Garden City Books, 1959.

Holmes, Urban T. *Chrétien de Troyes and the Grail.* Chapel Hill, NC: University of North Carolina Press, 1959.

Howarth, Stephen. *Knights Templar.* New York: Atheneum, 1982.

Insight Guides: France. Singapore: APA Productions, 1923.

Keyes, Francis Parkinson. *St. Theresa: Saint of A Little Way.* New York: Julian Messner, 1950.

Krehbiel, Henry E. *A Book of Operas.* New York: Macmillan, 1916.

Rowling, Marjorie. *Life in Medieval Times.* New York: G. P. Putnam's Sons, 1968.

Painter, Sidney. *French Chivalry.* Ithaca, NY: Cornell University Press, 1940.

Penguin Guide to France. New York: Viking Press, 1985.

Pyle, Howard. *The Story of the Grail: The Passing of Arthur.* New York: Charles Scribner's Sons, 1902.

White, Freda. *Three Rivers of France.* New York: Little, Brown, 1952.

Wilkins, Ernest Hatch. *Life of Francesco Petrarch.* Chicago: University of Chicago Press, 1971.

17. BRITTANY

Andersen, Wayne. *Gauguin's "Paradise Lost."* New York: Viking Press, 1971.

Costello, Peter. *Jules Verne.* New York: Charles Scribner's Sons, 1978.

Gaunt, William. *Impressionism: A Visual History.* New York: Praeger, 1970.

Goldwater, Robert. *Gauguin.* New York: Abrams, 1976.

Guizot, M. (Francois). *L'Histoire de France.* New York: AMS Press, 1969.

Bibliography

Hanson, Lawrence. *Noble Savage: Life of Paul Gauguin.* New York: Random House, 1954.

Lapre, Victor. *France in the Age of Louis XIII and Richelieu.* New York: Macmillan, 1974.

Locke, John. *Travels in France.* New York: Clarkson N. Potter, 1990.

Looby, Chris. *Benjamin Franklin.* New York: Chelsea House, 1990.

Loti, Pierre. *Iceland Fisherman.* New York: Alfred A. Knopf, 1946.

Lottman, Herbert R. *Jules Verne.* New York: St. Martin's Press, 1996.

McCarta, Robertson. *Brittany: Nelles Guide.* Munich: Nelles Verlag, 1993.

Perruchot, Henri. *Gauguin.* New York: World Publishing, 1964.

Pool, Phoebe. *Impressionism.* New York: Oxford Press, 1981.

Rewald, John. *History of Impressionism.* New York: Museum of Modern Art, 1973.

Thorley, Wilfrid. *Fleurs-de-Lys.* Boston: Houghton Mifflin, 1920.

18. AUVERGNE

Augutus, Antonia Valentin. *Mirabeau.* Clifton, NJ: M. Kelly, 1973.

Casanova, Jacques-Donat. *America's French Heritage.* Quebec: La Armour Landry Documentation Française, 1976.

Dumas, François Ribadeau. *Bulletin de la Société Historique Du Vie Arrondissement de Paris.* Paris: Place Saint Sulpice, 1975–1976.

Hargrove, Jim. *Encyclopedia of Presidents.* Chicago: 1987.

Hester, Conoly. On the Trail of Lafayette. *Georgia Journal* (spring issue), 1989.

Hooding, Carter. *Marquis de Lafayette.* New York: Random House, 1958.

Loobt, Chris. *Benjamin Franklin.* New York: Chelsea House, 1990.

Loth, David. *The People's General.* New York: Charles Scribner's Sons, 1951.

Maurois, André. *Lafayette in America.* Boston: Houghton Mifflin, 1960.

Moscow, Henry, and Dumas Malone. *Thomas Jefferson and His World.* New York: American Heritage, 1960.

Shennan, J. H. *Philippe, Duke of Orléans.* London: Thames and Hudson, 1979.

Wibberley, Leonard. *Man of Liberty: Thomas Jefferson.* New York: Farrar, Straus, Giroux, 1968.

Yalom, Marilyn. *Blood Sisters.* New York: HarperCollins, 1993.

19. BERRY

Le Verrerie

Cassavetti, Eileen. *The Lion and the Lilies.* London: Macdonald's and Jane's Publishing, 1977.

Milne, James Lee. *The Last Stuarts.* New York: Charles Scribner's Sons, 1984.

Scott, Sir Walter. *Waverly Novels.* New York: Viking Penguin, 1981.

Bibliography

Bourges

Bridges, John S. C. *History of France from the Death of Louis XI*, Vol. 1. New York: Octagon Books, 1978.

Brown, Leslie. *Indian Christians of St. Thomas*. Cambridge, UK: Cambridge University Press, 1956.

Chaucer, Geoffrey. *Canterbury Tales* ("Man of Law"). New York: MacMillan, 1971.

Eyre, Vale. *Charles VII*. London: Malcolm Graham, 1974.

Fournier, Alain. *The Wanderer*. New York: Houghton Mifflin, 1928.

Heldesheim, John. *The Story of the Three Kings: Melchior, Balthasar, and Jasper*. New York: Metropolitan Museum of Art, 1978.

Hennecke, Egar. *New Testament Apocrypha*, Vol. II. Philadelphia: Westminster Press, 1964.

Holinshed, Raphael. *Outline of Great Books: Chronicles of England*. London: Wise and Co., 1936.

Knecht, R. J. *Louis XII*. Cambridge, UK: Cambridge University Press, 1982.

Laugh, John. *Introduction to Seventeenth Century France*. London: Longmans, Green, 1954.

Miller, Dorothy. *Renaissance and Reformation Times*. New York: G. P. Putnam's Sons, 1939.

Neill, Stephen. *History of Christianity in India*. Cambridge, UK: Cambridge University Press, 1985.

———. *History of Christianity in India, the Beginning to A.D. 1707*. Cambridge, UK: Cambridge University Press, 1984.

———. *Reign of Charles VIII Regency of Anne Beaujeu*. New York: Farrar Straus Giroux, 1978.

Peattie, Donald Culhoss. *Lives of Destiny*. New York: New American Library, 1954.

Salmon, H. M. *Society in Crisis*. New York: St. Martin's Press, 1975.

Young, Mary. *Singing Windows*. Nashville, TN: Abingdon Press, 1962.

Meillant and la Commanderie

Barber, Richard. *The Knights and Chivalry*. New York: Harper and Row, 1974.

Bradford, Ernle Dusgate. *Shield and The Scimitar*. New York: Dutton Putnam, 1973.

———. *Sundered Cross: The Story of the Fourth Crusade*. Inglewood Place, NJ: Prentice Hall, 1967.

Bridge, Anthony. *The Crusaders*. New York: Franklin Watts, 1982.

Bridge, John S. C. *History of France from the Death of Louis XI*, Vol. 1. New York: Octagon Books, 1978.

Collis, Louise. *Medieval Woman: The Life and Times of Margery Kempe*. New York: Harper and Row, 1964.

Currie, Jean. *The Travelers and Guide: Rhodes*. London: Jonathan Cape, 1984.

Bibliography

Davidson, Mickie. *Louis Braille: The Boy Who Invented Books for the Blind.* New York: Hasting House, 1971.
de Troyes, Cretien. *The Story of The Grail.* Chapel Hill, NC: University of North Carolina Press, 1952.
Gillingham, John. *Life and Times of Richard I.* London: Weidenfeld and Nicholson, 1973.
Howarth, Stephen. *Knights Templar.* New York: Atheneum, 1982.
Knecht, R. J. *King Louis XII and Anne of Brittany.* Cambridge, UK: Cambridge University Press, 1982.
Lewis, Dominic Bevan. *Some Aspects of Louis XI, King Spider.* New York: Coward-McCann, 1929.
Partner, Peter. *The Knights Templar: Murdered Magicians.* Oxford, UK: Oxford University Press, 1982.
Recimen, Stephen. *The First Crusade.* Cambridge, UK: Cambridge University Press, 1980.
Reign of Charles VIII. *Regency of Anne Beaujeu.* New York: Farrar Straus Giroux, 1978.
Rowling, Marjory. *Everyday Life in Medieval Times.* New York: G. P. Putnam and Sons, 1968.
Seward, Desmond. *Eleanor of Aquitaine: The Mother Queen.* New York: Time Books, 1979.
Simon, Edith. *Piebald Standard.* Boston: Little, Brown, 1959.
Tapie, Victor L. *France in the Age of Louis XIII.* Old Topping, NJ: MacMillan, 1974.
Vaughn, Richard. *Valois Burgundy.* London: Allen Lane, 1975.
Wilkinson, Burke. *Frances in All His Glory.* New York: Farrar Straus Giroux, 1972.
Wilkinson, Clennel. *Coeur de Lion.* New York: Appleton-Century, 1933.

Nohant

Barry, Joseph. Goncourt Brothers. *Horizon Magazine,* vol. 2, 1948.
Brower, Harriet. *Story Lives of Master Musicians.* Philadelphia: J. B. Lippencott, 1965.
Fournier, Alain. *The Wanderer.* Clifton, NJ: Augustus M. Kelley, 1973.
Gavoty, Bernard. *Frederic Chopin.* New York: Charles Scribners Sons, 1977.
Goncourt, Frances V. (Frances Winar, [pseud.]). *Life of the Heart: George Sand and Her Times.* New York: Harper and Brothers, 1945.
Gordon, Mel (ed.). *Theatre of Fear and Terror.* New York: Amok Press, 1988.
Judson, Clara Ingram. *Ben Franklin.* New York: Follett, 1969.
Maindron, Ernest. *Marionettes and Guignols.* Paris: 1990.
Melchior, Ib. *Grand Guignol.* New York: Dodd Mead, 1987.
Orga, Ates. *Chopin: His Life and Times.* Tunbridge Wells, UK: Midas Books, 1978.
Prideaux, Tom. *World of Eugène Delacroix.* New York: Time-Life Books, 1972.

Bibliography

Sand, George. *The Story of My Life: The Autobiography of George Sand.* Albany, NY: State University of New York Press, 1991.

20. TOURAINE

Churchill, Winston. *Joan of Arc.* New York: Dodd-Mead, 1956.
De Monvel, Mauric Boutet. *Joan of Arc.* New York: Viking Press, 1981.
Domrêmy. *The Basilica of Bois-Chenu.* Ingersheim, France: Ingersheim.
Gies, Frances. *Joan of Arc: Legend and Reality.* New York: Harper and Row, 1959.
Johnston, Johanna. *Joan of Arc.* New York: Doubleday, 1961.
Lucie Smith, Edward A. *Joan of Arc.* New York: W. W. Norton, 1976.
Ross, Nancy W. *Joan of Arc.* New York: Random House, 1953.
Twain, Mark. *Personal Recollections of Joan of Arc.* New York: Harper and Brothers, 1899.
Williams, Jay. *Joan of Arc.* New York: American Heritage, 1963.

21. LORRAINE

Casame, H.. *Patton: A Study in Command.* New York: Charles Scribner's Sons, 1978.
Champion, Pierre. *Louis XI.* London: Cassell, 1929.
Cleugh, James. *Chant Royal King Louis of France.* Garden City, NY: Doubleday, 1970.
Cowley, Robert. *Lorraine World War I.* Horizons, 1972.
Etienne, Jean-Louis. *L'Est Republicain.* Nancy, France: 1994.
Ettinger, Albert M. A. *Doughboys with the Fighting Sixty-ninth: A Remembrance of World War I.* Shippensburg, PA: White Main Publishing, 1992.
Filliette, Edith. *St. Mary Magdalene.* Fountain Inn, SC: Society of St. Mary Magdalene.
Kendall, Paul Murray. *Louis XI, Universal Spider.* New York: W. W. Norton, 1971.
Lewis, D. B. Wyndham. *King Spider.* New York: Coward-McCann, 1929.
Lorenz, Otto. *Art Nouveau.* London: Bartley and Jensen, 1987.
Lynch, Rev. John W. *Bernadette: The Only Witness.* Boston: S. M. St. Paul Editions, 1981.
Newark, Tim. *Emile Gallé.* Secaucus, NJ: Chartwell Books, 1989.
Peck, Ira. *Patton.* New York: Scholastic Book Services, 1970.
Savage, Katherine. *Story of the Second World War.* New York: H. Z. Walk, 1958.
Tyrrell, Joseph M. *Louis XI.* Boston: Twayne, 1980.

22. BURGUNDY

Andrews, Allen. *The Flying Machine.* New York: G. P. Putnam's Sons, 1977.
Baxin, Jean Francois. *Wonderful Burgundy.* Paris: Ouest, 1988.
Coates Clive. *Côte d'Or.* San Diego, CA: Orion, 1997.
English, Sarah Jane. *Vin Vignettes.* Austin, TX: Eakin Press, 1984.

Bibliography

Fielden, Christopher. *France: Travellers Wine Guide.* New York: Sterling, 1990.
Fried, Eunice. *Burgundy.* New York: Harper and Row, 1986.
Jackson, Michael. Ballooning Adventures: Aloft in Burgundy. *Travel and Leisure,* April 1983.
Johnson, Hugh. *The World Atlas of Wine.* New York: Mitchell Beazley, 1985.
Johnson, Hugh, and Duijker Hubrecht. *The Wine Atlas of France.* New York: Simon and Schuster, 1987.
Kladstrup, Don, and Petie. *Wine and War.* New York: Broadway Books, 2001.
Laby, Micheline. *Burgundy: The Magic of a Word.* Dijon, France: Les Editions Du Bien, 1988.
Laby, Micheline. *Dijon: A City of Art and History.* Dijon, France: Les Editions du Bien, 1990.
Lichine, Alexis. *Alexis Lichine's Guide to the Wines of France.* New York: Alfred A. Knopf, 1967.
Parker, Robert M. *Parker's Wine Buyers Guide.* New York: Simon and Schuster, 1990.
Sichel, Seyd, Lanson, Cook, Mackenzie, and Langenbach. *A Guide to Good Wine.* London: Murrays, 1970.
Turner, Jane. *The Groves' Dictionary of Art.* Oxford, UK: Oxford University Press, 1998.

23. PROVENCE

Allentuck, Harriet. *A Portrait in Letter.* CT: Greenwood Press, 1978.
Bercovici, Konrad. *The Story of the Gypsies.* New York: Cosmopolitan Book Corp., 1928.
Chamson, André. *Francois Mauriac, Frédéric Mistral, Theodore Mommsen* (Nobel Prize Library Series). New York: A. Gregory, 1971.
Clébert, John Paul. *The Gypsies.* New York: Harmondsworth Penguin, 1967.
Cuttriss, Frank. *Romany Life.* London: Mills and Boon, 1915.
Davenport, William. The Camargue. *National Geographic.* Vol. 143, 1973.
Filliette, Edith. *St. Mary Magdalene.* Fountain Inn, SC: Society of Saint Mary Magdalene.
Hahn, Emily. *Romantic Rebels.* Boston: Houghton Mifflin, 1967.
Harding, James. *Gounod.* New York: Stein's Day, 1973.
Hecht, Paul. *The Wind Cried.* New York: Dial Press, 1968.
Leland, Charles. *English Gypsies and Their Language.* Detroit, MI: Gale Research, 1969.
Les Saintes Maries de la Mer. New York: Columbia University Press, 1998.
Memoirs of Frédéric Mistral. New York: New Directions Book, 1986.
Mistral, Frédéric. *Mirèio.* Paris: Alphonse Lamartine, 1859.
More, James. *The Mediterranean.* Ontario: Mika Studio, 1972.

Bibliography

Mossiker, Frances. *Madame de Sévigné*. New York: Alfred A. Knopf, 1983.
Penguin Guide to France. New York: Viking Penguin, 1991.
Pope's Birthday Celebration. New York: *Brooklyn Tablet*, Sept. 30, 1965.
Seward, Desmond. *Eleanor of Aquitaine*. New York: Dorset Press, 1978.
Starkie, Walter. *In Sarah's Tents*. New York: Dutton, 1954.
Stephens, James. Raggle Taggle Family of Mr. Cesareo Had Petrovich. *Wall Street Journal*, Feb. 12, 1968.
United Press International. French Delta Rivals America's West. Aug., 1973.
United Press International. Gypsies Keep to Old Customs. Aug. 27, 1973.
Williams, Charles. *Mme. de Sévigné*. Boston: Twayne, 1981.
Yoors, Jan. *Gypsies*. New York: Simon and Schuster, 1967.

Jean Henri Fabre

Anderson, Margaret. *The Children of Summer*. New York: Farrar, Straus and Giroux, 1997.
della Fazia Amoia, Alba. *Edmond Rostand*. Boston: Twayne, 1978.
Doorley, Eleanor. *The Insect Man*. New York: Appleton Century, 1937.
Eberle, Irmengarde. *Wide Fields*. New York: Thomas Y. Crowell, 1943.
Fabre, Abbé Augustin. *Life of J. H. Fabre the Entomologist*. New York: Dodd Mead, 1961.
Fabre, Jean Henri. *Social Life of the Insect World*. New York: Century, 1920.
Grant, Madeleine P. *Louis Pasteur: Fighting Hero of Science*. New York: McGraw Hill, 1959.
Teal, Edwin. *The Insect World of J. Henri Fabre*. New York: Dodd Mead, 1961.

24. THE GRAND DUCHY OF LUXEMBOURG

Barnow, Adriaan J. *The Pageant of Netherlands' History*. New York: Longmans, Green, 1950.
The Making of Modern Holland. New York: W. W. Norton, 1944.
Best, Thomas. *Reynard the Fox*. Boston: Twayne, 1983.
Carrick, Noel. *Let's Visit Belgium*. Bridgeport, CT: Burke, 1984.
Carson, Patricia. *The Fair Face of Flanders*. Ghent: E Story Scientia, 1969.
Egan, E. W. *Belgium-Luxembourg*. New York: Sterling, 1976.
Farago, Wadislaw. *The Last Days of Patton*. New York: McGraw Hill, 1981.
Fodor's Belgium-Luxembourg. New York: D. McKay, 1991.
Gerson, Noel. *A Tumultuous Life*. New York: D. McKay, 1971.
Geyl, Pieter. *Orange-Stuart 1641–1672*. New York: Charles Scribner's Sons, 1969.
Goolrick, William K. *Battle of the Bulge*. New York: Time-Life Books, 1979.
Goolrick, William K. *World War II*. Alexandria, VA: Time-Life Books, 1980.
Grand Duchy of Luxembourg. Luxembourg: 1993.

Bibliography

Houston, John Porter. *Victor Hugo Doré*. Old Tappan, NJ: Twayne, 1974.
Huddleston, Sisley. *Louis XIV in Love and in War*. New York: Harper and Brothers, 1929.
Hugo, Victor. *Les Misérables*. New York: Dodd Mead, 1825.
Huggett, Frank E. *Modern Belgium*. New York: Praeger, 1969.
Josephson, Mathew. *Victor Hugo*. New York: Doubleday, 1942.
Koning, Hans. *World of Vermeer*. Alexandria, VA: Time-Life Books, 1990.
Krispyn, Egbert, ed. *Reynard the Fox*. Boston: Twayne, 1983.
Landheer, Bartholomew. *The Netherlands*. Berkeley, CA: University of California Press, 1946.
Luxembourg National Tourist Office. *Battleground Luxembourg: Remember 44 the Bulge*. 1983.
Lyon, Margot. *Belgium*. New York: Walker, 1971.
Luxembourg Grand Ducal Family. Information and Press Service Luxembourg City.
Maurois, André. *Victor Hugo and His World*. New York: Viking Press, 1966.
de Meeus, Adrien. *History of the Belgians*. New York: Praeger, 1962.
Miller, Townsend. *Castles and the Crown*. New York: Coward McCann, 1963.
Nelson, Nina. *Belgium-Luxembourg*. London: B. T. Batsford, 1980.
Newcomer, James. *Grand Duchy of Luxembourg*. Fort Worth, TX: Texas Christian University, 1984.
Owens, Harry J. *Reynard the Fox*. New York: Alfred A. Knopf, 1945.
Petrie, Sir Charles. *Philip II of Spain*. New York: W. W. Norton, 1963.
PNEW Michelin Firm. *Belgique: Grand Duché de Luxembourg*. France: Clermont-Ferrand, 1979.
Prawdin, Michael, and George Allen. *The Mad Queen of Spain*. London: Unwin, 1938.
Putnam, Ruth. *William the Silent, Prince of Orange*. New York: G. P. Putnam, 1895.
Rachlis, Eugene. *The Low Countries*. New York: Time-Life Books, 1963.
Swinburn, Algernon. *A Study of Victor Hugo*. Folcroft, PA: Folcroft Library Edition, 1976.
Toland, John. *Battle Story of the Bulge*. New York: Random House, 1959.
Tomes, John. *Blue Guide Belgium-Luxembourg*. London: A and C Black, 1990.
Schiller; Freidrich. *Don Carlos Infante of Spain*. New York: Ungar, 1959.
Wedgwood, C. V. *William-the-Silent, 1533–1584*. New Haven, CT: Yale University Press.

25. BELGIUM

Black, A. and C. *Blue Guide of Belgium and Luxembourg*. New York: W.W. Norton, 1993.
Leanne Logan. *Brussels, Bruges and Antwerp*. Victoria, Australia: Geert Cole, 1999.

Bibliography

McDonald, George. *Insight Pocket Guide*. Brussels: Hans Hofer, 1997.

Snoeck, Ducaju, and Zoom. *Belgium at the Heart of Europe*. Ghent: 1967.

Steinbicker, Earl. *Day Trips in Holland, Belgium and Luxembourg*. Mamaroneck, NY: Hastings House, 1990.

Time Out Guide. London: Penguin Books Universal House, 1998.

27. DELFT

Barnouw, Adrian Jacob. *Making of Modern Holland*. New York: W.W. Norton and Co., 1944.

Edwards, Charles S. *Hugo Grotius, Miracle of Holland*. Chicago: Nelson Hall, 1958.

Egan, E.W. *Belgium and Luxembourg*. New York: Sterling, 1976.

Hargrove, Jim. *Belgium: Enchantment of the World*. Chicago: Children's Press, 1988.

Hugget, Frank E. *Modern Belgium*. New York: Frederick A. Praeger, 1969.

Lyle, Keigh. *Take a Trip to Belgium*. London: Franklin Watts, 1985.

Murat, Ines. *Colbert and Louis XVI's War Against the Dutch*. Charlottesville, VA: University Press, 1984.

Rocquet, Claude-Henri. *Bruegel: The Workshop of Dreams*. Chicago: University of Chicago Press, 1991.

———. *The Netherlands*. Berkeley, CA: University of California Press, 1946.

———. *William the Silent*. New Haven, CT: Yale University Press, 1958.

Rose, Barbara. *Golden Age of the Dutch*. New York: Frederick A. Praeger, 1969.

Strong, Roy. *Van Dyck: Charles I on Horseback*. New York: Viking Press, 1972.

The Low Countries. Alexandria, VA: Time-Life, 1963.

The World of Rubens. Alexandria, VA: Time-Life, 1977.

The World of Vermeer (1633–1675). Alexandria, VA: Time-Life Books, 1990.

Vreeland, Hamilton. *Hugo Grotius*. New York: Oxford University Press, 1917.

28. KRAKÓW

Adodaher, David. *Warrior of Two Continents: Kosciuszko Thaddeus*. New York: Julian Messner, 1968.

Age of Faith. New York: Time Life Books, 1970.

Anders, Wladyslaw. *An Army in Exile*. New York: Macmillan, 1949.

Ascherson, Neal. *The Book of Lech Walesa*. New York: Simon and Schuster, 1982.

Coleman, Marion. *Young Mickiewitz*. Cambridge Springs, PA: 1969.

Collins, David R. *Casimir Pulaski Soldier on Horseback*. Gretna, LA: Pelican, 1996.

Davies, Norman. *Heart of Europe: A Short History of Poland*. Oxford, UK: Clarendon Press, 1984.

Fodor's Eastern Europe. New York: Fodor Travel, 1944.

Kelly, Eric P. *The Trumpeter of Krakow*. New York: Macmillan, 1966.

Landau, Ron. *Ignace Paderewski*. New York: Thomas Y. Crowell, 1934.

Bibliography

Lengyel, Emil. *Ignace Paderewski, Musician and Statesman.* New York: Franklin Watts, 1972.

Majka, Julian. *Wieliczk Salt Mine Guide Book.* Wieliczka, Kraków: Tourist Route, 1998.

Mickiewicz, Adam. *Poetry and Prose.* Warsaw: Polonia, 1955.

Olszer, K. M. *Kosciuszko: For Your Freedom and Ours.* New York: Frederick Ungar, 1981.

Tuohy, Frank. *Ice Saints.* New York: Scribner, 1964.

Wójcicki, Bohdan. Kraków, What, Where, When. *General Director* (Spring/Summer) vol. 6, no. 2, 1999.

29. GREECE

Adler, Mortimer J. *Aristotle for Everybody.* New York: Macmillan, 1978.

Clapham, Francis M., and Abigail Frost. *Ancient Civilizations.* New York: Warwick Press, 1978.

David, Ephraim. *Aristophanes Athenian Society of Early Fourth Century B.C.* Leydens, The Netherlands: Brill, 1984.

Grene, David. *Complete Greek Tragedies Series.* Chicaco: The University of Chicago Press, 1959.

Hadas, Moses, and John McLean (trans.). *Euripides.* New York: Bantam Books, 1960.

Lattimore, Richard. *Aeschylus' Oresteia.* Chicago: University of Chicago Press, 1953.

Mantinbond, James H. *Four Plays of Aristophanes.* Washington, DC: University Press of America, 1963.

Ruskin, John. *Sesame and Lilies.* London: J. M. Dent and Sons, 1907.

Spatz, Lois S. *Aristophanes.* Boston: Twayne, 1979.

Sterrenson, James L. *Ancient Greece: Universal History of the World,* Vol. 2. New York: Golden Press, 1966.

Webb, Robert Henning (trans.). *Peace.* Charlotte, NC: University Press of Virginia, 1964, (translated by)

White, Anne Terry. *Aesop's Fables.* New York: Random House, 1964.

More Thank You's

BALTIMORE, MARYLAND
Joe Reynolds, Society of Saint Sulpice, Province of the United States of America

LONDON
Judith Dagworthy, Mary Willis, and Lucinda Buxton, The Savoy Group

PARIS
Rita Dinman, President of Vichy Cosmetics

Jean Guy and Rosiana Venezian, Guide Interprete

Marie and Michel Popov, Federation Europeans Des Sciences Sociales

Sandrine, Danielle and Georges Lebard

Fr. Joseph Cornineau and Father Raymond de Ville, Compagnie des Prêtres de Saint Sulpice

Father Henry Ptanissek, CSSP Congregation of Holy Ghost

M. et Mme. Patrice Mengin

Fr. Francis Girard, Jr. and Fr. Jacques Perrier, curés de la Cathédrale Notre Dame de Paris

Professor Dr. Franz Caurth, Der Rektor, Philosophy-Theology Hochschule Valenar, Germany

Roger de Brantes et Cie

Joe Jackson, Lewisville, Texas

M. Bernard Etienne, The Lido

Frederic Pousseur, Proprietor of Café Procope

TOURS
Michel Boudon—our miraculous tour guide

PROVINCE OF BERRY
Castle Ainay le Vieil

Comtesse Marie France de Peyronnet Director, Jacques Coeur Tour

More Thank You's

Le Verrerie Château
Count and Comtesse Antoine Vogüé

Auberge de la Commanderie
Count and Comtesse B. de Jouffroy-Gonsans

Castle Meillant
Marquise Jeanne de Mortemart

BOURGES
Sandrine Constant, LaLangagerie Services Linguistiques

ANGOULÂME
Mlle. Colette Tassel, Quiz Tour, Paris

SAINT ÉMILION
M. et Mme. Alain Querre, Musée de la Poterie
Dr. Roy Renfroe, Director, T.V. Munson Memorial Vineyard, Denison, Texas
François Chandou, Dallas, Texas, Saint Émilion Jurat
Dennis Swift, Fort Worth, Texas, Saint Émilion Jurat
Peter Handler, Santa Fe, New Mexico, Saint Émilion Jurat
David M. Munson, Denison, Texas
Peter Forbes, Wine Director, Centennial, Dallas, Texas
John Clift, Herald-Democrat, Sherman, Texas
Victor Wzviak, Neiman Marcus, Dallas, Texas
Jasper Russo, French Wines, Marty's, Dallas, Texas
Susan Graham, Sigel's, Dallas, Texas
Martin Sinkoff Wines, Inc.

LE PUY EN VELAY
M. Michel Chambon, Director Chavaniac-Lafayette
M. François Gilbert, President
M. Jean Paul Grinaud, Office de Tourisme

PAU
R. La Bastie, Hotel Regina

VENDÔME
Connie Aubert

NÎMES
Francis and Sylvian Mercier

More Thank You's

MARSEILLES

Dr. Don Simoni-Godefroy, Faculté de Médicine Cochin Port Royal

LOURDES

Breda and all the Irish ladies who peeled carrots

GERMANY

Gabrielle and Greg Rossingnol

ORLÉANS

Mlle. Naitine Gomez, Office de Tourisme
Danielle Habitzreider

STRASBOURG

Mme. Paulette Amrhein
M. et Mme. Robert Carpentier and Francis
M. et Mme. Phan Viet Tuyen, President du Centre European du P.E.N. Vietnamien a l'Etranger de l'Internation P.E.N.
Christian Fleith, Alsace Tourist Authority for Northern Alsace

ORANGE

Mireille Finnegan, Hotel Cigaloun
Pierre Téocchi, Harmas de J. H. Fabre, Serignan-du-Comtat

AVIGNON

J. Granier Museum Réquin Histoire Naturelle

ST. MAXIMIN

The Dominican Sisters and Edmond Filliette, Director, Saint Mary Magdalene Society

BEAUNE

B. Craig Phillips, Manager, Buddy Bombard Balloon Society, Château de Laborde Meursanges
Michel and Claude Jaboulet Vercherre, Pommard Chteau et clos de la Commaraine

DIJON

Mme. Micheline Laby, Françoise, and Christian

TALANT

Jill and Nadja Boucquemont

More Thank You's

BRUSSELS

Nick Le Jeune, Itineraries
Marion Lemesre, Deputy Mayor for Tourism
Mr. Serge Schultz, General Manager, Hôtel Metropole
Ms. Mathieu, Belgian Trade Commission, Houston, Texas

BRITTANY

Le Naour Gildas, Vannes
Canuta Le Henaff, Larmor-Plage

LUXEMBOURG

Pierre Gramegna, Consul General of Luxembourg
Byron Cain, President of International Intermediaries
Anne Bastian, Director of Luxembourg National Tourist Office, New York
Dr. Raymond Frisch, Mayor of Vianden, Chairman of Luxembourg National Tourist Office, Luxembourg City
Jean Claude Conter and Romain Schwartz, Luxembourg National Tourist Office, Luxembourg City
Mr. Fernand Cravat, Grand Cravat Hotel, Luxembourg City
Thierry Meyrat, Director of Trade Finance, World Trade Center, Dallas, Texas
Quesada-Tristian Ligia, Radio Luxembourg
Carin Fagan—Harvard University Graduate School of Business Administration
Dr. James Newcomer, Vice Chancellor Emeritus, Texas Christian University
Carla van derUhell, VVV Delft, Markt 85, 2611 GS Delft, Tel. (015) 12.61.00

NANCY

Jean Louis Etíenne, Professor of History—Lycée Poincaré
Jean Marie Cuney, History Specialist
Monique Grandgeorges, Attachée de Direction

Index

Page numbers in boldface refer to photographs.

Acropolis, the, 285, 293–295, 298
Adams, John, 27, 133, 252, 308n9, 320n53, 320n61
Adams, Samuel, 131
Adoration of the Shepherds (Rubens), 257
Aeschylus, 288, 289, 335n3
Aesop, 299, 300, 303
Agamemnon, 287–288
Agamemnon (Aeschylus), 288
Agincourt, Battle of, 8
Ainay le Vieil, Château, 140, **161**, 161–162, 165, 323n62
Anne d'Auray, Saint, 121–122
Anne of Austria (queen), 64, 122, 306n7, 309n8
Anne of Beaujeu, 140, 141, 326n25
Anne of Brittany, 113, 140, 162, 316n2, 322n38
Anselm, Saint, 218
Anthony, Saint, 92
Aristophanes, 290–292
Aristotle, 17, 266, 301–302
Arnold, Benedict, 131, 272, 334n5 (chap. 28)
Art Nouveau, 46, 181–183
Arthur (king of England), 100, 102, 113

balloon flight, 47, 118, 206–207
Balzac, Honoré de, xix, 16, 67, 79–84, 177–178
  Cousin Bette, 82–83
  Human Comedy, The, 83
  mistress Madame de Berny, 83
  wife Evelina de Hanska, 83–84, 177, 178, 314n10
Barber of Seville, The (Beaumarchais), xix, 73, 75
Battle of Nancy, The (Delacroix), 183
Battle of the Bulge, the, 229, 230, 234–38
Baudricourt, Robert de, 189–90
Bavon, Saint, 258, 333n13
Beauharnais, Josephine de. *See* Josephine (consort of Napoléon Bonaparte)
Beaumarchais, Pierre Caron de, xix, 73–78, 87, 176, 313n2 (chap. 12)
  Barber of Seville, The, xix, 73, 75
  Marriage of Figaro, The, xix, 73, 76–77, 313n10
Becket, Thomas à (archbishop of Canterbury), 7, 96
Beethoven, Ludwig von, 332n26
Benedict, Saint, 112
Benedict XI (pope), 159
Berlioz, Hector, 44, 47, 68, 84, 231
Bernard, Saint, 154, 188, 209
  role in Second Crusade, 155, 156
Bernhardt, Sarah, 182, 254
Bernini, Gian, 317n18
Berry, duc Jean de, 146, 151, 321n24
Berry, duchesse Marie-Caroline de, 115–117, 145
Bizet, Georges, xix, 46–50
Black Prince, the (later Edward III, king of England), 200
Blanche of Castile (queen), 97
Bly, Nelly, 316n15 (chap. 17)
Bombard, Buddy, 206–207
Boniface VIII (pope), 159

Index

Bourbon(s), 65, 66, 115, 130, 137, 326n25
  restoration, 36, 51, 90, 137
Bourhis, Abel le, **x**, 119–121, **120**
Brandywine, Battle of, 26, 131, 274
Breugel, Peter, 242
Byron, Lord, 16, 276

Caesar, Julius, 46, 104, 130, 172
Café Procope, 25
Calixtus III (pope), 149
Calvinist(s), 92, 314n11
  Pacification of Ghent, 246, 258
  sacking of churches, 245, 256, 267, 333n5
  uprising, 242, 245–250, 266
Carmen (Bizet), xix, 46, 48, 49, 50
"Carmen" (Merimée), 10, 46, 48, 49
Carpeaux, Jean-Baptiste
  Danse, La, **43**, 44
Caruso, Enrico, 3
Cathars, 158
Catherine of Alexandria, Saint, 189, 327n44
Catherine of Fierbois, Saint, 190, 191, 327n48
Catherine of Siena, Saint, 278–279
Cézanne, Paul, 317n20
Chagall, Marc, 42–44
Champs Elysées, 11
Charlemagne, 94, 96, 141, 173, 209, 210
Charles I (king of England), 23, 143, 320n10, 333n40
Charles II (king of England), 143, 320n11
Charles III (king of France), 94
Charles VII (king of France), 8, 148–149, 183
Charles VIII (king of France), 113, 140
Charles the Rash, Duke of Burgundy, 183–188, 239, 258
Chaucer, Geoffrey, 1
Chavaniac, Château, 127–129, **128**, 132–133, 134, 135
Chevalier, Maurice, 3, 144
Chopin, Frédéric, xix, 58–62, 166, 167
  artistic circle of, 15–16, 58, 61
  compositions, 50, 311n5, 324n75
  portrait of, 16
  and Sand, George, xix, 59–62, 165, 166, 312n7 (chap. 9)
Chrétien of Troyes, 100, 102–103
  Grail, The, 102–103
Churchill, Winston, 4, 119, 188

Citizen Egalité, 51, 65, 66
Citizen King. *See* Louis Philippe (king of France)
Clement V (pope), 160, 221
Clos Vougeot, 209
Clouds, The (Aristophanes), 290–292
Coeur, Jacques, 140, 148–152, 153
Colbert, Jean Baptiste, 114–115, 152, 162–165, 175
Colette, Sidonie-Gabrielle, 63, 312n3
Comédie Française, 25, 75, 76, 307n1 (chap. 4)
Comic Strip Museum, 255
Communards, 10, 48, 232
Corday, Charlotte, 308n3 (chap. 4)
Cornwallis, Charles, 1st marquis, 132
Count of Monte Cristo, The (Dumas), 210
Count Sigfrid, 230
courtly love, 100–103
Cousin Bette (Balzac), 82–83
Coward, Noel, 3, 5
Cromwell, Oliver, 143, 333n40
Cronkite, Walter, 229–30
Crusade(s), 7, 97–98, 100, 153–160, 234
Cyrano de Bergerac (Rostand), 228

Dante Alighieri, 83, 100, 160
Darius (Persian emperor), 297–298, 335n3
David, Jacques-Louis, 306n12
Degas, Edgar, 317n20
de Gaulle, Charles, 11–12, 44, 199, 306n20
Delacroix, Eugène, 15–19, 38–40
  Battle of Nancy, The, 183
  Liberty Leading the People, 17–18
  Sainte Anne Reading to the Virgin, 170
Demosthenes, 302–303
Depardieu, Gerard, 254
Deportes, François, 141
Descartes, René, 71–72
Desmoulins, Camille, 31–32, 308n17
Dionysius of Athens, Saint, 146
Don Juan of Austria, 246–47
D'Oyly Carte, Richard, 2–3
Drouet, Juliet, 232–233
Dudevant, Maurice, xix, 60–61, 167–170, 324n74
  Marionette Theatre, 167–170, **168**
Dumas, Alexandre *fils*, 169, 311n6
Dumas, Alexandre *père*, 68, 119, 210

Index

artistic circle of, 16, 61, 117, 165, 231–232
Count of Monte Cristo, The, 210
described by son, 312n11
philanthropy of, 311n6, 312n11
political involvement of, 67
Three Musketeers, The, 26, 210

Edict of Nantes, 113, 164
Eiffel, Alexandre Gustav, 202–204
Eiffel Tower, 11, 13, **203**, 203–204
Einstein, Albert, 254
Eleanor of Aquitaine, 112, 322nn48–49
   accused of poisoning Rosamond, 315n7 (chap. 15)
   children, 96, 112, 140, 305n1
   in Crusades, 156
   imprisonment of, 96–97
   marriage to Henry II, 8, 104, 112, 140, 156
   marriage to Louis VII, 7, 101, 110, 156, 316n17
Elizabeth I (queen of England), 208
Emery, Jacques André, 34–36
Escoffier, Auguste, 2–3, 305n8
Eudes III, Duke of Burgundy, 199
Eugene (pope),
Eugénie (empress), 13, 41, 47, 49, 51, 52, 122, 310nn2–4 (chap. 8)
   flight and exile, 13, 41
   political involvement, 56–57, 309n3, 311n19
   survival of bombing, 42, 55
Euripides, 289–290
Ezekiel (prophet), 335n6

Fabre, Jean Henri, 223–28
   Souvenirs Entomologiques, 224, 225
Félibres, 218, 223
Finsen, Niels, 208
Flaubert, Gustave, 124
   Madame Bovary, 124
Fontevraud abbey, **111**, 111–112
Fouquet, Nicolas, 114–115, 162, 164
Francis I (king of France), 8, 113, 143, 240
Francis, Duke of Anjou, 248–249
Francis of Assisi, Saint, 44, 100, 158,
Francis of Loyola, Saint, 158
Franklin, Benjamin, 25, 76, 274
   admirers of, 129, 166
   children, 119, 317n16
   and Lafayete, 128
   and Mirabeau, 32
   Poor Richard's Almanac, 166, 323n70
   travels in France, 26
Frederick II (king of Germany), 158–159, 323n58

Gabriel (angel), 317n8
Gallé, Émile, 181–183
Garnier, Charles, xix, 41–44, 45, 51
Gatianus, Saint, 324n2 (chap. 20)
Gautier, Théophile, 47, 166–167, 170
Géricault, Theodore, 13–15, 16
   Raft of the Medusa, The, 13–15, 16
Gershwin, George, 3
Gilbert, Sir William Schwenk, xix, 2, 3–4, 305n3 (chap. 1)
Gilbert and Sullivan operettas, 2, 3–4
Girl with a Pearl Earring (Vermeer), **263**, 263–264
Gobelin tapestries, 233
Goodman, Benny, xix, 5
Gounod, Charles, 44, 47, 68, 219
Grignan castle, 213, **214**
Grimm brothers, 177
Grotius, Hugo, 266–267
Gwynn, Nell, 320n11

Harold the Saxon, 94, 95
Henri of Navarre. *See* Henri IV (king of France)
Henri IV (king of France), 20–21, 22, 200
   as father, 143, 21
   love letters of, 86
   marriage to Marguerite de Valois, 8
   marriage to Marie de' Medici, 19, 20–21
   statue of, 1
Henry II (king of England), 7, 19, 157
   children, 96, 112, 305n1
   marriage to Eleanor of Acquitaine, 8, 104, 140
   See also Richard the Lion-Heart; John II (king of England)
Henry III (king of England), 1, 19, 104
Henry V (king of England), 8, 305n4 (chap. 2)
Henry VIII (king of England), 240, 320n9
Henry Plantagenet. *See* Henry II (king of England)

Index

Heraclius, 7–8
Herakles, 286–287, 293
Holy Ghost Fathers (Sulpicians), 33, 34–36, 309n19
Homer, 286, 287–288, 335nn1–2
   Iliad, The, 287–288
Hôtel Dieu, 55, **207**, 207–209
Hugo, Victor, 10, 68, 231–233
   on Art Nouveau style, 183
   artistic circle of, 16, 84, 165
   Hunchback of Notre Dame, The, 10, 232, 306n13, 331n4
   on Louis Philippe, 67
   Misérables, Les, 138, 232, 323n68
   political involvement of, 10, 55, 232–233
Huguenot(s), 8, 19, 63, 98, 173, 197, 200, 249, 307n12
Hunchback of Notre Dame, The (Hugo), 10, 232, 306n13, 331n4

Iliad, The (Homer), 287–288
Innocent III (pope), 155, 158

Jacqueline, countess of Hainaut and Holland, 239, 332n15
James, Saint, 104, 147, 151, 257
Jefferson, Thomas, 27, 308n9, 308n14
   and Lafayette, 129, 133
   on Louis XVI, 314n2 (chap. 14), 318n15
Joan of Arc, 178–179, 183, **194**
   death and sainthood, 11, 148, 197
   divine mission of, 127, 140–141, 189–195
   early life, 188–189
   likenesses of, 140, 182, 196, 197, 198, 233
   military exploits of, 8, 129, 148, 179, 187–197
   mother, 127, 197
John II (king of England), 104, 305n1 (chap. 1)
John II (king of France), 1, 200, 305n2 (chap. 2), 328n6
John Paul II (pope), 316n14 (chap. 16)
John of Gaunt (John II, king of France), 1, 200, 305n2 (chap. 2), 328n6
John the Blind, 230
John the Fearless, Duke of Burgundy, 205
Josephine (consort of Napoléon Bonaparte)
   daughter Hortense, 52, 53, 87, 88, 91, 252
   divorce from Napoléon, 35, 196
   later life and death, 91
   marriage to Napoléon, xix, 10, 86–89, **90**
   meets Napoléon, 85
   tomb of, 52, 53
   See also Napoléon Bonaparte
Jurade, 104, 107–109, 316n13 (chap. 16)
Jurats, 104, 107–109, **108**

Keroualle, Louise de, 143, 320n12
Knights Hospitallers, 153–154, 157–158, 160
Knights of Malta, 153–154, 157–158, 160
Knights Templar, 104, 153, 154–155, 157–160
Kosciuszka, Thaddeus, 271–273

Lafayette, marquis de, 53, 274, 276, 308n11, 319n48, 319n52
   American Revolution, involvement in, 26, 29, 130–133, 318n27
   "Declaration of the Rights of Man, A," 25, 29, 128, 133
   description of, 319n44
   French Revolution, role in, 28–29, 65–67, 133–134, 319n43
   home (Chavaniac), 127–129, **128**
   imprisonment of, 135–136
   later life, 136–138
   National Guard, commander of, 30–31, 134, 137, 308n11
   Washington, association with, 131–134, 138
   wife Adrienne, 130, 132, 133, 135–138, 318n12
Lalique, René, 182–83
Langtry, Lily, 2
Leclerc, Général, 11, 306nn19–21, 307n23, 324n2 (chap. 21)
Lenoir, Alexandre Marie, 306n8
Leonardo da Vinci, 152
Libermann, Francis, 36–40, **37**, 309n19
Liberty Leading the People (Delacroix), 17–18
Liszt, Franz, 165, 310n2 (chap. 7)
   artistic circle of, 16, 58, 166
   mistress Marie d'Agôult, 59, 166
   sex appeal of, 68
Louis, Saint. *See* Louis IX (king of France)
Louis VII (king of France), 7, 101, 140, 156–157
Louis IX (king of France), 8, 97–98, 159

Index

Louis XI (king of France), 150, 173, 322n39, 324n4, 325n15
  ascension to throne, 185
  childhood and youth, 183–185
  children, 140, 316nn2–3
  piety of, 183, 187, 193, 325n17, 325n19, 326n33, 327n41
  reign, 185–188, 326n33, 327n41
Louis XIII (king of France), 69, 266–267, 307n14, 319n50
  childhood of, 21, 307n2 (chap. 3)
  death of, 333n6
  marriage to Anne of Austria, 9,122, 309n8, 319n47
  musketeers of, 34, 309n6
  and Richelieu, 23, 63, 162, 309n6
  See also musketeers
Louis XIV (king of France), 141, 210, 314n2 (chap. 14), 324n5
  birth and parentage, 9, 34, 306n7, 334n6
  extravagance of, 71, 162–163, 204–205
  and finance ministers, 114–115, 152, 162, 175
  lechery of, 215, 216
  as Molière's patron, 70–71, 313n3 (chap. 11), 313n8 (chap. 11)
  political activities of, 143, 307n12, 312n5, 320n12, 329n6
  rivalry with relatives, 64–65
  Netherlands, conquest of the, 176, 216, 251, 264, 333n39
  See also Mazarin (cardinal); Montespan, Madame de
Louis XVI (king of France), 9, 10, 65, 66, 134, 169, 206
  and American Revolution, 130, 132
  and Beaumarchais, 75, 76
  description of, 25
  as patron of the arts, 76, 310n3 (chap. 7)
  revolt against and execution of, 9, 30, 31, 145
Louis XVIII (king of France), 10, 45, 116,
  death, 67
  reign of, 137
  restoration of, 36, 51, 66
Louis Napoléon. *See* Napoléon III
Louis Philippe (king of France), 66, 116, 145, 170
  ascent to throne, 65–67, 68, 137
  flight from France, 10, 54, 117
  reign, 17, 52–53, 58, 65, 67–68
Louisiana Purchase, 88, 314n2 (chap. 14), 319n40
Louvre, the, 9, 13, 16, 24, 74, 176, 310n5 (chap. 6)
  construction and renovation of, 55, 157, 165
  as living quarters, 21, 22, 64

Madame Bovary (Flaubert), 124
Maduro, George, 333n1 (chap. 26)
Magna Carta, the, 104
Maid of Orléans. *See* Joan of Arc
Maintenon, Madame de, 308n4 (chap. 5)
Malmaison, Château, xix, 52, 85, 86–90, 310nn3–4
Marat, Jean-Paul, 25, 26, 29, 78, 135
  murder of, 51, 308n3 (chap. 4)
Marathon, Battle of, 297, 298, 335n3
Marie Antoinette, 25, 65, 78, 162
  and Beaumarchais, 75, 76
  execution of, 9
  and Lafayette, 130, 134
  marriage, 9
Marie Louise of Austria, 196
  marriage to Napoléon Bonaparte, 10, 35, 89
Marionette Theatre, 167–170
  See also Dudevant, Maurice
Marriage of Figaro, The (Beaumarchais), xix, 73, 76–77
Martel, Charles, 322n41, 327n48, 327n53
Martin of Tours, Saint, 110, 165, 172–173, 324n2 (chap. 20)
Marx, Karl, 10, 55
Mary Magdalene, 220–223
Mary Queen of Scots, 8, 143, 197, 246
Mary Tudor (queen of England), 240, 332n27
Mazarin (cardinal), 114–115, 162, 251, 316n4 (chap. 17)
Medici, Catherine de', 8, 19–20, 307n2 (chap. 3)
  children of, 8, 19, 20, 197, 241, 248
Medici, Cosimo de', 148
Medici, Lorenzo de', 185, 186
Medici, Marie de', 19–24, 122, 307n4
  marriage to Henri IV, 19–20

387

Index

Meillant, 152–153
Melba, Nellie, 2
Mergenthaler, George, 237
Mérimée, Prosper, 10, 46, 48–49, 86
Michael, Saint, 127, 161, 256
  appears to Joan of Arc, 189
  as dragon slayer, 38, 92
  and Mont Saint Michel, 93, 98, 187
Mickiewicz, Adam, 275–276, 277
Mill, John Stuart, 224
Mirabeau, comte de Honoré Gabriel Riqueti, 26–32
Mistral, Frédéric, 218–20, 222–223, 227–28
  Mirèio, 218–219, 222–223
Molière, 63, 171, 175, 176, 215
  death, xix, 312n1 (chap. 11), 313n8 (chap. 11)
  life and career, 69–72
  Malade Imaginaire, Le, xix, 69, 71–72
  Tartuffe, Le, 71
  wife Armande, 25, 34, 70, 313n7 (chap. 11)
Monbousquet, Château, 106–107
Monet, Claude, 2, 124
Monroe, James, 34, 133, 135, 136, 137
Mont Saint Michel, 92–99, **93**, 187
Montespan, Madame de, 64, 312n7
Morris, Gouverneur, 135
Mozart, Wolfgang Amadeus, 44, 62, 310n2 (chap. 7), 313n8
Mucha, Alphonse, 182
Munson, Thomas Volney, 106
musketeer(s), 34, 115, 130
  See also Louis XIII (king of France)
Mystic Lamb of God Who Redeemed the World from Sin (van Eyck), 258

Napoléon III, 42, 68, 98, 106, 224
  ascent to throne, 54–56, 117, 232
  early life, 51–54
  era of, 202
  overthrow and death, 41, 47, 56–57
  marriage to Eugénie, 13, 57
  political stance, 10, 311n17
Napoléon Bonaparte, 65, 66, 78, 80, 137, 208, 276, 306n10
  achievements of, 314n1 (chap. 14)
  coronation of, 9–10, 306n12
  exile and death, 51–52, 68, 90, 258, 308n16
  feud with church, 34, 35–36, 98
  and Lafayette, 136
  marriage to Josephine, 10, 56, 85–90
  marriage to Marie Louise of Austria, 10, 89, 196
  military exploits, 56, 86–89, 176, 273
  Napoléon's Farewell to Josephine, 90
  and the Netherlands, 252
  reign, 9–10, 252, 256, 309nn15–16
  See also Josephine (consort of Napoléon Bonaparte)
Nazis, 68, 119, 199, 211, 234, 278
  France, invasion of, 11, 42, 98, 198
  Luxembourg, invasion of, 236
  Poland, invasion of, 270, 281
Nicholas V (pope), 149
Night Watch, The (Rembrandt), 262
Notre Dame de Paris, xvii, 6, 7–12, 19, 25, 160

Olier, Jean, 34, 309n9
Opéra Comique, 45–46, 50
Opera House (Paris), xix, 41–42, 55, 116,
Our Lady of Luxembourg (cathedral), 230–31

Paderewski, Ignace, 271, 276–278, 334n1 (chap. 28)
Paine, Thomas, 131, 308n13, 318n23
Palais Royal, xix, 69, 241
  history of, 63–68
  as theater, 69, 70
Pasteur, Louis, 54, 182, 224, 330n28
Patience (Gilbert and Sullivan), 4
Patrick, Saint, 173
Patton, General George S., Jr.
  Avranches, liberation of, 98–99
  and the Battle of the Bulge, 229, 234, 235–237
  death of, 331n1
  Nancy, liberation of, 180–181
Pavlova, Anna, 3
Payens, Hugh de, 155
Peace (Aristophanes), 292
Père Lachaise Cemetery, 62, 84,
Pericles, 288, 292, 293, 299
Perrault, Charles, 162, 164, 175–177
  Sleeping Beauty, 175
  Tales of Mother Goose, 176–177

388

Index

Peter the Hermit, 322n43
Petrarch, 100
Philip II (king of France), 112, 157, 316n17, 323n53
Philip II (king of Spain), 240–250
Philip IV (king of France), 159–160
Philip IV (king of Spain) 9, 251
Philip of Macedon (king), 300, 301, 302–303
Philip the Bold, first Duke of Burgundy, 200, 204, 205, 239, 257
Philip the Good, second Duke of Burgundy, 204, 205, 326n27
   deterioration and death of, 186
   and Louis XI, 184, 185
   power mongering of, 185, 205, 239
Philippe II (regent of France), 64–65, 315n8
Philippe Augustus, 64–65, 315n8
Philippe Egalité (Citizen Egalité), 51, 65, 66
Pisistratus, 286, 296
Pissarro, Camille, 317n20
Pius VI (pope), 309nn12–13
Pius VII (pope), 35, 306n11, 309n16, 309n18
Plato, 301
Poe, Edgar Allan, 118, 316n13 (chap. 17), 323n68
Pompadour, Madame de, 210
Pompidou, Centre, 6
Poor Richard's Almanac (Franklin), 166, 323n70
Pulaski, Count Casimir, 273–275

Rabelais, François, 8
Rachel (actress), 13, 307n1 (chap. 3)
Raft of the Medusa, The (Géricault), 13–15, 16, 17
Reign of Terror, 25, 32, 34, 65, 135
Rembrandt van Rijn, 257, 262–263, 317n18, 334n8 (chap. 26)
   Night Watch, The, 257, 334n8 (chap. 26)
René II, Duke of Lorraine, 183, 187–188
Richard the Lion-Heart (King Richard I of England), 104, 109, 112, 161
   alliance with Philip II of France, 157
Richelieu (cardinal), 22–23, 63, 162, 251, 309nn6–7
Ritz, César, 2–3
Robespierre, Maximilien-François-Marie-Isidore de, 66, 78, 135, 308nn12–13

Rochambeau, Général, 132, 318n27, 318n30
Rodin, Auguste, 10, 79, 231–232
Rossini, Gioacchino, 42, 46, 55, 166
Rostand, Edmond, 228, 331n36
Rousseau, Jean-Jacques, 129
Ruark, Robert, 233
Rubens, Peter Paul, 15–16, 244, 250, 257
   Adoration of the Shepherds, 257
   and Marie de' Medici, 19–20, 23–24
   Scourging at the Pillar, The, 257

Saché, Château, 173, 177–179
Saint Augustin, church of, 51
Saintes Maries de la Mer, Les, 218, 220–222, **221**
Saladin, 8, 155, 156–158
Salle Favart. *See* Opéra Comique
Sand, George (Aurore Dudevant), xix, 59–62, 67, 323n67
   and Chopin, xix, 59–62, 165, 166, 312n7 (chap. 9)
   on Chopin, 15–16
   daughter Solonge, 60, 61, 62, 324n72
   descriptions of, 311n2, 323n70
   home (Nohant), 165–170
   portrait of, 16
   son Maurice. *See* Dudevant, Maurice
   writing career, 61, 166–167
Sarah the gypsy, 220, 330n18
Saratoga, Battle of, 76, 131, 272
Savoy Hotel, the, xix, 1–5, **4**, 305n4 (chap. 1)
Savoy Theater, the, 2, 305n4 (chap. 1)
Scourging at the Pillar, The (Rubens), 257
Seine river, 7, 38, 160, 165, 200
Seton, Elizabeth Ann, 34–35, 309n14
Sévigné, marquise de, 122, 213–17
Shakespeare, William, 16, 23, 303, 305n4 (chap. 2)
   era of, 257, 317n18
   quoted, 182, 311n14
Shaw, George Bernard, 148, 189
Sleeping Beauty (Perrault), 173–175
Sleeping Beauty castle, basis for, 173–174, **174**
Sluter, Klass, 205
Solon, 296
Solonge, Saint, 146
Song of Roland, The, 96

389

Index

Sophocles, 288–289, 303
Sorel, Agnes, 148, 322n31
Spider King. *See* Louis XI
Spiridion, Saint, 316n10 (chap. 17)
Staël, Madame de, 26, 308n5 (chap. 4)
Stephen, Saint, 146, 147
Strauss, Johan, II, 296
Strauss, Johan, III, 3
Strauss, Richard, 254
Strickler, Colonel Daniel, 331n11
Sullivan, Sir Arthur, xix, 2, 3–4, 305n3 (chap. 1)
   See also Gilbert and Sullivan operettas
Sulpicians, 33, 34–36, 309n11, 309n19
Sun King. *See* Louis XIV

Taillifer, 96
Tales of Mother Goose (Perrault), 176–177
Talleyrand, Charles-Maurice de, 31, 86, 88, 308n16
Tartuffe, Le (Molière), 71
Tetrazzini, Luisa, 2
Themistocles, 297, 298–299
Third Estate, 27–28
Thomas, Saint, 147
Three Musketeers, The (Dumas), 22, 26, 67, 210, 255–256
Toone's Puppet Show, 255–256, **255**
Toulouse-Lautrec, Henri, 317n20
Trinitarian Order, 234
Troyes, Chrétien de, 100, 102–103
Tuileries (palace and gardens), 9, 13, 32, 35, 55
   attacks on, 78, 134–135
   construction of, 307n2 (chap. 3)
Tussaud, Madame, 26, 308n3 (chap. 4)
Twain, Mark, 68, 188, 191, 328n54

Ussé, Château, 173–174, **174**, 177, 324n5

Valentinian (Roman emperor), 172
Vallière, Louise de la, 312n7 (chap. 10), 323n64
van Eyck, Jan and Hubert
   Mystic Lamb of God Who Redeemed the World from Sin, 258
van Gogh, Vincent, 220, 264
Velasquez, Diego, 317n18
Verdi, Giuseppi, 44, 169, 244, 310n2 (chap. 8)
Vermeer, Jan, 263–264
   Girl with a Pearl Earring, 263–264, 263
Verne, Jules, 47, 117–119, 182, 316nn13–15
Verrerie, Château le, 142–144
Versailles palace, 29–30, 115, 137, 197
   renovation and decoration of, 163–164, 176, 216, 280
Victoria (queen of England), 2, 333n45
Vikings, 7
Villandry Gardens, **179**
Vincent de Paul, Saint, 34, 35, 307n12, 309n9, 329n2
Voltaire, 26, 31, 61, 129

Wagner, Richard, 44, 113
Washington, George, 66, 73, 127, 129, 272, 274, 318nn19–20
   described by de Toqueville, 318n19
   Kosciuskza, association with, 271–272
   Lafayette, association with, 131–134, 138
Waterloo, Battle of, 36, 90, 137, 196, 252
William the Conqueror (king of England), 94, 95, 96, 142
William the Silent, prince of Orange, 240–53
Willibrord, Saint, 238
Worth, Charles Frederick, 51

Here's the buzz about Mary Jane Wilson's first book,
Europe with a Busy Body!

"Mary Jane Wilson is a Dallas actress and tour guide and has appeared in several TV commercials and programs. She has also taken her travel talks to conventions and professional groups in Dallas–Fort Worth. The author [offers] her hints for traveling 'busybodies.'"
—Sarah Pattie, *San Antonio Light*

"Mary Jane Wilson is not your typical busload journalist . . . *Europe With a Busybody* . . . features all the tantalizing details the guides never tell you. Mary Jane, a trim and neat hurricane of zeal, explained: 'I've just fallen in love with all these dead people.'"
—Travel Detective Peter Rose, *Arizona Republic*

"The history under the sugar-coating of fun is all there."
—Joseph Palamountain, Jr., President Emeritus, Skidmore College

"A Serendipist delight presented with a hilarious but incisive outlook."
—*Atlanta Constitution*

"Reading through your marvelous book, I encountered again and again those very interesting background stories short enough to incite you to more reading and research, which for my part, I am certainly going to do. Everywhere I will recommend it."
—Friederike Zeitlhofer, Austrian Institute, New York

"A combination of awe and humor make *Europe with a Busy Body* a hilarious adventure."
—*Birmingham News*

"An excellent travel writer. It's travel writing light years removed from the conventional travelogue."
—*Amarillo Globe*

"Simply bubbles with energy and honest-to-goodness shared pleasure."
—*Clarion Herald, New Orleans*

About the author

Mary Jane Wilson is a well-known speaker for conventions and professional groups in and out of Dallas. A graduate of Skidmore College, she has taught speech at Ursuline Academy and has been featured in a variety of movies and television commercials with the Kim Dawson Agency.